A GUIDE TO MENTAL TESTING

A GUIDE TO
MENTAL TESTING

For Psychological Clinics, Schools, and
Industrial Psychologists

By
RAYMOND B. CATTELL, M.A., D.Sc.

Research Professor of Psychology, University of Illinois
Formerly Director of School Psychological Service and Clinic, City of Leicester

WITH A FOREWORD BY
WILLIAM MOODIE, M.D., F.R.C.P., D.P.M.
Medical Director, London Child Guidance Clinic

New Edition

UNIVERSITY OF LONDON PRESS, Ltd.
WARWICK SQUARE, LONDON, E.C.4

FIRST PRINTED 1936
SECOND EDITION 1948

Printed in Great Britain for the UNIVERSITY OF LONDON PRESS, LTD.
by HAZELL, WATSON AND VINEY, LTD., London and Aylesbury

DEDICATED TO MY CO-WORKERS IN THE
PSYCHOLOGICAL CLINIC AND
THE EXPERIMENTAL SCHOOL.

CECILIA BAKER.   RICHARD DEWHIRST.
JESSEY LOWE.   WINIFRED MILLER.
DIANA MILLIS.   MARJORIE RAILTON.
MARGARET WALTON. JAMES WILLSON.

FOREWORD

FOR some time there has been a lull in the progress of mental testing as a practical procedure. After the first wave of enthusiasm in the so-called Intelligence Tests, and their indiscriminate and often unintelligent application, this was bound to happen. It became evident that the results of these tests were influenced by factors other than intelligence, which seemed to elude measurement even if they were taken into account at all.

The psychotherapist, faced with problems of behaviour dependent on forces much more instinctive than intellectual, found the estimation of mental endowment alone of only limited value, especially since variations in mental capacity were always complicated by disturbances of the personality.

This was also the lot of the educational psychologist. Attainments often showed a marked discrepancy with test rating. Something obviously remained unexplained.

So the problem was thrown back and forth from one to the other, without any definite solution being arrived at.

In this book we have a much-needed and remarkably successful attempt to end this state of affairs. Looking on his subject from a wide angle, Dr. Cattell has sifted all those methods which aim at estimating, so far as can be, the various activities of the mind, using the term in a broad sense. He has wisely selected for detailed description only those whose value has been proved, and which are suitable for practical application. He has been critical and selective, and necessarily so, and he has substantiated his work with ample references.

Here, for the first time, is collected under one cover,

reliable information on all aspects of the subject. This book fills a long-felt want, and all practical psychologists, whether in educational, child guidance, or medical fields, will welcome it.

WILLIAM MOODIE, M.D., F.R.C.P., D.P.M.,
Medical Director, London Child Guidance Clinic.

CONTENTS

G.M.T.—I*

CHAPTER II

CHAPTER III

CHAPTER IV

CHAPTER V

CHAPTER VI

CHAPTER VII

CHAPTER VIII

INTRODUCTION

For some unaccountable reason the expression ' Mental Testing ' has been understood by many teachers and even a few psychologists as if it were written ' Intelligence Testing.' Text-books and articles dealing only with intelligence tests, or at the most with cognitive material, still appear bearing the title " Mental Tests." Obviously ' mental ' should refer to the mind in all its aspects, intellectual and emotional, and that is the sense it bears in the title of this book, which deals with tests and diagnostic methods in regard to intelligence, attainment, special aptitudes, interests, emotional structure, temperament, and character.

My aim has been to provide (1) A handbook which shall contain between its covers sufficient instructions, test materials and norms to aid the psychometrist in assessing the principal aspects of personality so far made accessible to exact examination. Without a practical handbook of this kind the psychologist is reduced to the time-consuming inconvenience of having to consult many different reference books and of carrying with him portfolios of obstinately errant test material.

Naturally the exactness and reliability vary considerably between such fields as intelligence testing, where research has long provided a sound theoretical basis, and the latest essays at character analysis which tread closely on the heels of pioneer research and can only be tentatively interpreted. With this explanation perhaps no apology is necessary for presenting relatively untried tests in the character-temperament section. They have promise in a region where most tests are of low validity and their publication may at least stimulate further research.

(2) A guide to most other available tests of any value (and from which the above are a selection), with brief

comments on their origin, validity, and source of publication. In general, only one or two tests are given in each field. Where American and English Tests are of equal goodness, the latter are usually given, since American standardisations are in some fields inapt to testing purposes in this country; but always the test based on sounder research is given first consideration. Tests of doubtful value are generally given no more space than suffices to print their titles. Even so, a complete catalogue of every test described in journals or placed on the market has not been attempted. Such a complete list already exists in Dr. G. Hildreth's *A Bibliography of Mental Tests and Rating Scales* (Psychological Corporation, N.Y., 1933), where over four thousand titles are recorded. A slightly less exhaustive but even more valuable survey and commentary on available tests—valuable particularly because it is constantly kept up to date—is O. K. Buros' *Mental Measurements Yearbook*.

The psychology of measurement is still greatly beset by growing pains. Only a thoroughly trained professional psychologist can hope to get a right perspective on the value and use of recent developments. But, since many psychometrists with lesser training have to use tests, some explanation or summary of basic principles cannot be omitted in a book of this kind. Although it is intended primarily as a handy tool for the busy practical psychologist and as a guide for the inquirer after new tests, it prefaces each set of tests with a condensed account of the present position of research in the field concerned. Since this must be very brief, it is necessarily more dogmatic in tone than one would ideally like it to be. There is also a section on the interpretation and synthesis of test findings. These statements of the general background should be of considerable help to teachers and psychometrists, whilst even the fully qualified psychologist will sometimes find it convenient to have at hand ready references to the research sources of his accepted techniques.

Two eccentricities require explanation. I have omitted detailed description of the Binet Scale and its revisions because, in spite of its continued use by medical officers and others, I find no scientific evidence for its being as valid as most of the tests devised since Spearman's principles were discovered. Besides which, it has too few pass or fail items, does not include tests for higher mental ages, contains tests of low ' g ' validity, and is overloaded with life experience and scholastic skill. It is presented, therefore, only as one test among many of equal worth. Secondly, I have used everywhere ' Consistency Coefficient ' as well as ' Reliability Coefficient.' To the layman, at least, ' reliability ' conveys more than that the test correlates highly with itself, and I am inclined to think that even to many psychologists it is subtly misleading. Consistency, on the other hand, expresses exactly what the coefficient measures. Probably the best system would be to apply the term Consistency Coefficient to self-correlations obtained by the ' split-half ' method or from two testings in quick succession, and to reserve the term Reliability Coefficient for correlations obtained from testings separated by long intervals of time. In that case the Consistency Coefficient would be the measure of the self-consistency of the test, whilst the Reliability Coefficient would indicate in addition the degree of variability (with time) of the quality assessed, i.e. its " functional fluctuation."

All being well, this handbook will be revised at intervals in response to the progress of research and the publication of new tests. I shall be greatly indebted to anyone bringing to my notice tests which he considers ought to be included or supplying new and more extensive norms for tests already described. Much arduous work has in the past been unnecessarily repeated, and research inquiries duplicated through the lack of some central co-ordinating body, but with the recent establishment of the British Committee on Human Mental Measurements, to which the writer has the privilege to belong, this confusion should give way to a progressive organisation of test material, norms, and standards which it is hoped will be reflected in future editions of this or similar books.

I am greatly indebted to Professor Burt for permission to reproduce certain items from his classical *Mental and Scholastic Tests*, to which some sections of the present book are an introduction.

RAYMOND B. CATTELL.

UNIVERSITY OF ILLINOIS,
1946.

CHAPTER I

THE MEASUREMENT OF INTELLIGENCE

1. The Nature of Psychological Measurement in General

MENTAL testing is concerned with defining the individual personality at a given moment, i.e. with diagnosis. The art of guidance, of therapy, of prediction and control of behaviour in various applied fields, goes far beyond this and requires a systematic knowledge of developmental psychology through which the significance of the given measurements can be appreciated. A layman holding a mental-testing handbook is not a psychologist. It is necessary to stress this fact, because the present work, in order to retain a reasonable size, is compelled to confine itself rather strictly to the problems of description and measurement, assuming at every point that the reader is supplementing the bare statements of measurement with a wealth of implication from his psychological training.

The immediate task of description and measurement is presided over by two domestic gods—the reliability coefficient and the validity coefficient. Every measuring device must demonstrate that it is consistent with itself when applied on subsequent occasions and that, in addition, it measures the aspect of personality it is supposed to measure. These seemingly simple requirements are, however, much confused in current practice and it behoves us to define them more precisely.

Before we can validate a test we have to define the trait which it is designed to measure. Accurate qualitative description therefore has to precede measurement. In other words, psychology has to explore the characters of the unitary traits of man before mental testing can begin. Some traits are absolutely unique to individuals—like a six-fingered hand—and cannot be expressed in any scale common to all human beings. Mental testing is at present concerned with common traits; those of which every human being possesses a certain amount. Common traits are established by correlation studies correlating restricted manifestations of behaviour which we may call ' trait elements.' When a group of trait elements vary together we say that they constitute a unitary trait.

Unitary traits are of two kinds—surface traits or syndromes and source traits. The former are revealed by a cluster of positively intercorrelating elements, in which each correlates with every other member of the group. Most of the syndromes of psychiatry are correlation clusters, as also are most of the old ' types.' An exhaustive review of known correlation clusters has been published elsewhere.[1]

Source traits, on the other hand, may be regarded as the basic independent influences behind the clusters. They are discoverable by factor analysis, which reveals the distinct factors or vectors required to account for the observed correlations. Not all factors are psychologically meaningful source traits. A special technique is required in research to ensure that the mathematical analysis shall reveal the root psychological entities.[2]

A correlation cluster seems to be sometimes the result of a single factor, as, for example, in the Dominance syndrome or the Intelligence-General Talent Cluster; but more frequently it is due to the cumulative effects of two or more overlapping factors. The ' extraversion ' cluster, for example, seems to be the consequence of at least three factor endowments, in cyclothymia, in dominance and in surgency. The source trait is thus interpretative—it penetrates below the surface of behaviour to the underlying unitary influence—whereas the surface trait is almost purely descriptive, being simply a statement that a certain

[1] " The Principal Trait Clusters for Describing Personality," R. B. Cattell, *Psychological Bulletin,* xlii, 161–192, 1945.
[2] This technique and all the theoretical background of the present section is discussed at length in *The Description and Measurement of Personality,* R. B. Cattell, World Book Co., Yonkers-on-Hudson, New York, 1946.

group of behaviour manifestations go together, for reasons unknown, or at least neglected.

Surface traits, as research shows and the theory of structure might lead us to expect, are decidedly more numerous than source traits. For this and other reasons, applied psychology is likely to deal more with source traits than surface traits. Of course, the two systems of description and measurement are not mutually exclusive, but are actually alternative means of dealing with and resolving exactly the same set of observations. Unfortunately, a good deal of applied psychology up to the present has dealt with neither surface traits nor source traits, but with arbitrary, ' logical ' trait definitions. These ' traits ' are taken from the dictionary or manufactured in the mind of the psychometrist—e.g. clerical aptitude, social intelligence, ' paragraph comprehension '—and have generally never been demonstrated to correspond to any natural entity. To attempt to validate a test against such a composite is strictly meaningless. It is like asking for a compass that will simultaneously point north, south, east, and west.

If we deal with the measurement and prediction of behaviour performances in terms of source traits, i.e. factors, the procedure reduces to that expressed by the following basic formula:

$$P_{jk} = a_k F_{1j} + b_k F_{2j} \ldots + m_k F_{nj}$$

where P_{jk} is the estimated performance of the individual j in the situation k; F_{1j} is the endowment of the individual j in the source trait F_1 (and similarly for the source traits F_1, F_2, etc.); and a_k is the loading of the factor F_1 in the performance k, i.e. its rôle and importance in respect to k. For the fuller understanding of factor analysis and factorial representation the reader is referred to the several excellent expositions now available.[1] The formula at least suffices

[1] Burt, C. L., *The Factors of the Mind* (London: University of London Press, 1940) ; Guilford, J. P., *Psychometric Methods* (New York: McGraw-Hill Book Company, Inc., 1936); Holzinger, K. J., and Harman, H. H., *Factor Analysis* (Chicago : University of Chicago Press, 1940); Thomson, H. G., *The Factorial Analysis of Human Ability* (London: University of London Press, 1939), Revised Edition, 1946; Thurstone, L. L., *The Vectors of the Mind* (Chicago: University of Chicago Press, 1935), Revised Edition, 1944.

to remind one that the prediction of any performance—in school, occupation, therapeutic situation, etc.—normally requires measurements of several source traits, if the range of individual variation in the performance in question is to be fully accounted for.

2. Validity, Reliability, Consistency

The validity of a test aiming to measure a source trait is its factor loading in the factor concerned. With independent, orthogonal factors this is the correlation of the test with the pure factor as criterion.

The validity of a test aiming to measure a surface trait is the correlation of the test with a weighted or unweighted pool of the trait elements in the cluster. The well-known process of ' item analysis ' is, at its best, the validation of test items in terms of a surface trait. Unfortunately, in many instances of item analysis no attempt has first been made to ascertain that the test as a whole constitutes a single cluster, and in many important instances later research has shown the criterion to be a composite of two or more distinct clusters and any number of factors.

One may seek to establish the reliability of a test either by correlating odd with even items at a single administration or by correlating one administration with a later one. There are important differences between these results which justify calling them by different names, and the writer would suggest ' odd-even consistency ' for the first and ' quotidian reliability ' for the second. If the odd-even consistency coefficient is low, the test is bad; but if the quotidian reliability is low, it may show only that the ability which the test measures does indeed fluctuate from day to day. The latter tendency, intrinsic to certain traits, e.g. in a marked degree to surgency and to neuroticism, has been called ' function fluctuation,' or ' quotidian variability.' The relation between the odd-even (' split-half') consistency coefficient and the reliability (test-retest) coefficient permits one to calculate how much of the variance in measurement is due to each source—experimental error of measurement and function fluctuation. This analysis of source trait measurements with respect to validity, experimental error, and function fluctuation is illustrated in more detail below with respect to the measurement of intelligence. The problem of validation itself is discussed in more detail, with respect to ' internal ' and ' external ' validation, in Chapter V.

Ideally we should record validity, consistency, and reliability coefficients systematically for every test examined and described in this compendium. Actually we have been compelled to handle the evaluation more flexibly and inexactly. The recording of such coefficients, where they have been published, would at present merely operate to create a false impression of precision and of the relative merits of tests. For, as statisticians well know, the consistency coefficient can always be made to reach a ' satisfactory ' level by taking a population sample with sufficiently high scatter. Until all published coefficients have been systematically corrected to some standard scatter, preferably that of the total population, it will be pointless and misleading to set them out here. The same applies *a fortiori* to validities, and with the added complication that very few tests have yet been validated against estimated pure factors.

3. The Nature of Intelligence

The problem of measuring intelligence may well be taken as a paradigm for the treatment of most other source traits. *Historically* it can scarcely constitute a model, for the gropings and errors which occurred in attaining to clarity need not be repeated with other factors.

So long as controversy existed as to what was meant by intelligence no test could truly be validated, and the design of tests perforce remained a matter of personal taste. However, the researches which began with Spearman and were refined by Thurstone, as well as the more naturalistic studies of Terman with the Binet, demonstrate that abilities in general may be conceived as (1) a general ability entering into almost all performances, but far more into complex relation eduction than other performances; (2) certain group factors each covering an area such as verbal, number, spatial, musical, etc., performance; and (3) certain abilities which are absolutely specific to one performance.

The analyses of Thurstone differ from those of Spearman and Holzinger in giving less weight to the general ability. For Thurstone first resolves the performance wholly into the equivalent of group factors, namely into ' Primary Abilities,' and then takes the general factor as whatever the primary abilities have in common.

The techniques of measuring primary abilities *per se* are discussed in the next chapter, which is concerned with group and specific abilities. Here we shall discuss the measurement of the general factor, which corresponds—if anything corresponds—to what the general public alludes to by the term ' intelligence.'

If we agree that intelligence is the most general ability, i.e. the ' g ' factor, the choice of ' intelligence tests ' is no longer on an arbitrary basis. A good sub-test in an intelligence test battery is one that correlates very highly with ' g ' and has only a small specific ' s.' The same technique enables one to decide to what extent ' g ' is important in various school subjects and adult occupations, i.e. to predict from tests the fields in which a person may be successful and to what extent.

Measurements of ' g ' show that it increases rapidly in early years, then more slowly towards 14, and remains constant after about 15 years of age. The exact age of cessation of growth is still a matter for inquiry, but there are indications [1] that in the normal child intelligence ceases to grow after 16 years, in the subnormal after 14 years, and in the supernormal after 18 years.

' g ' is primarily expressed in terms of mental age. The child who scores as many points on a given test as, say, the

---

[1] " Occupational Norms of Intelligence and the Standardisation of an Adult Intelligence Test," by R. B. Cattell, *Brit. J. Psychol.*, xxv, 1, 1934.

average child of 11, is said to have a mental age of 11. His intelligence quotient (I.Q.) is obtained by dividing his mental age by his chronological age. To avoid fractions, the quotient is multiplied by 100. Thus a child with a mental age of 8 and an actual age of 10 would possess an I.Q. of 80:

$$I.Q. = \frac{8 \times 100}{10} = 80$$

This intelligence quotient remains remarkably constant for any given individual both during childhood and in adult life.[1] Differences of mental exercise and even of nutrition seem to affect it but little, though certain diseases may result in a reduction of I.Q.[2]

4. Technique of Measurement

Although one aims at measuring inborn capacity, there is no reason why it should not be accurately measured inferentially through the medium of some acquired ability, e.g. reading and verbal ability, provided all the persons to be measured have had equal training, i.e. have been equally exposed to opportunities for acquiring verbal skill. Indeed, experiment has shown that verbal tests may be decidedly more ' saturated ' with ' g ' than most non-verbal and performance tests. Stephenson[3] has shown, however, that there is probably a verbal factor over and above ' g ' running pretty evenly through most verbal sub-tests, and that non-verbal tests are free from this. Nevertheless, having regard to the high saturation of the former with ' g ' and to the fewness of satisfactory non-verbal sub-tests, there is little inaccuracy in using a verbal test whenever a normal level of verbal education can be taken for granted, i.e. whenever one can be certain that the vocabulary demanded by the test is well within the vocabulary of even the most backward of the subjects.

[1] " The Constancy of ' g,' " by C. S. Slocombe, *Brit. J. Psychol.*, xxvi, 17, 1926.
[2] *Physique and Intellect*, by Paterson, 1930.
[3] *J. Educ. Psychol.*, March 1931.

In any other circumstances, as when a child has missed much schooling, or in testing foreigners not fully skilled in the language, or in all testing of young children below the age of 8, or especially with deaf and dumb children, a non-verbal or performance test is indispensable.

Tests may be classified in various ways, and the division into verbal and performance tests or into group and individual tests is by no means exhaustive. There are verbal tests which require no reading or writing; there are verbal tests requiring only reading ability (no speaking or writing), and there are non-verbal tests which do not differ in any significant way from performance tests, except that they are done on paper and require movements of a pencil instead of movements of a wooden model. Again, even within the class of non-verbal paper tests, there is a very significant difference between 'pictorial' tests on the one hand and on the other 'perceptual' tests which deal only with lines and figures having no meaning or associations other than those directly given to perception. The latter could be used in inter-racial comparisons, even of civilised and uncivilised peoples, whereas the former, though suitable for peoples speaking different languages, could not be used where the pictures would be differently interpreted.

Everything considered, the most useful classification for the practitioner is into paper tests on the one hand and performance tests on the other. For the latter are almost exclusively individual tests, and their bulkiness frequently precludes their use outside the clinic or laboratory; whilst the former, whether verbal or non-verbal, can be used either as group tests or individual tests and are conveniently applied almost anywhere.

5. Test Material

(A) PAPER TESTS—VERBAL AND NON-VERBAL PICTORIAL

There are at least four criteria by which a good intelligence test can be judged: (1) It should contain only sub-tests highly saturated with 'g.' These are such as Synonyms,[1] Classification, Instructions, Completion, Opposites, Analogies, Inferences, etc., and their various modifications, together with others yet to be devised and assayed. Some tests, e.g. Substitution, are good at low mental ages but not so g-saturated higher up. (2) It should be finely graded, i.e. have a large number (100–200) pass or fail items, which should be arranged in order of increasing difficulty. (3) It should be nicely adjusted in difficulty to the age of the subjects, and should not attempt to extend over too wide a range. (4) It should be adequately standardised on a truly representative sample of the population. That it should be intrinsically interesting goes without saying, though it is part of the psychologist's technique, in administration, to make every test entertaining.

Intelligence tests, like most Attainment tests, may be designed to permit either of ' selective ' or ' inventive ' answers. In the latter, the subject supplies the answer himself, whereas in the former he chooses the answer from a number of given alternatives. Although the selective system allows a certain number of correct responses to be obtained by sheer chance, it renders the test more objectively evaluated and eliminates the factor of mere ability to recall items stored in memory, a factor which is certainly quite distinct from intelligence. Most researches indicate that the selective form is more effective for the majority of uses,[2] and the principle is now followed in all good tests.

Granted that the strongest possible motives—competition, desire to please an adult, self-regard, curiosity—have been enlisted, and a sense of pleasurable anticipation aroused, the administration of most tests is a relatively straightforward proceeding. Nevertheless, the experience of most psychologists shows that many teachers have to be warned to resist the teacher's impulse to give help or instruction, and instead to follow the directions with unmitigated exactness. Not only is it necessary to get chil-

[1] " Three Points of Interest to Mental Test Constructors," by C. S. Slocombe, *Brit. J. Psychol.*, xxviii, 19.
[2] " An Enquiry into the Relative Values of the Inventive and Selective Forms of Group Tests of Mental Capacity," by J. G. Cannon, *Austral. J. Psychol.*, iv, 25.

dren uniformly interested, but also to give confidence to those who are nervous. In general, when one knows which is the duller and which the brighter section of the class, the former should be put at the front in order that one may watch lest they go widely astray, give them encouragement, and prevent copying—all of which errors of testing are more common in the duller sections.

Most tests have a time limit, which also should be exactly observed. The imposition of a time limit is in theory sound, since, granted the intention to work quickly, intelligent individuals are quicker [1] and consequently are penalised in a test without time limits by having to dally while the duller ones catch up. Nevertheless, temperamental slowness or quickness to some extent breaks through the intention to work quickly, and in any case nervous individuals may be flustered by the awareness that they will have to work at undue speed. Consequently the time limit has been adjusted in the author's tests to permit the average child just sufficient time to complete the test easily. With adults an exacting time limit is open to still greater objections, for experiments have shown that the performance of adults on speeded tests declines from about the age of 25, whereas ' power,' i.e. the ability granted adequate time, does not.[2] The general ability with adults becomes invested more in particular skills and fields of ability. The individual differences due to the general ability become less important and those due to the group factors become more important. But even the general ability loses some of its fluidity. In fact, there are quite a number of differences between the manifestations of general ability in children and in adults, which led the writer to propose the theory of two forms of ' g '—' fluid ' and ' crystallised.'[3] It is important to be aware of these

[1] See *Quickness and Intelligence*, by E. Bernstein, *Brit. J. Psychol. Monog. Suppl.* No. 7. Also Vernon, P. E., "Intelligence Test Sophistication," *Brit. J. Educ. Psychol.*, 1938, viii, 237–44.
[2] See Lorge, I. "The Influence of the Test upon Mental Decline as a Function of Age," *J. Educ. Psychol.*, 1936, xxxii, 100–10.
[3] Cattell, R. B., "The Measurement of Adult Intelligence," *Psychol. Bulletin*, 1943, xl, 153–93.

in making any comparisons of children's and adults' mental measurements and in making predictions from them.

In many instances one wishes to retest a child's intelligence after the lapse of some months or years. When more than a year elapses it is quite safe to use the same test, for the test items are almost invariably forgotten, and in any case the child's growing intelligence encounters the critical questions within a new region of the scale.

But for purposes of more immediate retesting, the best-known tests are always prepared in an A and a B Form of equal difficulty and similar construction—the B Form being for retesting shortly after the A Form has been used. The layman is frequently suspicious as to the effects of practice in intelligence testing. Since practice does not increase intelligence itself, the better the intelligence test—i.e. the more it is saturated with ' g '—the less it is susceptible to practice effects. Experiment shows that in repeated testings the score goes up very slightly between the first and second testings, but that thereafter the increase is quite negligible. This first increase through practice, as also, to some extent, that resulting from coaching, is nothing more than the settling down to that type of examination situation, and is only appreciable in the lower intelligence levels, or among very young children and with adults who have never been in an examination situation. In these cases—or still more where these cases are in a mixed group with practised individuals—it is wise to give a short 'practice' or 'buffer' test (the results of which are thrown away) before the test proper, when any accurate results are required.[1] For this reason the scores (but, of course, not the I.Q.) on the B Forms which are intended to be given last, are slightly higher than the equivalent scores on the A Forms, at least over the lower ranges of intelligence.

To see the meaning of an intelligence test score in full

[1] See e.g. C. S. Slocombe, " The Influence of Practice on Mental Tests," *Forum of Educ.*, xxvi, 3.

perspective we may represent it by the following formula [1]

$$\text{Performance} = G + dG + c + t + f + fv + e + R$$

in which G is the innate general ability; dG the environmentally produced change in general ability; c the cultural gain through the test being in informations or skills advantageous to the individual in question; t the effect of training specifically in intelligence test situations; f the 'function fluctuation' through psychological change or fatigue, etc.; fv the function fluctuation through changes in will and interest; e the experimental error in measurement from all other causes, extrinsic to the subject; and R the influence of specific abilities unavoidably included with the general ability measure.

(i) *Test Material Available* (*Detailed*)

At present some two dozen group and individual tests in Britain and America satisfy the above demands. Particulars of the age-ranges for which they are suitable and the time required are set out below. Since details of administration and norms are given in the respective handbooks issued with the tests, no further instructions in regard to the use of these tests need be given here (except in the case of the author's own tests, where new norms are set out more recent than those available in the handbook). The Binet-Simon scale or any of its modifications is not included among them, for reasons given in the Foreword. Its component test items are frequently more tests of scholastic attainment and life experience than of ' g,' [2] and the pass or fail items are far too few. The personal relationship that arises between tester and tested in the course of the testing, and which is sometimes claimed to give greater reliability to this type of individual test, is just as likely to

---

[1] Cattell, R. B., "A Culture-Free Intelligence Test, I and II," *J. Educ. Psychol.*, 1940, xxxi, 161–80, and 1941, xxxii, 81–100.
[2] See e.g. " Intelligence Tests for Children of 4 to 8 Years," R. B. Cattell and H. Bristol, *Brit. J. Educ. Psychol.*, iii, 1933.

introduce errors because of shyness and other temperamental effects in the child [1] and because the examiner is
likely to be affected in doubtful cases by the appearance
and bearing of the child.[2]   It is certainly true that the
examiner gains evidence of temperament and character
traits in administering the Binet intelligence scale which he
would not gain with paper tests, but when definite temperament tests are available it is a mistake to vitiate the
intelligence test by roughly blending the two.   The reten-
tion of the Binet tests in a good deal of clinical work to-day
is alike a great tribute to the early genius of Binet and to
the conservatism, rather than the scientific conscience, of
the present generation of clinical psychologists.

The following is a list of some good available tests, in
alphabetical order.   When inspecting the descriptions of
tests it is necessary to remember that, generally speaking,
an intelligence test should not have less than 30 minutes'
duration (more with young children).   Teachers are often
inclined to use shorter and shorter tests, whilst still hoping
to use the results as a basis for important decisions—sometimes affecting the candidate's whole career.   Fifty minutes is not too much when such decisions are in question.
The tests have been arranged according to age levels, i.e.
according to the *mental ages* for which they are suitable,
and are provided with brief comments on their structure.
Certain tests, notably the Northumberland, the National
Institute, and the Cattell Tests, provide a complete series
of uniform tests, one for each age-range section.   With the
exception of the Otis Test, they are all English, since the
wording and standardisation of American tests are often
unsuitable for English children.

---

[1] See also the evidence in Chapter VII, p. 302.

[2] Too strong a motivation in intelligence testing—as in most cognitive performance
—may be disadvantageous.

A group test would seem to produce quite adequate attention and interest.   Over
a wide range of motivation strength there is practically no variation of score on intelligence tests.   Maller and Zubin (" The Effect of Motivation upon Intelligence Test
Scores," *J. Genet. Psychol.*, xli, 136) found that very strong motive led to (i) no increase
of score, (ii) increase in number of items attempted, balanced by (iii) increase in
number of errors.   See also A. Wild, " The Effect of Conation upon Cognition,"
Brit. J. Psychol.

Infancy: 0–4-year Range

Gesell's Norms of Development from birth to the sixth year. Available in *The Mental Growth of the Pre-school Child* (Macmillan). No unusual apparatus needed. These test situations are by no means always tests of intelligence, but are probably fairly saturated with ' g ' during the first and second year, especially those items in the " Adaptive Behaviour " section (chap. x). (No investigations on ' g ' value have been made.) They enable one to fix mental age to within about two months. Carefully selected and standardised, but the norms in the upper ages are a little low for English children.

BRIEF ' MENTAL CAPACITY ' SCALE FROM GESELL (MAINLY ' ADAPTIVE BEHAVIOUR ' ITEMS) FOR 0–4 YEAR RANGE

4 months
- 85 to 100%. Can lift head when lying on back. Resist pressure to move head.
- 65 to 85%. Follow slowly-moving plate or bright light with eyes.
- 20 to 50%. Move arms in an attempt to shift piece of paper (letter size) placed over face when prone on back.

6 months
- 85 to 100%. Pick up spoon from table.
- 65 to 85%. Sit up with slight support.
- ,, ,, ,, Express recognition of strangers as being different from familiar faces.
- 20 to 50%. Look round for fallen spoon.
- 0 to 20%. Sit up alone.

9 months
- 85 to 100%. Sit up alone.
- 65 to 84%. React to mirror images (of self) shown. Some response indicating interest or recognition counts as a pass.
- ,, ,, ,, Clasp and pull down ring dangled on string just above head.
- ,, ,, ,, Can say ' Mama ' and ' Dada ' and one other word.
- 20 to 50%. Lift inverted cup to recover cube after seeing cube placed under cup.

12 months
- 65 to 75%. Place cube in cup when told (without assistance by gesture)
- 50 to 65%. Climb (crawl) up stairs.
- 20 to 50%. Walk alone.
- ,, ,, ,, Can pile *three* blocks (cubes) on top of each other to make a stable pile, after once seeing it done.

18 months
- 65 to 85%. Make attempt to turn knob when wanting door open.
- 50 to 65%. Make single vertical stroke (distinct from scribble) after seeing one made as a model.
- 20 to 50%. Put cube in plate or in cup according to instructions (i.e. discriminate between plate and cup).
- ,, ,, ,, Point to two parts of body (out of eye, nose, mouth).
- ,, ,, ,, Pile *four* blocks in a stable pillar (see above).

orting of junior children.   Time required, 45 minutes.
standardised.   Stencil keys.   Obtainable from
srs. G. Harrap & Co.

eight. Non-verbal.—Ten short sub-tests of good
dity. Age-range 6–11 years.   Time required, about 35
utes (18¼ minutes' testing time, remainder instructions,
).   Soundly standardised. Obtainable from Messrs. G.
rrap & Co.

ior and High School School Range: 11–17 years inclusive

(Tests for scholarship examinations at 11 years should be
osen from the 11–14 mental age-range, since most
holarship candidates between whom it is desired to dis-
nguish finely fall at a 12–13 mental age.)

*American Council on Education Psychological Examination for
igh School Students*.—Companion test to adult form (see
elow).   Designed by L. L. and T. G. Thurstone and
evised each year. High validity as tested by internal
actorial composition.   One hour.   Machine scorable.
Obtainable Co-operative Test Service (see below).

Cattell Test, Scale II.   Verbal with non-verbal items.
Group or Individual. Ages 11–15 years.   (Quite suitable
for average and sub-average adults.)—Six sub-tests, giving
151 pass or fail items.   The validity of these individual
sub-tests ranges [1] from 0·65 to 0·85. Standardised on
2,070 cases supplied from various parts of Great Britain.
Time required, 70 minutes. The first sub-tests have a
generous time limit to give subjects a sense of confidence.
A and B Forms provided.   Preliminary 'practice' test
supplied to eliminate 'test sophistication.' The test can
be given in a much shortened form requiring 24 minutes
and correlating with the full scale [1] 0·88. Stencil key.
Obtainable from Messrs. G. Harrap & Co.

Chelsea Tests.   (P. B. Ballard.)   Verbal ages 11–14
years.   Group or Individual.—Four sub-tests giving 100
pass or fail items. First test timed, but others unlimited.
Total time therefore varies, but about an hour generally

[1] Halstead, H., and Chase, V. E., "Review of a Verbal Intelligence Scale on
Military Neurotic Patients," *Brit. J. Med. Psychol.*, xx, 195–201, 1944.

---

2 years

65 to 85%. Pile *four* blocks in a stable pillar (see above).
„ „ „   Make single vertical stroke, with pencil, in imitation (see above).
50 to 65%. Obey propositions:
  Put the ball on the box.
  Put the ball in the box.
  Put the ball behind the box.
  Put the ball in front of the box (or chair).
  Put the ball under the chair.
  (getting *three* correct.)
20 to 50%. Make tolerable drawing of a circle after seeing one drawn.
„ „ „   Build ' bridge ' with three bricks after seeing one made.
„ „ „   Can name *three* objects in a picture (Dutch Home Scene, (" Tell me what you can see ").

3 years

65 to 85%. Use pronouns, plurals, and past tense in speech.
„ „ „   Presented with several cubes and cup. " Put just *one* block into the cup." Respond correctly.
50 to 65%. " Put *two* blocks in cup " (as above and after doing one successfully). Respond correctly.
20 to 50%. Copy a cross just recognisably from a model + presented (but not drawn in their presence).
„ „ „   Can carry out three commissions without asking further. " Here's a key; I want you to put it on that chair over there; then I want you to shut that door, and then bring me the box which you see over there." (Pointing in turn to these objects.) Repeat, stressing: *First* put the key on the chair; *then*, etc.

4 years

65 to 85%. Successfully respond to instructions to put only two cubes in cup. (See 3-year test above.)
„ „ „   Answer reasonably two out of three:
  " What must you do when you are sleepy ? "
  " What ought you to do when you are cold ? "
  " What ought you to do when you are hungry ? "
20 to 50%. Copy a square (recognisably) from a model (but not drawn in their presence).
„ „ „   Provide two oblong cards, one divided by a diagonal cut into two triangles. Child presented with two triangles and asked to " Put them together so that they look exactly like this (pointing to rectangle).' Allow three attempts of 1 minute each. Pass if two of three are successful.
„ „ „   Give an answer to " What must you do if you have lost something ? " which shows that expression ' lost ' is fully understood.
0 to 20%. Give a correct answer on three out of four ' missing feature ' pictures. " What is left out of the face ? " (Four pictures of faces as in Binet 7 year. One with mouth, one with nose, one with ear, and one with eye missing.)

The percentages on the left indicate the number of children found by Gesell to pass this test at the age concerned. A child should have the mental age indicated on the left when he passes the tests on which 50% (say 40–60%) of the children of that age succeed. But unfortunately Gesell's norms are not arranged in 50% categories. With the arrangement of items made above a child should pass for a given year when he succeeds in more than a half of the items for that year (except in the Fourth year, when just a half will suffice).

The Measurement of Intelligence in Infants and Pre-school Children.   Psyche Cattell, Psychological Corporation, 1940.

This is a test which, in part, is developmental, as in Gesell's scale, and in part describes tests requiring some apparatus. It is, perhaps, the most useful and generally valid set of tests yet proposed for the 0–4-year range, and is well standardised.

Merrill Palmer Test for children of 21 to 63 months (effective range 2–6 years). Time required $\frac{3}{4}$ hour to $1\frac{1}{4}$ hours, according to child.—A medley of some 38 verbal and non-verbal tests, giving 93 separate diagnostic items. The test is not constructed on intelligence test principles in so far as the constituents are selected on grounds of *low* mutual correlation (see Stutsman, *Mental Measurement of the Pre-School Child*, 1922). Probably not a very sound measure of ' g,' but rather of general development. Interesting to children and highly practicable to administer. Correlates ·78–·79 with Binet score. Recently standardised for this country by Hilda Bristol (details published in Prof. Hamley's section [1] on " Mental Tests " in the *Education Year Book*, 1935), on 530 children, with the following results:

Age in Months:	21	24	27	30	33	36	39	42	45	48	51	54	57	60	63	66	68
Points:	11	17	23	30	34	44	51	57	63	69	73	76	79	62	64	66	67

The American norms, on 631 cases, are about 5 points lower than these over the whole range. Apparatus (fairly extensive) obtainable from Messrs. Stoelting, or from Raper, Psychological Laboratory, University College, Gower St., London.

Minnesota Pre-School Scale (Goodenough, Foster, Van Wagener). Range 18 months to 6 years.—Not so attractive to children as is the Merrill Palmer. Available, Educational Test Bureau, Minneapolis.

The California First-year Mental Scale.—A series of test items selected from various sources. Standardised on 61 infants over range 1 to 21 months. Consistency coefficient ·62 (0–3 months) to ·86 (4–18 years). Validity unestablished. Described in University of California Syllabus Series, 1933, No. 243.

[1] Or " The Testing of Intelligence," H. R. Hamley. Evans Bros., 1935.

On the whole, one is forced to a yet no very satisfactory tests of ' age-range.

Kindergarten Period: 4–8 *years*

Dartington Intelligence Scale (Cattell Scale 0). Individual test, 4–8 years.— tests.[1] 96 pass or fail items. Standard on well-sampled group. American s Psyche Cattell. Time required—$\frac{3}{4}$ hour 25 minutes. Obtainable from Messrs. (

Junior School Range: 8–11 *years*

Ballard's Junior Test (*New Examiner*, p. 23 of test types, some of which involve a cert general knowledge. 100 items. No time for elementary school children of 8–14 years.

Cattell Test, Scale I. Non-verbal. Group For ages 8–11 years.—Eight sub-tests of g 106 pass or fail items. Standardised on 620 se including individuals of known mental age. quired, 45–50 minutes. A and B Forms prov test can be given in a shortened form requiring 2 Stencil key. Preliminary practice given in Obtainable from Messrs. G. Harrap & Co. (Th places the verbal Scale I, the verbal test having be not entirely satisfactory for children of 8–11.)

Otis Primary.—Eight non-verbal subjects of good Ages 6–10 years. Norms too low for English (about 11 points of I.Q.). English norms recent pared. Results expressed in Indices of Brightness are not comparable with Intelligence Quotients, generally not so useful. Time required, about 35 mi Obtainable from Messrs. G. Harrap & Co.

Simplex Junior.—Group or Individual. An ' omni type of test. Age-range rather large (7–14 years) for acc

[1] See " Intelligence Tests for Children of 4–8 years," by R. B. Cattell H. Bristol, *J. Educ. Psychol.*, iii, 1933.

suffices.   Permits of inventive as well as selective answers.
Tentative norms which do not cover low 11- and 12-year-
olds or high 13- and 14-year scores.   Material and norms
in *Group Tests of Intelligence* (Ballard).

Columbia Test.   (P. B. Ballard.)   Verbal.   Ages 10–14.—
Six sub-tests.   Four or 5 minutes each; two untimed.
Tentative norms not extending to mental ages below
10 or above 14.   Material in *Group Tests of Intelligence*
(Ballard).

Group Test 34.   Verbal, with non-verbal items.   Group
or Individual.   Age range 10–15 years.—Nine sub-tests
of good validity, giving 200 pass or fail items.   Rather
large vocabulary demand on two tests.   Timed on each
sub-test.   Total test time, 38 minutes.   Well standardised.
Available from National Institute of Industrial Psychology.

Moray House Test 10.   (Godfrey Thomson.)   Verbal.
Group or Individual.   Ages 10·6–12.—Fifteen sub-tests
representing five distinct types of sub-test.   100 items, some
on only a two-response basis.   Sub-tests not timed.   Total
time, 45 minutes, plus 10 minutes for a 'shock absorber
test.'   Very soundly standardised.   Available from University of London Press.

Moray House Test IIa.   (Godfrey Thomson.)   Verbal.
Group or Individual.   Ages 10·6–12.—An 'omnibus' test,
without distinct sub-tests, the instructions being given
afresh on each item.   Seventy-five items.   Forty-five minutes, plus 10 minutes for 'shock absorber' test.   Very
soundly standardised, over small age range.   Available
from University of London Press.   This test and test 12
were originally twin tests (i.e. A and B Forms), but the
latter has been converted into the Scottish Mental Survey
Test.

Northox Group Intelligence Test.   (G. P. Williams.)   Ages
11–12 years.—Five sub-tests, one requiring arithmetical
knowledge.   Time, 30 minutes.   Obtainable from Messrs.
G. Harrap & Co.

Northumberland Mental Tests, No. 1.   (Godfrey Thomson.)
Group or Individual.   Verbal.   Ages 10–12·6.—Twelve

sub-tests. Time required, 1 hour. Very soundly standardised on 2,500 children in Northumberland. Supplied with 10 minutes' practice 'introduction' test. Obtainable from Messrs. G. Harrap & Co.

Northumberland Standardised Tests — III, Intelligence. (Burt.) Group or Individual. Verbal. Ages 10–12, but quite effective a year above and below these limits.— Nine highly valid sub-tests. Time—10 minutes for preliminaries; 1 hour for test. Time limit on each sub-test. Soundly standardised. Obtainable from University of London Press.

Northumberland Mental Tests, No. 2. (Godfrey Thomson.) Group or Individual. Verbal. Ages 12·6 and over.— Fourteen sub-tests, giving 60 pass or fail items. Time, 1 hour, notified every $\frac{1}{4}$ hour, but no limit on each sub-test. Soundly standardised. Obtainable from Messrs. G. Harrap & Co.

Otis Advanced Test. Verbal. Group or Individual. Ages 10 to about 13.—Ten sub-tests of good validity. Possibly not yet adequately standardised for English children. Results expressed as Indices of Brightness or as Intelligence Quotients. A and B Forms available; also an abbreviated test. Time required, about 1 hour 10 minutes. Obtainable from Messrs. G. Harrap & Co.

Scottish Research Council Mental Survey Test (1932). Verbal and Pictorial. Age range 10–12 years.—Mixed items. One demanding large vocabulary. Time required, 50 minutes. Very soundly standardised (on 87,000 Scottish children). Obtainable from University of London Press.

Simplex Group Test. Group or Individual. Verbal. Age range 10–14 years.—Twenty-six sub-tests. (Rather big vocabulary demand.) Time required, 1 hour. Obtainable from Messrs. G. Harrap & Co.

Spearman's " Measure of Intelligence." Verbal. Booklets not required. Age range 10–14 years.—Seven highly valid sub-tests. Time required, about $1\frac{1}{4}$ hours. Soundly standardised. (See *Forum of Education*, 1929.) Obtainable from Methuen & Co.

Adult Tests, i.e. 14 *Years and Upwards*

(*Note.*—Most of these tests are better adapted to 'superior adults.' For getting accurate measurements of the lower mental ranges among adults—e.g. among unskilled workers —it is advisable to use tests from 11–14-year ranges. In the case of adult defectives, the 4–8-range, e.g. the Dartington Scale, will be found most effective.)

American Council on Education Psychological Examination for College Freshmen.—Six sections; one hour; yields distinct scores in (1) verbal and (2) quantitative-numerical abilities. Designed by L. L. and T. G. Thurstone. New form published each year. Machine scorable. Obtainable Co-operative Test Service, 15, Amsterdam Avenue, New York.

Cattell Test, Scale III. Verbal with non-verbal items. Group or Individual.—Six highly valid sub-tests, giving 151 pass or fail items. Preliminary practice test. Time required, 1 hour 10 minutes. Time limit for each of sub-tests. Standardised on 2,000 adults, with additional occupational norms.[1] A and B Forms available. The test can be given in a much shortened form (24 minutes), especially suitable for subjects of limited reading vocabulary. Stencil keys. Obtainable from Messrs. G. Harrap & Co.

Crichton Test. (Dr. Ballard.) Verbal. Group or Individual.—Omnibus test of 28 items. Inventive and selective answers. No time limit. Rough norms. Material in *Group Tests of Intelligence* (Ballard).

Group Test 33. Verbal. Group or Individual.—Five sub-tests. Synonyms require too large a vocabulary for average adult. Time required, 30 minutes. Obtainable from National Institute of Industrial Psychology.

Otis Self-administering Tests of Mental Ability. Higher Examination. Group and Individual.—One test of 75 items. Scored on 20 or on 30 minutes. A useful rough test of short duration. Obtainable from World Book Co., Yonkers, N.Y.

[1] See " Occupational Norms of Intelligence and Standardisation of an Adult Intelligence Test," *Brit. J. Psychol.*, xv, 1, July 1934.

Stanford-Binet, 1937 revision, has two forms, L and M, as described above, and has had sufficient ' top ' added to make a sound test for superior adults, but is still founded on the questionable theory of the original Binet.   Obtainable from Houghton Mifflin, Boston.

Wechsler-Bellevue.   Age 10 and over.   Individual, verbal. —Shares the unsatisfactory theoretical foundation of the Binet and is rather heavily loaded with ' V ' factor and general knowledge.   Obtainable from Psychological Corporation, Fifth Avenue, New York, 1939.

Tests of very brief duration (and therefore low reliability) are available in the 12-minute Otis and the abridged Otis by Wonderlic (Wonderlic, E., and Hovland, C. I., *J. Appl. Psychol.* xxiii, 685–702, 1939).

Measurement of Deterioration in Intelligence

A special case of the measurement of intelligence is that in which one is measuring the ability of some person in whom, through epilepsy or other psychotic conditions, or even through old age, deterioration is believed to have taken place temporarily or permanently.   One wishes to measure both the present intelligence (which can be done in the ordinary way with a suitable ' g ' test) and the original level of intelligence.   The task of assessing the latter is like reconstructing the dimension of some ancient building from its present ruins.   Size of vocabulary is known to correlate closely with intelligence among people of reasonably similar education.   The researches of Simmins,[1] Babcock,[2] Shipley, Davies Eysenck,[3] and others show that the vocabulary, at least in patches, persists at its original degree of elaborateness after intelligence has gravely declined.   Score on a suitable vocabulary test, therefore, is the best means yet known to determine what ability a person once had.   The research of Davies Eysenck[3]

---

[1] Constance Simmins, " Deterioration of ' g ' in Psychotic Patients," *J. Mental Sci.*, October, 1933.

[2] E. Babcock, " An Experiment in the Measurement of Mental Deterioration," *Arch. of Psychol.*, No. 117, N.Y., 1930.

[3] M. Davies Eysenck, " An Exploratory Study of Mental Organisation in Senility," *J. of Neurol. and Psychiat.*, viii, 15–22, 1945.

and the inquiries of the present writer[1] indicate that the measurement of intelligence where deterioration has occurred is best handled by the concepts of ' fluid and crystallised ability,'[2] according to which *two* scores are finally used to define the individual's general ability.

The Terman Vocabulary Test, being standardised for adults, was used in the above researches, but other suitable tests will be found in the vocabulary section of " Attainment Tests," though they will need to be standardised afresh for this purpose—namely, in relation to I.Q.s among adults.

(ii) *Other Tests (Not Detailed)*

Measurement of Intelligence by Drawings (F. L. Goodenough). —Owing to the very large specific factor in drawing ability, it is not a means by which one would normally choose to estimate intelligence. Scored in the particular manner worked out by Goodenough, however, correlations as high as ·76 with intelligence may be obtained. For details, see Special Aptitudes, p. 62, of next chapter.

Bristol Group Reasoning Tests. (Dr. Barbara Dale.)— Inferences only. Well graded. A test which has been shown to involve a rather extensive special ability.[2] University of London Press.

Evesham Intelligence Test. (Dr. Haselhurst, Grammar School, Evesham.)

Leeds Intelligence Test. (Dr. Terry Thomas.)—Nos. 1–4 for boys of 11 plus. Extension for 15-16 years. Bell & Co.

Oxton Group Intelligence Test. (G. P. Williams.)—For children of 11–14. Mainly general knowledge, as devised for certain Education Committees.

Porteus Maze Tests. Individual. Paper mazes, 6–15 years, one for each year. Excellent for inter-cultural comparisons, but involve a personality stability factor additional to intelligence.

Tomlinson's " West Riding Tests of Mental Ability."—

---

[1] Cattell, R. B., " The Measurement of Adult Intelligence," *Psychol. Bull.*, xl, 153–93, 1943.

[2] See Spearman's *Abilities of Man*, p. 225, for summary of evidence.

NORMS FOR CATTELL

READY RECKONER FOR

Score on Complete Test		10	14	16	18	20	22	24	26	28	30	32	34	36	38	40	42	44	46
Score on Abbreviated Form		8	10	11	12	14	15	16	17	18	19	20	21	22	23	25	26	27	28
ACTUAL AGE OF CHILD IN YEARS AND MONTHS	4.0	84	90	94	97	100	103	106	110	113	117	120	123	127	131	135	139	143	148
	.6	75	80	83	86	89	92	95	98	101	104	107	110	113	116	120	123	126	131
	5.0	67	72	74	77	80	83	86	89	91	94	96	99	102	105	108	111	114	118
	.6	61	65	68	70	73	75	78	80	82	85	88	90	93	95	98	101	104	107
	6.0	56	60	63	65	67	69	71	73	75	78	80	82	85	87	90	92	95	98
	.6	51	55	57	59	61	63	65	68	70	72	74	76	78	80	83	86	88	91
	7.0		51	53	55	57	59	61	63	65	67	69	71	73	75	77	79	82	84
	.6					53	55	57	59	61	63	65	66	68	70	72	74	76	79
	8.0					50	51	53	55	57	59	61	62	64	66	68	70	72	74
	.6							52	53	55	57	58	60	62	64	66	67	69
	9.0										52	53	55	57	59	60	62	64	66
	10.0													51	52	54	56	57	59
	11.0															49	50	52	54
Adults 15 +																40	41	43	44

Pick out the column which bears the score and the row marked by the age of

SCALE O (DARTINGTON SCALE)
CALCULATING INTELLIGENCE QUOTIENTS

48	50	52	54	56	58	60	62	64	66	68	70	72	74	76	78	80	82	84	86	88	90
29	30	32	33	34	36	37	38	40	41	43	44	46	47	49	51	52	54	55	56	57	59
152	157	161	164																		
135	140	144	148	153	158	164	169														
122	127	131	134	138	143	148	153	158	164												
111	115	118	121	125	128	134	139	144	150	155	161	167									
101	105	108	111	115	119	123	128	132	137	142	147	152	158	165							
93	97	100	103	106	110	114	118	122	126	131	136	141	146	152	158	164	170				
87	90	93	96	99	102	106	110	113	117	122	127	132	137	141	146	152	158	164	170		
81	84	87	89	92	96	99	102	105	109	114	118	122	127	132	137	142	147	153	159	165	171
76	79	81	84	86	89	93	96	99	103	107	111	115	119	124	128	133	138	144	149	155	160
72	74	76	79	81	83	87	90	93	97	100	104	108	112	116	120	125	130	135	140	145	150
68	70	72	75	77	79	82	85	88	91	95	99	103	107	110	114	119	123	127	132	137	142
61	63	65	67	69	71	74	76	79	82	85	88	91	95	99	103	106	110	115	119	123	128
56	57	59	61	63	65	67	69	72	75	77	80	83	86	90	93	97	100	104	108	112	116
46	47	49	51	53	54	55	56	57	58	59	62	64	66	69	71	73	75	77	79	81	84

the person tested. At their junction will be found his intelligence quotient.

NORMS FOR

DIRECTIONS.—Pick out the column which bears the score and the row marked by the
the examinee expressed in

SCORE

	FORM A	16	20	23	25	26	27	28	29	30	31	32	33	34	35	36	37	38
	FORM B	20	25	29	31	32	33	34	35	36	37	38	39	40	41	42	43	44
	7 (6·9–7·2)	86	93	97	100	101	103	105	106	107	109	110	111	112	113	114	115	115
	7½ (7·3–7·8)	80	87	91	94	95	96	97	99	100	102	103	104	104	105	106	106	108
	8 (7·9–8·2)	75	81	85	88	89	90	91	93	94	95	96	97	98	99	100	100	101
	8½ (8·3–8·8)	71	77	80	83	84	85	86	87	88	90	91	92	92	93	94	95	96
	9 (8·9–9·2)	67	73	76	78	79	80	81	82	84	85	86	87	87	88	89	89	90
	9½ (9·3–9·8)	63	68	71	75	75	76	77	78	79	80	81	82	83	83	84	84	85
	10 (9·9–10·2)	60	65	68	70	71	72	73	74	75	76	77	78	78	79	80	80	81
	10½ (10·3–10·8)	57	62	65	67	68	69	70	71	71	72	73	74	74	75	76	76	77
	11 (10·9–11·2)	55	59	62	64	65	65	66	67	68	69	70	71	71	72	73	73	74
	11½ (11·3–11·8)	52	56	59	61	62	63	64	65	65	66	67	68	68	69	70	70	71
	12 (11·9–12·2)	50	54	57	58	59	60	61	62	63	64	64	65	65	66	67	67	68
	12½ (12·3–12·8)		52	54	56	57	57	58	59	60	61	62	62	63	63	64	64	65
	13 (12·9–13·2)		50	52	54	55	56	56	57	58	59	59	60	60	61	61	62	62
	14 (13·9–14·2)			45	50	51	52	52	53	53	54	55	56	56	57	57	57	58
	Adults (17·9–)																57	58

	FORM A	55	56	57	58	59	60	61	62	63	64	65	66	67	68	69	70	71
	FORM B	61	62	62	63	64	65	66	67	67	68	69	70	71	72	73	74	75
	7 (6·9–7·2)	141	142	143	144	145	147	149	152	154	157	159	161	163	165	167	170	173
	7½ (7·3–7·8)	131	132	133	134	136	137	139	141	143	145	148	150	152	154	156	159	162
	8 (7·9–8·2)	123	124	125	126	127	128	130	133	135	137	139	141	142	144	146	149	152
	8½ (8·3–8·8)	116	117	118	119	120	121	123	125	127	128	130	132	134	136	138	140	142
	9 (8·9–9·2)	109	110	111	112	113	114	116	118	119	121	123	125	126	127	129	132	135
	9½ (9·3–9·8)	103	104	105	106	107	108	110	112	114	115	117	118	120	121	123	125	127
	10 (9·9–10·2)	98	99	100	101	102	103	105	106	107	109	111	112	113	115	117	119	121
	10½ (10·3–10·8)	93	94	95	96	97	98	100	101	103	105	106	107	108	109	111	113	115
	11 (10·9–11·2)	89	90	91	92	94	95	96	97	99	100	101	102	104	105	107	108	110
	11½ (11·3–11·8)	86	87	88	89	90	90	91	92	93	95	96	97	99	100	102	103	105
	12 (11·9–12·2)	82	83	84	85	86	87	88	89	90	91	92	93	95	96	97	99	101
	12½ (12·3–12·8)	78·6	79	80	81	81·6	82	84	85	86	87	89	90	91	92	93	95	97
	13 (12·9–13·2)	75	76	77	78	78	79	80	82	83	83	85	86	87	88	90	91	93
	14 (13·9–14·2)	70	71	72	72	73	74	75	76	77	78	79	80	81	82	83	84	85
	Adults (17·9–)	67	68	69	69	70	71	72	73	73	74	75	75	76	77	78	79	80·6

AGE IN YEARS

This standardisation is based on measurements of some 1,200 persons as described
elementary and secondary school scores, as described

SCALE I

age of the person tested.   At their junction will be found the intelligence quotient of relation to a normal of 100.

39	40	41	42	43	44	45	46	47	48	49	50	51	52	53	54	FORM A
45	46	47	48	49	50	51	52	53	54	55	56	57	58	59	60	FORM B
117	119	120	122	123	125	126	128	129	131	132	133	135	136	137	139	7 (6·9–7·2)
109	110	112	113	115	116	117	119	120	122	123	124	126	127	128	129	7½ (7·3–7·8)
102	104	105	106	107	109	110	111	112	114	115	116	117	119	120	122	8 (7·9–8·2)
97	98	99	100	101	103	104	105	106	107	108	109	110	112	113	114	8½ (8·3–8·8)
91	92	93	94	95	96	98	99	100	101	102	103	104	105	106	108	9 (8·9–9·2)
87	88	89	90	91	92	93	94	95	96	97	98	99	100	101	102	9½ (9·3–9·8)
82	83	84	85	86	87	88	89	90	91	92	93	94	95	96	97	10 (9·9–10·2)
78	79	80	81	82	83	84	85	86	87	88	89	90	91	92	93	10½ (10·3–10·8)
75	75	76	77	78	79	80	81	82	83	84	84	85	86	87	88	11 (10·9–11·2)
72	73	73	74	75	76	77	77	78	79	80	81	82	83	84	85	11½ (11·3–11·8)
69	69	70	71	72	72	73	74	75	76	77	77	78	79	80	81	12 (11·9–12·2)
66	66	67	68	69	70	70	71	72	73	74	74	75	76	77	78	12½ (12·3–12·8)
63	64	65	65	66	67	68	68	69	70	71	71	72	73	74	75	13 (12·9–13·2)
59	59	60	61	61	62	63	63	64	65	66	66	67	68	69	69	14 (13·9–14·2)
58	59	60	61	61	61	62	62	63	64	65	65	66	66	66	67	Adults (17·9–)

72	73	74	75	76	77	78	79	81	83	86	89	93	97	101	105	FORM A
76	77	78	79	80	81	82	84	85	87	90	93	97	100	104	108	FORM B
165	168															7 (6·9–7·2)
155	158	161	164	167												7½ (7·3–7·8)
145	148	151	154	158	162	167										8 (7·9–8·2)
137	140	143	146	149	153	158	168									8½ (8·3–8·8)
130	133	136	138	141	145	150	159	168								9 (8·9–9·2)
123	126	129	131	134	137	142	151	160	170	176	179					9½ (9·3–9·8)
117	120	123	125	128	131	135	144	152	162	167	170	181				10 (9·9–10·2)
112	115	117	119	122	125	129	137	145	155	160	163	173				10½ (10·3–10·8)
107	109	111	114	117	120	123	131	139	148	152	155	165	185			11 (10·9–11·2)
103	105	107	110	112	115	118	126	134	142	147	149	158	176			11½ (11·3–11·8)
99	100	102	105	107	110	113	121	128	136	141	143	152	170			12 (11·9–12·2)
95	97	99	100	104	106	109	116	123	131	136	138	146	163			12½ (12·3–12·8)
87	90	92	94	96	98	101	108	114	121	126	128	131	152	190		13 (12·9–13·2)
81	83	84	85	88	88	90	95	100	103	107	109	113	123	143	154	14 (13·9–14·2)
																Adults (17·9–)

elsewhere.   The typical population is reconstructed from a combination of in the *Brit. J. Psychol.*, January 1936.

NORMS FOR

SCORE

FORM A	39	41	44	47	52	55	58	61	64	67	69	71	73	74	75	76	77	78
FORM B	40	42	45	48	53	57	60	63	65	69	71	73	75	76	77	78	79	80
7½ (7·3-7·8)	93	100	106	113	120	123	127	130	134	137	140	144	147	149	151	153	156	158
8½ (8·3-8·8)	83	88	94	100	106	109	112	115	118	122	124	126	129	131	134	136	138	139
9½ (9·3-9·8)	73	79	84	89	95	97	100	103	105	108	110	113	116	118	119	121	123	125
10½ (10·3-10·8)	67	72	76	81	86	88	90	93	95	98	100	102	105	106	108	110	111	113
11 (10·9-11·2)	64	68	73	77	82	84	86	88	91	94	96	98	100	101	103	104	106	108
11½ (11·3-11·8)	62	66	69	74	78	80	82	85	87	89	91	93	96	98	99	100	101	103
12 (11·9-12·2)	58	63	67	72	75	77	79	82	84	86	87	89	91	92	94	96	98	99
12½ (12·3-12·8)	56	60	64	68	72	74	76	78	80	82	84	86	88	89	91	92	93	95
13 (12·9-13·2)	54	58	62	65	69	71	73	75	77	79	81	83	85	86	87	88	89	91
13½ (13·3-13·8)	52	56	59	63	67	69	71	72	74	76	78	79	82	83	84	85	86	88
14 (13·9-14·2)	50	54	57	61	64	66	68	70	72	74	75	77	79	80	81	82	83	85
14½ (14·3-14·8)	50	54	57	60	63	64	66	67	69	71	72	74	76	77	78	79	80	82
15 (14·9-15·2)	50	54	57	60	63	64	66	67	69	71	72	73	74	75	76	77	78	79
15½ (15·3-15·8)	50	54	57	60	63	64	66	67	69	71	72	73	74	75	76	77	78	79
16 (15·9-16·2)	50	54	57	60	63	64	66	67	69	71	72	73	74	75	76	77	78	79
Adults (17·9-)	50	54	57	60	63	64	66	67	69	71	72	73	74	75	76	77	78	79

FORM A	96	97	98	99	100	101	102	103	104	105	106	107	108	109	110	111	112	113
FORM B	98	99	100	101	101	102	103	104	105	106	107	108	109	110	111	112	113	114
7½ (7·3-7 8)																		
8½ (8·3-8·8)																		
9½ (9·3-9·8)	162	163	166	169	171	173	174											
10½ (10·3-10·8)	147	148	150	153	155	156	157	159	161	162	164	165	167	168	170	172		
11 (10·9-11·2)	140	141	143	145	147	149	150	152	153	155	156	157	159	160	162	163	165	166
11½ (11·3-11·8)	134	135	137	139	141	142	144	146	147	148	149	150	152	153	154	156	157	159
12 (11·9-12·2)	128	129	131	133	135	136	138	139	140	142	143	144	145	146	148	150	152	153
12½ (12·3-12·8)	123	124	126	128	130	131	132	134	135	136	137	138	140	141	143	144	146	147
13 (12·9-13·2)	118	119	121	123	125	126	127	129	130	131	132	133	135	136	137	139	140	141
13½ (13·3-13·8)	114	115	117	119	120	121	122	123	124	125	127	128	130	131	132	133	134	135
14 (13·9-14·2)	110	111	113	114	115	117	119	119	120	121	122	123	125	126	127	129	130	131
14½ (14·3-14·8)	106	107	109	110	112	113	114	115	116	117	118	119	121	122	123	124	125	126
15 (14·9-15·2)	102	103	105	107	108	109	110	111	113	114	115	116	117	118	119	120	121	122
15½ (15·3-15·8)	99	100	102	103	104	105	107	108	109	110	111	112	113	114	115	116	117	118
16 (15·9-16·2)	97	98	99	100	101	102	103	104	105	106	107	108	109	110	111	113	114	115
Adults (17·9-)	97	98	99	100	101	102	102	103	104	105	106	107	107	108	109	109	110	111

AGE IN YEARS

This standardisation is based on measurements of some 2,700 people, sampled from *J. Psychol.*, January 1936. The principle of the 'shifting denominator' (as The psychometrist should note that from the score of 114 and upwards

SCALE II

79	80	81	82	83	84	85	86	87	88	89	90	91	92	93	94	95	FORM A
81	82	83	84	85	86	87	88	89	90	91	92	93	94	95	96	97	FORM B
160	162	164	167	169	171	174											7½ (7·3-7·8)
141	143	145	147	149	151	153	155	157	159	161	163	165	168	171			8½ (8·3-8·8)
127	129	130	132	134	135	137	139	141	142	144	145	147	150	152	158	160	9½ (9·3-9·8)
114	116	117	119	121	122	124	125	127	128	130	131	133	136	138	143	145	10½ (10·3-10·8)
109	111	112	114	115	117	118	120	121	123	124	126	127	130	134	136	138	11 (10·9-11·2)
104	106	107	109	110	112	113	115	116	118	119	121	122	124	126	130	132	11½ (11·3-11·8)
100	102	103	104	105	106	108	109	111	112	113	115	117	119	121	125	127	12 (11·9-12·2)
96	98	99	100	101	103	104	105	107	108	109	111	112	114	116	120	122	12½ (12·3-12·8)
92	94	95	96	97	99	100	102	103	104	105	107	108	110	111	115	117	13 (12·9-13·2)
89	91	92	93	94	95	96	98	99	100	101	103	104	105	107	111	113	13½ (13·3-13·8)
86	88	88	89	90	92	93	94	95	96	97	99	100	102	104	107	109	14 (13·9-14·2)
83	84	85	86	87	89	90	91	92	93	94	96	97	99	100	103	105	14½ (14·3-14·8)
80	81	82	83	84	86	87	88	89	90	91	92	93	95	97	100	101	15 (14·9-15·2)
80	81	82	83	84	85	86	87	87	88	89	90	90	91	93	96	97	15½ (15·3-15·8)
80	81	82	83	84	85	86	87	87	88	89	90	90	91	93	95	96	16 (15·9-16·2)
80	81	82	83	84	85	86	87	87	88	89	90	90	91	93	95	96	Adults (17·9-)

114	115	116	117	118	119	121	125	127	130	133	136	139	142	145	147	148	FORM A
115	116	117	118	119	120	122	126	128	130	133	136	139	142	145	147	148	FORM B
																	7½ (7·3-7·8)
																	8½ (8·3-8·8)
																	9½ (9·3-9·8)
																	10½ (10·3-10·8)
168	169	169	170	171													11 (10·9-11·2)
161	162	162	163	164	164	166	170	172	174								11½ (11·3-11·8)
155	156	156	157	157	157	160	163	165	167	170							12 (11·9-12·2)
148	149	149	150	150	150	152	156	158	160	164	168	172					12½ (12·3-12·8)
142	143	144	145	145	145	147	150	152	154	158	161	165	167	170	172	173	13 (12·9-13·2)
137	138	138	139	139	139	142	145	146	148	152	156	159	161	164	166	167	13½ (13·3-13·8)
132	133	133	134	134	135	137	140	142	143	146	150	154	156	159	160	161	14 (13·9-14·2)
127	128	129	129	130	130	132	135	137	138	141	144	148	150	153	154	155	14½ (14·3-14·8)
123	124	124	125	125	125	127	130	132	133	137	140	144	146	148	149	150	15 (14·9-15·2)
119	120	120	121	121	122	124	126	127	129	132	135	139	141	143	144	145	15½ (15·3-15·8)
116	117	117	118	118	118	120	122	123	125	128	131	134	136	138	140	141	16 (15·9-16·2)
111	112	112	113	113	113	114	116	117	118	120	122	124	126	126	127	128	Adults (17·9-)

elementary and secondary school children in Great Britain, as described in the *Brit*.
described for Scale III) has been employed on the upper reaches of intelligence.

these norms are modified from those in the earlier edition of this book.

NORMS FOR

															SCORE			
FORM A	29	31	35	38	42	44	46	48	50	52	54	56	58	60	61	62	63	64
FORM B	39	41	43	45	48	50	51	52	54	56	58	60	62	64	65	66	67	68
12½ (12·3–12·8)	58	64	68	72	80	88	92	96	100	104	108	112	116	118	120	124	128	132
13 (12·9–13·2)	55	61	65	69	77	85	88	92	96	100	104	108	111	113	115	120	123	127
13½ (13·3–13·8)	53	59	63	66	74	81	85	85	92	96	100	104	107	109	111	115	118	122
14 (13·9–14·2)	50	57	60	64	72	78	82	85	89	93	96	100	103	105	107	110	114	118
14½ (14·3–14·8)	50	57	60	64	70	75	79	82	86	89	93	96	100	102	103	107	111	114
15 (14·9–15·2)	50	57	60	64	70	75	79	80	83	85	90	93	96	98	100	103	106	110
15½ (15·3–15·8)	50	57	60	64	70	75	79	80	83	85	87	90	93	95	97	99	103	106
16 (15·9–16·2)	50	57	60	64	70	75	79	80	83	85	87	90	93	95	97	99	101	103
16½ (16·3–16·8)	50	57	60	64	70	75	79	80	83	85	87	90	93	95	97	99	101	103
17 (16·9–17·2)	50	57	60	64	70	75	79	80	83	85	87	90	93	95	97	99	101	103
17½ (17·3–17·8)	50	57	60	64	70	75	79	80	83	85	87	90	93	95	97	99	101	103
18 (17·9–18·2)	50	57	60	64	70	75	79	80	83	85	87	90	93	95	97	99	101	103
18½ (18·3–18·8)	50	57	60	64	70	75	79	80	83	85	87	90	93	95	97	99	101	103
19 (18·9–19·2)	50	57	60	64	70	75	79	80	83	85	87	90	93	95	97	99	101	103
19½ (19·3–19·8)	50	57	60	64	70	75	79	80	83	85	87	90	93	95	97	99	101	103
20 (19·9–20·2)	50	57	60	64	70	75	79	80	83	85	87	90	93	95	97	99	101	103

FORM A	81	82	83	84	85	86	87	88	89	90	91	92	93	94	95	96	97	98
FORM B	84	85	86	87	88	88	89	90	91	91	92	93	94	94	95	96	97	97
12½ (12·3–12·8)	178																	
13 (12·9–13·2)	171	173	175	177														
13½ (13·3–13·8)	164	166	168	170	172	174	177											
14 (13·9–14·2)	158	161	163	164	166	168	171	173	175	176	178							
14½ (14·3–14·8)	153	155	157	158	160	162	165	166	168	170	172	174	177					
15 (14·9–15·2)	148	151	152	153	155	157	160	161	163	163	166	168	171	173	174	175	176	177
15½ (15·3–15·8)	143	145	146	148	150	152	154	156	158	160	162	163	165	167	168	169	170	172
16 (15·9–16·2)	139	141	142	143	145	147	150	151	153	154	156	158	160	162	163	164	165	166
16½ (16·3–16·8)	135	136	138	139	140	142	145	146	148	149	151	153	155	157	158	159	160	161
17 (16·9–17·2)	131	133	134	135	136	137	141	142	144	145	146	149	151	153	154	155	156	157
17½ (17·3–17·8)	127	128	129	130	131	132	136	138	140	141	142	144	145	148	149	150	151	152
18 (17·9–18·2)	127	128	129	130	131	132	133	134	135	136	137	138	139	140	141	142	143	148
18½ (18·3–18·8)	127	128	129	130	131	132	133	134	135	136	137	138	139	140	141	142	143	144
19 (18·9–19·2)	127	128	129	130	131	132	133	134	135	136	137	138	139	140	141	142	143	144
19½ (19·3–19·8)	127	128	129	130	131	132	133	134	135	136	137	138	139	140	141	142	143	144
20 (19·9–20·2)	127	128	129	130	131	132	133	134	135	136	137	138	139	140	141	142	143	144

AGE IN YEARS

This table is based on norms from over 2,000 adults, sampled from a variety of occupations. and Standardisation of an Adult Intelligence Test," by R. B. Cattell (Brit. J. Psychol., developing a little longer with children of higher intelligence, so that there is a

SCALE III

65	66	67	68	69	70	71	72	73	74	75	76	77	78	79	80	FORM A
69	70	71	72	73	74	75	76	77	78	78	79	80	81	82	83	FORM B
136	139	141	144	146	150	154	156	159	162	164	166	168	170	172	176	12½ (12·3–12·8)
130	133	136	138	141	143	146	149	153	155	157	159	161	164	166	170	13 (12·9–13·2)
126	128	130	133	135	139	140	144	148	149	151	153	155	157	160	163	13½ (13·3–13·8)
121	124	126	128	130	133	135	139	143	144	146	148	150	152	154	157	14 (13·9–14·2)
117	119	121	124	126	128	131	134	138	139	141	142	144	146	148	151	14½ (14·3–14·8)
113	115	117	120	122	124	126	129	132	134	136	138	140	142	144	146	15 (14·9–15·2)
109	111	113	115	117	120	122	125	128	130	132	133	135	137	139	141	15½ (15·3–15·8)
105	106	108	111	114	116	118	120	124	126	128	129	131	133	135	137	16 (15·9–16·2)
105	106	108	109	110	111	113	115	120	122	124	125	127	129	131	133	16½ (16·3–16·8)
105	106	108	109	110	111	113	115	117	119	120	121	122	123	125	129	17 (16·9–17·2)
105	106	108	109	110	111	113	115	117	119	120	121	122	123	125	126	17½ (17·3–17·8)
105	106	108	109	110	111	113	115	117	119	120	121	122	123	125	126	18 (17·9–18·2)
105	106	108	109	110	111	113	115	117	119	120	121	122	123	125	126	18½ (18·3–18·8)
105	106	108	109	110	111	113	115	117	119	120	121	122	123	125	126	19 (18·9–19·2)
105	106	108	109	110	111	113	115	117	119	120	121	122	123	125	126	19½ (19·3–19·8)
105	106	108	109	110	111	113	115	117	119	120	121	122	123	125	126	20 (19·9–20·2)

99	100	102	104	106	108	110	112	114	116	118	120	122	124	126	128	130	FORM A
98	99	100	102	105	106	108	110	112	113	115	117	118	120	122	125	127	FORM B
																	12½ (12·3–12·8)
																	13 (12·9–13·2)
																	13½ (13·3–13·8)
																	14 (13·9–14·2)
																	14½ (14·3–14·8)
																	15 (14·9–15·2)
																	15½ (15·3–15·8)
174	176	178															16 (15·9–16·2)
168	171	174	176	178													16½ (16·3–16·8)
163	165	167	169	172	174	176	177	178									17 (16·9–17·2)
158	160	163	166	168	169	171	172	173	174	175	176	177	178				17½ (17·3–17·8)
154	156	159	161	163	164	166	167	168	169	170	171	172	173	174	175		18 (17·9–18·2)
150	152	154	156	158	160	162	163	164	165	166	167	168	169	170	171	172	18½ (18·3–18·8)
145	146	147	148	149	154	157	158	159	160	161	162	163	164	165	166	167	19 (18·9–19·2)
145	146	147	148	149	150	151	152	153	154	155	156	157	158	159	160	161	19½ (19·3–19·8)
145	146	147	148	149	150	151	152	153	154	155	156	157	158	159	160	161	20 (19·9–20·2)

The manner of its derivation is explained in "Occupational Norms of Intelligence, vol. xxv, July 1934). It embodies the notion that intelligence goes on 'shifting denominator' to the I.Q. between 14 and 19 years of age.

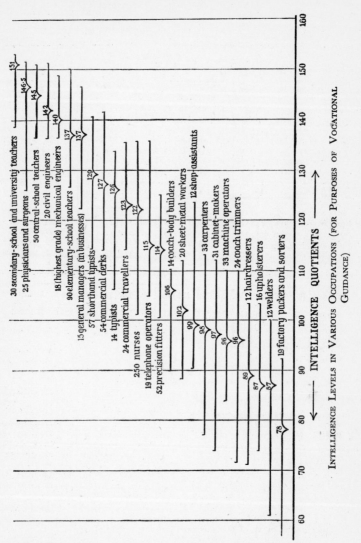

The central figure and ⟩ on each line indicates the average I.Q. for the sample taken. The length of the line subtends the scatter of I.Q. for the middle 50 per cent. in that occupation.

Abstracted from measurements on more than a thousand adults, as reported in " Occupational Norms of Intelligence and Standardisation of an Adult Intelligence Test," by R. B. Cattell (*Brit. J. Psychol.*, vol. xxv, July 1934).

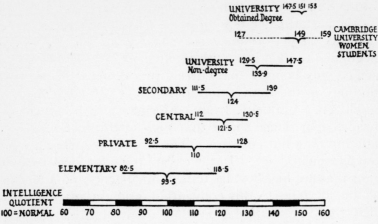

INTELLIGENCE RELATING TO EDUCATIONAL GROUP

Highly valid sub-tests. Standardised. University of London Press.

Wiltshire Intelligence Tests.—(Not published for general use.)   (Prof. Hamley and Dr. Philpott.)—A test based on recent research towards non-linguistic sub-tests. Institute of Education, London.

(B) PERFORMANCE TESTS

As already indicated, the term ' performance test ' is used to cover a great variety of intelligence tests whose only common feature is that they require apparatus. Yet logically and psychologically they may sometimes present just the same situation as paper tests. For example, the Healy Picture Completion Tests, in which wooden pieces cut out of a picture pasted on a board have to be put back again, is not different from several tests classified with the paper tests above in which the subject indicates with a stroke of the pencil where necessary items from a picture should be replaced.

Nevertheless, it is a proven fact [1] that, especially with

---

[1] " Intelligence Tests of Children of 4–8 years," *Brit. J. Educ. Psychol.*, i. See also " The Use of Performance Tests of Intelligence in Vocational Guidance," *J. Inst. Indus. Psych.*, xxix, 4.

young children, greater interest is spontaneously aroused by the performance type of test. Unfortunately the great majority of performance tests have quite low and even negligible correlations with intelligence.

The only homage that current practice pays to research findings is the convention that one shall not calculate intelligence quotients from performance tests—since the briefest experience shows that such intelligence quotients are anything but constant. The score is therefore always left as a mental age. In the case of those few performance tests that are highly valid tests of intelligence, no attention should be paid to this convention, and the usual I.Q. is best used.

Until the recent progress in temperament and character research has made itself felt in applied tests, there will still be good reason for using performance tests of even poor ' g ' validity—because of the insight they give into temperament and character reactions in face of opportunities, difficulties, and frustrations.[1] The readiness of a child to get angry or to give up; the planfulness shown in moving the blocks in the Passalong test; the tendencies to excitability and impulsiveness in the Seguin Form Board; the confidence or hesitation in Knox's cube movements; the absence of self-criticism and foresight in maze tests, are revelations very helpful to the psychologist in getting at the root of a behaviour problem. Even the mental age itself, or rather its comparison with the mental age on a good (non-verbal) paper test, gives valuable evidence. A relatively high score on the Seguin board is definitely associated with, among other factors, high ' g,' i.e. general strength of character (see p. 213). In many performance tests, however, the discrepancies between true mental age and apparent mental age on the performance test are more often due to special aptitudes, mechanical aptitude, or manual dexterity.

There are, as has been indicated, innumerable perform-

---

[1] See e.g. " Interpretation of Reactions to the Pintner-Paterson Performance Scale," by E. M. Wires, *J. Educ. Res.*, 1931, xxiv, 53.

ance tests available (Healy, Bronner, Low, and Shimberg, for example, record 100), and many of them have been developed for limited purposes in vocational guidance, or nursery schools, or from some enthusiastic personnel manager's inner consciousness, without 'g' validation,

SUBJECT.

FIG. 1.—Seguin Form Board: Positions of Pieces in Three Heaps Ready for Re-insertion.

without norms, and without research in regard to effective methods of scoring.

I shall therefore give full descriptions, norms, etc., only for a few tests of good validity which will provide the average psychologist with all he needs for most occasions. This section is followed by another merely listing, without detailed descriptions, most other important performance tests. The use of these can be read up in such books as Pintner and Paterson: *A Scale of Performance Tests*; or Healy, Bronner, Low, and Shimberg: *A Manual of Mental Tests and Testing*.

(i) *Test Material Available (Detailed)*

The Seguin (also called, when slightly modified, the *Goddard*) *Form Board* should be arranged to face the subject, as shown on p. 35. The pieces are placed in three heaps (not spread out) at the back of the board in the particular order indicated. The subject is told to replace the pieces as quickly as possible (using either or both hands). He does this three times, and is timed with a stop-watch on each trial. The result can be scored either on time or on time and errors. Since the judgment of errors is somewhat subjective, and since no better ' g ' correlation results from including them, the time score alone is generally taken. This may be either the average of the three trials or the shortest of three. Probably the latter system is slightly better, since it relates itself to quickness of learning.

Norms.—There are two main sources of norms for this test: those obtained by Gaw and given in the *Industrial Fatigue Research Board Report,* No. 31, and those obtained on still bigger samples by Arthur [1] in America. The figures are practically identical over the 5–10-year range, but thereafter Earle's and Gaw's results give decidedly shorter times. This is of little importance, since the test is in any case not a good one in that upper range. The norms below are compounded of these two standards, and are further slightly modified in accordance with some additional results for which the writer is indebted to P. E. Vernon. Since this test is probably most diagnostic between $2\frac{1}{2}$ years and 6 years, it is a pity that norms are lacking at this lower limit. The present writer has attempted to remedy this matter contingently by collecting scores from $3\frac{1}{2}$- and $4\frac{1}{2}$-year-old elementary nursery-class boys and girls, which have been averaged and included in the table below, producing a further modification (reduction) of times.

[1] *A Point Scale of Performance Tests,* by G. Arthur, N.Y.

NORMS

Mental Age.			3½	4	4½	5	5½	6	6½	7	7½
Shortest of 3 trials (secs.)		.	56	46	40	35	31	27	25	23	21½
Total of 3 trials (secs.) .		.	216	161	133	123	114	105	98	90	83

Mental Age.	.	.	8	8½	9	9½	10	10½	11	11½	12	12½
Shortest of 3 trials (secs.)	20	19	18½	17½	16½	16	15	14½	14	13½		
Total of 3 trials (secs.) .	77	72	68	64	61	58	55	52	49	46		

Mental Age.	.	.	13	13½	14	14½	15	16	17	18	19	20
Shortest of 3 trials (secs.)	13	12½	12½	12	12	11½	11	10½	10½	10		
Total of 3 trials (secs.) .	43	41	39	37	36	35	35	34	34	34		

The Seguin Form Board is a fairly valid ' g ' test only below mental ages of about 10 (i.e. with children and adult feeble-minded). With greater capacities, in accordance with Spearman's " Law of Diminishing Returns," it becomes only a test of manual dexterity. Obtainable from Messrs. Stoelting, Chicago.

Ferguson Form Board.—A much more difficult Form Board suitable for older children and adults. A graduated series of six boards, the pieces in five of which are divided into two sections and otherwise complicated. Continue until subject fails on two consecutive boards. Present so that no two pieces belonging together are in juxtaposition. Time limit for each board, 5 minutes.

Score.—Record time on each board. Convert time into score according to table on p. 38, and then convert score to mental age according to second table.

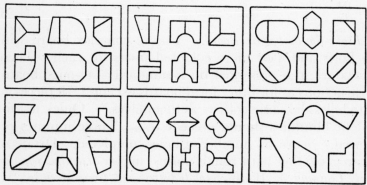

FIG. 2.—Ferguson Form Boards.

For critical examination of its value see E. D. MacPhee

and A. J. Brown: " An Enquiry into the Standardisation
of the Ferguson Form Boards," *J. Educ. Psychol.*, xxx, 21.
Found reliable, but increases of score not much related to
mental age and low correlations with intelligence tests.
Obtainable from Messrs. Stoelting.

FERGUSON FORM BOARD
TABLE

Values.		10	9	8	7	6	5	4	3	2	1	0
Board I.	Time in Seconds	0 to 16	17 19	20 21	22 24	25 27	28 29	30 36	37 51	52 66	67 300	F
Board II.	,,	0 to 68	69 72	73 76	77 81	82 86	87 89	90 92	93 97	98 104	105 300	F
Board III.	,,	0 to 79	80 88	89 95	96 102	108 112	113 127	128 144	145 163	164 186	187 300	F
Board IV.	,,	0 to 117	118 130	131 140	141 155	156 178	179 197	198 205	206 208	209 212	213 300	F
Board V.	,,	0 to 167	168 181	182 197	198 216	217 232	233 242	243 253	254 264	265 271	272 300	F
Board VI.	,,	0 to 223	224 248	249 262	263 267	268 269	270 272	273 277	278 285	286 294	295 300	F

NORMS: VALUES INTO MENTAL AGES

Sex.	Age:	9	10	11	12	13	14	15	16
M.	. . .	12	18	24	30	36	42	48	54
F.	. . .	12	18	24	30	36	34	38	41

Leake-Smith Figure Board.—A more complex board with
12 holes and 3 or more coloured insets for each. These
insets are also presented on a standard ' lay-out ' board.
Instructions as for other form boards except " All pieces go
into holes the same colours as themselves." Quick test for
colour blindness should precede test. Three minutes required. Score by number of holes completed. Details of
board, together with rough norms, in *The Scientific Selection
and Training of Workers in Industry and Commerce*, by M.
Martin-Leake and Thyra Smith (Pitmans).

Knox Cube Imitation Test.—Material required: Five one-inch cube blocks of the same colour and material. Four are placed in a row in front of the subject, about two inches apart.

SUBJECT

4 3 2 1

EXAMINER

The examiner, holding the fifth cube in his hand, says, " Watch carefully, and then do as I do." He then taps the blocks with the fifth cube in a prescribed definite order (and at about one tap per second), always beginning with the cube at the subject's left. He then lays the fifth cube down in front of the child between the third and fourth cube and says, " Do that." The following lines, in increasing complexity, are followed:

A. 1234	C. 1432	G. 13124
X. 12343	D. 1423	H. 143124
Y. 12342	E. 13243	I. 132413
B. 1324	F. 14324	J. 142341

(This order is Pintner's modification and extension of Knox's. X and Y follow on A as shown; thereafter one proceeds alphabetically.) The examiner proceeds until there are at least four successive failures, and gives one point for each line correct.

Mental Age			4	5	6	7	8	9	10	11	12	13	14	15	16
Score			1	2½*	4	5	5½*	6	6½*	6½*	7	7	7½*	8	8

Healy Picture Completion Tests. Picture 1 (see Fig. 3a).
—Place test before child with 48 pieces (10 correct and 38 alternatives) in irregular order at the back. Ask child to fill in pieces to make pictures look sensible and right (illustrate with ' wheel ' block). Allow 10 minutes; most children finish in 5 or 6 minutes.

Scoring.—This is based on credit given to each piece as follows:

---

* There are, of course, actually no half scores, but these are means—after Pintner and Paterson.

There is apparently no increase after 16 years.

Broken Windows.

Broken windows .	100
Closed windows .	32
Blank . . .	2
Cage . . .	1

Dog.

Dog . . .	64
Barley . .	2
Blank . . .	2
Departing cat .	2
Broken windows .	1
Cat . . .	2
Hatchet . .	1
Mouse . . .	1
Standing bird .	1
Stool . . .	1

Log.

Log . . .	52
Hatchet . .	6
Stool . . .	2
Blank . . .	1

Basket.

Basket . .	55
Cherries . .	7
Bucket . .	2

Cat.

Cat . . .	81
Barley . .	4
Chicken . .	2
Milk bottle . .	4
Flying bird . .	2
Sleeping cat .	2
Cup . . .	1
Fruit . . .	1
Standing bird .	1
Stool . . .	1

Football.

Football . .	84
Baseball . .	21
Cherries . .	2
Flying bird . .	1
Pumpkin . .	1

Flying Bird.

Flying bird . .	87
Standing bird .	18
Cage . . .	7
Cherries . .	3
Basket . .	2

Hat.

Hat . . .	65
Barley . . .	4
Purse . . .	3
Mouse . . .	2
Cat . . .	2
Books . . .	1
Flying bird . .	1
Chicken . .	1
Dog . . .	1

Chicken.

Chicken . .	58
Cat . . .	2
Cherries . .	2
Standing bird .	2
Barley . . .	1
Cage . . .	1
Departing cat .	1
Flying bird . .	1
Hatchet . .	1
Mouse . . .	1

Norms

Score .	80	160	240	320	400	440	470	495	505	518	522
Mental Age	5	6	7	8	9	10	11	12	13	14	15

Picture 2 (see Fig. 3b).—Place board before child with 60 pieces in standardised places (given with apparatus). Say, " Picture begins here where the boy is getting dressed. A piece is missing from each picture. Pick out the one piece that makes the picture look more sensible and right and put it in the space. Begin here (examiner shows demonstration picture). Study each carefully." Time limit, 20 minutes. A value is given for each piece as shown. Where *no* figure appears opposite in the following table, —5 is the value allowed.

HEALY PICTURE 2

Picture No.	Hole No.									
	1	2	3	4	5	6	7	8	9	10
1 . .	—	—	—	—	2	—	—	—	—	12·5
2 . .	0	0	1	2	—	0	0	0	0	0
3 . .	—	—	—	—	—	—	1	12·5	—	—
4 . .	—	—	—	—	—	—	—	—	—	0
5 . .	—	—	—	—	—	—	0	0	0	—
6 . .	0	—	—	0	—	—	—	—	—	—
7 . .	0	0	1	2	—	0	0	0	0	0

FIG. 3 (a). HEALY PICTURE COMPLETION TESTS, PICTURE 1.

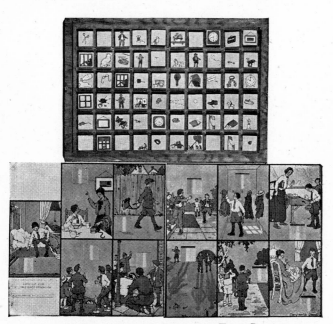

FIG. 3 (b). HEALY PICTURE COMPLETION TESTS, PICTURE 2.

HEALY PICTURE 2 (Continued)

Picture No.	Hole No.										
8	o	—	—	2	—	—	—	—	—	—	—
9	—	5	o	—	o	—	—	—	—	—	o
10	o	—	—	—	—	—	—	—	—	—	—
11	1	—	—	8	—	—	—	—	—	—	—
12	—	o	—	—	o	—	—	—	—	—	1
13	—	5	o	—	3	—	—	—	—	—	1
14	—	—	—	—	—	—	1	6	—	—	—
15	—	—	1	—	—	1	o	o	o	—	—
16	—	—	—	—	—	—	o	o	o	—	—
17	—	—	—	—	—	—	1	6	—	—	—
18	—	—	o	—	—	9·5	—	o	—	—	—
19	—	2	—	—	o	—	—	—	—	—	o
20	—	—	—	—	—	—	—	—	—	—	—
21	—	o	—	—	1	—	—	—	—	—	o
22	—	—	—	—	2	—	—	—	—	—	o
23	1	—	—	18	—	—	—	—	—	—	—
24	—	—	—	—	o	—	2	—	—	—	o
25	—	—	—	—	—	—	o	o	o	—	—
26	—	—	o	—	—	4	—	—	o	—	—
27	—	—	o	—	1	—	—	—	o	—	o
28	—	—	o	—	—	4	o	o	o	—	—
29	—	—	—	—	—	—	—	—	—	—	o
30	2	—	—	2	—	—	—	—	—	—	—
31	—	—	—	8	—	—	—	—	—	—	—
32	—	o	—	—	1	—	—	—	—	—	o
33	—	—	—	—	—	—	—	—	—	—	—
34	—	—	—	—	—	—	5·5	o	o	—	—
35	—	—	11	—	o	o	—	—	—	—	o
36	—	—	1	—	—	—	o	o	o	—	—
37	—	o	4	—	o	o	—	—	—	—	o
38	—	—	—	—	—	—	—	—	—	—	o
39	—	—	—	—	—	—	o	o	1	—	—
40	—	—	—	—	—	—	—	—	—	—	1
41	—	o	—	—	2	—	—	—	—	—	o
42	o	—	—	2	—	—	—	—	—	—	—
43	—	o	—	—	2	—	—	—	—	—	o
44	—	—	1	—	—	1	o	o	o	—	—
45	5	—	—	2	—	—	—	—	—	—	—
46	o	o	o	o	o	o	—	—	—	—	o
47	—	5	o	—	1	—	—	—	—	—	2
48	—	—	—	—	—	—	o	o	5	—	—
49	—	10	o	—	1	—	—	—	—	—	2
50	o	—	—	—	—	—	o	o	1	—	—
51	o	o	1	2	—	o	o	o	o	—	o
52	1	—	—	8	—	—	—	—	—	—	—
53	o	o	1	2	—	o	o	o	o	—	o
54	—	—	—	—	—	—	o	o	o	—	—
55	—	—	o	—	o	o	—	—	—	—	o
56	—	—	—	—	—	—	2	o	o	—	—
57	—	—	—	—	—	—	o	o	1	—	—
58	o	o	1	2	—	o	o	o	o	o	o
59	—	—	—	—	—	—	o	o	2	—	—
60	—	o	2	—	o	o	—	—	—	—	o

Norms from 1,542 cases (Healy, Bronner, Low, and Shimberg):

Ages	7	8	9	10	11	12	13	14	15	16	17–20	20–50
75th percentile	24	41	48	59	63	66	69	72	76	75	76	78
Median	9	27	37	47	54	55	58	62	64	66	65	65
25th percentile	6	7	23	32	41	45	50	52	54	54	54	54

A recent enquiry by Stephenson shows this test to be quite low in ' g ' saturation.

Passalong Test.—A performance test particularly suitable for the upper ranges of mental age (8–16) years. It consists of nine graded box problems, in each of which a given arrangement of red and blue blocks has to be converted (by sliding the pieces about) into another arrangement shown on a model (card). Scoring is straightforward, on successes and times. Time required, 29 minutes maximum, but generally less, and seldom more than 15 minutes. Having regard to the time taken, this is one of the more valuable performance tests, for it involves no manual dexterity, is not obviously affected by general life experience, and correlates with intelligence tests to the extent of about $0.55 \pm .06$ (consistency 0.74). Soundly standardised.

Score Table for Reference [1]:

Sub-Test or Box No.	\	Time taken (seconds).										NORMS.	
	0 30	31 60	61 90	91 120	121 150	151 180	181 210	211 240	241 270	271 300		Age.	Score.
1	2	2	1	1								7 years 6 months	11
2	3	3	2	1								8 years 6 months	13
3, 4, 5, 6, 7	5	5	4	3	2	1						9 years 6 months	16
8	7	7	7	6	5	4	3	2				10 years 6 months	19
9	8	8	8	8	7	6	5	4	3			11 years 6 months	21
												12 years 6 months	24
Possible score: 45												13 years 6 months	27
												14 years 6 months	29
												15 years 6 months	32
												16 years 6 months	35
												17 years 6 months	37
												18 years 6 months	40

Apparatus obtainable from the National Institute of Industrial Psychology, Aldwych.

Drever-Collins Performance Scale. Scale A.—A selection of eight performance tests, some of which are modifications of tests outlined below and some of which are newly devised by Drever and Collins. Consists of Koh's blocks design (modified), Knox's Cube (modified), Drever-Collins Domino. Size-weight test; Manikin, Feature Profile, Two Figure

---

1 A second method of scoring, more finely graded for timing and requiring fresh norms, is given in *Intelligence Concrete and Abstract*, p. 155, by W. P. Alexander (Camb. Univ. Press).

Board (modified), Healy and Fernald Completion Puzzle A (modified), Drever and Collins' Cube Test, Healy and Fernald P.C. Test 1; Drever and Collins' ' Bo Peep ' Test.

A supplementary test without language (3 from Series A and 3 new ones), entitled Series B, has been standardised for younger children (6 and under). Material obtainable from Baird, scientific instrument maker, Lothian Street, Edinburgh. Directions in *Performance Tests of Intelligence*, by Drever and Collins, published Oliver & Boyd, 1928.

A new Drever-Collins Performance Scale is now issued, as a result of extensive research carried out on performance tests under the ægis of the Scottish Council for Research in Education.

Alexander Performance Test.—A scale of three tests; the Passalong, the Block Design (Koh's), and the Cube Construction, requiring about 45 minutes to administer. Alexander's monograph [1] shows this to be pretty good measure of ' g ' and to measure in addition a group factor ' K ' (practical ability). The battery is a very promising one, and is well standardised (see p. 165 of Monograph).

Porteus Maze Tests. Vineland Revision (1919).—A series of thirteen mazes on paper, one for each year from 3–4 inclusive (except 13) and two for adults. A good test for observing impulsiveness, irresolution, planfulness. Boys tend to make slightly better scores than girls, so that temperament is probably being measured to some extent as well.

(ii) *Other Tests (not Detailed)*

(a) *Form Boards*

Cornell Form Board.—Shapes as Seguin, but portions of holes can be changed about (Whipple's modification).

---

[1] A second method of scoring, more finely graded for timing and requiring fresh norms, is given in *Intelligence Concrete and Abstract*, p. 155, by W. P. Alexander (Camb. Univ. Press).

FIG. 4.

Dearborn Form Boards. (Dearborn and Anderson.)— Series of three: (1) triangle; (2) four irregular holes with pieces cut into smaller sections; (3) regular, with several insets to each hole, allowing four problems with different degrees of difficulty.

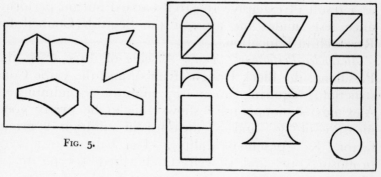

FIG. 5.

FIG. 6.

Casuist Form Board. (Sprague and Knox. Pintner-Paterson modified.)—Suitable for older children and adults. Five sectionised pieces.

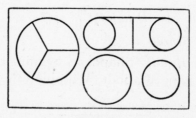

FIG. 7.

Two-figure Board.   (Pintner-Paterson.)—For young children.   Two pieces; one in five and the other in four sections.   (Modification by Drever and Collins.)

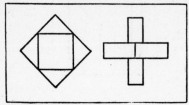

FIG. 8.

Gesell's Three-figure Board.—For infants.

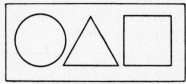

FIG. 9.

Five-figure Board.—Five pieces each divided into two or three pieces; also arranged in one straight row of holes.

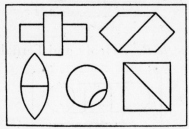

FIG. 10.

Triangle Test.—Gwyn's.   Young children.

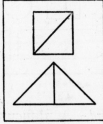

FIG. 11.

Diagonal Board.—Kempf's.   Older children and adults.

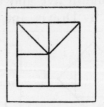

FIG. 12.

Construction Puzzle A.   (Healy and Fernald.)—Probably more 'g' saturated than most Form Board Tests.   Older children and adult defectives.   (Modified also by Drever and Collins.)   Scored on time, number of moves, and repetition of impossible moves.

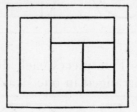

FIG. 13.

Construction Puzzle B.   (Healy and Fernald.)—Adults.

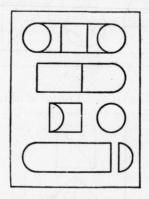

FIG. 14.

Moorees Form Board.—A difficult form board suitable for adults and standardised for English subjects.

Details with Dr. P. E. Vernon, The University, Glasgow.

Oakley Form Board.—A complex form board involving colours and consequently revealing colour blindness if present. Suitable for older children and adults. No ' g ' validation yet presented, but use over long period suggests this test may be more useful than most form boards in throwing light on temperament and character. Detailed description by C. A. Oakley, in *Human Factor*, March 1935. Obtainable from The Bar-Knight Model Co., 15 Margaret Street, Glasgow, C.1. No thorough standardisation yet, but preliminary results on 102 cases show range of average times $3\frac{1}{2}$ to $4\frac{1}{2}$ minutes.

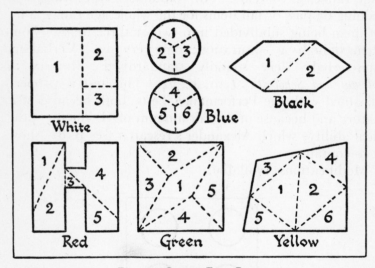

FIG. 15.—OAKLEY FORM BOARD.

(b) General Performance Tests

Arthur's Performance Tests.—A very widely standardised test, which also has the advantage of being available in two forms: (a) Form I, and (b) Form II for re-testing. On the other hand, relative to its length, it shows no advance in ' g ' validity, since it includes some of the older and weaker tests. Suitable for mental ages from 6 years to 21 years.

Form I includes: (1) Knox Cube; (2) Seguin; (3) Two

Figure; (4) Casuist; (5) Manikin and Feature Profile; (6) Mare and Foal; (7) Healy P.C. I; (8) Porteus Maze; (9) Koh's Block Design.

Form II includes: (1) Knox Cube (series reversed); (2) Seguin (board inverted); (3) Gwyn's Triangle Test; (4) Paterson's Five Figure; (5) Glueck's Ship; (6) Healy P.C. II; (7) Porteus Maze (number at left of subject); (8) Koh's Block Design (designs inverted). See present text for details of these. For particulars of standardisation as a whole see " A Point Scale of Performance Tests," by G. Arthur, *Commonwealth Fund Publications, N.Y.*, vols. i and ii.

Binet-Simon Scale.—Burt's Translation. Individual Test. Age range, 3–16 years. An ' omnibus ' type of test containing 65 pass or fail items for the whole age range, a few of them being subdivided into two or three items. Some items of high ' g ' saturation; some very low. Verbal and non-verbal. Very soundly standardised. Material in *Mental and Scholastic Tests*, p. 24. This test is properly classified with the Performance Tests, both because of its nature and because of the fair amount of ' F ' factor (practical ability) which Alexander's research (see p. 81) shows it to contain.

Modifications Available:

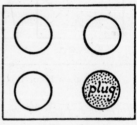

Burt Revision of the Binet Scale. Contingently standardised.

The most recent revision in America is the Terman-Merrill Scale, with two equivalent forms L and M, published by the Houghton Mifflin Co., Boston.

Vineland Revision and Extension of the Binet Scale.

Yerkes' Point Scale Revision and Extension of the Binet Scale.

Adaptation Board: Vineland.—A board (Fig. 16) with four holes and a block which will fit only one of them. Subject has to follow this hole when the board is rotated in various ways. Probably a good test of ' g,' but not sufficient possible variation of score. Standardised. (Messrs. Stoelting.)

Wallin Peg Boards.—Four graded boards, similar to form boards. Suitable only for nursery school infants or for low-grade imbeciles of any age. (Messrs. Stoelting.)

Designs Test (part of the American Army Performance Test Scale).—Six designs shown to subject for 10 seconds each and then to be reproduced. Points according to completeness of reproduction.

Digit Symbol Test (American Army Performance Scale). —Extensive norms. Nine digits and symbols form a key, from which seventy-five digits have to be keyed. A substitution test similar to those included in many intelligence tests.

Koh's Blocks.—Imitation and construction of coloured models with coloured cubes. Well standardised. Whole range of childhood. Modifications in Drever-Collins Test and in Stutsman Sixteen-Cube Test. Correlates quite highly with ' g ' (about ·8), but not included in first line of tests (above), because takes rather much trouble and time to administer.

Mazes—Young's.—Slot maze (metal) 4–9 years. Standardised.

Cube-Construction Test.—Three-inch cube, painted in various parts to be reconstructed from parts. Three models. Correlation with ' g ' of about 0·8. Well standardised.

Pyramid Test.—Stutsman. Imitating building block construction (for pre-school children).

Little Pink Tower.—Stutsman. Imitating building block construction (pre-school children).

Hollow Square.—Lincoln's (Fig. 17). Eight separate problems, one minute limit to each. Children and adults.

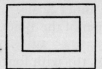

FIG. 17.—ELEVEN
PIECES PROVIDE
DIFFERENT WAYS
OF FILLING THE
HOLLOW SQUARE.

Decroly Matching Game.—Matching sixteen silhouette pictures on cards. Young children.

Atkins' ' Object-fitting ' Test.—(Fitting familiar objects.) Consistency ·79–·96. Instructions by Pantomime. 1½–5 years. Well standardised and pretty well ' g ' saturated. 10–20 minutes required. Obtainable from Messrs. Stoelting.

Kent Shakow Complex.—For industrial purposes.

Kent Shakow Clinical.—Children and adults.

Worcester Form Board.—Four boards, but last two can be given in six different ways, i.e. eight boards are really available. Coloured suitable for adults and school children and pre-school children.

Picture Completion Form Boards.—

Mare and Foal. (Healy and Fernald.) Very young children.

Manikin. Conventionalised figure of man, in six pieces. Suitable pre-school children.

Feature Profile Test. (Knox and Kempf.)—Older children.

FIG. 18.   FIG. 19.

Ship. (Glueck.)—Children.

(C) PERCEPTUAL, CULTURE-FREE TESTS

For most purposes for which performance tests were used (illiterates, aliens, primitive people, comparisons of social classes and races), one would now use ' perceptual tests,' which avoid verbal skills without running into manual skills or pictorial interpretations. Here are available the Progressive Matrices of Raven and Penrose and the Culture-free Intelligence Test Scales of the present

writer, each requiring about one hour and being standardised in percentiles on mental ages.   The Cattell Culture-
free Test [1] has a scale for adults applicable through
University student level and a scale for Junior High School,
suitable for the range 11–15 years.   These tests have been
shown to have as good a ' g ' saturation as verbal tests,
and to be as free from cultural influences as performance
tests.[2]

NOTE ON SCATTER IN PURER ' G ' TESTS

Psychometrists used to the lesser scatter of I.Q.s with
the Binet, or in intelligence tests much loaded with scholastic and general information, will be surprised at the
frequency with which the norms on these scales bestow
high and low I.Q.s.   It must be remembered (a) that the
trend has been for more recently developed tests to give
greater scatter.   The early Binet gave a standard deviation
around 11 points of I.Q.   Later it climbed to 15 and 16,
and in the recent revisions as high as 19.   The Cattell
Scales have an S.D. of about 20 (in certain extensive
samples—e.g. that made in the city of Leicester published
in *The Fight for Our National Intelligence*, P. S. King
& Co., 1937—the standard deviation has been found
as high as 24·5), and variability quite as great is found
with the Culture-free Perceptual Tests, which are still
more recent.   (b) The general effect of classroom teaching, and of age itself, is to advance the dull and ' level
down ' the bright, as far as knowledge is concerned.
Consequently, the more a test involves knowledge, as
distinct from mental capacity, the less will be the scatter
obtained on it in terms of mental ratio (I.Q.).   The
following frequencies are approximately correct for Scales
I, II, and III.

Below 70	.	.	.	.	4·5%	100–110	.	.	.	.	21·0%
70–80	.	.	.	9·0%	110–120	.	.	.	15·0%
80–90	.	.	15·0%	120–130	.	.	.	9·0%
90–100	.	.	21·0%	130–140	.	.	.	3·5%
		Above 140	.	.	2·5%			

[1] Published by the Psychological Corporation, 522 Fifth Avenue, New York.
[2] Cattell, R. B., Feingold, S. N., and Sarason, B., " A Culture Free Intelligence
Test, II ; Evaluation of Cultural Influence on Test Performance," *J. Educ. Psychol.*,
1941, xxxii, 81–100.

CHAPTER II

TESTING SPECIAL APTITUDES—MECHANICAL, MUSICAL, ARTISTIC, DEXTEROUS, ETC.

1. Nature of Special Aptitudes

OUR understanding of the special aptitudes—their limits, their measurement, and their natural history—is, so far, by no means in such a satisfactory state as that concerning intelligence. A good many tests devised for vocational guidance and purporting to make measurements of a person's gifts in special directions, e.g. manual dexterity, would not stand a moment's scientific psychological investigation. Even a well-planned test, such as Stenquist's Test of Mechanical Aptitude, proved on analysis to be testing manual dexterity as well as mechanical understanding, and to be strongly affected alike by practice and the extent to which a child's interests in mechanical things had had opportunity to develop.

Probably many aptitudes are not constitutional, like ' g,' but rather matters of acquired skill, which in turn may have been derived partly from the kind of temperament or character structure possessed by the individual during the formative years of his interests. (In such instances, it is an arbitrary matter whether the tests for aptitudes be placed in this chapter or in the next chapter on " Attainment Tests.") Thus, with our present deficiency of knowledge on the inborn and acquired factors in mathematical skill, it seems best to classify tests for it under "Attainment Tests," but later research may enable us to have tests both for the inborn aptitude and for the extent to which it has been clothed in trained knowledge.

Even though there is uncertainty as to whether the tests are tapping inborn aptitudes, it may still be of importance to take measurements, for, in the circumstances of most lives, the mind does not remain indefinitely plastic, and the investments of time and interest that have been made by, say, the age of 20, are rarely completely obliterated. A group of persons obtaining poor scores on a mechanical aptitude test administered at that age is therefore unlikely ever to catch up to a group with higher scores. Certainly for selecting the best workers during the years directly succeeding the test, the employer does well to select according to the test results. Cox [1] has shown that even in manual skills, a type of ability highly susceptible to practice, the order of the candidates after a fairly long period of practice differs little from that obtained at a first testing, but this is probably true only under normal conditions of life, where there is no reason to suspect that some candidates have had opportunities for intensive practice.

To forget that special aptitudes may be susceptible to change through training and emotional readjustments is, however, not so dangerous an error—because not so common—as that of measuring special aptitudes where no special aptitudes exist. In the field of vocational guidance and industrial selection, as already mentioned, this *ad hoc* designing of tests supposedly measuring supposed special aptitudes has run riot. The most comprehensive single research on special abilities or group factors is that of Thurstone,[2] who isolated ten which he called ' Primary Abilities.' Thurstone adopted a different statistical analysis from that underlying other descriptions of ability in these two chapters, in such a way that what we have called ' g ' or general ability was divided up among the ' primary abilities.' Consequently, these last are not completely independent, but are positively correlated. However, even when in theory we separate the group factors completely from ' g,' most actual tests of them inevitably contain an admixture of ' g.'

Probably the group factors in ability are quite numerous, but most of those which are of practical importance in education and many of those operative in industry are probably comprised by the set of about twelve confirmed by the overlapping studies of Burt, Thurstone, Stephenson, Alexander, Cox, Seashore, and others. These we may summarise as follows: (1) Verbal ability[1]; (2) Fluency (verbal and pictorial imagination); (3) Numerical (arithmetic facility); (4) Reasoning (logical, inductive inferential ability); (5) Memory; (6) Spatial thinking and geometrical aptitude; (7) Practical ability ('K'); (8) Mechanical aptitude (of uncertain independence from 7); (9) Manual dexterity; and (10) Musical ability, in four major factors.

The above special abilities will now be treated in detail, except in the case of Fluency, which is dealt with in the chapter on "Temperament." The above list is not exhaustive. Thurstone found twelve primary abilities (but made tests only for the six most important above); Karlin,[2] following Seashore, split musical ability or aptitude into even more numerous factors, and special studies have split the dexterities, mathematical ability, and memorising into more numerous subsidiary influences.

The psychometrist needs to be principally on guard against the widespread assumption that a special aptitude exists corresponding to each occupation or human interest, e.g. clerical ability, ability to deal with people. These latter are ' logical trait divisions '—mere collections of functionally disparate abilities outcropping in a certain arbitrarily bounded field. As pointed out fully elsewhere,[3][4] the psychologist does best to measure and predict from more permanent and real trait unities, which are

---

[1] See W. Stephenson, "Tetrad Differences for Verbal Sub-tests relative to Non-verbal Sub-tests," *J. Educ. Psychol.*, 1931, xxii; W. P. Alexander, *Intelligence, Concrete and Abstract* (Camb. Univ. Press, 1935); and Thurstone, L. L., *Primary Mental Abilities* (Univ. of Chicago Press, 1938).

[2] Karlin, J. E., "A Factorial Study of Auditory Function," *Psychometrika*, vii, 251-79, 1942.

[3] Cattell, R. B., *The Description and Measurement of Personality*, World Book Co., New York, 1946.

[4] Cattell, R. B., "Personality Structure and Measurement—I. The Operational Determinations of Trait Unities," *Brit. J. Psychol.*, 1946.

either *environmental mould* traits or *constitutional* traits.[1] The boundaries of a real trait unity, of either of these kinds, are likely to extend beyond those of the conventional title. For example, 'numerical ability' might also be a factor in success as a telephone operator or have some connection with exactness in spelling. Research on these special abilities, their ranges, and the fields in which they are useful to performance is, however, only in its infancy. One is lucky if even an adequate set of tests, with properly standardised norms, is available for the ability itself. To expect exact information about all the everyday situations in which the ability can predict, is premature.

Though scepticism is necessary in regard to many so-called 'special aptitudes,' we have admitted tests for some, of a practically important nature, even where no well-founded psychological factor is yet known. It is certain at least that they measure something over and above 'g,'[2] and if the work in which success is to be predicted is practically identical with the activity of the test, the measurement is at least significant for the immediate purpose. In some cases general psychological considerations indicate that later research is almost certain to find a definite ability in the region concerned.

For the sake of clarity it will be most helpful to speak of 'abilities' when the emphasis is on the arbitrary categories of human activity (e.g. clerical 'ability') and of factors when we refer to the natural fundamental functional units in human mentality, e.g. mechanical aptitude factor, speed factor, which are revealed by statistical methods, e.g. tetrad analysis. Any 'ability' related to some job or confined to some academic subject is probably in most cases the resultant of 'g' and of two or three 'factors.'

2. Notes on Methods of Converting Raw Scores into Significant Units

Once more, as in intelligence testing, we are faced with

[1] Cattell, R. B., *op. cit.*
[2] I.e. a specific, narrow factor is present even though a group factor cannot be proved.

the problem of converting the number of marks [1] scored on any particular test—the raw score—into terms which will be immediately intelligible in a wider sense and applicable to standards already established in the field of application with which we happen to be concerned, e.g. vocational guidance. With intelligence tests we used units of mental age, but now we are dealing with abilities that do not necessarily vary in any regular way with age. Moreover, many of the tests are most frequently needed for purposes of discriminating within the adult population.

Generally, the experimenter is faced with the problem of having to convert the individual's raw score into some figure which will signify at once that individual's position relative to others of the same age or class, or with regard to the population as a whole; and which can be added to or used with calculations of other scores obtained by the same individual. Three of the simplest methods of doing this, most widely used in applied psychology, are as follows:

(1) One may work out the standard deviation (or the mean deviation) for the population concerned, and say how many units of standard deviation any individual lies above or below the mean.[2] Thus, if the standard deviation should work out at, say, 4·5 points, a person having a raw score 9 points above the mean would have a final score of + 2 standard deviations; one having a raw score of 13·5 below the mean would have a score of − 3. Such scores are called standard or normal (z-scores) and permit of many variations, e.g. the T-score, in which the σ is divided into ten divisions, the mean being called 50.

The chief advantages of standard scores are: (1) Measures in different raw units and different dimensions are rendered comparable, and (2) the frequency of occurrence of various standard scores is known in a normal distribu-

[1] Some tests may not be scored in points even at the beginning. Such tests are based on the method of 'median samples' discussed in Chapter III, p. 62. But what follows here is equally applicable to tests first scored in those terms.

[2] The standard deviation "σ" is obtained by subtracting each individual's score in turn from the mean score. These differences are then squared; the scores are summed up and the total thus obtained is divided by the number of cases, and the square root of the resulting figure is found.

tion and is approximately known in most actual samples, so that scores have immediate general meaning.

(2) Percentile method, in which the score is given as the rank position among a hundred persons.

(3) Various hybrid methods between (1) and (2) are known. The most valuable is that which begins with percentiles and converts them into scores representing approximately equal units along a difficulty continuum. The grading of students' achievement into A, B, C, D, etc., grades is based on this principle.

The method assumes normal distribution of the steps of difficulty in the subject, not necessarily of the raw scores. If we take equal steps of difficulty along the base of the normal, the proportions of the population cut off follow a certain law. Actually they have ratios fixed by the terms of a binomial expansion. This expansion must be chosen with regard to the number of points that one wishes to have in one's point scale. Thus, if one wishes to score a manual dexterity test on a scale of five units, each unit being theoretically equivalent to any other, then one builds up a score distribution diagram (histogram) for, say, 2,000 people, and finds the position of the vertical lines which will divide up its area into portions having the following ratios, reading from end to end 1, 4, 6, 4, 1. (The coefficients of the binomial expansion of $(1 + 1)^4$.) With this population of 2,000, the numbers would be 125, 500, 750, 500, 125. Perhaps the lines cutting these numbers will fall at scores of 78, 72·5, 69, and 64 marks. By such a method, 78 marks or over, therefore, has a score of 5 on this five-point scale; similarly, anyone between 69 and 72·5 would have a score of 3, and so on. If a ten-point scale had been needed, it would have been sufficient to divide the distribution according to the successive terms of the expansion $(1 + 1)^9$. The fact that equal steps on the raw scores do not in fact mean equal steps in value is obvious from this example, in which a difference in raw score of $5\frac{1}{2}$ marks (between 72·5 and 78) means at one part of the scale a difference of only one unit, whereas in another part (in the 69 to 72·5 region) it means more than two units.

Each of the three methods—standard deviations, percentile ranks, equal unit intervals—has its advantages. The real issue to be faced in deciding which to adopt is whether the results from various tests may need to be added together afterwards to produce a summed resultant. If so, the percentile method is useless, because the interval between, say, 100 and 90 is really greater than that between, say, 40 and 50. For such purposes, as also for falling into line with the common classification (average, good, very good, poor, very poor) which tends to follow the normal distribution, the method of equal unit intervals is best. For results to be examined from the point of view of probable error, etc., the standard deviation method is best. For most other purposes the percentile method is easily first. Norms of the last-named kind can be very readily established, on populations of any size; they show the position of the subject at a glance; they contain the median and the quartiles within themselves; they are of especially good use in vocational guidance, where one frequently has to proceed to selection knowing that a certain percentage of the population is admitted to a particular kind of employment, e.g. if 2 per cent. of the population can earn a living at music the person advised to take it up must fall roughly above the ninety-seventh percentile on musical aptitude tests. Most of the norms which follow in this section are given in percentiles.

A far more complete discussion of scoring and scaling devices is available, most recently, in P. E. Vernon's *The Measurement of Abilities*, University of London Press.

3. Tests of Aptitudes

The various aptitudes to be discussed are arranged in alphabetical order. In each instance a brief résumé of present knowledge on the matter is followed by an account of the test material available.

ARTISTIC ABILITY

There have been no adequate investigations into the nature of this ability, into the relations of various branches of plastic art talent, into the connection of artistic appreciation with creative capacity, or into the emotional or hereditary roots of these abilities. It is only certain that some of the abilities (ability to draw and paint) are not closely correlated with intelligence,[1] and that a big special factor or factors must be involved.

Meier-Seashore Art Judgment Test.—Based on the reasonable assumption that æsthetic judgment, resting upon fine discrimination, feeling, and insight, is basic to success in art, whether it be sculpture, painting, etching, or some form of applied art. It consists of 125 pairs of drawings, the members of each pair differing from each other in some slight respect, which is, however, crucially important for composition, etc. (reproductions of the less well-known Old Masters, Japanese prints, etc.). Consistency Co-efficient ·71 to ·85. Correlation with ' g ' negligible. Validity roughly established by comparing score of talented children, of art students, and of persons of good intelligence, but no artistic capacity.[2] Time required, 45–50 minutes. Norms from 1,850 high school (13 years and over) and art school students. *Material:* Picture-book, manual, record sheets. From Bureau of Education Research, University of Iowa, U.S.A. The following approximate norms for English children have been obtained by the writer with 125 12- and 13-year-old elementary school children (a year or so of age difference does not appreciably affect the norms).

Deciles	10 (highest)	9	8	7	6	5	4	3	2	1
Score	Above 91	87–91	85–86	83–84	81–82	79–80	77–78	74–76	68–73	Below 68

Burt's Test in Æsthetics.—Nine pairs of photographs (Applied Art—jars, rugs, armchairs, etc.) for comparisons as in Meier-Seashore. These pictures were published in *The Listener*, and results are based on some 6,000 replies. Burt found the following mean scores (out of nine) for the follow-

---

[1] See e.g. H. F. Mannel, *Talent in Drawing.*
[2] See H. A. Currall, " What do the Meier-Seashore and the McAdory Art Tests Measure?" *J. Educ. Res.*, 1932, p. 26 who found these two tests to correlate only ·27 ± ·06.

ing groups. A basis for more detailed norms on children of 7 to 18 years will be found in the *Brit. J. Educ. Psychol.*, iv, June 1934, in " Æsthetic Judgments of Children," by M. H. Bulley.

	Men.	Women.
Artists	7·0	7·5
Art Teachers	8·1	7·9
Teachers (Science)	6·8	6·7
Army and Navy	5·8	—
Clerks	5·8	6·3 .
Labourers and Servants	4·4	4·7

A useful ' snap ' test, lasting only a few minutes, but necessarily rather unreliable on account of fewness of items.

The pictures were chosen by M. H. Bulley, and are taken from a fuller list of nineteen pairs published in " Have you Good Taste ? " (1933). A similar excellently selected set of pictures, but in pure instead of applied art, will be found in M. H. Bulley's *Art and Counterfeit*.

Cattell-Reynolds Test of Artistic Aptitude. (Small groups or individuals.)—A test with five distinct sections, separately assessable: (1) discrimination of colours and saturations (10 items); (2) memory for colour and shades (over short intervals) (10 items); (3) appreciation of composition (as in Meier-Seashore); (4) sense of colour harmony, measured by 10 pairs of pictures identical in form, differing in colour combinations; (5) motor ability in drawing. An objective test of twenty items to test the subject's ability to draw what he has already conceived.[1] Time required, about 30 minutes. 60 items. Contingent standardisation. It is not claimed for this test any more than for others available in this field, that it is anything but tentative and based on *a priori* analysis of the capacities required in art. This test was devised with the help of the Leicester College of Art, and was divided into sections with regard to skill required in applied art in local industries.

Material: not yet made generally available, but will be published if further experiments prove the test satisfactory.

---

[1] Currall, *op. cit.*, found Meier-Seashore poor correlation with estimates of active artistic ability and McAdory test even poorer.

CLERICAL APTITUDE

Although in vocational guidance an estimate of aptitude for clerical work would be most valuable, nothing is known as to the nature of the abilities involved. A suitable temperament and a particular level of ' g ' are obviously of first importance. So-called ' clerical aptitude ' tests are partly measures of intelligence and partly examinations in attainment in the skills—sorting, indexing, recording, English, arithmetic—involved. The National Institute of Industrial Psychology's clerical test has been withdrawn as a test of clerical aptitude, but the following attainment tests exist:

Minnesota Vocational Test for Clerical Workers.—Details in *Personnel J.*, 1932.

Benge's Clerical Aptitude Test (Paper).—Obtainable from Messrs. Stoelting.

J.E.R. Clerical Test.—Institute of Educational Research, Columbia University, New York.

O'Rourke's Clerical Aptitude Test.—(1) Reasoning Problems. (2) Reasoning Test. Educational and Personal Publishing Co., Washington.

DRAWING ABILITY

It has long been established that ability to draw involves a big special factor in addition to intelligence; indeed, the former is far more important than the latter (Spearman [1] judges it approximately four times as important), so that borderline defectives may sometimes draw extremely well, and highly intelligent adults be unable to do so. Much indirect evidence suggests that this aptitude is largely inborn. In most children it develops very little after the age of 9 or 10.[2] There is some evidence that drawing skill is related to surgent temperament and the emotional instability of factor D.[3] [4]

[1] C. Spearman, *Abilities of Man.*
[2] F. Childs, *J. Educ. Psychol.*, 1915, vi.
[3] C. J. Earle, " The Figure Drawings of Adult Defectives," *J. Mental Sci.*, April 1933.
[4] Cattell, R. B., " Personality Traits associated with Abilities—I. Drawing Ability," *Educ. and Psychol. Measurement*, 1945, v, 131–47.

Tests Available

No extensive diagnostic standardised tests are yet available. For children the best test is:

Burt's Drawing of a Man described on p. 116 of the chapter on Attainment Tests. A valuable median samples scale.

Measurement of Intelligence by Drawing, by F. L. Goodenough. Chicago '26. This test, the standardisation and scoring of which is based on a detailed, part by part analysis, rather than on the ' whole ' median samples method used by Burt, is intended as a test of intelligence [1] through drawing and is consequently less suited than it might be for testing drawing ability *per se*. Nevertheless, it provides a good measure of capable and intelligent, if not of artistic, drawing performance. About 10 minutes, but no time limit. Child's drawing of a man. Chiefly for mental ages 4–10. Reliability ·8 to ·9; ·75 with Stanford Binet. No arbitrary decision as to what does or does not constitute intellectual merit in drawing. Artistic standards disregarded and alleged to be not a test of artistic ability. Criterion of validity is correlation with actual and mental age (rather begging the question as to whether an intelligence test). Scoring requires careful study. Assessed on 50 points, e.g. fingers present, head shown, eye detail, free from clothing transparencies, etc.; girls score slightly higher than boys.

MIDLAND DRAWING SCALE FOR ADULTS

This is a brief scale of adult drawing ability, on the same lines as, and supplementing, Burt's scale for children.

The adult is given pencil and quarto-sized paper, and asked to draw a man, in the most effective manner he can conceive. He is given 10 minutes to do so. The following five-point scale of samples is based on drawings from 100 adults (men and women). It is based on the statistical device of the equal unit intervals, i.e. the general population

[1] See Spearman, *Abilities of Man*.

distributes itself into these five grades in the ratios indicated by the following numbers:

Grade I II III IV V

Number 1 4 6 4 1

The drawing to be assessed is compared with the samples in each of the five categories, and given the mark of the sample which it most nearly rivals. Note the tendency to bring in movement in the better samples.

DEXTERITY (MOTOR ABILITY)

The measurement of dexterity is of great importance in industry, because of the relatively large proportion of workers engaged in assembly, packing, machining operations, etc. With the increased attention now given in education to the developing of manual skills the diagnosis of ability in this direction promises to be of importance also in schools.

Although the measurement of dexterity might appear a simple matter, and although industrial workers have complacently 'measured' it in personnel selection for some time, there are many theoretical and practical difficulties.

Early work (e.g. that of Perrin,[1] Earle and Gaw[2]) seemed to show no group factor of 'dexterity'—it looked as if each particular skill must be measured separately by *ad hoc* tests. Garfiel[3] took into account, not only manual dexterity, but also dexterity of the whole body, legs, head, etc., and found some indications of a very slight group factor.

Cox's recent work[4] practically clears up the issue. Success in manual operations is partly a matter of 'g,' partly of 'm' (mechanical aptitude), but also partly of a group manual dexterity factor and a specific dexterity factor. The influence of 'g' and 'm' in routine work is practically negligible, so that the measurement of dexterity there assumes importance. We must distinguish between routine as-

[1] " An Experimental Study of Motor Ability," *J. Exp. Psychol.*, 1921.
[2] " The Measurement of Manual Dexterities," Report No. 4. National Institute of Industrial Psychology, 1930.
[3] " The Measurement of Motor Ability," *Arch. of Psychol.*, 1923, No. 62.
[4] *Manual Skill, its Organisation and Development*, Camb. Univ. Press, 1934.

sembly and packing work on the one hand and mechanical assembly—requiring solutions of problems as to how parts must be assembled—on the other. The latter involves some ' g ' and more ' m ' (see p. 68). The former is largely a matter of group and specific dexterity factors. When the work is complex (not intellectually complex, but complex in movement), the group manual dexterity factor is most important, but when it is simple (as in Perrin's experiment) the specific factors are alone important.

Therefore for complex routine assembly of any kind a test of the manual dexterity factor will be valuable, but selection for simple operations is better made on a test resembling as closely as possible the operations to be carried out.

Little is known as to whether we are dealing in manual dexterity with an inborn or an acquired ability factor (though systematic interest is, of course, important in developing the actual ability), but Cox's results show definitely that the order of skill obtained on dexterity tests with unpractised subjects remains essentially unchanged after any period of practice. The absolute difference is, however, reduced, owing to those with poor initial ability being relatively more improvable. Boys do better than girls in tests in which strength and speed of movement are required, but girls do better when independent finger control is concerned.

Any of these tests may be invalidated by practice.

TESTS OF MANUAL DEXTERITY

The following three tests are the best arising from Cox's recent research, and may be used as one battery requiring about 30 minutes (median) and yielding a very fair measure (·8 correlation) of manual dexterity factor.

Eye-board Test I.—Individual test, but can be used with a group up to about 6 persons. A board 15 × 16 inches containing 10 rows of 9 eyes in a row. A spool with a lace round it lies at the end of each row, and a clip stands at

GRADE I

FIG. 20.

GRADE II

FIG. 21.

GRADE III

FIG. 22.

GRADE IV

FIG. 23.

GRADE V

Fig. 24.

both ends of each row. Subject is required to unclip the lace, unwind it from the spool, thread it through the eyes, and clip it up at the other end of the row—for each of the 10 rows. Scored (a) on time to complete, or (b) on number of eyes threaded in 3 minutes. This is perhaps the best test yet devised for measuring the general manual dexterity factor running through manual assembly tests. It correlates ·80 with this factor 'd' (among school-leavers 14 years), has a consistency coefficient of ·90, and no correlation with 'g' (see J. W. Cox's research in *Manual Skill*, Camb. Univ. Press). Apparatus from J. W. Cox, c/o Methuen & Co., Essex Street, London.

Norms.—(a) Time Method. Median for 14-year-old elementary school boys : 14 minutes 10 seconds.

(b) Number of eyes in 3 minutes : Twelve-year-old elementary school boys. Median, 85 eyes. Upper quartile, 93 eyes. Lower quartile, 74 eyes.

Fourteen-year-old intermediate school boys. Arranged in five equal intervals (binomial expansion), (i) 67 eyes and under, (ii) 68–87 eyes, (iii) 88–99 eyes, (iv) 100–115 eyes, (v) 116 and over.

A shortened form of this test. Eye-board Test II is available, in which a short practice period is included.

Pin-board Test.—Consists of a board 12 × 12 inches furnished with 64 brass pins and a terminal clip. Subject is required to wind with right hand a given ball of string, held in left hand, over each pin until the terminal clip is reached. Score = time to complete, thrice.

Norms.—Median for 14-year-old elementary school boys : 8 mins. 55 secs. Consistency, 0·90. Correlation with general manual factor, about ·5. Material from J. W. Cox, c/o Methuen & Co.

Pin-stick Test.—Consists of a stick 12 inches long, 1 inch square, mounted on a handle. 10 'pins' (nails) along each side of the stick. Subject winds string round the nails with right hand while holding stick with left hand. Done thrice. Score = total time taken.

Norms.—Median for 14-year-old elementary school boys. 6 mins. 26 secs.

The following tests have negligible correlation with the general dexterity factor, but are of value in measuring specific dexterities [1] (closely related to the test itself).

1. *Nut and Bolt.*—A test having a correlation of ·3 to ·4 (the best of Earle's and Gaw's tests) with skill in the work of smith, fitter, carpenter, and electrician. Two small cardboard boxes each containing 10 small screw-bolts and 10 nuts made to fit these. Nuts and bolts unfastened and all mixed together, placed in heap on table. Instruction " Screw these nuts on the bolts—until they are tight—as quickly as you can " (show how to ' spin ' the nuts with the finger).

Score = average time for two trials (i.e. two boxes).

The following deciles are for 14-year-old elementary school children and are derived from the histograms of Earle and Gaw for 200 children.

Decile	1	2	3	4	5
Boys . .	Below 78	78- 84	84- 92	92- 96	96-102
Girls . .	Below 101	101-111	111-119	119-130	130-141
Decile	6	7	8	9	10
Boys . .	102-111	111-119	119-127	127-143	143 and over
Girls . .	141-148	148-160	160-169	169-181	181 and over

2. *Peg Board.*—A test correlating ·34–·38 with skill as smith or carpenter. Apparatus: a board, slightly more than 10 inches square, with 10 rows of holes, 10 holes in each, 1 inch apart. Set of wooden pegs (10 or more), 2 inches long, $\frac{1}{4}$ inch in diameter, round. Board placed in front of subject and clamped to the table. Half of the board (5 rows of holes) nearest to the subject is covered with piece of paper fixed by drawing-pins. Instructions: " Begin here (top left), and put pegs in top row (indicate), using only your thumb and middle finger." Pegs to be picked up separately. Repeat (1) with thumb and third finger, and (2) with thumb and fourth finger. Record time taken and number of pegs dropped. Score = time for all three performances, plus 3 seconds for each peg dropped. The following norms (after Earle and Gaw's

[1] Earle and Gaw, *op. cit.*, p. 55.

histograms for 200 children) are for 14-year-old primary school children.

Decile	1	2	3	4	5
Boys . .	Below 90	90–97	97–101	101–108	108–111
Girls . .	Below 88	88–94	94– 99	99–102	102–109

Decile	6	7	8	9	10
Boys . .	111–117	117–122	122–128	128–150	150 and over
Girls . .	109–118	118–125	125–135	135–148	148 and over

The Seguin Form Board (see p. 36), and the

Leake-Smith Figure Board (see p. 39) have also been found to yield useful correlations with skill in packing and sorting. For adult norms see *The Scientific Selection and Training of Workers in Industry and Commerce*, by M. Martin-Leake and Thyra Smith (Pitmans).

Macquarrie Test for ' Mechanical Ability.'—A widely standardised test, largely of manual dexterity rather than mechanical ability, of pencil and paper form, suitable for group testing of dexterity. Published by California Test Bureau, 5916 Hollywood Boulevard, Los Angeles, California, U.S.A.

OTHER DEXTERITIES

Press, Foot, and Hand Co-ordination.—An instrument devised and standardised by the National Institute of Industrial Psychology for testing dexterity of press machine workers. Obtainable from Messrs. Stoelting.

Touch Placing Test.—An instrument devised and standardised by the National Institute of Industrial Psychology to measure a subject's skill in placing and adjusting objects without visual aid, as in various industrial processes. Obtainable from Messrs. Stoelting.

LOGICAL ABILITY

As has been stated at the opening of this chapter, there are good grounds for supposing that ability to deal with evidential relations is partly a specific ability. It is commonly assumed that this logical ability is more highly developed in men and women, and the few researches so far carried out would appear to confirm this.

The tests described below will obviously be pretty highly

saturated with ' g.'   It is suggested that a measure of the
' logical ability ' which they also contain would best be
gained simply by dividing the ' Reasoning ' score by the
mental age, previously determined by an intelligence test.

Probably the most valid single test of the R (Reasoning
Ability) factor to-day is found in Thurstone's battery.
(See p. 82.)

Bristol Group Reasoning Tests.—For children.   A and B
Forms, fifteen items on each.   Practice Sheet by Barbara
Dale (University of London Press).

Burt's Graded Reasoning Tests.—Two inference items
for each year from 7 to 14 inclusive.   Well standardised
and carefully freed from specialised knowledge.   Material
and instructions in *Mental and Scholastic Tests*, pp. 237–42.

Noll, J. H., " Measuring Scientific Thinking," *Teachers'
Coll. Record,* 1934, No. 35.   Describes a test of 134 items to
test five habits of thought: accuracy, suspended judgment,
open-mindedness, intellectual criticalness, habits of looking
for cause-and-effect relationships.   Reference to an incomplete standardisation.

Watson-Glaser Tests of Critical Thinking.—Sub-tests on
generalisation, inference, recognition of assumptions, etc.,
in which the non-' g ' element is stressed (' r ' with ' g '
equals ·3 or ·4).   Probably measures to a considerable
extent the C factor of freedom from emotionality and
emotional distortion, as well as the ' logical ability.'
Published in two forms, for group testing, by World Book
Co., Yonkers-on-Hudson, New York, N.Y.

MECHANICAL APTITUDE

Most tests of ' Mechanical Aptitude' have in the past
been, at least in part, tests of mechanical knowledge and
experience—or even of manual dexterity—and have
accordingly been classified in the " Achievement Tests "
section of this book.   The only really satisfactory test—at
least in this country and probably in America too (with
the recent possible exception of the Minnesota Mechanical
Aptitude Test)—is that of Cox, based on the very

thorough investigation described in his monograph *Mechanical Aptitude, its Existence, Nature, and Measurement.*

Battery for Boys 11–14 *Years.*—The following tests— Test I, Test II, Test D, and Paper Folding A—are the only tests which are easy enough for Junior Scholarship children. It is suggested that they be used as one battery, but since each is standardised separately, one or two can be chosen and, in the writer's experience, Test I and Test D form quite a useful combination.

Test I.—Five wooden models. Can be used with groups or individuals. Selective answers (on printed diagrams). Fifteen answer items. Time required, 20 minutes. Norms for primary school children 11–14 years and technical schools 13–16 years.

Test II.—Five models supplementing the above. Fifteen (selective answer) items (printed diagrams) in booklets. Time, 15 minutes. Norms as for Test I.

Test D.—Six diagrams. Insight into mechanism. Scored on 30 answer items. Time, 35 minutes. Norms for Technical Schools.

Paper Folding A.—Cutting of folded papers (as in Binet Test). Score of 79 items. Time, 35 minutes. Norms for primary school children 11–14 years, and technical schools 13–16 years.

Battery for School Leavers, 14–16 *years*

*Test M.*1.—Ten mechanical (wooden) models. Selective answers on diagram booklets. Scored on 46 items. Time 35 minutes. Norms for primary school children 12–14 years (for whom it is rather on the difficult side) and for adult students.

Norms for Secondary School Leavers, Boys, 16 years (from F. C. Thomas)

Decile	1	2	3	4	5	6	7	8	9	100
Score	4–7	7–9	9–12	12–13½	13½–15	15–17	17–19	19–21	21–26	26–4

Test D.—As above.

*Test E.*3. (Form B) (superseding shortened Form A).— Mechanical Explanation. Selective answers in booklets. Score 49 on 31 items. Time, about 40 minutes. Norms for 14–15-year-old boys.

Paper Folding B.—As Folding A above, but more difficult. *Norms* for a shortened test (1 hour 10 minutes) for 14-year-old boys. The following five-point (method of equal units) division is based on the scores of over 400 elementary and intermediate school boys divided into five sections according to a normal distribution curve, i.e. in the proportion 1 : 4 : 6 : 4 : 1 :

Point Score	I	II	III	IV	V
Raw score in marks (Models and Diagrams combined) .	0-6	7-12	13-20	21-31	32 and upwards

Battery for Selection among Engineers

Test M.2.—Ten mechanical models. Selective answers, giving score on 66 items. Time, 40 minutes. *Norms* for Technical College Students 14–16 years.

Test C, Form B.—Mechanical completion test on diagrams, etc., in booklets. Score on 48 items. Time required, 35 minutes.

Paper Folding B.—As above.

Each of the above three batteries includes a model test, a diagrams test, and a paper-folding test, and requires about 1 hour 50 minutes to administer (which includes time for distribution, etc.). It is inadvisable to cut the battery down to less than 1 hour.

All the above models, diagrams, booklets, etc., may be obtained from Dr. J. W. Cox, c/o National Institute of Industrial Psychology.

Bennett-Fry Mechanical Comprehension Test.—This is a very varied and carefully worked-out test, containing items both of the kind already established as measures of mechanical aptitude and of a kind which may involve more straight *knowledge* of mechanical and scientific processes. It has a wide range of difficulty, making it suitable for adults and school children, a good reliability and internal validity, and is entirely on paper, for group administration. Form AA for school children and adults. Form BB for engineers. Time 20–40 minutes. Forms available Psychological Corporation, 522 Fifth Avenue, New York,

N.Y. Other ' mechanical aptitude ' tests are rather tests of knowledge and achievement, and are classified in that section below.

MUSICAL APTITUDE

Research indicates clearly a specific factor, or rather a group of specific factors over and above ' g ' in determining success in music. Indeed, this special factor weighs the issue in musical success almost as much as ' g.' Nevertheless, there is yet no evidence as to whether such talent is innate or acquired. The experiments of Professor C. E. Seashore and his school stand out above all others in this field, and present a very complete investigation which has led to the only test available, viz.:

Seashore's Musical Talent Test.[1]—A set of six phonograph records testing the following essential capacities with the consistencies indicated by the coefficients.[2] Pitch Discrimination, ·71; Intensity Discrimination, ·65; Time sense, ·48; Consonance Appreciation, ·43; Memory for melodies, ·59; Rhythm sense, ·29. Of these, memory correlates most highly with music teachers' estimates of ability. The correlation of estimates with all tests together (pooled) appears to be about 0·4, but this may be no reflection on the tests. The effect of musical training on test performance is not marked.

Stanton and Koerth[3] found correlations of ·45–·83 ± ·02 between test scores before and after training the group.

The test, which, of course, is one of appreciation, not of motor performance on musical instruments, is a group test, and can be used with adults and older children down to the age of about 11 years. Norms permit of allowance for practice, age, and intelligence. Material obtainable from Messrs. Stoelting.

[1] See e.g. C. E. Seashore and H. Mount, *Psych. Monog.*, No. 108, 1918.
[2] A. W. Brown, " The Reliability and Validity of the Seashore Tests of Musical Talent," *J. Appl. Psychol.*, 1928, xii.
[3] " Musical Capacity Measures of Adults repeated after Musical Education," *Univ. of Iowa Studies*, 1930, xxxi. See also J. Kwalwasser, " Tests and Measurements in Music," *Psychol. Bull.*, 1928, xxv; D. L. Larson, " An Experimental Critique of the Seashore Consonance Test," *Psychol. Monthly*, 1928, xxxviii.

MEMORY

Although a ' good memory' is a factor constantly considered in selecting for employment and a ' bad memory '
is a symptom to be assessed in borderline neurotic conditions, research shows that we are dealing with a complicated function rather than the single ability in which the
above expressions would lead one to believe.

Effect of Intelligence.—Most reports on mental defectives
include the remark, " Has a very poor memory." Statistical enquiry shows medium correlation of intelligence and
memory. Actually, with meaningful material (e.g. prose
passages, commissions) the correlation with ' g ' reaches
·3–·4, but with unrelated or sensory material (objects,
colours, strings of numbers) or mechanical skills, it is
practically zero, i.e. good memory is as likely to occur with
low as with high I.Q.s.

Varieties of Memory.—One must distinguish first between
committing to memory (amount remembered immediately)
and retentivity as such. The latter is most simply measured
by the ' Memory Ratio ' (Moore) which compares the
amount known immediately after memorising with the
amount known some considerable time after.

It is the latter which is most independent of ' g.' But
we may scarcely speak of retentivity as a whole since
there is only a slight general factor running through
retentivity (about ·1–·2 intercorrelation), whilst group
factors are quite large. The known group factors are:
(1) sensory memory, common e.g. to sensory memories
from auditory and visual sources. Intercorrelation about
·3–·4; (2) verbal memories. Intercorrelation ·4–·5; (3)
non-verbal symbolic memories, e.g. for digits. Inter-
correlation ·6–·7. Apparently there is no ground for supposing that long-distance and short-distance memory are
distinct abilities.[1]

To predict a person's capacity to memorise in any particular field would seem to be possible from a measure of his

[1] This conclusion and the above figures are based mainly on Spearman's *Abilities of Man,* chapter xvi on " Retentivity of Dispositions."

intelligence, his general retentivity, and his specific retentivity. General psychological considerations suggest, however, that a person's retentivity is not a fixed measurement like his intelligence, but something likely to alter with any considerable change of health or emotional adjustment. Again, we are dealing with something highly responsive to the emotional forces of the person's conscious and unconscious purposes and life plan. A man of good intelligence and retentivity may yet forget his own name.

With these modifying factors in mind, the following test of the general retentivity factor may be used to give fairly significant predictions. The psychometrist should also keep in mind the test of ' M ' available in Thurstone's battery (p. 82).

It is important that the same strength of motive to remember should as far as possible be stimulated in all.

RETENTIVITY TEST

Consists of four parts. In each the subject is simply instructed to commit as much as possible to memory. (1) Page of Pictures. Expose for 30 seconds. Test number of items recalled immediately afterwards. (2) Page of Nonsense Syllables. Expose for 30 seconds. A series of twenty cards is then exposed, in an irregular mass, and the subject is asked to pick out those which occurred on the sheet. See cards on p. 76. (3) A Page of Shapes. See p. 77. (4) The following list of words is read out twice, at rate of about 1 per second: Horse, Laugh, Strong, Cruel, Car, Brave, Love, Fight, Talk, Boy.

In each sub-test 1 minute is allowed for recall, and the score is the number of items right minus the number wrong.

The recall is tested again after the lapse of 1 hour (the subject not being specifically informed of this intention— only ' memorise ').

Retentivity Score = Number of first recall subtracted from number on second (all tests pooled). Therefore negative and numerically greater for poorer retentivity.

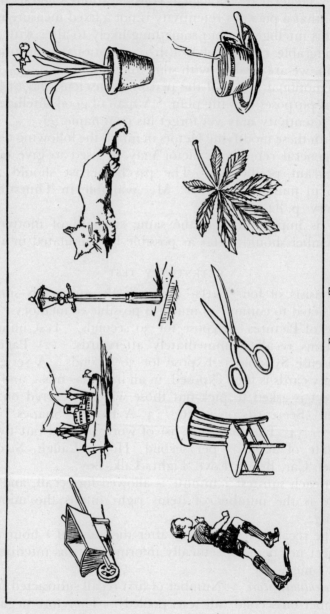

Fig. 25.—Test 1

Norms.—There are as yet no adequate norms. For children between 10 and 14 years the mean is about — 5 and the quartiles at — 2½ and — 8. Ability to memorise, plus Retentivity, i.e. 'power of memory,' goes on increasing throughout childhood and up to about 30 years of age, after which it declines slightly, but Retentivity probably shows lesser growth variation.

SOCIAL INTELLIGENCE

Owing to its importance for vocational guidance and the selection of persons for administrative and human contact occupations, 'social intelligence' has been the subject of a considerable number of tests, though none has been standardised in this country. No one has proved the existence of or defined this social intelligence, and experiment reveals that the tests are in fact merely more or less

DAG ROF MUN KIBB PEL

LON MEZ PLAF LIF SEG

FIG. 26.—TEST 2.—Memorise these syllables.

good measures of ordinary ' g.' Thus Strang[1] found a correlation of ·44 with ordinary intelligence tests and concluded that apart from this the tests were measuring only the informational side of social intelligence.

Probably social intelligence is, over and above ' g ' itself, essentially a matter of information and skill relating to psychological situations, depending on experience gained

[1] R. Strang, "Relation of Social Intelligence to Certain Other Factors," *School and Soc.*, 1930, xxxii, pp. 268–72.

1 DAG	2 NID	3 ROF	4 TIB
5 MUN	6 WUL	7 KIBB	8 STEN
9 PEL	10 KAS	11 LON	12 FOL
13 MEZ	14 VEE	15 PLAF	16 THUL
17 LIF	18 RET	19 SEG	20 HAR

FIG. 27.—TEST 2.—Pick out the cards bearing the syllables you have already seen.

through temperamental bent and early interests. Almost certainly a measure of cyclothyme temperament (p. 169) would correlate with success in handling social situations (among people of equal ' g '). An additional test will be found in the social and human interests section of the Interests Test (p. 147).

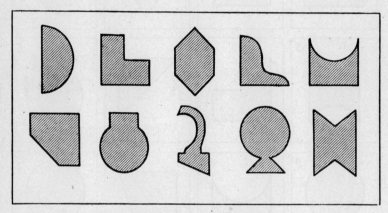

FIG. 28.—TEST. 3.—Memorise these shapes.

The basis for further tests in a composite battery lies in the picture interpretation tests of Binet,[1] the suggestions of Spearman,[2] and the sequence tests of Decroy.[3] (Most of the Picture Completion Tests—Healy, Fernald, Pintner— seem to the present writer not to be sufficiently replete with psychological relationships to be included in a Social Intelligence battery.) There are also the Problematical Situations tests of Webb [4] which might readily be extended and standardised to form part of a battery for adults. Finally, there are Ruckmick's (listed below) and others' tests of ability to judge emotional expression—an essential part of practical social intelligence, but also possibly largely ordinary ' g.'

The tests described below, although not necessarily as

---

[1] *Annee Psycho.*, 1905, xi, " Interpretation." A. Binet.
[2] Spearman's *Abilities of Man*, picture facing p. 181.
[3] *Annee Psycho.*, 1914, xx.
[4] *Brit. J. Psychol. Monog., Suppl.*, 1915, No. 3.

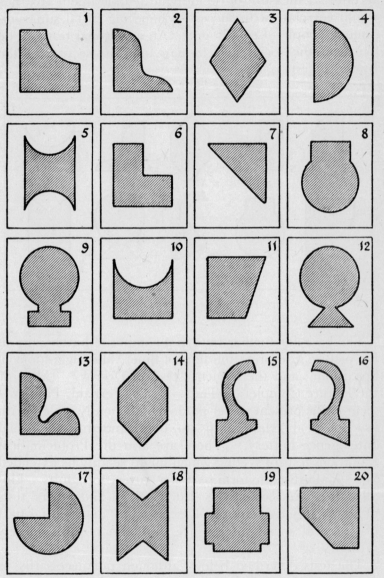

FIG. 29.—TEST 3.—Pick out the cards bearing the shapes you have already seen.

sound as the battery suggested here, are already in a prepared (and generally in a standardised) form.

Clearly much research remains to be done both in proving the existence and nature of psycho-social aptitude and in devising tests.

For Children

Schwartz's Social Situation Picture Test.—For boys and girls of 9–13 years. Six pictures for girls and 8 pictures for boys. " What is the boy (girl) thinking of (or about to do)? " Standardised presentation but not standardised scores from the point of view of social intelligence. First part of question on each picture could be used as group or individual test and readily standardised. Second part definitely intended for individual psychiatric interview (see Projection Tests, p. 196), and not usable for above purpose. About 15 minutes required. Material: Messrs. Stoelting.

For Children and/or Adults

Test of Social Intelligence.—(Partially Standardised.) Bureau of Public Personnel Administration Staff; *Public Personal Studies*, 1930, U.S.A.

George Washington University Social Intelligence Test (Secondary School and College).—Obtainable: Centre for Psychological Service, Washington, D.C. See also " Ethical Discrimination Tests " (Chapter VI).

Ruckmick's [1] *Emotional Expression Pictures.*—A series of 32 photographs of a female face expressing laughter, scorn, fear, grief, etc., etc. They are of sufficient difficulty for the average adult to fail in about 50 per cent. of his judgments as to the emotion depicted, but can be made still more difficult by covering the upper or lower half of the face. Kindergarten children nevertheless pass quite a number—especially those dealing with primary emotions.[2] No norms are yet available. These could be readily built up, the present writer suggests, on a basis of 30 seconds'

---

[1] See Ruckmick, " A Preliminary Study of the Emotions," *Psych. Monog.*, xxx, 1922.
[2] See Gates, " An Experimental Study of the Growth of Social Perceptions," *J. Educ. Psychol.*, xiv, 1923.

exposure of each picture (including time to write down word describing the emotion). Group or individual test. Ruckmick's key supplied with material. Material from Messrs. Stoelting. (In this connection there are also photo series by Rudolph (18 male expressions), perhaps not so satisfactory as the above, and Feleky (24 female).) Also Hickson's and others' photos of delinquents, etc., for judging ability to judge character. Obtainable: Messrs. Stoelting.

SPATIAL ABILITY

This is one of the factors brought out by Thurstone's research and measurable by his test described at the end of this chapter. It is centred in the ability to recognise shapes in different positions and rotations and perhaps in the sheer ability to recognise or hold in mind spatial forms. A test of this kind standardised in Britain is the *Form Relation and Memory for Designs Test* of the National Institute of Industrial Psychology. It consists of eight sub-tests of ability to recognise the ' fit ' of plane and solid shapes along with a ninth test of ability to memorise shapes. It is frequently used as a test of aptitude for dress-making or to measure other abilities in girls corresponding to mechanical ability in boys, but how successfully no one knows. It can be used for 12–14-year-olds or adults, requires about 40 minutes to give, and is intended for use as a group test. Booklets from National Institute of Industrial Psychology.

Norms (from N.I.I.P.) for 13–14-year-old children:

Deciles	1	2	3	4	5
Score on Form Relations .	Below 18	18–19	19–21	21–23	23–25
Score on Memory for Designs	Below 25	25–28	28–30	30–32	32–34

Deciles	6	7	8	9	10
Score on Form Relations .	25–27	27–29	29–31	31–34	34–upwards
Score on Memory for Designs	34–36	36–38	38–40	40–42	42–upwards

For 15–16-year-old children:

Deciles	1	2	3	4	5
Score on Form Relations .	Below 24	24–27	27–29	29–32	32–34
Score on Memory for Designs	Below 31	31–34	34–36	36–37	37–38

Deciles	6	7	8	9	10
Score on Form Relations .	34–36	36–38	38–40	40–43	43–upwards
Score on Memory for Designs	38–40	40–41	41–42	42–44	44–upwards

PRACTICAL ABILITY

An ability which may or may not have some relation to the above is the very definite and important practical ability isolated by Alexander,[1] Stephenson,[2] and El Koussy,[3] and generally called ' k ' factor.[4] It appears principally in the ability to handle performance tests and the fitting of spatial patterns. It operates additional to intelligence in Alexander's Passalong Test (which see), and is the special object of several very adequate tests developed for military selection purposes during the war.

VERBAL ABILITY

Since the researches of Kelley and of Stephenson during the last seven years, it has been known that most intelligence tests are measuring a verbal group factor ' v ' in addition to ' g.' Professor Burt, many years earlier, spoke of ' verbalisers '—children whose ability for verbal expression was obviously far in advance of their intelligence. It is obvious that the measurement of this verbal factor is going to be of the greatest importance in vocational guidance. At present, however, we are far from knowing what its exact limits are, whether it is constitutional, or acquired, or what standards of ' v ' endowment are required in various occupations. The trend of research evidence at the moment would seem to indicate that ' v ' is a facility, not only with words, but with any form of mental operation with symbols, as distinct from things in themselves. The most widely used and best standardised test at present available for measuring this factor (with ' g ') is that of Thurstone (see below). Alexander [5] found a ' v ' factor particularly heavy in Thorndike's Reading Test and in the Terman Group Test of Mental Ability. A measure of ' v ' might therefore be obtained roughly by observing the

---

[1] *Intelligence, Concrete and Abstract*, W. P. Alexander (Camb. Univ. Press).
[2] Stephenson, W., " A Note on the Purification Technique in Two-factor Analysis," *Brit. J. Psychol.*, xxvi, 2, 1935.
[3] *The Visual Perception of Space*, A. H. El Koussy (Camb. Univ. Press).
[4] Not to be confused with the personality ' K ' factor, Chapters V and VI.
[5] *Intelligence, Concrete and Abstract*, p. 96, W. P. Alexander (Camb. Univ. Press).

differences between scores on these two tests on the one hand and on some satisfactory non-verbal test, e.g. Sleight non-verbal Test (p. 18), Cattell Scale I, Non-verbal Test (p. 17), or Culture Free Test (p. 51) on the other.

WIT

The quickness and the creativeness of wit we know to be related to the 'A' and 'F' factors of temperament. Fairly good correlations should be obtained between wit and estimates of cyclothymia and surgency (see p. 172) or wit and measures of fluency of association (see p. 176). As to the variation of wit with age we know little, whilst questions of quality and of individual and social conditions lead one quickly into profound problems of the unconscious and of social psychology. Nevertheless, a rough measure of the amount of wittiness which a person possesses may at times be needed.

A measure of intelligence should first be made, and then a measure of 'A' and 'F' which determine the extent to which intelligence is able to issue as wit. To the impression thus gained may be added for greater reliability a direct measure of wit on the " scale of wit " very carefully selected and standardised by Dr. Wynn Jones in his recent book, *An Introduction to the Theory and Practice of Psychology.* Two series available (p. 101), 18 points in each. Scored on degree of insight and quickness of response. Norms for adult students, secondary and primary schoolboys.

A foundation for a still better test, based on a clearly defined general factor of wit appreciation, will be found in Eysenck's *The Dimensions of Personality.*

OTHER SPECIAL ABILITIES

The theoretically most complete and practically most widely standardised test for measuring some of the above abilities (where indicated) and others now to be mentioned is Thurstone's *Chicago Test of Primary Mental Abilities* (published by the American Council on Education, 744

Jackson Place, Washington, D.C.). It deals with six abilities: verbal (V), spatial (S), memory (M), and reasoning (R), as discussed above, and, also, numerical (N), and word fluency (W). 'N' is not general mathematical ability, and not problem arithmetic, but facility with numbers, and, as such, may also be measured by an arithmetical attainment test, described in the next chapter. 'W' is the verbal outcropping of 'general fluency,' the nature and measurement of which is described in Chapter V.

The test is in two forms, one for college students and one for children of 11 to 17 years. It is a group test and can be machine-scored. Each of the six ability measures requires a 40-minute session, and it is recommended that they be given at the same time on six successive school days.

Among the less confirmed special abilities may be mentioned Eysenck's [1] two factors of æsthetic appreciation (quite distinct from drawing or artistic ability discussed above).

[1] Eysenck, H. J., " Personality Factors in Preference Judgments," *Nature*, cxlviii, 246, 1941.

CHAPTER III

ATTAINMENT TESTS: SCHOLASTIC AND GENERAL

1. The Purpose of Attainment Tests

THE attainment test grew up in the first place out of the attempt, associated in this country principally with the names of Ballard and Burt,[1] to make more reliable and exact the ordinary scholastic examination. In the hands of the psychologist, such tests have acquired a wider use, and may be said to assess any kind of information accomplishment or skill, from size of vocabulary to speed of typewriting or accuracy of shooting. A very thorough survey of the theory, practice, and statistical treatment of scholastic attainment tests and ability measures is now available in Vernon's *The Measurement of Abilities* (University of London Press, 1940), the reading of which will help the non-psychologist in understanding matters dealt with in condensed fashion in this and the preceding chapter.

In spite of the now notorious unreliability of the essay type of examination it may be worth while to summarise the arguments concerning these tests.

(1) The questions in the attainment test are such that answers (usually selective or on the true-false plan) are definitely either right or wrong. Partial scoring and subjectivity arising from the personal factor of the examiner's mood or individuality does not enter.

Consequently, the correlation of markings by different examiners is perfect, whereas with the essay type of examination it is rarely more than 0·6 (Ballard).

(2) Instead of answering four or five questions in an

---

[1] Since Burt's *Scholastic Tests* and Ballard's *New Examiner* are in every clinic and most schools, I have not thought it necessary to arrange for the reproduction of their tests here.

hour, the examinee now has to answer (without being forced to hurry) perhaps two hundred. The element of luck, through the examiner's picking on favourable or unfavourable questions, is now eliminated, for the examinee has to answer questions concerning the whole range of his course. Where questions are of the true-false type, i.e. having only two alternative answers (and in the more recent attainment tests this is avoided wherever possible), the examinee, admittedly, has an even chance of being right on a large number of questions, but each examinee tends to profit equally from this source of credit. Experiment shows that the reliability (i.e. correlation coefficient) of consecutive testings remains very high, even when this source of error goes uncorrected. By doubling the number of wrong answers and subtracting the figure from the number of right answers, a score is obtained which, on an average, is the number that would have been correct if no answers had been correct through lucky shots.

(3) The attainment test tests attainment only, or, in the words of critics, it fails to test intelligence, the power of organising information, the power of sustained effort, the ability to initiate trains of thought and to express oneself in words. One may doubt whether the power of sustained effort should be included in the list, but, apart from this, it is true that the attainment test, like the intelligence test, tests only one aspect of what is measured by the ordinary examination. Now it is precisely this analytical power of the new tests which recommends them to the teacher-psychologist. If one wishes to test intelligence in a scholarship examination, the proper course is to use an intelligence test. The results may afterwards need to be combined with those from an attainment test, but it is desirable to know how much is contributed by each, for, in a scholarship at 11+, a low attainment score is not significant if the child happens to come from a school lacking normal teaching advantages, whereas at the university scholarship stage it might be imprudent to admit a scholar, however bright, who was completely lacking in knowledge of some subject

which he would need to bring to degree standard in three short sessions.

Other qualities which it is alleged (nothing more) that ordinary examinations test may be more certainly measured by temperament and character tests (e.g. " ability to initiate trains of thought," by ' fluency of association ' tests, p. 176, steadiness of character by ' perseveration ' tests, p. 234).

Doubtless at the root of the irrational passive resistance [1] to the objective attainment test is the fact that many teachers try to use the examination, not as a means of assessment, but as an instrument of training. If examinations are frequent, it is perhaps as well to make them a training in organising and expressing ideas (for admittedly if children are to cram for examinations they will do more harm by cramming for the attainment test than for the essay type of examination [2]); but if ample training in these habits is already given in the course of education proper, there is every reason to make the examination a reliable attainment assessment only.

2. Technique of Construction

Attainment is frequently expressed in terms of attainment age, the units of which are fixed by the achievement of the average child in that subject at each age. One must never lose sight of the fact that these attainment ages do not rest on a stable and regularly developing biological basis as do mental ages. The latter are different only for different races, but the former vary with every difference of school system, of curriculum or method of teaching. Provided this is borne in mind, it is nevertheless highly valuable to determine attainment standards in age units, especially if the standardisation is based on a system of education that is reasonably widespread, e.g. the primary-school system in this country.

[1] Not marked everywhere. In America the College of Physicians and Surgeons has already set examinations in this form, with conspicuous success. See Wood, " New Type Examinations in the College of Physicians and Surgeons," *J. Person. Res.*, 1926, v.

[2] Two or three teachers who have read these words in manuscript point out, however, that the ordinary examination, often repeated, can, unlike the attainment test, do considerable damage to style.

Here the concept of the Accomplishment or Attainment Quotient (A.Q.$= \frac{\text{Attainment Age}}{\text{Mental Age}} \times$ 100) and the Educational Ratio (E.R.$= \frac{\text{Attainment Age}}{\text{Chronological Age}} \times$ 100) will be found useful, especially in comparing group results. The E.R. will have a fairly close agreement with the I.Q., but the A.Q. is more likely to vary inversely with the I.Q. The quotients need to be used cautiously and by those who are not likely to make rash and unpsychological deductions.

When results are not expressed in attainment ages they may be expressed in percentiles or units of standard deviation in the manner described in the last chapter (p. 56). Such methods are preferable in standardising tests for adults.

Attainment tests permit of being scored in two distinct ways: (1) the method of point scores, and (2) the method of direct comparisons. By the method of point scores one gives points or marks for each item correct and transforms the total score by means of a graph into an attainment age or percentile rank. But some attainments, e.g. handwriting[1] and drawing, speech and deportment, do not readily admit of being dismembered and scored point by point. Then it is that one has to fall back on direct comparisons with a series of models each of which represents a definite step upwards in quality from its next neighbour. Thus Burt obtained drawings of ' a man ' from a large number of children and selected from each year the drawing most typical of that age. A child's drawing attainment age can be assessed by sliding his drawing of ' a man ' over this gauge until one reaches the model to which it is most comparable.

Similarly, Ballard has devised a ten-point scale of legibility of script writing, though here the steps are based neither on age nor on percentile distribution, but on the estimates of a committee of art teachers and others. Whether one uses point scores or median samples the steps employed may be on a basis of percentiles, equal units, or age equivalents. It is the manner of assessment—whether by total impression or piecemeal and point by point—which

---

[1] Though Freeman has attempted an analytical scale for this purpose.

distinguishes the direct comparison or ' median samples ' method from the point score method.

This direct comparison or sample method has the disadvantage that it introduces once more the personal equation of the examiner, though not nearly to such a disastrous extent as in the ordinary examination. Some accomplishments can be assessed by either method. Goodenough has produced norms for drawing based on point scoring; whilst on the other hand English essays have been assessed, more accurately than by a marking technique, through direct comparison with ranked samples.

Obviously the highest ranges of accomplishment in art and literature cannot be assessed by attainment tests in the terms so far evolved for the work of children.

In most attainment tests, the answers are of the selective rather than the inventive type, because of the certainty of scoring which, as pointed out (see p. 9), this method alone gives. Naturally, a person answers more on a selective than on an inventive test, since most people can recognise more than they can recall, but there is no evidence that the ranking of persons by the two methods differs in any way. It is highly desirable that there should be five or six alternative answers to each item, and it is also apparently good technique to give spurious attractiveness to the wrong answers that the ignorant may be tempted by them.[1] Even the position (in order) of the answers seems to affect the frequency with which they are chosen by the ignorant.[2]

Occasionally the material does not admit of five-response answers, and one has to fall back upon three-response or on true-false answers (two response) in which there is a fifty-fifty chance of being right, even when the examinee is entirely ignorant. Then greater accuracy is obtained by subtracting from the number of items right the number of items wrong, for the latter is probably equal in number to the answers obtained correct by luck.

[1] H. L. Arnold, " Analysis of Discrepancies between True, False, and Simple Recall Examinations," *J. Educ. Psychol.*, 1927, xviii.
[2] " The Effect of Printed Response Words upon Children's Answers to Questions in Two-response Types of Test," by C. O. Matthews, *J. Educ. Psychol.*, 1927, xviii.

Although the last-mentioned device practically eliminates differences due to the subjects' greater or lesser temperamental tendency to risk a guess, experiment shows that it
is desirable in all selective type tests to issue definite instructions to all examinees either to guess or not to guess.
The evidence as to which is better is conflicting. On the
whole, and particularly on multiple response tests (say,
four alternatives or more), the instruction not to guess
seems to produce more valid and consistent measurements.
Even if the instruction to make a guess on every item is
given, to apply afterwards a correction for guessing is
hardly worth the trouble with a five- or six-response test;
for the chance of right answers by luck is small, and multi-
plying the wrong answers by four or five to get a figure to
subtract from the number right is a questionable procedure.

Although the instruction not to guess produces slightly
better consistency correlations, it is still doubtful whether
the validity of the attainment test itself is increased thereby,
for we may now be measuring a temperament factor too:
the inclination to risk a guess when told not to guess.

To sum up: the instruction to guess is essential in two-
response tests, whether guessing correction is applied or
not (and generally it should be), but in multiple response
tests it is a matter of indifference, though where the multiple
responses are numerous (say, six or more alternatives) the
instruction not to guess is probably better.

3. Available Material

Since it is in the various branches of English and of
arithmetic that measurements are most frequently made,
these branches are set out first and in greatest detail. All
other tests are classified under subject-headings alphabetically. The material of Burt and of Ballard is not
printed here in detail, since it is already issued in other
books [1] available in almost any library. We also have not

---

[1] *Mental and Scholastic Tests*, by C. Burt (P. S. King & Son): *The New Examiner*, by
P. B. Ballard (Univ. of London Press).

listed, except sporadically, the uniform and very comprehensive *Co-operative Achievement Tests*, published by the
Co-operative Test Service, 15 Amsterdam Avenue, New
York. These are mainly of high school difficulty, require
about 40 minutes each, permit of machine-scoring, and are
well standardised. They include English, foreign languages, science, mathematics, etc., and are too numerous
for separate recording here.

(A) English and Arithmetic

ENGLISH

Ability in English includes many distinct kinds of
skill and knowledge. For general purposes, as well as
for diagnosing causes of backwardness, it is desirable to
assess each separately. There is the skill to read quickly,
the ability to spell, the extent of the vocabulary understood; the sense of style and habit of correct grammatical
usage and, finally, knowledge of literature and classical
speech enrichments. Even these are not strictly defined
powers: reading, for example, may mean either the ability
to comprehend a passage silently read, or the ability to read
words out aloud correctly and quickly with or without
understanding. For one purpose we need to assess comprehension; for another, just speed of reading.

Ballard has rightly said that, apart from purposes of
diagnosing backwardness, the essay must be the central test
of attainment in English, and he has devised an objectively
scored test—his ' construction test '—to measure the kind
of artistic skill required in good essay writing.

To assess the attainment age in English of children referred
for general backwardness (and with whom the psychologist
can only spend a few minutes), the writer has found it best
to use a test of Reading Comprehension and of Vocabulary.
These are parts of a complete battery of English and
arithmetic tests standardised by the writer under the title of
Midland Attainment Tests (because they have been stan-

dardised in Midland schools, mainly in the City of Leicester). This battery consists of the following parts:

English	*Arithmetic*
Reading Comprehension, 10 minutes.	Mechanical skill, 10 minutes.
Reading Vocabulary, 5 minutes.	Information (Method), 60 minutes.
Spelling, 10 minutes.	
Grammar, Style, Construction, 20 minutes.	
Knowledge of Literature, 15 minutes.	

It permits of being administered and scored in two ways: (1) as a group test, when the score is the number of items right within a certain time limit. This score is converted to an attainment age by means of a table of norms; (2) as an individual test, when, for convenience and for economy of time, the child is stopped when he fails on three successive items. (The items have been graded in order of increasing difficulty.) His attainment is indicated by the point which he reaches when these failures begin.[1] This can be read off at once, for, as in Burt's tests, the attainment ages in years and fractions of a year are set out alongside the items.

The available tests in English are as follows :

(a) Reading

A great deal of research has been done on the analysis of reading ability and disability. Unfortunately, much of it has been logical rather than naturalistic, empirical, and factorial. The published tests are proportionately numerous and overlapping, and it is difficult to make a selection of them which is more useful and valid than another, for general purposes. The psychometrist interested in fine diagnosis should certainly be familiar with the researches of Gates, Pressey, and those published notably from the Universities of Iowa, Minnesota, and Columbia.

1. Comprehension

Ballard's Test.—Silent reading. Twenty-two brief passages on completion test principle (with little demand on

---

[1] Example of scoring: A child who answers, with only one or two scattered errors, up to and including " Does a boy wear a hat? " and then fails on *three successive items*, would have an attainment age of 7½ years.

intelligence). Possible score of 50 words. Time, 15 minutes (10 for adults). Norms for ages 9–14 inclusive. *New Examiner*, p. 163.

Burt's Test.—" Read what is on the card (not aloud) and do what it says." Demands on intelligence as far as possible eliminated. Seventeen items. Years, 5–13 inclusive. Most finely diagnostic around 6 and 7 years. (*Mental and Scholastic Tests*, p. 345.[1]) This and all the other attainment tests of Professor Burt have been very soundly standardised on at least 500 children at each age in London schools.

Iowa Silent Reading Tests, by H. A. Greene, A. N. Jorgensen, and V. H. Kelley.—These analyse reading comprehension into rate-comprehension, untimed comprehension, poetry comprehension, word meaning, sentence meaning, paragraph meaning, etc. They are printed in elementary, advanced, and re-test forms, each with widely based norms (for American children). Obtainable: World Book Co., Yonkers-on-Hudson, New York.

Minnesota Speed of Reading Test, for College and High School Students, by A. C. Eurich.—A comparatively brief test of paragraph comprehension, available in A and B forms. Published by University of Minnesota Press, Minneapolis, Minn., U.S.A.

Midland Test (*Cattell*).—Items up to $5\frac{1}{2}$-year level not included in the group test. In the individual test these items are merely read (aloud), whereas the rest is a test of silent comprehension. Ten minutes allowed for group tests. (*Scoring:* 2 marks for each completely correct answer. Where two or more words have to be underlined in an item *all* must be correct for that item to be counted (i.e. no half marks).[2] In the individual test the attainment age is the point reached when three successive failures ensue, no regard being paid to one and two item failures earlier.

---

[1] The material for all Burt's tests described here will be found in *Handbooks of Tests* by Burt (P. S. King); also in a much larger volume with research findings, in *Mental and Scholastic Tests*, by Burt (P. S. King). The smaller book has not norms for all tests.

[2] Example of scoring: A child who answers, with only one or two scattered errors, up to and including "Does a boy wear a hat?" and then fails on *three successive items*, would have an attainment age of $7\frac{1}{2}$ years.

Material

4 *Years*

(·5)   A   B   O   I   T

(·5)   to   we   in

5 *Years*

(·25)   on by it

(·25)   bun dog ball the

(·5)   Can a cat see ?   { yes
                             no

6 *Years* (·25 per question)

Put a dot in this ring ◯

We hold a pen between our { fingers
                            toes
                            teeth

Is it true that a sister is always { no
     a girl ?   yes
                                     sometimes

How many legs has a dog ? { none
                            two
                            four
                            lots

7 *Years* (·5 per question)

Does a boy wear a hat ? { sometimes
                          no
                          always

When robbers break into a house they { sleep
  generally come to { steal
    { play

8 *Years* (·5 per question)

A cow is bigger than a { kitten
  { horse
  { tram

Put a cross in the oblong that follows this full stop. ▭ △ ○

9 *Years* (·5 per question)

If you lift your hands above your head are { yes
  they above your shoulders ? { no
  { nearly

The land was so flat that the rain which { heaps
  fell lay on the ground in great { rivers ·
  { pools

10 *Years*

Take this paper and turn it right round, so that the bottom is at the top. Then write a capital letter P in this square ▢ . After that turn the paper the right way again.

11 *Years* (·5 per question)

Draw as quickly as you can a straight line under the last word in this sentence.

Which of the following animals is most commonly kept as a pet in civilised countries ?

    Camel   Cow   Dog   Horse

12 *Years*

Natural, barbarian, again, plate.

Each of these words has the letter ' a ' in it. Find out which contains it the largest number of times and draw a line under the whole word.

13 *Years* (·5 per question)

At first the swan left its nest and swam angrily in little circles around the intruder, beating the water with its wings, but, finding its efforts useless, it soon rose in the air and flew swiftly away.

It had $\begin{cases} \text{built} \\ \text{abandoned} \\ \text{eaten} \end{cases}$ its own nest.

The preceding examples have required you to indicate one answer only.   In this instance, however, you are asked to underline two words, namely, ' preceding ' and ' required ' above.

14 *Years*

> He rose at dawn and fired with hope,
>   Shot o'er the seething harbour bar
> And reached the ship and caught the rope
>   And whistled to the morning star.
>
> And while he whistled long and loud,
>   He heard a fierce mermaiden cry,
> " O boy, though thou art young and proud,
>   I see the place where thou shalt lie."

The mermaid's prophecy would most likely bring to the boy a sense of $\begin{cases} \text{hope.} \\ \text{adventure in foreign parts.} \\ \text{danger from drowning.} \\ \text{pride in his ship.} \end{cases}$

Norms for Group Test

Attainment age .	6	7	8	9	10	11	12	13	14
Score in marks .	1·3	10·0	14·1	17·8	21·0	24·2	27·5	30·4	34·0

Gates's Primary Reading Tests (see *Teachers' Coll. Record,*[1] 1926, xxviii) for diagnosis of reading disability.   Arbitrary sub-divisions as into (i) paragraph mastery, (ii) reading to predict outcome of future events, (iii) reading to understand precise directions, (iv) reading to note details.

Northumberland Standardised Tests. (1925 series) Burt, Set II, English.   Group or individual.   49 minutes. (7 on each sub-test.)   Ages 7–14 years.—Obtainable from University of London Press, Ltd.

Williams's Junior Scholarship Tests, I English.   (*b*) Reading.   Obtainable from Messrs. G. G. Harrap & Co.

2. Speed, Accuracy, etc.

Burt's Test.—(*a*) *Accuracy.*—Ability to read aloud cor-

---

[1] See also Gates's *The Improvement of Reading*, Macmillan.

rectly. 110 words in graded series. Ages 4–14 years inclusive. Ten words at each age. Attainment age that at which child passes more than half of items. An individual test. Also a sub-test of accuracy of knowledge of figures and letters.

(*b*) *Speed.*—200 monosyllables, continuous and uniform in difficulty. Norms for number of words read aloud in 60 seconds. Instruction to read rapidly. Individual test.

(*c*) *Speed, Accuracy, and Comprehension Combined.*—A paragraph, timed, with questions to follow to test comprehension. Mainly monosyllables.

Ballard's Test.—*Accuracy.*—One-minute reading scale. Mainly monosyllables (158 words), but graded to larger words. Instruct to read aloud rapidly. 1 minute allowed. Norms for $5\frac{1}{2}$ years to 16. (*New Examiner*, p. 145.) One scale for boys; another for girls.

Northumberland Test.—See above, p. 95.

3. Vocabulary

Midland Test 2 (*Cattell*).—A silent reading test to determine the size of vocabulary in respect of understanding the meaning of words seen (note that speaking vocabulary is smaller than the ' understood ' or reading vocabulary). Group or individual test. 5 minutes allowed.

Group Test Scoring.—1 mark for each correct item.

Norms for Group Test

Attainment age	6	7	8	9	10	11	12	13	14
Score in marks	3·4	6·8	10·9	12·8	14·7	16·1	16·9	17·5	18·1

Individual Test Scoring.—As shown below, e.g., a child who stops [1] after answering the first seven items has an attainment age of $7\frac{1}{2}$.

Materials for Reading Vocabulary Test

6 *Years* (·2 per question)

$$1. \text{ A King is a } \begin{cases} \text{dog} \\ \text{man} \\ \text{flower} \end{cases}$$

---

[1] i.e. fails on three successive items. This is taken as the point of failure in all the Midland Tests when given individually.

2. A peach is a { fruit / place / toy }

3. Copper is a kind of { bird / wood / metal }

4. To drip means to { sing / drink a lot / fall in drops }

5. Newts are found in { fireplaces / pools / coal-mines }

7 *Years* (·25 per question)

6. Haste means the same as { flour / straw / hurry }

7. A dungeon is a { ship / prison / club }

8. Reins are used on a { ship / horse / motor-car }

9. Impolite means { silly / quick / rude }

8 *Years* (·5 per question)

10. A juggler is a { wild animal / man / pirate }

11. To insure means to $\begin{cases} \text{make certain} \\ \text{hurt someone} \\ \text{lose money} \end{cases}$

9 *Years* (·5 per question)

12. To conceal means to $\begin{cases} \text{make} \\ \text{break} \\ \text{hide} \end{cases}$

13. Hysterics are a kind of $\begin{cases} \text{flower} \\ \text{fit} \\ \text{instrument} \end{cases}$

10 *Years* (·5 per question)

14. Shrewd means $\begin{cases} \text{cross} \\ \text{tired} \\ \text{clever} \end{cases}$

15. To quake means to $\begin{cases} \text{shake} \\ \text{talk} \\ \text{run} \end{cases}$

11 *Years*

16. Candid means $\begin{cases} \text{sugary} \\ \text{frank} \\ \text{tinned} \end{cases}$

12 *Years*

17. To repose is to $\begin{cases} \text{rest} \\ \text{reply} \\ \text{make a face} \end{cases}$

13 *Years*

18. A declivity is a $\begin{cases} \text{part of a ship} \\ \text{liking} \\ \text{slope} \end{cases}$

14 *Years*

19. Tedious means $\begin{cases} \text{ill} \\ \text{tiresome} \\ \text{cross} \end{cases}$

(b) Spelling

Ayre's Spelling Scale.—Compiled of the 1,000 most common words in the English language, classified in 26 sections of increasing difficulty. A sound scale for making a very thorough examination of spelling achievement and requiring about an hour. Well-founded norms, arranged for school standards. Material in Ballard's *Group Tests of Intelligence.*

Burt's Test.—(a) Actually labelled *Vocabulary Test.* No time limit. Ages, 5–14 inclusive. Ten words at each age. Attainment age that at which more than one-half of words are correctly written. Words dictated by teacher with repetition when necessary. (*Mental & Scholastic Tests,* pp. 287 and 402 for norms.)

(b) *Dictation.*—No time limit. Use of phrases and sentences instead of isolated words, to avoid ambiguity. Continuous, but graded material scored by number of letters correct. Norms (*Mental & Scholastic Tests,* p. 403), ages 6–14 inclusive.

Midland Test 3 (*Cattell*).—Each word to be read out twice. (Since 10 minutes is allowed for the whole test, this means spending about 15 seconds on each word.) Group or individual test. In the individual test the child scores the indicated attainment age when he passes *all* the words opposite that age before failing in three consecutive items, e.g. failure in ' blind,' ' family ' and ' point ' gives a seven-year performance.

5 years.	in we do go out
6 years.	can may did door grow
7 years.	ball last about child
8 years.	blind family point perhaps
9 years.	protection motion frighten
10 years.	punishment continue portion
11 years.	construct wander lonely
12 years.	passenger shepherd
13 years.	manufacture deceiving
14 years.	intelligent impatient

These additional graded words are to be used for higher attainment ages and are to be added to the above list in the group test:

community, guardian, referring, liquefy, ecstasy, marriageable, unnecessary, spatial.

Scoring.—1 mark for each correctly spelt word.

Norms for Group Test

Attainment age	5	6	7	8	9	10	11	12	13	14
Score in marks	0·5	7·0	12·0	16·5	20·0	23·0	26·4	29·0	31·0	33·1

Note that the norms at 5 and 6 in this test will vary greatly with the general aims and methods of the infant school, notably with the age at which formal reading and writing begin.

Schonell's Tests.—A series of standardised spelling tests and graded remedial material. Based on extensive research, and probably offering the best test available in this country for diagnosing and remedying the causes of spelling disabilities. Material in *Essentials in Teaching and Testing Spelling*, by J. Schonell (Macmillan, 1932).

(c) Grammar, Style

Here one aims, not at testing explicit knowledge of grammar or grammatical nomenclature, but at assessing acquired skill in grammatical usage and the (psychologically closely related) sense of style.

Ballard's Test. (Called English ' Comprehension,' p. 172 of the *New Examiner*.)—This test also includes tests of vocabulary. 100 items. A matter of indicating better alternatives in sentences, etc. 1 hour required. Norms for ages 10–14 inclusive.

Midland Test 4 (Cattell).—Deals with general knowledge of how English should be written—grammar, style, phrase arrangement, punctuation. Not arranged for scoring by ' point of failure ' method. 20 minutes required.

Items

Put a line under the best word, wherever two or more words are given.

1. $\begin{Bmatrix} \text{Wear} \\ \text{Where} \\ \text{Were} \end{Bmatrix}$ are we ?

2. $\begin{Bmatrix} \text{There} \\ \text{Their} \end{Bmatrix}$ is no more.

3. They knew $\begin{Bmatrix} \text{we} \\ \text{us} \end{Bmatrix}$ two had done it, for they saw $\begin{Bmatrix} \text{we} \\ \text{us} \end{Bmatrix}$ come.

4. " I $\begin{Bmatrix} \text{shall} \\ \text{will} \end{Bmatrix}$ drown," cried the distressed swimmer.

" No one $\begin{Bmatrix} \text{shall} \\ \text{will} \end{Bmatrix}$ save me."

5. If you are tired $\begin{Bmatrix} \text{lay} \\ \text{lie} \end{Bmatrix}$ down.

6. He had neither hat $\begin{Bmatrix} \text{nor} \\ \text{or} \end{Bmatrix}$ coat.

7. The chieftain, with ten warriors, $\begin{Bmatrix} \text{was} \\ \text{were} \end{Bmatrix}$ there.

8. Everybody likes to see $\begin{Bmatrix} \text{their} \\ \text{his} \\ \text{one's} \end{Bmatrix}$ name in print.

9. $\begin{Bmatrix} \text{These} \\ \text{This} \\ \text{Those} \end{Bmatrix}$ sort of people $\begin{Bmatrix} \text{is} \\ \text{are} \end{Bmatrix}$ no good.

In some of the following sentences one or more words are wrong. Put a line under the incorrect words.

10. How much are them apples ?
11. He is the man what done it.
12. I have bought me a new hat.
13. I teached him to read.
14. He don't do what he should.
15. In the park were a row of tall trees.
16. All of us play cricket.
17. Mary and myself will call at the shop.

18. I beseeched him to return.
19. He does it well.
20. None of the boys had a bat of their own.
21. You did not ought to have gone.
22. Each is right.
23. He came with father and I.
24. The boy and not the girls are to blame.
25. Which is the best of the two ?
26. He plays most careful.

27. Punctuate and insert any capital letters that are needed:

the duke dashed up shouting all is lost whats the hurry said lord growley hurry exclaimed the dukes standard bearer why if were not in france before sunday we shall all be dead men so they rode off in haste hoping to reach the ships.

In some of the following sentences the meaning is not clear. Underline the words that are in the wrong position:

28. My friend spent Easter shooting at the country house of Lord and Lady Molton.
29. Away he went, like the wind.
30. Please return the book I lent you quickly.
31. I only like him when he is good.
32. " Fast car wanted by a sportsman with four cylinders."
33. " Boy wanted to sell eggs under sixteen years of age."
34. " Lighting fireworks is forbidden in the streets."
35. This is the man whom I sent for.
36. He was glad constantly to tend the fire which burnt well.

Which of the following is the better style ? Indicate by a cross.

37. (a) The man was told to thoroughly clean the garage.

(b) The man was told thoroughly to clean the garage.

(c) The man was told to clean the garage thoroughly.

38. (a) Who knows, but in this solitary place
There lies a heart that burnt with fire divine;
A hand of iron, a stern imperial face,
Or skill to turn the sweet melodious line.

(b) Perhaps in this neglected spot is laid
Some heart once pregnant with celestial fire;
Hands, that the rods of Empire might have swayed,
Or waked to ecstasy the living lyre.

39. (a) The pearls of the morning dew have fled never to be found again.

(b) The pearls of the morning dew have fled never to come back at any future date.

Scoring.—1 mark for each completely correct answer.

Norms

Attainment age	6½	7	8	9	10	11	12	13	14
Score in marks	4	6·8	8·8	11·0	16·0	19·6	21·3	22·0	22·7

(d) Composition and Construction

A good part of this ability is assessable by the Midland Grammar Style Test above, but Ballard has devoted one test entirely to attempting the objective assessment of ability in English Composition as such. His test, and others now available, are given below.

Ballard's ' Construction ' Test.—Fourteen graded passages, each to be rearranged. One hour required. Norms for years 10–14.

Burt's Test.—' Median Samples ' of children's compositions, from age 7 to 14 years inclusive. Material in *Mental and Scholastic Tests*, p. 395.

Northamptonshire Composition Scale (G. P. Williams).—A series of median samples. Obtainable Messrs. G. G. Harrap & Co.

(e) Knowledge of Literature and Classical Speech Enrichments

Midland Test 5 *(Cattell)*.—This test is intended primarily for purposes of vocational guidance for determining especial interest in, or familiarity with, literature, in younger children. Time required, 15 minutes. To be read silently by subjects.

Items

1. Robinson Crusoe is about a man on a(n) { Aeroplane. / Submarine. / Island.

2. " Oh, what big ears you've got " was said in { The Sleeping Beauty. / Little Red Riding Hood. / Jack and the Bean Stalk.

3. "Peter Pan" is a story about a little boy who { wouldn't grow up. / ate a lot of pancakes. / kept a pet lion.

4. The Pied Piper played his tunes to { Kings and Courtiers. / Rats and Children. / The Queen of the Fairies.

5. Scrooge comes in a tale called { A Christmas Carol. / King Midas. / Ghosts.

6. Shakespeare wrote a play called { The Tempest. / She Stoops to Conquer. / Spears and Swords.

7. Samson was { a strong man / a king } described in the { New Testament. / Old Testament. / Tempest.

8. "Treasure Island" was written by { Kipling. / Dickens. / Stevenson.

9. " Alice in Wonderland " was written by
{ Angela Brazil.
Stevenson.
Lewis Carroll.

10. " Westward Ho! " is a story about
{ Hereward the Wake.
The Spanish Main.
Christopher Columbus.

11. Write the number of the Proverb against the sentence that explains it:
   1. Birds of a feather flock together.
   2. One swallow does not make a summer.
   3. Beware of buying a pig in a poke.
   Don't be misled by insufficient evidence.
   Don't take a thing till you've examined it thoroughly.
   A man is known by the character of his friends.

12. "Ivanhoe" is a story about
{ Race Horses.
Knights.
Pirates.

13. The Stories of Sherlock Holmes were written by
{ Edgar Wallace.
Conan Doyle.
Rider Haggard.

14. Choose an author responsible for each of the following quotations, and put the number of the quotation at the end of his name:
   (a) " Of all beasts he learned the language, learned their names and all their secrets."   Burns.
   (b) "Scots, wha hae wi' Wallace bled."   Macaulay.
   (c) " But I have felt a presence that disturbs me with the joy of elevated thought."   Wordsworth.
   (d) "Then out spake brave Horatius."   Longfellow.

15. " The Elephant's Child " is described in
{ Just-so Stories.
The Heroes.
Memories of a Lion Hunter.

16. " The Everlasting Mercy " was written by
{ Conan Doyle.
Ibsen.
Masefield.

17. " The Forsyte Saga " was written by $\begin{cases} \text{Walpole.} \\ \text{Synge.} \\ \text{Galsworthy.} \end{cases}$

18. " The Time Machine " is a story by $\begin{cases} \text{Jules Verne.} \\ \text{H. G. Wells.} \\ \text{Bernard Shaw.} \end{cases}$

19. " Man and Superman," was written by $\begin{cases} \text{Carlyle.} \\ \text{G. B. Shaw.} \\ \text{Oscar Wilde.} \end{cases}$

20. Emerson is famous for his $\begin{cases} \text{plays.} \\ \text{poems.} \\ \text{essays.} \\ \text{novels.} \end{cases}$

21. Choose an author responsible for each of the following quotations, and put the number of the quotation at the end of his name:

    (a) " If I should die, think only this of me."   Tennyson.

    (b) "My heart aches and a drowsy numbness steals."   Hood.

    (c) " I come from haunts of coot and hern."   Brooke.

    (d) " I remember, I remember, the fir trees dark and high."   Keats.

22. Put these characters in their right plays or stories by writing the number of the appropriate play after them:

    1. Macbeth   Orlando
    2. The Spectator Club   Mr. Micawber
    3. The Rivals   Banquo
    4. As You Like It   Sir Roger de Coverley
    5. David Copperfield   Bassanio
    6. The Merchant of Venice Dugald Dalgetty
    7. A Legend of Montrose Mrs. Malaprop

23. Write the number (1, 2, 3, 4) of the expression against the words that explain it.

(a) More honoured in the breach than in the observance		Do as you please.
(b) Vice versa	means	The other way about.
(c) Mutatis mutandis		Other things changing appropriately.
(d) Laissez faire		Not strictly kept.

24. Choose an author responsible for each of the following quotations, and put the number of the quotation at the end of his name:

  (a) " This they all with a joyful mind bear through life like a torch in flame."   Browning.

  (b) In Xanadu did Kubla Khan, a stately pleasure dome decree.   Newbolt.

  (c) " Oh, to be in England, now that April's there."   Shelley.

  (d) " The warm sun is failing, the bleak wind is wailing."   Coleridge.

25. Write the number of the expression against the words that explain it:

(a) A pyrrhic victory	A tale of woe.
(b) A jeremiad	Something gained at immense loss.
(c) A metonym	A figure of speech.
(d) An iambic foot	A metrical form in poetry.

26. To what object, living or dead, does each of the following passages refer ?

   " He clasps the crag with crooked hands,
   Close to the sun in lonely lands,
   Ringed with the azure world he stands.
   The wrinkled sea beneath him crawls,
   He watches from his mountain walls
   And like a thunderbolt he falls."
         A(n).........................

" Like a glow-worm golden in a dell of dew."

A(n).........................

" This royal throne of kings; this sceptred isle."

....

Scoring.—1 mark for each correct sentence; 3 marks (1 for each item) in questions 11 and 26; 4 marks (1 for each item) in questions 14, 21, 23, 24; 7 marks (1 for each) in question 22.

Norms.

Attainment age	6½	7	8	9	10	11	12	13	14
Score	2·0	2·4	5·0	8·0	11·0	16·0	19·9	23·0	26·5

Nelson-Denny Reading Test. Separate sections on vocabulary and paragraph comprehension. For colleges and high schools. Two forms, for re-test. Published: Houghton Mifflin, Boston, U.S.A.

Pressey Test of Reading Comprehension. Tests of speed and comprehension for school and college. Published: Ohio State Dept. Educ., Ohio, U.S.A.

Traxler Reading Tests. Rate and comprehension. A and B forms, for high school and college. Published: Public School Publishing Co., Bloomington, Illinois, U.S.A.

Diagnostic Tests of Reading Disability.

Monroe, *Diagnostic Reading Tests.* Record Blanks, Manual, and Material. Obtainable from Messrs. Stoelting.

Gray's *Oral Reading Paragraphs* (Mixed Aspects assessed). Obtainable from Public School Publishing Co., Bloomington, U.S.A.

Diagnostic Examination of Silent Reading Abilities, by M. van Wagenen and A. Dvorak.—For schools and colleges. Analyses into speed comprehension, vocabulary, central thought, general information, etc. Published: Educational Test Bureau, Minneapolis, Minn.

ARITHMETIC

The most common and the most useful division of arithmetical ability is into knowledge of arithmetical methods on the one hand and actual speed and accuracy—' skill '— in the four fundamental processes, on the other.   For performance in these two branches may be at entirely different levels. A university student, for example, may be at an extremely high level in acquaintance with methods, yet below the level of a ' special ' class child in sheer speed and accuracy of addition, multiplication, etc. In vocational guidance quite different lines of work may be indicated according to the relative proficiency shown in these distinct aspects of mathematical ability.

In diagnosing the causes of backwardness in arithmetic, however, this division is not enough, though it provides a useful preliminary analysis.   As is well known to the psychologist, who works in the educational field, backwardness in arithmetic, more than in any other subject, is liable to arise through the child having missed one small process in the sequence of his arithmetical education. The recovery of the necessary link is essential to rectifying the general backwardness. It may be he has never reached proficiency with a certain range of multiplication tables, or has never understood long division, or has an erroneous habit in cancelling fractions. The psychologist must proceed like the geologist to examine the strata until he detects the ' faulty lie ' which indicates a missing layer.

For this purpose a qualitative analysis of the errors in a well-graded methodology test is usually sufficient to lead up to the specially devised testing sums with which the psychologist must eventually probe in such cases.

(a) ' Knowledge of Method' Tests

Burt's Test (1) *Mental.* (Individual.) Ages 4–14.— Ten questions to each year (5 mechanical, 5 problems in each year). Soundly standardised for London children.

(2) *Written.* (Group or Individual.)—Ages 7–14. Five questions to each year. *Mental and Scholastic Tests*, p. 363.

Ballard's Test. (Arithmetical Reasoning.) (*New Examiner*, p. 193.)—100 graded questions. Time required, 1 hour.

Midland Test (Cattell). (Individual or Group.) Oral or Written.—In either method paper is provided on which rough calculations can be made. The questions are graded and arranged in the order most commonly found in primary school work. Time allowed, 1 hour.

Scoring.—1 mark for each correct answer (total 49).

Norms

Attainment age	6½	7	8	9	10	11	12	13	14
Score	3·1	4·0	9·3	15·0	21·0	27·0	33·1	39·2	46·0

Items

4 *Years.* (Basic level, before any questions at all are answered.)

Add ⅓ of a year per question answered.

1. How many fingers am I holding up? (hold up 3).
2. How far can you count? (pass if counts up to 5).
3. If you had 2 pennies in this hand, and I gave you one more, how many would you have then?

5 *Years.* (Level attained when the above three questions are correctly answered.)

Add ⅓ of a year per question answered.

4. I had 3 potatoes on my plate and my mother gave me two more; how many had I then?
5. I had 5 rabbits, 1 died; how many have I left?
6. Tom had 9 oranges. He gave 4 to Jane. How many has he left?

6 *Years.*

Add ⅓ of a year per question answered.

7. What are twice 3?
8. How many do 6 and 5 make?
9. 9 apples were divided equally among 3 children. How many did each have?

7 *Years.*

Add ¼ of a year per question answered.

10. I had seventeen apples and lost eight. How many are left?

11. How many halfpennies are there in fivepence?

12. My brother has ten nuts, my sister has thirteen, and I have eight. How many have we got together?

13. I have thirty apples. If they are divided equally among five boys, how many will each get?

8 *Years begin here.*

Add ⅙ of a year per question answered.

14. How many days are there in six weeks?

15. Milton is 23 miles away; a man gave me a lift in his car for 15 miles. How many miles have I still to walk?

16. My brother is five feet high. How many inches is that?

17. What do 25 and 26 make?

18. What number is half-way between 11 and 17?

19. There were 104 sailors and only 8 could go in one boat. How many boats would be wanted?

9 *Years.*

Add ⅙ of a year per question answered.

20. John had 14 coupons. He lost 8, but his mother gave him 11 more. How many had he then?

21. In my pocket are six halfpennies, three pennies, and half-a-crown. How much is that altogether?

22. What are nine eights?

23. How many ounces are there in one and a half pounds?

24. 16 companies of soldiers marched to the fort (there were 250 in each company). 7 men were killed on the march. How many arrived?

25. How many thirteens are there in 65?

10 *Years*. (Henceforth add fractions of a year for each question in the manner indicated above.)

26. A hunter shot 47 lions in one year, 123 in the next, and 196 in the next. How many did he shoot altogether?

27. An airman rose 1,000 feet in the air, fell 63, rose 111, and fell 254. What is his present height?

28. Captain Scott was born in 1868 and died at the South Pole in 1912. How old was he when he died?

29. I buy 8 penny stamps and 9 halfpenny ones. How much change shall I have from 2 shillings?

30. How many minutes are there in 3 hours?

31. The airman had to be in his machine a quarter of an hour before the flight started. The flight started at five-and-twenty to one. When had he to be in his machine?

11 *Years*.

32. If apples are seven for sixpence, how many could I buy for half-a-crown?

33. How many inches in 3 yards 1 foot?

34. A boxer weighed 10 stone 3 pounds, but he lost five pounds while training. What is his weight now?

35. A boxer had £2 given him as a prize. With this he bought a book for 7s. 6d., and six tennis balls at tenpence each.
How much had he left?

36. How much is a quarter of £5 10s.?

37. How many separate triangles can I make with 25 matches, and how many matches will be left over?

12 *Years*.

38. What is $\frac{4}{21} \div \frac{8}{7}$?

39. How much do $\frac{1}{5}$ and $\frac{2}{3}$ make?

40. What is $\frac{2}{8}$ of $2\frac{1}{4}$?

41. What is $\frac{1}{3}$ of $\frac{1}{4}$?

13 *Years*.

42. A man earned £131 3s. 10d. a year in wages. How much is that a week? (52 weeks in a year.)

43. My car uses a pint of oil every 100 miles. How many miles can I go with two gallons of oil?

44. How much is left if you take $\frac{1}{3}$ from $1\frac{1}{4}$?

14 *Years.*

45. In one case of apples 6 out of every 50 were bad, and in another case 4 out of 40 were bad. Which case contains the greater proportion of good apples?

46. What is $1\frac{5}{9} \times 1\frac{10}{35}$?

47. What is the shortest length of ribbon from which I can cut off either 4-inch, 6-inch, or 8-inch lengths an exact number of times?

48. What is six times 1·31?

49. A boy sold a knife for 1s. 3d., gaining 3d. on what he gave for it. What fraction of the cost price was his profit?

KEY TO ARITHMETIC TEST

1.	3	13.	6	25.	5	37.	8 triangles 1
2.	5	14.	42	26.	366	38.	$\frac{1}{8}$ [over
3.	3	15.	8 miles	27.	794	39.	$1\frac{2}{15}$
4.	5	16.	60 ins.	28.	44 yrs.	40.	$1\frac{9}{10}$
5.	4	17.	51	29.	$11\frac{1}{2}d.$	41.	$1\frac{1}{3}$
6.	5	18.	14	30.	180 mins.	42.	£2 10s. 5½d.
7.	6	19.	13	31.	12·20	43.	1,600
8.	11	20.	17	32.	35	44.	$1\frac{1}{2}$
9.	3	21.	3s.	33.	120	45.	2nd Case
10.	9	22.	72	34.	9 st. 12 lb.	46.	2
11.	10	23.	24 oz.	35.	£1 7s. 6d.	47.	2 lb.
12.	31	24.	3,993	36.	£1 7s. 6d.	48.	7·86
						49.	$\frac{1}{4}$

Northumberland Standardised Tests. (1925 Series.) (Burt.) I. Arithmetic. (Group or Individual.) 49 minutes. Ages 7–14 years.—Test has seven sub-tests, each of which admits of separate assessment by its own norm table. They are: (1) Addition (speed and accuracy, but also knowledge of method in most compound systems); (2) Subtraction (speed, accuracy, and knowledge of methods as (1)); (3) Multiplication (speed, accuracy, and method knowledge); (4) Division; (5) Mental arithmetic; (6) Rules (knowledge); (7) Reasoning (knowledge of method, plus speed, skill, and intelligence). Norms also for test as a whole. Soundly standardised. Manual of Instructions with Norms for group testing obtainable from University of London Press, Ltd.

(b) Mechanical Skill

Burt's Tests. 1. *Mechanical Graded Test.*—This avoids ' problems,' but is to a large extent also a measure of ' method knowledge ' rather than of speed and accuracy. Five items for each year from 7 to 14.

2. *Ungraded Test.*—A continuous test for each of the four rules—addition, subtraction, etc. Five minutes allowed for each paper. Score by number of correct figures.

Ballard's Test. (*New Examiner*, p. 190.)—A graded test similar to Burt's above, avoiding problems, but testing knowledge of method in addition to mechanical speed and accuracy. 100 items. Time allowed, 50 minutes. Also (*op. cit.* p. 147) 1 minute oral addition test, 1 minute subtraction test. Norms for 5–12 years.

The Southend Attainment Test in Mechanical Arithmetic.—Standardised for junior and senior school levels.

Midland Test (Cattell). (Group or Individual.)—Testing speed and accuracy in the four rules. To avoid fatigue and for greater reliability of measurement, each section (adding, etc.) is in two parts, i.e. eight parts in all. Exactly 1 minute is allowed on each part.

Scoring.—$\frac{1}{2}$ mark for each *figure* correct. Score from all parts included in one total.

Norms

Attainment age .	6½	7	8	9	10	11	12	13	14
Score . .	1·1	3·0	12·8	21·5	30·9	40·0	50·0	58·4	65·7

Material

1. *Addition.*

95	74	63	76	27	39
56	29	79	31	18	84
18	86	32	39	10	71
37	32	45	46	92	20

2. *Subtraction.*

7385	8435	9254	5106	4871	3598
6244	6317	5617	3967	2904	2719

3. *Multiplication.*

1713	2435	2302	5941	4586	7664
2	3	4	5	6	7

4. *Division.*

2)14524 3)17814 4)33700 5)16420 6)31728 7)52052

5. *Addition.*

95	59	39	46	93	28
63	28	63	47	23	41
39	45	58	12	72	93
42	79	77	24	49	64

6. *Subtraction.*

9844	9263	7431	6057	3056	5641
9578	2325	6914	2884	2217	3172

7. *Multiplication.*

8679	5878	7049	2093	4136	7120
8	9	3	5	7	9

8. *Division.*

8)46624 9)84033 2)18752 4)92504 6)31782 8)50072

Williams's Junior Scholarship Tests. II, Arithmetic : (*a*) General; (*b*) Speed and accuracy. Obtainable from Messrs. G. Harrap & Co.

Achievement Test in Other Subjects.—The remaining subjects, i.e. other than English and Arithmetic, follow in alphabetical order.

(B) *Other Accomplishments and Skills*
Algebra

Ballard's Test. (*New Examiner,* p. 200.)—100 items, graded. Time, 2 hours. Norms (for Central School boys from 11 to 14 years) for 1–4 years of Algebra study.

Douglas's Diagnostic Tests for Elementary Algebra.—See H. R. Douglas, " A Series of Standardised Diagnostic Tests in the Fundamentals of Elementary Algebra," *J. Educ. Res.*, 1921, p. 396.

Institute of Educational Research Algebra Test.—Form A, Elementary, to Quadratics. Form B, Quadratics and beyond. Bureau of Publications, Columbia University, N.Y.

Biology

Richards's Achievement Test in Biology. (Dr. Richards's Biology Department, Clarke University.)—Based on extensive preliminary questionnaire investigation as to biology courses. Suitable for higher secondary schools and intermediate university students. Multiple response. Stencil key. Sound norms. Obtainable: Messrs. Stoelting.

Drawing

The measurement of drawing ability is one frequently made in the course of clinical examination of children, because it throws valuable light on the emotional and ideational make-up of the child; it requires little time; it is interesting to the child, and the observation of his method of approach and ultimate product offer evidence as to his general maturity.

Burt's Test is by far the most commonly used. The child is asked simply to ' draw a man.' No time limit is set. The finished product is compared with the members of the following series [1] of median samples (see p. 87 as to meaning of median sample) and allotted to the appropriate year. For valuable detailed notes on qualitative interpretations of drawings see Burt's *Mental and Scholastic Tests*, pp. 318–25.

An attainment scale for adults is reproduced on p. 62 of the chapter on " Special Aptitudes."

Economics

American Council Economics Test.—Secondary school and university.

---

[1] Reproduced here by kind permission of Professor Burt.

Electrical Inclination Test.—A test of information and interest in practical electrical problems. Messrs. Stoelting.

French

American Council Alpha French Test 1926.—Range: Secondary school and college. Available from World Book Co., Yonkers, N.Y.

American Council Beta French Test.—Range: Junior school and secondary school. World Book Co., Yonkers, N.Y.

French Aural Comprehension Test.—Available from Bureau of Publications, Columbia University, N.Y.

General Knowledge

(1) *For Children.*

" *Northampton Group Intelligence Test.*" (G. Perrie Williams.)—A test of general knowledge (geography, history, literature, general science, everyday observation) for children of 11–14 years. Time, 35 minutes. Norms as yet limited to medians on each sub-test for 11–12 years. Messrs. G. Harrap & Co.

Probst's Kindergarten Test.—Two forms, each of 32 questions (time, number, simple mechanics), correlation ' g ' ·64 consistency, ·94; rough norms. See "A General Information Test for Kindergarten Children," *Child Development*, 1931, ii, 81.

(2) *For Older Children and Adults.*

A test of general knowledge, including mechanical and constructional dress-making, scientific and mathematical, business and financial, artistic and musical, rural and farming, furnishing, literary, sport, geographical, social, philosophical, and religious knowledge is provided by the Interest Tests on p. 134 of Chapter IV. Use only sections 1, 2, 3, 4, 5, 6, 7, 8, 10, 11, 12, 14, 15. The total time is rather less than half an hour. Each section is timed separately as indicated on p. 153. The subject's relative familiarity with each branch can be determined separately, but his score on the whole can also be assessed by the norms below.

Norms.

For 14-year-old children (based on 250 cases):

Decile	1	2	3	4	5	6	7	8	9	10
Raw Score	Below 21·5	29·5	34·5	39·1	42·5	47·5	52·5	58·5	66·5	Above 66·5

For Adults.—No results for average adults available. These are from student groups (University and W.E.A.):

Decile	1	2	3	4	5	6	7	8	9	10
Raw Score	Below 38·5	44·5	49·5	54·5	59·5	65·5	71·5	79·5	88·5	Above 88·5

A second *General Knowledge Test*, of a rather more difficult kind, suitable for students, but designed to measure a very wide range of information, is given in the appendix of this book. Norms may be available by 1947.

Whipple's Range of Information Tests.—Suitable for adults. 100 words. Blanks obtainable Messrs. Stoelting.

Geography

Ballard's Test. (*Op. cit.*, p. 211.)   100 items. Time, 45 minutes. Largely the geography of England and Wales, but including questions on physical and economic geography. Norms (incomplete) according to year of study.

Northumberland Standardised Tests. (Geography.)—See p. 113.

German

American Council Alpha German Test. Vocabulary. Secondary school and college.   World Book Co., Yonkers, N.Y.

Geometry

See *J. H. Minnich.* (*Minnich's Geometry Tests*), " A Scale of Measuring Pupils' Ability to Demonstrate Geometrical Theorems," *School Review*, 1919, p. 101.

Handwriting

Ayres Handwriting Scale:
(1) Primary schools.
(2) Adults.
Available from Russell Sage Foundation, New York.

AGE 3

FIG. 30.

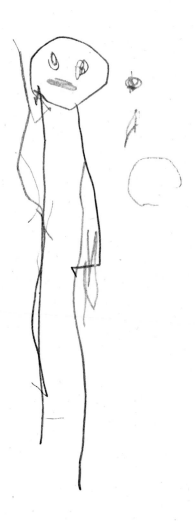

FIG. 31.

AGE 5

FIG. 32.

AGE 6

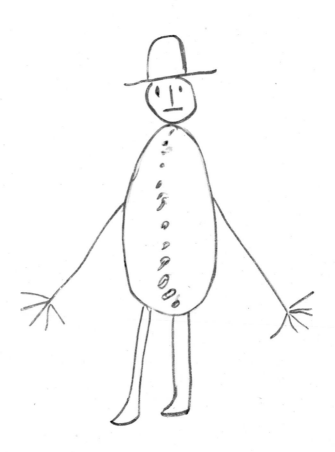

FIG. 33.

FIG. 34.

FIG. 35.

FIG. 36.

FIG. 37.

AGE 11

FIG. 38.

German Soldier

FIG. 39.

KING ' GEORGE

FIG. 40.

AGE 14

FIG. 41.

Ballard's Script-writing Norms. For children. A series of steps, arbitrarily chosen, with four specimens at each step for comparison. Available in *New Examiner.*

Burt's Test of Goodness of Cursive Handwriting.—Median samples for each age, from 5 to 14 years inclusive. *Mental and Scholastic Tests,* p. 371.

Courtis's Standard Research Tests in Handwriting.—Senior departments of primary schools. Obtainable from S. A. Courtis, Detroit.

Freeman Chart for Diagnosing Faults in Handwriting.—All standards of primary schools. Houghton Mifflin Co., Boston.

Midland Test (Cattell).—The following scale in cursive style, on the median samples' principle, is intended for use with school-leavers of 13–15 years. It is graded only into five stages, since finer grading is not wanted and wastes time in most vocational guidance work. The steps are on an ' equal unit intervals ' basis, i.e. the sections of the normal distribution, of which each is a typical sample, are in the proportions 1 : 4 : 6 : 4 : 1. These norms are from 200 elementary school children of 14 years. Two boys' and two girls' samples are given in each section. This may be regarded as a continuation of Burt's Scale above. See Figs. 42–6, pp. 120–4.

History

Ballard's Test. (P. 224, *op. cit.*, p. 89.)—History of England since accession of Henry VII. 100 items. Time, 45 minutes.

Columbia Research Bureau American History Test.—Secondary school and university. World Book Co., Yonkers, N.Y.

Northumberland Standardised Tests (History).—See p. 95.

Van Wagenen's History Scales.—See " Historical Information and Judgment in Pupils of Elementary Schools," *Columbia Contrib. Educ.,* No. 101, 1919.

American Council European History Test.—Secondary school and university. World Book Co., Yonkers, N.Y.

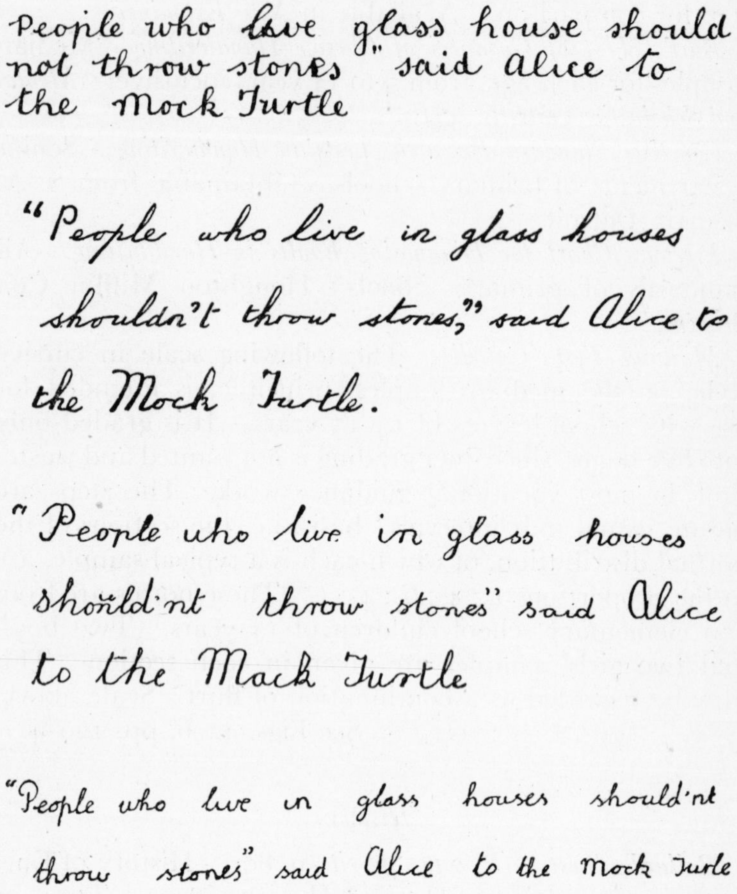

People who have glass house should
not throw stones " said Alice to
the Mock Turtle

"People who live in glass houses
shouldn't throw stones," said Alice to
the Mock Turtle.

" People who live in glass houses
should'nt throw stones" said Alice
to the Mack Turtle

"People who live in glass houses should'nt
throw stones" said Alice to the Mock Turle

FIG. 42.—GRADE I.

On this and subsequent pages the specimens of handwriting by boys are at the top
and by the girls underneath.

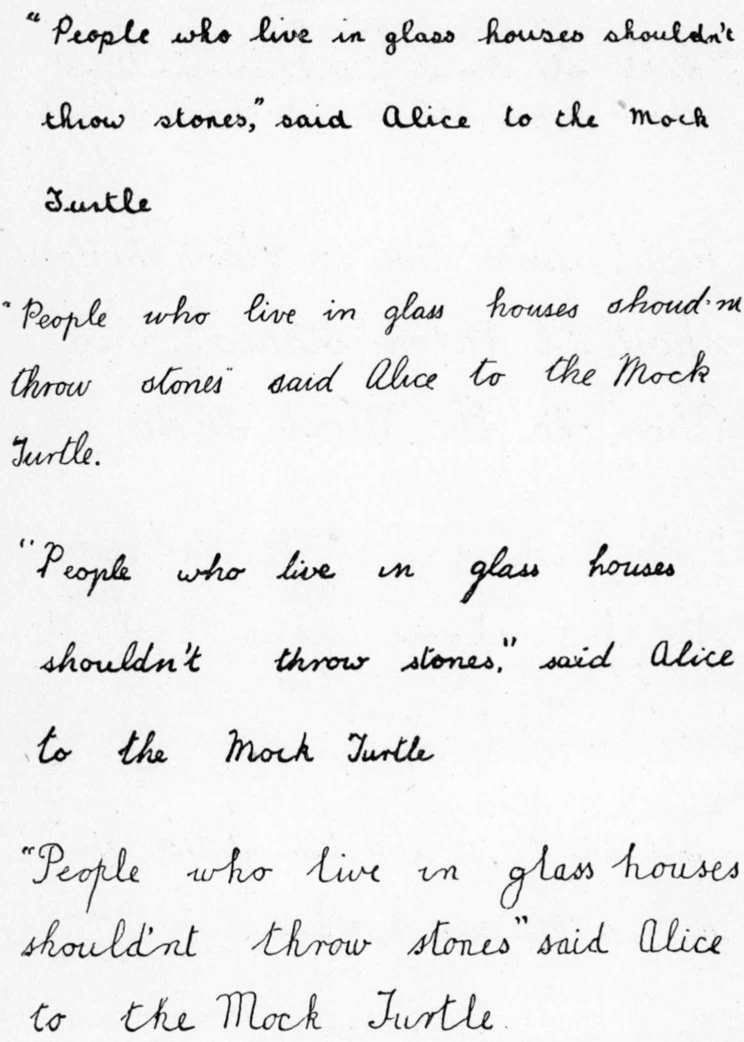

" People who live in glass houses shouldn't throw stones," said Alice to the Mock Turtle

" People who live in glass houses shoud·n throw stones" said Alice to the Mock Turtle.

" People who live in glass houses shouldn't throw stones." said Alice to the Mock Turtle

"People who live in glass houses should'nt throw stones" said Alice to the Mock Turtle.

FIG. 43.—GRADE II.

" People who live in glass houses should not throw stones", said Alice to the Mock Turtle

"People who live in glass houses shouln't throw stones," said Alice to the Mock Turtle.

"People who live in glass houses shouldn't throw stones," said Alice to the Mock Turtle.

"People who live in glass houses shouldn't throw stones," said Alice to the Mock Turtle.

FIG. 44.—GRADE III.

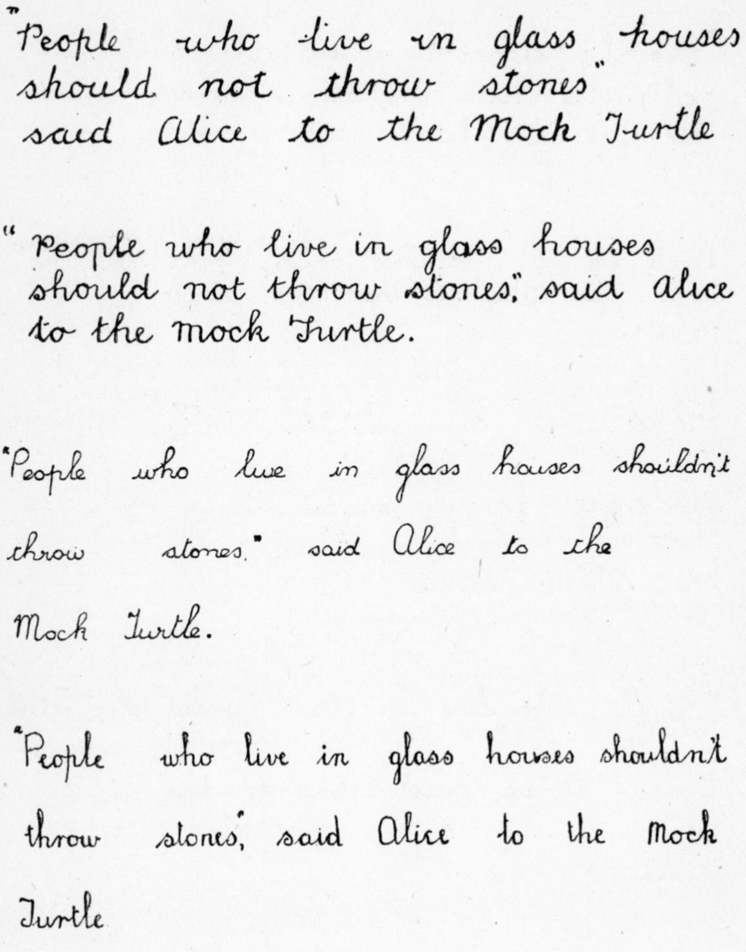

"People who live in glass houses
should not throw stones"
said Alice to the Mock Turtle

" People who live in glass houses
should not throw stones." said Alice
to the Mock Turtle.

"People who live in glass houses shouldn't
throw stones." said Alice to the
Mock Turtle.

"People who live in glass houses shouldn't
throw stones", said Alice to the Mock
Turtle

Fig. 45.—Grade IV.

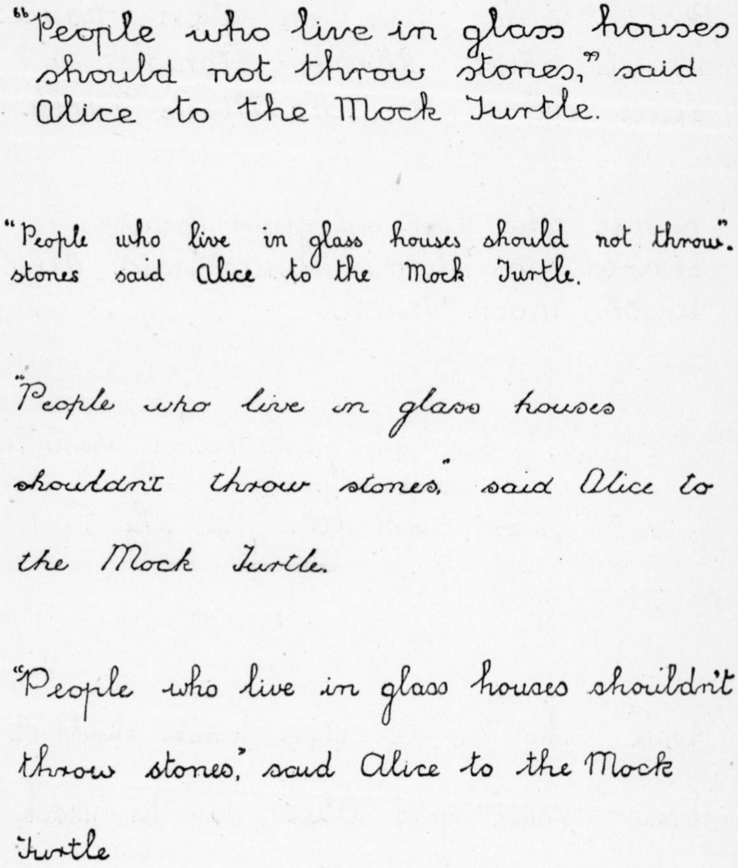

"People who live in glass houses should not throw stones," said Alice to the Mock Turtle.

"People who live in glass houses should not throw". stones said Alice to the Mock Turtle.

"People who live in glass houses shouldn't throw stones" said Alice to the Mock Turtle.

"People who live in glass houses shouldn't throw stones" said Alice to the Mock Turtle

FIG. 46.—GRADE V.

Italian

American Council Tests in Italian.—Secondary school and college. World Book Co., Yonkers, N.Y.

Latin

Henmon's Latin Tests.—See "The Measurement of Ability in Latin," *J. Educ. Psychol.*, 1917, pp. 515, 588; 1920, p. 121.

Co-operative Junior Latin Test } Available from Co-opera-
Co-operative Senior Latin Test } tive Test Service, New York.

Powers Diagnostic Latin Test.—First-year Latin. Available from Public School Publishing Co., Bloomington, U.S.A.

Mathematics

See also Arithmetic, Algebra, Geometry, Trigonometry.
Rogers and Thurstone's Tests of Mathematical Achievement.—N.Y., U.S.A.

Mechanical Knowledge

Stenquist's Mechanical 'Aptitude' Tests. Senior I and Senior II.—A paper test with pictures to test information with regard to tools and machines. Stoelting or World Book Co., Yonkers, N.Y.

Stenquist's Assembly Test. Series I and Series II (of practically equal difficulty).—Each has ten common mechanical objects which are to be assembled. May be regarded as a measure of attainment in skill in handling mechanical objects. Scored on errors and successes in a given time. Norms for ages 11–14 for adults. Obtainable from Messrs. Stoelting. Revised form available from the National Institute of Industrial Psychology.

Knowledge of Tools Test. (*Warnes.*)—Paper Test. Appropriate norms for technical schools. Obtainable from Messrs. Stoelting.

Religious Knowledge

Laycock's Test of Biblical Information for children over 11 and adults.—Seven sub-tests giving 100 items. Carefully worked out and widely standardised for Canadian children. Obtainable from University of Alberta Bookstore, Edmonton, Canada.

Science

Caldwell's Science Tests. (Botany, Chemistry, Zoology, and Physics.)—Secondary school. Obtainable: General Board of Education, New York.

A Test of Scientific Aptitude. (*J. Educ. Psychol.*, vol. 18, p. 27.) (D. L. Zyne.)—Recorded by author as an aptitude test, but probably attainment (in habits).

Co-operative General Science Test.—Secondary schools and university entrants. Co-operative Test Service, New York.

Spanish

American Council Alpha Spanish Test.—Secondary school and university.

American Council Beta Spanish Test.—Preparatory and secondary school, 1926.

Sports

Information Test. (Rogers.)—Messrs. Stoelting.

Stenography and Typing

Stenographic and Typing Test. (Rogers.)—Dictation and typing tests. See Link, *Employment Psychology*, Macmillan. Messrs. Stoelting.

Trigonometry

American Council Trigonometry Test.—Secondary school and University. World Book Co., Yonkers, N.Y.

(C) *General Scholastic Knowledge Profiles*

A profile of the individual's performances, relative to others, in all school subjects can be obtained by testing on all of Burt's Scholastic Tests, or the Midland Attainment Tests, or any of the tests listed under the separate headings above.   At the university level a very adequately standardised test is available in the Graduate Record Examination, published by the Carnegie Foundation for the Advancement of Teaching.   But there are also batteries aimed at a less thorough or analytical testing of the special subjects and directed to getting a single profile indicating the individual's weak and strong points in attainment.

CHAPTER IV

GAUGES OF INTEREST, ATTITUDE, AND OBJECT LIBIDO INVESTMENT

1. Importance of Interest Tests

THE psychoanalytic method of ' free association ' is the most widely used technique for exploring interests and emotional attachments, particularly with regard to those deeper currents of interest not realised and recognised by the conscious mind.

In circumstances where the free association technique is not possible, or, more commonly, as a brief preliminary survey to guide such proceedings, an objective interest test of a more systematic kind is highly valuable; indeed, I have known instances where the inference from the objective test has in the end proved to be more correct than the first psychoanalytic interpretations. Frequently, with children, an all-round assessment of interests, revealing in which directions these are abnormally strong or strikingly deficient, gives at once, along with an investigation of the home situation, a clue to the main causes of maladjustment. With adults, such a gauge of interests may be a measure only of the outer crust of the mind—of the object libido attachments—and may not be fine enough to detect narrow intensive concentrations even there. But in giving an objective picture of the adjustments at the conscious level—free from the bias of the analyst's own conception of those interests (which is often based on insufficient evidence)—the test result is a valuable contribution to the jig-saw puzzle of the personality picture.

Secondly, interest tests have considerable use in vocational guidance. It is true that about 50 per cent. of 14-year-old children change their conceptions as to what is the most desirable and interesting profession at least once within a bare twelve months; but this does not imply that their basic interests—mechanical, social, out-of-door—change with the same rapidity, and recent research [1] has shown that vocational guidance, based on the interest investments already made at that age, turns out to be as reliable as that based on test estimates of ability. Obviously both need to be taken into account in a systematic and intelligent synthesis.

In social psychology important deductions may be made from the application of scientifically standardised gauges of interest and attitude to whole groups and classes of people.

Interest and attitude tests are probably of greatest value to the psychologist, however, in the investigation of character and personality adjustment. For this reason there are difficulties in drawing the line between tests which should appear in the present chapter and those which appear under character and temperament. Our division rests on this basis: that interest and attitude tests gauge the person's conscious likes and dislikes, attitudes, opinions, and beliefs with regard to particular objects, whereas tests of temperament, character, and disposition in those respects in which they approach attitude tests, are measuring the general attitude to life as a whole. For example, Allport's Ascendance-Submission Test is classed as a test of disposition because it concerns attitude to life as a whole, whereas a gauge of superiority-inferiority towards, say, foreigners or women, would be regarded as an attitude test.

Obviously, even with this restriction, interest and attitude tests have great importance for personality, since, as McDougall has cogently shown, the particular investments of a person's instinct energy—his conscious sentiment structure (other than the self-regarding sentiment)—are a considerable part of his character. When we have mapped the individual's sentiments, we have gone a long way towards predicting his behaviour and towards understanding problems in the distribution of his energies.

---

[1] McHale (" An Information Test of Interest," *Psychol. Clinic*, 1930, xix) found high correlation between results on an interest and efficiency in line of work eventually followed.

In clinical work, particularly, a quantitative investigation of the field of conscious interests should be a basis for excursions into the unconscious and a check on the results.

2. Types of Test Employed

Since the whole subject is still in a chaotic state, largely through excessive practical applications having preceded serious research into sentiment structure, it is not surprising that the attempts to approach the matter vary enormously.

In America, particularly, measures of all manner of interests and attitudes—vocational interests, attitudes to various religions, to foreigners, to prohibition, to political parties, to birth control, free trade, to sex questions, Sunday observance, towards war, etc.—have been developed and standardised.[1]

Unfortunately, the majority make a very naïve, direct approach, asking the subject to rate himself on a scale, to state his preferences or underline his interests. With equal *naïveté* they have fallen foul of the danger of importing moral approval and disapproval into the question. Thus there are several tests of " Racial *Prejudice*." Ethical implications of this kind are proper to the technique of political propaganda, but are ridiculous in psychology; for it behoves the psychologist to preserve complete scientific detachment from the natural phenomena which he studies; indeed, 'prejudice' in the psychologist amounts to a complete betrayal and disqualification of his science. It is not for the psychologist as such to decide whether the attitude is sound. Apart from such implications in labelling tests, the measurement of attitude itself proves to be surprisingly free from effects due to the attitude of the designer himself.[2]

The failure to devise sufficiently ingenious indirect approaches which would measure the subject's interests or attitudes without his being aware of the fact is more serious. Experiment has shown that, as one would expect, subjects

---

[1] For a complete list of such standardised scales see G. Hildreth, *A Bibliography of Mental Tests and Rating Scales*, p. 165. Also the end of the present chapter.

[2] E. D. Hinckley, " The Influence of Individual Opinion on Construction of an Attitude Scale," *J. Soc. Psychol.*, 1932, iii.

consciously or unconsciously (1) give themselves flattering scores, and (2) in general give themselves less extreme scores than would result from the common opinion of their fellows.[1] Fundamentally honest persons may exist, but they are not very prevalent among persons seen by the practising psychologist. For research purposes, with groups of students having scientific consciences, such tests may temporarily be admitted, but even then the psychologist must face the reproach that he is not basing his conclusions on typical samples of human nature.

All this applies *a fortiori* to measures of temperament and emotional make-up based on the same direct self-revelation in questionnaires (see Chap. VI).

Those who are interested in such tests for research purposes or for the limited objects for which they are suitable, e.g. group differentiation, are referred to the extensive literature on their use and improvement.[2]

The three approaches which seem to be more promising than the above are: (i) use of the psychogalvanometer; (ii) observations of the selective action of attention and memory on material presented[3]; (iii) measurements of the individual's general knowledge, of the stores of information that have been accumulated around his particular interests. No standardised tests are available in (i) and (ii). McCrae[4] used the magnitude of the psychogalvanic reflex, when various instinct situations were presented to subjects, as a fairly successful measure of instinct strength. There is little doubt that, when the technique is correct,[5] the magnitude of the deflection is related to the conative strength of the interest aroused by the exposed object.

---

[1] C. W. Manger, " The Effect of Self-interest on Scores made on the Allport Test for Measuring Ascendance Submission," *Psychol. Clinic*, 1932, xxi.

[2] D. D. Droba, " Methods for Measuring Attitudes," *Psychol. Bull.*, 1932, xxix. D. Fryer, " Validating Measures of Interest," *Personnel J.*, 1932, xi. C. K. G. Wang, " Suggested Criteria for Writing Attitude Statements," *J. Soc. Psychol.*, 1932.

[3] E.g. Moore, in " Testing the Strength of Instincts," *Amer. J. Psychol.*, where stimulus words, e.g. many, career, achievement, are exposed, and the subject's quickness of response with an appropriate word is taken as a measure of the strength of that instinct.

[4] Colman and McCrae, "Measuring the Strength of Instincts," *Forum Educ.*, 1928.

[5] See suggestion in R. B. Cattell, " Experiments on the Psychical Correlate of the Psychogalvanic Reflex," *Brit. J. Psychol.*, xix, 4, 1929.

In measuring interest by the third method, the subject is presented with an objective (new type) achievement test which he believes to be a test of information and memory. The assumption behind the test is that a person is well informed in those subjects in which he has long had powerful, stable interests, and ill-informed in subjects which don't interest him. Occasionally, for examination purposes or because of the interests of friends, he will acquire information in subjects which would not otherwise have interested him, but the accessibility of his knowledge on those subjects will decline rapidly with time unless true interest appears. Much research is needed into methods (i), (ii), and (iii). The present writer obtains correlations of 0·4 to 0·5 between measurements of interests by the attention method (spontaneous attention to pictures) and the information method.[1] Super has obtained similar correlations between known occupational interests and information-attention tests, but not between the latter and self-assessments on interest.

3. Interest-Value Test Material Available

The measurement of interests or values, i.e. of what the individual considers the objects worthy of attention, is of importance to the psychiatrist, the vocational guidance worker, and the social psychologist. The study of direct occupational interests is postponed to section 5 of this chapter. The study of peculiar and specific emotional interests, such as is necessary in some aspects of psychiatry, is dealt with under association tests and free association. Here we deal with interests as they concern the total personality and, therefore, as they concern all applied psychology at some stage or in some aspect of prediction.

Classifying general interests, in order to begin measurement, has been the principal difficulty of psychologists. One can either take arbitrary, convenient, and perhaps logical fields of interest or one can seek, by factor analysis

[1] See *Journal of Character and Personality*, Jan. 1936.

and similar techniques, the groups in which interests in fact bunch themselves in our present population and culture.

Interest Test A.15, below, with its fifteen divisions of the whole field of possible interests, proceeds on an arbitrary basis of division, as also does the *Allport-Vernon Study of Values* (published by Houghton, Mifflin Co., Boston), which follows the logical categories of Spranger—political, religious, æsthetic, etc.

On the other hand, the *Attitude-Interest Analysis Test* of Terman and Miles (McGraw Hill Co., New York) is based on an established correlation cluster of interests that goes with masculinity-femininity, and further research may show it to measure a single masculinity-femininity factor. Brogden [1] has recently analysed a wide range of interest-factors and shown eight clear factors. There is some resemblance of these factors to the temperament factors of Chapter V, and we must envisage the possibility that the broad factors in interests will prove to be personality-temperament factors. At present, however, there is no published, standardised test of these eight interest-factors.

Tests fashioned on the original, arbitrary-type concepts of Spranger are available in the Allport-Vernon Study of Values and in the Maller-Glaser Interest Values Inventory, which use the ' theoretic,' æsthetic, social, and economic categories. The latter contains three sub-tests of preferences in three distinct fields, and is published by Bureau of Publications, Teachers' College, Columbia University, New York. Specifically *vocational* interest measures are considered in section 5 below.

*Interest Test A.*15 (First form of test, 15 sections)

This may be called a " Gauge of Object Libido Attachment," since in measuring interests we must bear in mind that we are in fact exploring the objective investments of libido, which should throw light on the libido investments generally.

---

[1] Brogden, H. E., *A Factorial Analysis of the Interest-Values Test* (in Press).

It is divided into fifteen sections, this division having been found suitable by preliminary research. For a discussion of the rationale of this division, see p. 132. It is arbitrary, but psychological rather than logical and philosophical. That is to say, it is a classification based on some of the main types of interest actually found in clinical work, and is intended to be most useful from the point of view of the significance of interests in individual adjustment.

The items in each section are roughly graded in order of increasing difficulty, and the time allowed is so chosen that only those who can answer each question instantly will succeed in doing all items. In some sections, notably that on sex interests, the sampling of knowledge has to be through indirect associations, and the extent of knowledge is discovered rather by questioning on unusual aspects than by a direct intensive survey. For instructions and norms see end of test.

I. Travelling, Holidaying, Geographical Interests

Dykes are very common in
- Italy.
- **Holland.**
- Assam.
- Canada.

Dr. Livingstone crossed { Australia / **Africa** } and met Stanley.

The Straits of Magellan run by
- Sicily.
- **S. America.**
- Iceland.
- Ireland.

Which of these holiday resorts is on the sea coast?
- Buxton.
- **Paignton.**
- Bath.
- Llangollen.

Which of the following is given on a passport?
- **the colour of your eyes.**
- the town of your destination.
- the names of your parents.
- your finger prints.

The one-inch ordnance survey map
- has contour lines only every 50 feet (sometimes with colours).
- has different colours for different heights.
- has contours only at 100 feet intervals (sometimes with colours).
- marks steep hills with a special sign.

The " land of the midnight sun " is
- Central Africa.
- Alaska.
- Tierra del Fuego.
- Norway.

The express from London to Birmingham leaves { King's Cross / Paddington } and goes by { G.W.R. / L.M.S. } in about { two / four } hours.

Which of the following represent associations concerned with travelling ?
- A.A.A.
- T.U.
- C.T.C.
- Y.H.A.

The following are the official annual holidays (for the whole year) allowed to the following people. Put a number to show the holiday which goes to each person:

about
- eight weeks   2   1. Policeman.
- three weeks   3   2. Elementary School Teacher.
- twelve days   1   3. Bank Clerk.
- thirty days   4   4. Lieutenant in the Army.

II. Sporting, Militaristic, and Primitive Masculine Excitements Generally

A try in Rugby football is gained by
- kicking the ball over the goal line.
- carrying the ball over the goal line.
- throwing the ball over the goal-keeper's head.
- dribbling the ball into the goal circle.

The first stroke won in a game of tennis gives $\begin{Bmatrix} 5 \\ 10 \\ \underline{15} \\ 12 \end{Bmatrix}$ points to the striker.

The length of a cricket pitch is $\begin{Bmatrix} 18 \\ 20 \\ \underline{22} \\ 24 \end{Bmatrix}$ yards.

The Derby comes $\begin{Bmatrix} \text{before} \\ \underline{\text{after}} \end{Bmatrix}$ the Grand National and is $\begin{Bmatrix} \underline{\text{before}} \\ \text{after} \end{Bmatrix}$ the Cesarewitch.

The Annual Race at the Isle of Man is for $\begin{Bmatrix} \underline{\text{motor-cycles}} \\ \text{motor-cars} \end{Bmatrix}$ and is known as the $\begin{cases} \underline{\text{Tourist Trophy.}} \\ \text{Schneider Cup.} \\ \text{Le Mans.} \\ \text{Duke of York's} \\ \quad \text{Cup.} \end{cases}$

A Lewis Gun fires $\begin{cases} \text{small shells.} \\ \text{shells from a moving belt.} \\ \underline{\text{bullets from a rotating drum.}} \\ \text{grenades.} \end{cases}$

A small-bore shot-gun for shooting rooks is known as $\begin{cases} \text{Two two.} \\ \text{Winchester.} \\ \underline{\text{Four ten.}} \\ \text{Twelve Bore.} \end{cases}$

The Grand National is a $\begin{cases} \text{flat race.} \\ \text{hurdle race.} \\ \underline{\text{steeplechase.}} \\ \text{point to point.} \end{cases}$

Grouse shooting begins on $\begin{cases} \text{September 1st.} \\ \text{October 1st.} \\ \underline{\text{August 12th.}} \\ \text{July 4th.} \end{cases}$

The main control of an aeroplane is called a(n) •

- joy stick.
- aileron.
- rudder wheel.
- dip rod.

III. Business, Commercial, Acquisitive Interests

A penny is $\left\{\begin{array}{l}\text{bigger}\\\text{smaller}\end{array}\right\}$ than a two-shilling piece. A pound note is $\left\{\begin{array}{l}\text{greener}\\\text{browner}\end{array}\right\}$ than a ten-shilling note.

The rate of interest on money in the P.O. Savings Bank is $\left\{\begin{array}{l}2\frac{1}{2}\%\\3\frac{1}{2}\%\\4\frac{1}{2}\%\\5\frac{1}{2}\%\end{array}\right.$

A receipt stamp is required for any amount over $\left\{\begin{array}{l}£1\\£2\\£3\\£4\end{array}\right.$

'Piece Work' is a system of wages in which a man is paid

- a bonus for overtime.
- so much for every hour's work.
- so much for every article made.
- extra for steady work.

An order cheque differs from a bearer cheque in that

- it needs a receipt stamp on the back.
- it cannot be paid unless crossed.
- it can be paid to anyone only when endorsed.
- it can be paid to anyone only when not endorsed.

The amount of rates a man pays depends on

- his income.
- the rent of his house.
- whether he has a car.
- his taxes.

Which of the following $\left\{\begin{array}{l}\text{is}\\\text{are}\end{array}\right\}$ taxed $\left\{\begin{array}{l}\text{houses.}\\\underline{\text{motor-cycles.}}\\\underline{\text{cinema performances.}}\\\text{ginger beer.}\\\text{letters.}\end{array}\right.$
in this country?

Put 1, 2, 3, and 4 against these names to show which earns most, next most, etc., and least (at 30 years of age) $\left\{\begin{array}{l}\text{4 Postman.}\\\text{3 Policeman.}\\\text{2 Secondary School}\\\quad\text{Teacher.}\\\text{1 Life Insurance Agent.}\end{array}\right.$

A man who wishes to depress the market is known as a $\left\{\begin{array}{l}\text{bull.}\\\text{contango.}\\\underline{\text{bear.}}\\\text{chequer.}\end{array}\right.$

A balance sheet must be signed by a $\left\{\begin{array}{l}\text{shareholder.}\\\text{solicitor.}\\\underline{\text{director.}}\\\text{cashier.}\\\underline{\text{auditor.}}\end{array}\right.$

IV. Mechanical and Constructional Interests

Fretwork is usually done with $\left\{\begin{array}{l}\text{deal.}\\\underline{\text{3-ply wood.}}\\\text{matchboarding.}\end{array}\right.$

A spanner is used for $\left\{\begin{array}{l}\text{turning screws.}\\\text{lifting cars.}\\\underline{\text{tightening nuts.}}\\\text{pulling out nails.}\end{array}\right.$

The skirt of a thick woollen frock is best —— the bodice to get a neat effect. $\left\{\begin{array}{l}\text{whipped}\\\text{smocked}\\\underline{\text{gathered}}\\\underline{\text{pleated}}\end{array}\right.$

A gudgeon pin is found in the $\left\{\begin{array}{l}\underline{\text{piston}}\\\text{camshaft}\\\text{wheel hub}\\\text{tyre}\end{array}\right\}$ of a motor-car.

The top rail of a door is fitted by
- a mortice tenon.
- a haunched mortice.
- a stamp tenon.
- copper screws.

The bias battery in a wireless set is connected to the
- valve.
- dial.
- aerial.
- high-tension circuit.

Stops on a camera regulate the
- aperture.
- shutter speed.
- size of film.
- focusing.

' Slip ' is used in
- photography.
- pottery.
- etching.
- joinery.

Which of these could you best make with 1½ yards of gingham?
- Nightdress for mother.
- Rompers for baby.
- Handkerchief satchet.
- Handkerchiefs for father.

The ' differential ' of a car is found in the
- back axle.
- gear-box.
- steering rod.
- engine.

V. Scientific and Mathematical Interests

The column of mercury held up by air pressure is highest
- on a mountain.
- at sea-level.
- in a deep mine.
- at the equator.

A planet differs from stars in that it
- is larger.
- moves in an orbit.
- twinkles a lot more.
- has rings round it.

In sunlight plants give out $\left\{\begin{array}{l}\text{chlorophyll.}\\ \text{air.}\\ \text{carbon dioxide.}\\ \underline{\text{oxygen.}}\end{array}\right.$

Water boils at $\left\{\begin{array}{l}200° \text{ Fahrenheit.}\\ 100° \text{ Fahrenheit.}\\ \underline{100° \text{ Centigrade.}}\\ 200° \text{ Centigrade.}\end{array}\right.$

Limestone is a(n) $\left\{\begin{array}{l}\text{igneous}\\ \underline{\text{sedimentary}}\end{array}\right\}$ rock and $\left\{\begin{array}{l}\underline{\text{does}}\\ \text{does not}\end{array}\right.$
contain fossils.

Mendel discovered a law concerning $\left\{\begin{array}{l}\text{plant growth.}\\ \underline{\text{heredity.}}\\ \text{natural selection.}\\ \text{photo-synthesis.}\end{array}\right.$

$a^2 + 2ab + b^2 = \left\{\begin{array}{l}(a-b)^2\\ \underline{(a+b)^2}\\ (a-2b)^2\\ (a+2b)^2\end{array}\right.$

Underline the element with the largest atomic weight. $\left\{\begin{array}{l}\text{Iron.}\\ \text{Oxygen.}\\ \underline{\text{Uranium.}}\\ \text{Hydrogen.}\end{array}\right.$

That current $= \dfrac{\text{voltage}}{\text{resistance}}$ is known as $\left\{\begin{array}{l}\text{Ampere's law.}\\ \underline{\text{Ohm's law.}}\\ \text{Boyle's law.}\\ \text{Volta's law.}\end{array}\right.$

The speed of sound depends upon $\left\{\begin{array}{l}\text{the pitch of the note.}\\ \text{the amplitude of vibration.}\\ \underline{\text{the temperature of the air.}}\\ \text{the pressure of the air.}\end{array}\right.$

VI. Things of the Mind : Philosophy ; Logic ; Language ; History

Aristotle was $\left\{\begin{array}{l}\text{A French writer.}\\ \underline{\text{A Greek philosopher.}}\\ \text{An Italian artist.}\\ \text{An ancient Roman.}\end{array}\right.$

A paradox is a(n) {
statement that seems to contradict itself.
particular kind of metaphor.
earthly story with a heavenly meaning.
kind of bird.
}

The Act which said that people must not be kept in prison indefinitely without trial was called {
Magna Charta.
Bill of Rights.
Habeas Corpus.
Emancipation Act.
}

Mutatis Mutandis means {
with necessary alterations.
change is for the best.
life is change.
willing or unwilling.
}

Utilitarianism is a system of {ethics / economics}. founded by {Plato. / Descartes. / Bentham.}

An {Analogy 2 / Aphorism 1 / Hyperbole 3} is a {(1) short statement of a general truth. / (2) parallel. / (3) exaggeration.}

Indicate the meaning of each of the three words by putting the number of the correct meaning against it.

A syllogism is a {
silly remark.
form in logic.
platitude in philosophy.
logical error.
}

Voltaire was to the French Revolution as {Lenin / Karl Marx / Trotsky / Rousseau} was to the Communist Revolt of Russia.

Solipsism is the belief that {
a good act is its own reward.
an idea that works in practice is true.
things exist only as ideas in the minds of the thinkers.
the sun is the centre of the universe.
}

Which of the following are systems
of philosophy ?
$\begin{cases} \underline{\text{stoicism.}} \\ \text{agrarianism.} \\ \underline{\text{nominalism.}} \\ \text{rationalisation.} \end{cases}$

VII. Rural, Naturalistic, Country Life Interests

Hazel catkins usually blossom in
$\begin{cases} \text{winter.} \\ \text{late autumn.} \\ \text{late summer.} \\ \underline{\text{early spring.}} \end{cases}$

Trout are
$\begin{cases} \underline{\text{brown}} \\ \text{grey} \\ \text{black and white} \\ \text{silver} \end{cases}$
in colour.

A setter is a
$\begin{cases} \text{lap dog.} \\ \text{racing dog.} \\ \text{sheep dog.} \\ \underline{\text{gun dog.}} \end{cases}$

A horse's back knees are called
$\begin{cases} \text{hocks.} \\ \underline{\text{fetlocks.}} \\ \text{pastern.} \\ \text{withers.} \end{cases}$

Wild bluebells grow best in
$\begin{cases} \text{marshy places.} \\ \underline{\text{woods.}} \\ \text{meadows.} \\ \text{heaths and moors.} \end{cases}$

A young hare is called
$\begin{cases} \underline{\text{a leveret.}} \\ \text{a cub.} \\ \text{a guilt.} \\ \text{a rabbit.} \end{cases}$

A pheasant's home is known as a
$\begin{cases} \text{covey.} \\ \text{wish.} \\ \underline{\text{covert.}} \\ \text{coppice.} \end{cases}$

Corn when first collected on the field is put in
$\begin{cases} \text{ricks.} \\ \text{stacks.} \\ \text{stooks.} \\ \text{mounds.} \end{cases}$

Which of the following birds is first to return to the British Isles in spring or summer ?
$\begin{cases} \text{Wild goose.} \\ \text{Cuckoo.} \\ \text{Swallow.} \\ \text{Peewit.} \end{cases}$

A beech leaf has a $\left\{\dfrac{\text{polished}}{\text{rough}}\right\}$ surface and a(n) $\left\{\dfrac{\text{irregular}}{\text{smooth}}\right\}$ outline.

VIII. Interest in Religion, the Supernatural, and Myths

The disciple who betrayed Jesus was $\begin{cases} \text{John.} \\ \text{Peter.} \\ \underline{\text{Judas.}} \\ \text{Andrew.} \end{cases}$

Practically all religions include a belief in $\begin{cases} \text{one god.} \\ \text{ten commandments.} \\ \underline{\text{immortality.}} \\ \text{saints.} \end{cases}$

" Of such is the Kingdom of Heaven " was said by Christ when speaking of $\begin{cases} \text{saints.} \\ \text{reformed sinners.} \\ \text{baptised heathen.} \\ \underline{\text{children.}} \end{cases}$

Valhalla was the name of the $\begin{cases} \text{temple} \\ \underline{\text{burial ground}} \\ \text{Heaven} \end{cases}$ of the $\begin{cases} \text{Greeks.} \\ \text{Norsemen.} \\ \text{Ancient Britons.} \end{cases}$

The Lord's Prayer contains $\begin{cases} \text{Father forgive them.} \\ \underline{\text{Thy Kingdom come.}} \\ \text{Ask and ye shall receive.} \\ \text{Blessed be they that mourn.} \end{cases}$

Orpheus was a $\left\{\dfrac{\text{sailor}}{\text{musician}}\right\}$ who $\begin{cases} \text{ascended to heaven} \\ \text{descended to the bottom of the sea} \\ \underline{\text{descended to hell}} \end{cases}$ to bring back Eurydice.

What prophet was becoming famous during the youth of Jesus ?

- St. Peter.
- Elijah.
- <u>John the Baptist.</u>
- St. Paul.

Who struck the rock and drew forth water miraculously ?

- Elijah.
- <u>Moses.</u>
- Abraham.
- Christ.

Which of the following was a great mystic ?

- St. Theresa.
- <u>St. Augustine.</u>
- St. Christopher.
- St. Francis.

Which of the following words have close religious connections ?

- sacrum.
- eramite.
- <u>Eli Sabacthani.</u>
- stalagmite.

IX. Literary, Dramatic (including Drama in the Press) Interests

" Peter Pan " is about a little boy who

- <u>wouldn't grow up.</u>
- ate a lot of pancakes.
- kept a pet lion.
- climbed a beanstalk.

Shakespeare wrote a play called

- She Stoops to Conquer.
- King Midas.
- <u>The Tempest.</u>
- Spears and Swords.

The stories of Sherlock Holmes were written by

- Edgar Wallace.
- Rider Haggard.
- H. G. Wells.
- <u>Conan Doyle.</u>

" Man and Superman " was written by

- <u>Bernard Shaw.</u>
- Galsworthy.
- Oscar Wilde.
- Carlyle.

Which of the following are characters from Dickens?
$$\left\{\begin{array}{l}\text{\underline{David Copperfield.}}\\ \text{Orlando.}\\ \text{Mrs. Malaprop.}\\ \text{Mr. Micawber.}\\ \text{\underline{Sir Roger de Coverley.}}\end{array}\right.$$

A play with exaggerated feelings is called a 4.
A play that ends happily is called a 3.
A play that ends sadly is called a 1.
Write 1, 2, 3, 4, or 5 at the end of each line above to show which of the words below will complete the sentence properly.

    1. Tragedy.
    2. Drama.
    3. Comedy.
    4. Melodrama.
    5. Masque.

In England, when someone has committed suicide, a(n)
$$\left\{\begin{array}{l}\text{\underline{inquest}}\\ \text{post mortem}\\ \text{court case}\end{array}\right\} \text{is held.}$$

Which of the following were notorious murderers?
$$\left\{\begin{array}{l}\text{John McCullen.}\\ \text{\underline{Charles Peace.}}\\ \text{Patrick O'Regan.}\\ \text{\underline{Crippen.}}\\ \text{Llewellyn Jones.}\end{array}\right.$$

In England, a person who has committed murder but is found insane, is sent to
$$\left\{\begin{array}{l}\text{Princetown.}\\ \text{Pentonville.}\\ \text{\underline{Broadmoor.}}\\ \text{Wormwood Scrubbs.}\end{array}\right.$$

X. Artistic, Musical Interests

The " Merry Widow " and the " Blue Danube " are
$$\left\{\begin{array}{l}\text{Fox Trots.}\\ \text{\underline{Waltzes.}}\\ \text{Tangos.}\\ \text{Sea Shanties.}\end{array}\right.$$

Put an ' L ' by the lowest and an ' H ' by the instrument with the highest pitch
$$\left\{\begin{array}{ll}\text{'Cello.} & \text{L.}\\ \text{Piccolo.} & \text{H.}\\ \text{Viola.} &\end{array}\right.$$

The choir sang
$\left\{\begin{array}{l}\text{Beethoven's} \\ \text{Bach's} \\ \underline{\text{Handel's}} \\ \text{Mozart's}\end{array}\right\}$
' Messiah.'

C sharp on the piano is
$\left\{\begin{array}{l}\text{a little below} \\ \underline{\text{the same as}} \\ \text{much above} \\ \text{above}\end{array}\right\}$
D flat.

An etching is a
$\left\{\begin{array}{l}\text{colour} \\ \underline{\text{black and white}}\end{array}\right\}$
from (a)
$\left\{\begin{array}{l}\underline{\text{copper-plate.}} \\ \text{wooden blocks.}\end{array}\right\}$
picture in

Which of these is the copy of a picture by a great painter?
(Indicate by a cross.)[1]

Michelangelo, who lived
$\left\{\begin{array}{l}\underline{\text{at the Renaissance,}} \\ \text{in the 19th century,} \\ \text{in the 18th century,}\end{array}\right\}$
was

famous as a(n)
$\left\{\begin{array}{l}\text{architect.} \\ \text{sculptor.} \\ \text{etcher.}\end{array}\right\}$

The Norman style of architecture is characterised by
$\left\{\begin{array}{l}\text{Doric column.} \\ \underline{\text{rounded decorated arches.}} \\ \text{pointed windows.} \\ \text{flying buttresses.}\end{array}\right\}$

Which of the following singers can reach the
highest note?
$\left\{\begin{array}{l}\text{baritone.} \\ \text{contralto.} \\ \text{tenor.} \\ \underline{\text{soprano.}}\end{array}\right\}$

[1] The solution here is the picture on the left. (Old Battersea Bridge. Whistler.)

What would be the best for a suit for a grey-eyed schoolboy?

- dark brown.
- light brown.
- check.
- <u>grey.</u>

Write W, G, P, or B after each of these precious stones to show whether they are white, green, purple, or blue.

Amethyst.   (P.)
Sapphire.   (B.)
Turquoise.   (B. or B.G.)

Spats are worn

- to keep a watch-chain in place.
- to clip trousers for cycling.
- to prevent the colour from rubbing.
- <u>to protect the ankles.</u>

The walls of a nursery are suitably coloured

- brown.
- red.
- lemon.
- <u>navy blue.</u>

Which of the following could be used as a shampoo for very fair hair?

- henna.
- belladonna.
- linseed oil.
- <u>camomile.</u>

A bandeau is worn

- on top of a hat.
- round the waist.
- round a stocking.
- <u>round the head.</u>

Which of the following artists introduced emphasis on shape and colour itself without trying to make an accurate representation of the object?

- Constable.
- <u>Whistler.</u>
- Reynolds.
- Leonardo da Vinci.

XI. Interests in Dress, Decoration, Furniture, and Adornment

Which of these would be the best material for a party dress?

- cambric.
- <u>taffeta.</u>
- gingham.
- drill.

A man's full even-   { striped grey }   trousers   { coat with tails.
  ing dress has   { black   }   and a   { black coat.

The heavy curtains over theatre   { cretonne.
  doors are usually made of   { casement cloth.
                                   { slub rep.
                                   { velour.

Jacobean furniture   { light wood and bulbous legs.
  is characterised   { dark wood and twisted legs.
  by   { fine inlaid work.
                      { dark wood and simple severe outlines.

XII. Sensual Pleasures and Comforts

"Humbugs" are usually flavoured with   { liquorice.
                                        { aniseed.
                                        { fruit.
                                        { peppermint.

Egyptian and Turkish   { a mellow perfumed smoke.
  cigarettes differ from { long cork tips.
  others in having   { a very flat oval shape.
                        { tobacco with a peculiar texture.

Eau-de-Cologne is a kind of   { disinfectant.
                              { scent.
                              { wine.
                              { silk.

Turkish Delight is a   { green   } sweet   { very hard.
                       { brown   } that is { like jelly.
                       { pink and white }   { nutty.

Stout differs from Ale   { fermented with hops.
  in being   { more bitter.
                         { stronger and more intoxicating.
                         { dark and frothy.

When indoors on a   { shoes?
  winter's evening { leather slippers?
  would you wear   { polished slippers with a soft sole?
                    { fur-lined soft slippers?

Bath salts are { first dissolved in hot water / put straight into a warm bath } to { replace soap. / make bath more pleasant. / drive out a cold. }

Talcum powder is used to { soothe the skin after shaving, etc. / clean teeth. / keep the scalp in good condition. / polish finger-nails. }

On a cold winter's evening, would you rather { go out to a dance? / visit the theatre? / go skating or walking? / sit in an easy chair by the fire? }

Mayonnaise is put on { roast turkey / boiled chicken / green salad } and has a { sweet / vinegary / salt } taste.

XIII. Sexual, Reproductive, Love Interests

Which of the following is a love story? { Westward Ho! / Coral Island. / The Blue Lagoon. / The Invisible Man. }

A woman generally knows that she must prepare for a baby { 1 year / 3 months / 7 months / 6 weeks } before its birth.

A wedding dress is usually { pink / white / green / black } with { no / short / puffed / long } sleeves.

An engagement ring is worn on the { first / second / third } finger of the { left / right } hand.

In which of the following does direct fertilisation of the female take place before offspring can be produced? { Cats. / Queen bees. / Sparrows. / Salmon. }

A marriage can be dissolved if a husband

admits { alimony / adultery / anomaly } and sometimes if he is { adolescent. / impotent. / indulgent. }

A eunuch was a { man / woman / girl } whose duty it was to look after

the { horses. / harem. / crown jewels. }

Hamlet called his uncle in-cestuous because he had married { in haste. / a woman older than himself. / a near relative. / without permission. }

Each of the Concubines of King Solomon, of whom there were { two / some hundreds / one } was a kind of { wife. / servant. / mistress. / nurse. }

King Solomon was { anomalous. / idolatrous. / adulterous. / polygamous. }

A man who { tells lies / makes love } in return for material gain can

reasonably be called a { prostitute. / thief. / seducer. }

XIV. Social, Human, and Club Interests

Do you usually spend a day's holiday { playing games with others ? / making or mending things ? / reading ? / going walks alone ? }

If an acquaintance gave you a present that you really didn't want, would you { give it back to him ? / tell him it was very nice but no good ? / thank him kindly ? / thank him and tell him you didn't want it ? }

If you saw a man and a woman quarrelling and shouting at each other in the street, would it be wisest to

- stand by in case violence is <u>threatened?</u>
- tell the man to leave her alone or you'll knock him down?
- put the woman under your protection and see her safely away?
- ask them what it's about?

The suit that gives the highest scores in auction bridge is

- hearts.
- diamonds.
- <u>spades.</u>
- clubs.

Underline any of these of which you have been at one time a member.

    Scouts or Girl Guides.
    Boys' Brigade or Y.M.C.A.
    Church or Church Choir.
    School Clubs.
        (Score for 3 or more.)

Public-houses are open in the middle of the day from

- <u>10.30 to 2 p.m.</u>
- 12.30 to 3 p.m.
- 11.0 to 1.30 p.m.
- 10.0 to 2.0 p.m.

(Score according to local bye-laws, but usually 10.30 to 2 p.m.)

People sometimes talk about themselves

- to make people like them.
- when they are very happy.
- <u>to get confidences in return.</u>
- to annoy others.

Consequences is a game played with

- cards.
- <u>pieces of paper and pencil.</u>
- dice.
- counters on a board.

Which of the following represent(s) nation-wide club
organisations? 1. R.A.O.B. 2. <u>Freemasons.</u> 3. Citi-
zens' Union. 4. <u>Travellers' League.</u> 5. Pansy Club.

Give the names (Christian names) of any of your friends
whom you have seen during the past week (5 names or
more count an answer to this question).

XV. Home Interests, Family, Parental Attachments

(Don't put down answers here unless you are certain of
them.) (For brother and sister, read father and mother
if you are an only child.)

What is the date of your (eldest) sister's birthday? (or of
your eldest brother if you have no sister). (Father or
mother if no brother or sister.)

What is your mother's favourite colour for her dresses?
(if you can definitely remember it).

How many evenings in the week do you spend with your
family (when you are at home)? (Count as ' correct '
if 3 or more.)

Do you know how old your mother and father were when they

were married ? $\begin{cases} \text{Yes} \\ \text{No} \end{cases}$ Give ages $\begin{cases} \text{Father} & \text{(Both given} \\ \text{Mother} & \text{to count.)} \end{cases}$

Name some interests that you share with your father or
mother, e.g. films. (3 at least.)

Name some hobbies of your brothers and sisters, or parents
if you have no brothers and sisters. (3 at least.)

Give the names of some friends of your brothers or sisters
(or parents if no brothers or sisters). (4 at least.)

How old were you when you began to choose your own
clothes, boots, hats, etc.? (11 years or over.)

Underline any of the following
that you discuss with your
parents (or children)
$\begin{cases} \text{sport.} \\ \text{your friends and enemies} \\ \text{religion.} \\ \text{motor-cars or clothes.} \end{cases}$

(Score for 4.)

Do you prefer to play with
$\begin{cases} \underline{\text{brothers and sisters.}} \\ \underline{\text{friends outside.}} \\ \text{parents.} \\ \underline{\text{yourself alone.}} \end{cases}$

(Score for either or both items underlined.)

Not every section need be given, since each has its own norms (occasionally one wishes to leave out Section 13, on sexual interests, in giving group tests to children).

The ten questions in each section are to be presented on a separate sheet.

Instructions for Administering

For children up to and including 15 years, 2½ minutes is allowed on each sheet (i.e. 37½ minutes in all) and for adults 2 minutes (i.e. 30 minutes in all). Subjects are instructed not to guess where they really do not know the answer.

Now the scores on any general information test are found to correlate quite highly with intelligence, so it becomes necessary to correct the score on each section to determine the extent of interest quite apart from the additional general " knowledge-ableness " due to high intelligence.

In all but three sections, ½ point is subtracted from the score for every 20 points of I.Q. which the subject has above I.Q. 100. (Anyone between 110 and 130 would have ½ point subtracted, 130–150 1 point, and so on.) Conversely, ½ point is added for each 20 points of I.Q. below 100. But in sections 6, 7, and 10, 1 point is equivalent to 20 points of I.Q. This ratio has been determined empirically by a comparison of the scores of groups of different average I.Q.

When the individual's scores have thus been corrected for I.Q., his relative interest in various sections may be determined by reference to the tables on pp. 154–5. The population has been divided up into five groups, each being a successive 20 per cent. of the population, from lowest to highest. By finding into which group the subject's score falls, one gives him a value from 1 to 5.

These norms are from 200 14-year-old primary school children.

The norms for boys and girls are distinct, since the interest pattern for the normal boy is widely different from that for the normal girl.

On the basis of these 1 to 5 scores, a profile can be constructed as shown on pp. 156–7. The 'normal' profile would, of course, be a straight line, down the middle section.

NORMS OF INTEREST TEST

No. of Section.	Interest (Name)	Pentile Scores (i.e. 20% of population fall in each section)				
		1.	2.	3.	4.	5.
	Boys					
1.	Travel	Below 2·5	to 3·18	to 3·6	to 4·25	and above
2.	Sports	Below 3·25	to 4·12	to 4·8	to 5·75	and above
3.	Commercial . . .	Below 1·75	to 2·3	to 3·12	to 3·95	and above
4.	Mechanical . . .	Below 2·6	to 3·25	to 4·12	to 4·75	and above
5.	Scientific . . .	Below ·6	to 1·25	to 1·8	to 2·6	and above
6.	Things of the Mind .	Below ·12	to ·75	to 1·5	to 2·25	and above
7.	Rural, Naturalistic .	Below 2·75	to 3·75	to 4·6	to 5·75	and above
8.	Religious . . .	Below 2·75	to 3·6	to 4·3	to 5·1	and above
9.	Literary . . .	Below 2·5	to 3·25	to 4·05	to 5·05	and above
10.	Artistic . . .	Below 1·5	to 2·3	to 3·05	to 4·12	and above
11.	Decorative . . .	Below 2·8	to 3·5	to 4·4	to 5·25	and above
12.	Sensual Pleasures .	Below 3·6	to 4·8	to 5·9	to 7·25	and above
13.	Sex	Below 1·12	to 1·75	to 2·2	to 2·8	and above
14.	Social . . .	Below 1·95	to 2·75	to 3·9	to 4·25	and above
15.	Home . . .	Below 1·5	to 2·25	to 3·0	to 3·6	and above
	Girls					
1.	Travel	Below 1·5	to 2·25	to 2·75	to 3·75	and above
2.	Sports	Below 1·25	to 2·05	to 2·6	to 3·75	and above
3.	Commercial . . .	Below 2·9	to 2·95	to 3·6	to 4·5	and above
4.	Mechanical . . .	Below 2·12	to 2·75	to 3·25	to 3·9	and above
5.	Scientific . . .	Below ·8	to 1·25	to 2·09	to 2·75	and above
6.	Things of the Mind .	Below ·12	to ·5	to ·9	to 1·4	and above
7.	Rural, Naturalistic .	Below 2·75	to 3·8	to 4·25	to 5·5	and above
8.	Religious . . .	Below 2·75	to 3·25	to 3·95	to 4·6	and above
9.	Literary . . .	Below 2·8	to 3·4	to 4·25	to 4·8	and above
10.	Artistic . . .	Below 1·6	to 2·12	to 2·6	to 3·4	and above
11.	Decorative . . .	Below 2·8	to 4·25	to 5·5	to 6·5	and above
12.	Sensual Pleasures .	Below 5·5	to 6·4	to 7·05	to 7·95	and above
13.	Sex	Below 1·65	to 2·6	to 3·25	to 3·95	and above
14.	Social . . .	Below 2·5	to 3·12	to 3·8	to 4·6	and above
15.	Home . . .	Below 1·5	to 1·95	to 2·5	to 3·5	and above

The same procedure is used for scoring adults, but the following norms are quite tentative, being based on only 54 cases.

Here the allowance for intelligence appears to be ½ point for 20 points of I.Q. on sections 1, 3, 4, 5, 8, 10, 13, and 15, and 1 for 20 points of I.Q. on 2, 6, 7, 9, 11, 12, 14.

NORMS OF INTEREST TEST FOR ADULTS

No. of Sec.	Name of Section	1.	2.	3.	4.	5.
				Men		
1.	Travel	Below 2·85	to 3·5	to 4·3	to 5·3	and above
2.	Sport	Below 5·4	to 5·8	to 6·5	to 7·4	and above
3.	Commercial	Below 3·85	to 4·85	to 5·8	to 6·75	and above
4.	Mechanical	Below 2·95	to 3·4	to 4·75	to 5·75	and above
5.	Scientific	Below 1·9	to 2·8	to 3·9	to 5·35	and above
6.	Things of the Mind	Below ·8	to 1·5	to 2·95	to 4·5	and above
7.	Rural, Naturalistic	Below 4·1	to 4·75	to 5·1	to 5·75	and above
8.	Religious	Below 4·25	to 5·25	to 5·9	to 6·8	and above
9.	Literary	Below 3·95	to 4·6	to 5·4	to 6·2	and above
10.	Artistic	Below 4·8	to 5·25	to 5·15	to 6·95	and above
11.	Decorative	Below 2·75	to 3·75	to 4·45	to 5·95	and above
12.	Sensual Pleasures	Below 5·85	to 6·25	to 7·1	to 7·75	and above
13.	Sex	Below 3·5	to 4·2	to 4·75	to 6·5	and above
14.	Social	Below 1·5	to 2·6	to 3·3	to 3·9	and above
15.	Home	Below ·95	to 1·75	to 2·1	to 3·25	and above
				Women		
1.	Travel	Below 2·65	to 3·45	to 4·35	to 5·45	and above
2.	Sport	Below 2·75	to 3·9	to 5·75	to 7·15	and above
3.	Commercial	Below 3·9	to 4·9	to 5·95	to 6·95	and above
4.	Mechanical	Below 2·35	to 3·85	to 4·75	to 5·9	and above
5.	Scientific	Below ·95	to 1·95	to 2·5	to 3·5	and above
6.	Things of the Mind	Below 1·35	to 1·85	to 2·5	to 4·2	and above
7.	Rural, Naturalistic	Below 2·75	to 4·25	to 5·75	to 6·85	and above
8.	Religion	Below 4·95	to 5·65	to 6·25	to 6·95	and above
9.	Literary	Below 3·8	to 4·5	to 5·25	to 6·5	and above
10.	Artistic	Below 4·25	to 5·25	to 5·8	to 6·75	and above
11.	Decorative	Below 5·25	to 6·3	to 6·8	to 7·3	and above
12.	Sensual Pleasures	Below 6·25	to 6·85	to 7·25	to 7·65	and above
13.	Sex	Below 3·25	to 3·95	to 5·6	to 6·75	and above
14.	Social	Below 2·3	to 2·85	to 3·35	to 4·98	and above
15.	Home	Below 2·65	to 3·1	to 3·45	to 4·3	and above

Attempts have been made to bring these fifteen interests under two or three main headings, but no such classification can be entirely satisfactory. Psychoanalytic findings show that interests logically utterly remote may spring from the same unconscious pattern and satisfy the same desires. All manner of classifications of interests, objective, subjective, social, material, group, etc., have been suggested, but none has been shown to contain grouped elements which actually correlate highly together. For different purposes, different arrangements are useful. We have chosen a classification of the fifteen interests which will be of value more especially in clinical work, and which is illustrated

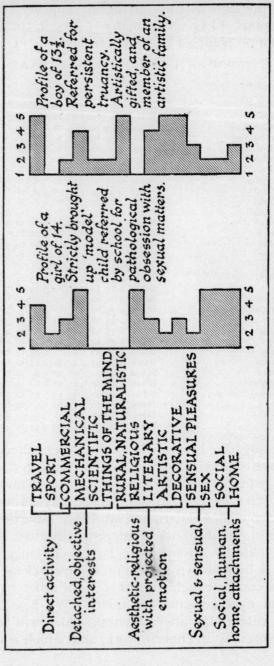

FIG. 47 (a). Children.

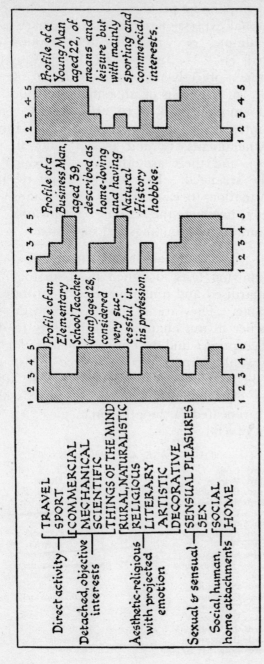

FIG. 47 (b). Adults.

in the accompanying profiles. It is based on the nature of the emotional expression achieved in the various interests, whether simple, or with projected emotion or highly sublimated, etc. (i) Interests in Direct Activity 1, 2, 3; (ii) Complex, objective, coldly intellectual interests, 3, 4, 5, and 6; (iii) Interests of an æsthetic-religious type with projected emotion, 7, 8, 9, 10, and 11; (iv) Sexual and sensual interests, 12 and 13; (v) Social, Human, and Home Attachments, 14 and 15. (i) and (ii) overlap in section (3), and there are other sections which might be differently arranged. The test is, therefore, best used, paying attention to each section as it stands, and only secondarily heeding the cruder classification into the simpler and larger groupings just suggested.

4. Measures of Attitude

The following tests, designed by Thurstone, form the best standardised and uniform series of attitude measures yet available. They are, of course, open to the objections raised earlier in this chapter (susceptibility to dishonesty and self-deception), and the norms, which are for American subjects, would almost certainly need revision for this country, being closely dependent on local atmosphere. A test on 650 students with one of these scales (Race Attitude) repeated a month later, gave a consistency coefficient of 0·88.

THURSTONE ATTITUDE SCALES

Attitude towards God	E. J. Chave and L. S. Thurstone.
Attitude towards War	D. D. Deoba.
Attitude towards the Negro	E. D. Hinckley.
Attitude towards the Law	D. Kalz.
Attitude towards Capital Punishment	R. C. Peterson.
Attitude towards the Chinese	R. C. Peterson.
Attitude towards the Germans	R. C. Peterson.
Attitude towards War	R. C. Peterson.
Attitude towards Censorship	G. C. Rosander and Thurstone.
Attitude towards the Constitution	G. C. Rosander and Thurstone.
Attitude towards U.S.A.	G. C. Rosander and Thurstone.
Attitude towards Prohibition	H. N. Smith and Thurstone.
Attitude towards Patriotism	M. B. Thick and Thurstone.
Attitude towards Communism	Thurstone.
Attitude towards Evolution	Thurstone.
Attitude towards the Church	Thurstone and E. J. Chave.
Attitude towards Immigration	Thurstone.
Attitude towards League of Nations	Thurstone.

THURSTONE ATTITUDE SCALES—*contd.*

Attitude towards Free Trade	Thurstone.
Attitude towards Monroe Doctrine . . .	Thurstone.
Attitude towards German War Guilt . .	Thurstone.
Attitude towards the Bible	Thurstone.
Attitude towards Economic Position of Women .	Thurstone.
Attitude towards Foreign Missions . . .	Thurstone.
Attitude towards Divorce	Thurstone.
Attitude towards Freedom of Speech . .	Thurstone.
Attitude towards Social Position of Women .	Thurstone.
Attitude towards Honesty in Public Office .	Thurstone.
Attitude towards Preparedness . . .	Thurstone.
Attitude towards Public Ownership . .	Thurstone.
Attitude towards Unions	Thurstone.
Attitude towards Birth Control . . .	Thurstone and C. K. A. Wang.
Attitude towards Sunday Observance . .	Thurstone and C. K. A. Wang.
Attitude towards the Treatment of Criminals .	Thurstone and C. K. A. Wang.

Also Allport's *Measurement of Students' Attitudes*, dealing with aspects of college life, obtainable from Messrs. Stoelting ; and Watson's *Public Opinion Test*—a means of measuring deviations from common opinion or ' fair-mindedness ' in religious, economic, and other issues, obtainable from Messrs. Stoelting.

5. Measures of Vocational Interests and Attitudes

Because of their importance in vocational guidance practice, occupational interests have come in for quite a disproportionate amount of detailed technical research. In this field it has been shown that the main outlines of interest in most people do not change much after late adolescence ; that there are appreciable hereditary correlations (e.g. of identical as opposed to fraternal twins) in interest, indicating presumably the dependence of interests on temperament ; that there are four large factor patterns which alone account for a good proportion of individual interest differences, and that apparently remote occupations, e.g. chemistry and psychology, may sometimes have a similar basic interest pattern. The chief test in this field is :

Vocational Interest Blank for Men, by E. K. Strong, for ages 17 years and over. Can be scored with respect to 4 factors, or 35 occupations, or 6 occupational groups; a single form having 400 items on which preferences can be indicated.   Time required : 40 mins.   Can be machine scored.   There has been a great deal of research on this test, showing consistencies between ·75 and ·88.

There is an equivalent *Vocational Interest Blank for Women*, but designed for work with respect to only 17 different occupations.   The validation of this test against occupational success has been thoroughly investigated and is discussed fully in E. K. Strong's *Vocational Interests of Men and Women*, Stanford University Press.

A similar test—relating interests as subjectively stated by the individual to success in occupations—is available in the *Kuder Preference Record*.   This is issued in an ordinary group test form and in a form suitable for machine scoring. Norms for a number of occupations and external validations against a few occupations are now available.[1] Published by Science Research Associates, 1700, Prairie Avenue, Chicago, Ill.

The Thurstone Vocational Interest Schedule is similar, but has the advantage of measuring the interests of college freshmen with respect to seven experimentally established reference factors.   Machine scoring.   Published by the Psychological Corporation, 522, Fifth Avenue, New York.

---

[1] See e.g. relation of number ability to computation interests in Adkins, D. C., and Kuder, G. F.   The relation of primary mental abilities to activity preferences. *Psychometrika*, v, 1940.

CHAPTER V

TESTS OF TEMPERAMENT AND DISPOSITION

1. What is to be Measured in Personality

THE problem of personality measurement is somewhat arbitrarily divided between the present chapter and the ensuing chapter on character ; but the foundation of both will be presented here.

In assessing personality the most difficult question has always been, " What is the important thing to measure ? "; for personality has an infinity of aspects. The question has been answered differently in different periods of psychological theory and in such diverse fields as those of psychiatry, education, and industrial and military personnel work. But if one deals with the real functional and structural unities in personality, rather than artificially-created, *ad hoc* unities, the same factors will always be relevant, in whatever field of personality expression is involved. They may have different relative importance in education, industrial personnel work or psychotherapy ; but they will be the same unitary, functional, temperament or character factors.

As indicated elsewhere,[1] the traditional attempt to define personality in terms of traits and types becomes, in modern mathematical terms, a process of searching for (1) correlation clusters and (2) statistical factors. A trait unity may be recognised, named, and used only when its parts have been shown to correlate together positively in a " cluster " or to go together in a factor. To the former kind of unity we have applied the term *surface trait* and to the factor the term *source trait*. These are alternative descriptive methods of dealing with the same individual differences in personality. The surface

[1] Cattell, R. B., *The Description and Measurement of Personality*. New York, 1946, World Book Co.

trait stops at a purely descriptive level, the source trait handles these descriptive surface traits in alternative, analytical, interpretative fashion.

Such terms as extrovert, introvert, somatotonic, cerebrotonic, anxiety hysteric, and many psychiatric syndromes, correspond to surface traits. A list of the established surface traits has been set out elsewhere.[1] Each of these, defined by the constituent behaviour there set out, can be used as a rating scale. However, because source traits account for the same facts more economically, are more widely useful, and more widely used by psychologists, the analysis of personality will be continued and completed here only with respect to factors.

A large-scale factor analysis of a very comprehensive set of personality variables[2] and a survey of all past work in this field[3] indicate that there are some twelve factors which can at present be considered established in terms both of ratings and questionnaire data. (There are rather more than twelve in questionnaire data alone.) The behaviour-rating factors can be considered the exterior and the questionnaire factors the interior views of the same unitary personality traits. These personality factors, in descending order of contribution to the variance of all personality traits, are listed in Table I.

TABLE I

THE TWELVE PRIMARY FACTORS OF PERSONALITY

Factor

A   Cyclothyme *v.* Schizothyme Temperament.

B   General Intelligence (Spearman's ' g ' in its personality manifestations) *v.* Mental Defect.

C   Emotionally stable character *v.* Demoralised General Emotionality.

[1] Cattell, R. B., " The Principal Trait Clusters for Describing Personality," *Psychol. Bull.*, 1945, xlii, 129–162.

[2] Cattell, R. B., " The Description of Personality, III.   Principles and Findings in a Factor Analysis," *Amer. J. Psychol.*, 1945, lviii, 69–91.

[3] Cattell, R. B., *The Description and Measurement of Personality*, World Book Co., New York, 1945.

Factor

D   Hypersensitive, Infantile, Sthenic Emotionality *v.* Phlegmatic Frustration Tolerance.

E   Dominance *v.* Submissiveness.

F   Surgency *v.* Melancholic, Anxious Desurgency.

G   Positive Character Integration *v.* Immature, Dependent Character.

H   Charitable, Adventurous, Rhathymia *v.* Obstructive, Withdrawn Schizothyme Temperament.

I   Sensitive, Imaginative, Anxious Emotionality *v.* Rigid, Tough Poise.

J   Neurasthenia *v.* Vigorous, ' Obsessional-Determined ' Character.

K   Trained, Socialised, Cultured Mind *v.* Boorishness.

L   Surgent Cyclothymia *v.* Paranoia.

Factor B has been dealt with in Chapter I ; factors A, D, E, F, H, and L will be dealt with here as variables which are more likely to have a constitutional rôle, i.e. as temperament and disposition factors, while C, G, I, J, and K will be considered in the next chapter as factors more dependent on environment and training, or else more definitely connected with character stability, personality integration, and moral control.

2. Methods of Measurement

Since the measurement of personality by objective test methods is still in its infancy, the psychometrist who requires a ready-made measurement method and who cannot afford the time to adapt and standardise devices still at the research stage, must depend on rating, self-rating by questionnaires, or examination of background, case-history data.

A few objective tests, already sufficiently tried by research and practice, are given in this and the following chapter. But a far greater array and variety of possible and promising objective tests, too unfinished to set out here, will be found surveyed and validated in Chapter 11 of the present writer's *Description and Measurement of Personality*. The writer is directing research toward producing during 1947 a battery of practicable objective tests —for use both in psychiatric diagnosis and in personnel work—of the chief personality factors that have been established to date. These tests will be published as research work proceeds. Practising psychologists interested in acquiring them should write to the author at the Psychology Department, University of Illinois, Urbana, Illinois.

The validation of a personality trait measurement, whether of an ability, a temperament trait, or a dynamic trait, is properly to be considered as having two aspects, which we may call central and peripheral, or internal and external. Standardisation, which must, of course, always follow and not precede validation, also has these two aspects.

Central and peripheral validation may be most quickly defined by reference to intelligence testing. An intelligence test is centrally and intrinsically validated by demonstrating that it is sufficiently loaded, i.e. correlated, with the general ability factor that runs through all performances involving relation eduction. Factors in any realm are established and defined with greater and greater purity by a kind of iterative procedure—a process of successive approximation in which, as we gradually perceive the essential nature of the factor, we construct better and better measures of it. By inspection of the most pure or saturated tests we arrive at its intrinsic nature.

At the same time, however, or closely on the heels of the above, we obtain correlations between success in the test performance and success in various everyday life landmarks, e.g. occupations, games, adjustments, scholastic progress. These give peripheral significance and validation to the factor measured. To attempt to define or validate a factor trait against these wider situations first is to invite the chaos which comes of ill-judged ambition, for the real-life situations are almost all more complex than those we can control in the laboratory. For example, to define intelligence grandiosely as ' that which makes for success in life ' would involve us in the absurdity of calling a boxer's weight his intelligence. Success depends on a great variety of personality factors, any one of which helps some real-life performances and impedes others. Strictly, what has been thought of as external or peripheral *validation* is actually an adding of significance, meaning, and predictive power to a unitary trait measurement already truly validated by internal validation.

By internal *standardisation* we refer to the first acquisition of meaning in raw scores through exploring their relation to the intrinsic characters of a population. It involves matching the raw scores with some necessary character such as age, sex, or frequency within the population. Central standardisation is achieved when we get age norms or percentiles. Peripheral standardisation, however, is never completely achieved. It proceeds as we establish the mean and scatter in the trait concerned for various occupations, classes, and real-life adjustments or critical points of success and failure. The peripheral standardisation of the objective tests of personality factors will naturally require many years of further work after their central validation as measures of the factors and their central standardisation in percentile scores. Reliable results and information concerning the scores on the chief personality factors found in various occupational groups, in successful and unsuccessful working groups, in successful and unsuccessful social adjustments, in various grades of neurotics and delinquents will be welcomed by the writer, who will endeavour in further editions to set up a peripheral standardisation for these factors of general utility to applied psychologists.

Although objective tests are available for *some* source

traits the only methods uniformly available for all are, as mentioned above, ratings, questionnaires, and case-history data, the range of use of which may now be examined more closely. During the war it was repeatedly demonstrated that knowledge of a person's past would predict his future where both rating and questionnaire failed to do so. Some of the most predictive items in 'questionnaires' were really items which, truthfully answered, could be considered case history—e.g. background data about grade reached in school, previous nervous breakdowns, having belonged to boy scouts, leadership rôles in athletic clubs, etc. Unfortunately most of these correlations were established directly between some test item and some further performance in a military career, since time did not permit factorisation and the relation to the main personality traits; so that this data, because of its ephemeralness, is lost as an aid to personality measurement.

It will be obvious, from implicit and explicit references, that the theory of measurement advocated in this book favours validating each test against a source trait factor, and then predicting from the individual's factor endowment his performance in a given life situation. External and internal validation are the prerequisites of this practice. On the other hand, a great deal of applied psychology has proceeded directly from test to situation prediction. The alternatives may be represented diagrammatically as follows :

$$\text{(Central)} \qquad \text{(Peripheral)}$$

(1) Test $\longleftrightarrow$ Factor $\longleftrightarrow$ Life situation.

(2) Test $\longleftarrow\qquad\qquad\longrightarrow$ Life situation.

The latter has a spurious air of economy; for actually the chief argument for the extra trouble required when using the former method is that it constitutes an ultimate saving. Tests come and go, often becoming obsolete in a few years, but personality traits (factors) are far more permanent. The regressions worked out between occupational success and a given test have to be thrown away with the test; those directly related to personality factors stay. The number of regression coefficients required in applied psychology, both in guidance and therapy, is so great that no science of applied psychology could ever be built up on specific, transitory tests.

However, when using factors, we are left, at present, only with ratings and the self-ratings of questionnaires. The following factor-by-factor description of the main source traits defining personality is therefore presented as:

(*a*) A list of traits which are the most highly loaded in the factor, and hence describe it.

(*b*) A list of traits which can be rated, and the ratings pooled, to give the best estimate of each factor uncontaminated by other factors.

(*c*) A reference letter for picking out from the complete questionnaire in the appendix the items specifically used for assessing the factor in question. Whether the question is to be answered 'yes' or 'no,' in order to be counted positively, is indicated on the questionnaire itself.

For reasons already set out—principally that the direct questionnaire is invalidated in critically motivated situations by the individual's lack of self-knowledge and honesty—the questionnaire is not recommended as a device for personality measurement. Most published, standardised questionnaires—e.g. the Humm-Wadsworth, the Minnesota Multiphasic, the Bell, Bernreuter and other inventories, and a host of other personality questionnaires—suffer from the additional defect that the unitary character of the traits they claim to measure has seldom or never been established by factorial analyses. Indeed, such analysis has almost invariably shown that the supposed 'neuroticism,' 'extraversion,' etc., are spurious entities.

The questionnaire items cover only ten factors—those which have been repeatedly rediscovered in factor analyses. These include eight of the present factors and two found in questionnaire work only. For many rating studies it may be best to confine rating to six factors, for

D, G, H, J, and L require confirmation, and B can always be measured best by test.

For assessments by ratings, through observations, the observers or judges should take the usual dictionary meaning of the separate traits on which ratings are to be made and average independent scores to get each factor. Preferably the definitions should be amplified into terms of several *actual behaviour manifestations* in a list circulated among all the judges. The usual precautions for valid and reliable ratings need to be enforced as follows :

(1) Begin with rankings and convert to ratings.
(2) Have as many judges as possible, to average, and do not have all judges standing in the same relation to the subjects (e.g. not all teachers rating children).
(3) Arrange time sampling, so that behaviour is observed a standard amount in diverse standard situations.
(4) Do not ask one judge to rank more than about thirty people.

The norms for rating obviously have meaning for, and can only be built up with respect to, the particular group and judges with which the experimenter is working.

Finally, it should be remembered that though the assessment of these dozen or half-dozen factors gives greater prediction of total personality than is obtainable with any other list of variables of comparable length, it still leaves untouched the specific factors, and therefore does not uniquely describe the individual. For example, factors C and G and B may account for about 60 per cent. of the variability among people (the ' variance ') in the cluster ' realistic, practical, persevering, facing life ' ; but there is still a certain amount (40 per cent.) of endowment in this cluster unaccounted for by these general factors and presumably due to specific, environmental moulding influences. It is suggested that all ratings be made on a continuum between two polar opposite traits, as below.

FACTOR A. CYCLOTHYME *v.* SCHIZOTHYME

Observer's Rating on :	*Temperament*
Co-operative	*v.* Obstructive.
Adventurous	*v.* Timid, withdrawn.
Grateful	*v.* Thankless.
Soft-hearted	*v.* Hard-hearted, embittered.
Easy-going	*v.* Short-tempered.
Friendly	*v.* Hostile.
Frank	*v.* Secretive.
Adaptable	*v.* Inflexible, rigid.
Genial, warm-hearted	*v.* Cold-hearted.
Optimistic	*v.* Pessimistic.

The above best describe and estimate the factor. But when it is desired to estimate a factor in company with others and yet avoid too much spurious correlation between the factors, it is necessary to choose trait elements which are not only highly saturated with the factor, *but also relatively free from any one other factor.* The following are not quite as highly saturated as the above, but give an estimate less correlated with other factors.

A +	A —
Friendly	*v.* Hostile.
Co-operative	*v.* Obstructive.
Frank	*v.* Secretive.
Trustful	*v.* Sadistic.
Reasonable	*v.* Suspicious.
Not sadistic	*v.* Mulish.
Adaptable	*v.* Inflexible.
—————	*v.* Extra-punitive (blaming others).
Gentle-tempered	*v.* Headstrong.
Submissive	*v.* Assertive.
Self-effacing	*v.* Exhibitionistic.
Self-dissatisfied	*v.* Conceited.

Questionnaire : 20 items under A.

This is the well-known cyclothyme-schizothyme (sometimes called introvert-extrovert) temperament factor. Cyclothymes are usually more pyknic [1] in body build, more successful in dealing with people, less interested in theories and principles and more in facts and detail, given to mild swings of mood in terms of depression and elation, etc. The full implications of this temperament factor for guidance, adjustment, etc., may well be obtained from such a summary as that of Kretschmer.[2]

FACTOR D.   HYPERSENSITIVE, INFANTILE, STHENIC EMOTIONALITY *v*. PHLEGMATIC, FRUSTRATION-TOLERANT TEMPERAMENT

Observer's rating on :

Exhibitionistic	*v*. Self-effacing.
Self-pitying	*v*. Emotionally mature.
Emotional	*v*. Unemotional.
Excitable	*v*. Phlegmatic.
Impatient	*v*. Patient.
Changeable	*v*. Stable emotionally.
Reckless	*v*. Self-controlled.
Self-deceiving	*v*. Realistic.
Hypochondriacal	*v*.
Nervous habits	*v*.

Less inter-factor correlation with :

D +	D −
Self-pitying	*v*.
Thankless, unappreciative	*v*. Grateful.
Easily jealous	*v*.
Emotional	*v*. Unemotional.

---

[1] Pyknic refers to a body build with large girth, broad face, soft, rounded features, etc.   The correlations obtained in Britain and the U.S.A. between the breadth factor in body build and cyclothyme temperament have not been more than about 0·4. See, however, Sheldon, W. H., *The Varieties of Physique*, 1942.

[2] Kretschmer, E., *Physique and Character*.

D +	D —
Excitable	*v.* Phlegmatic.
Impatient	*v.* Patient.
Infantile	*v.* Mature emotionally.
Exhibitionistic	*v.* Self-effacing.
Headstrong	*v.* Gentle-tempered.

Questionnaire : 20 items marked D.

It is possible that this is related to what is popularly called ' artistic ' temperament and to artistic ability.

FACTOR E.   DOMINANT *v.* SUBMISSIVE DISPOSITION

Observer's rating on :

Assertive	*v.* Self-submissive.
Boastful	*v.* Modest.
Headstrong	*v.* Gentle-tempered.
Exhibitionist	*v.*
Extra-punitive (blaming others)	*v.* Self-critical.
Sophisticated	*v.* Simple.
Tough	*v.* Sensitive.
	v. Introspective.
Hard-hearted, embittered	*v.* Soft-hearted.
Short-tempered	*v.* Easy-going.

Less inter-factor correlation with :

E +	E —
Assertive	*v.* Self-submissive.
Boastful	*v.* Modest.
Conceited	*v.* Self-critical.
Energetic, spirited	*v.* Languid.
Self-confident	*v.* Self-distrustful.
Debonair	*v.*
Adventurous	*v.* Inhibited.
Curious	*v.* Uninquiring.
Sophisticated	*v.* Simple.
' Smart '	*v.*

Questionnaire : 20 items marked E.

FACTOR F. SURGENT TEMPERAMENT *v.* MELANCHOLIC, CYCLOID DESURGENCY

Observer's Rating on :

Cheerful	*v.* Gloomy.
Genial	*v.* Cold-hearted.
Optimistic	*v.* Pessimistic.
Enthusiastic	*v.* Apathetic.
Placid	*v.* Worrying.
	v. Hypochondriacal.
Sociable (forward)	*v.* Shy.
Sociable (gregarious)	*v.* Seclusive.
Responsive	*v.* Aloof.
Imaginative (original)	*v.* Habit-bound.

For less inter-factor correlation :

Optimistic	*v.* Pessimistic.
Genial	*v.* Cold-hearted.
Enthusiastic	*v.* Apathetic.
	v. Hypochondriacal.
Placid	*v.* Worrying.
	v. Melancholic.
	v. Introspective.
Tough	*v.* Sensitive.
Lethargic	*v.* Hurried.

Questionnaire : 20 items marked F.

A high degree of surgency is found in those who succeed in social situations, who give a positive impression on meeting, who show imagination and resource in dealing with situations, especially social situations requiring inventiveness and quickness. There is evidence [1] that at its positive extreme this factor is found in conversion hysteria, and at its negative extreme in dysthymic [1] neuroses and melancholia. It is slightly negatively related to character.

[1] Eysenck, H. J., *Dimensions of Personality*, London, 1947.

FACTOR H. CHARITABLE, ADVENTUROUS RHATHYMIC *v.*
OBSTRUCTIVE, WITHDRAWN SCHIZOTHYMIC TEMPERAMENT

Observer's Rating on :

Co-operative	*v.* Obstructive.
Friendly	*v.* Hostile.
Idealistic	*v.* Cynical.
Grateful	*v.* Thankless.
Soft-hearted	*v.* Hard-hearted.
Adventurous	*v.* Timid, withdrawn.
Frank	*v.* Secretive.
	v. Superstitious, given to obsessive fears.
Lusty	*v.* Queasy, inhibited.
Spirited	*v.* Languid.

It is difficult to reduce the correlation of this factor
estimate with that of A, except by taking a more numerous
set of elements, as follows :

H +	H —
Grateful	*v.* Thankless.
Soft-hearted	*v.* Hard-hearted.
Friendly	*v.* Hostile.
Intrusive	*v.* Reserved.
Impulsive	*v.* Deliberate.
Frank	*v.* Secretive.
Self-effacing	*v.* Exhibitionistic.
Natural	*v.* Affected.
Musical and æsthetic interests	*v.*
Emotional	*v.* Unemotional.
Impatient	*v.* Patient.
Adventurous	*v.* Inhibited.
Bold	*v.* Timid.

The correlations of this factor with vocational, social,
and educational adjustment have not yet been investi-

gated. Clinically, the low loadings in this factor are in the direction of catatonic schizothyme make-up.

FACTOR L.   SURGENT CYCLOTHYME *v.* PARANOIA

Genial	*v.*	Cold-hearted.
Soft-hearted	*v.*	Hard-hearted.
Easy-going	*v.*	Short-tempered.
Co-operative	*v.*	Obstructive.
Adventurous	*v.*	Timid, withdrawn.
Friendly	*v.*	Hostile.
Trustful	*v.*	Suspicious.
Reasonable	*v.*	Mulish.
Adaptable	*v.*	Inflexible.

Again, correlation with A is difficult to avoid, and there is some doubt as to the independent existence of this factor. However, since it seems clinically a clear syndrome, it is included, with the following wide variety of elements, to avoid spurious correlation.

L +		L −
Extra-punitive	*v.*	
Inflexible	*v.*	Adaptable.
Hard-hearted, embittered	*v.*	Soft-hearted.
Short-tempered	*v.*	Easy-going.
Cynical	*v.*	Idealistic.
Obstructive	*v.*	Co-operative.
Withdrawn	*v.*	
Cold-hearted	*v.*	Genial.
Emotional	*v.*	Unemotional.
Dissatisfied	*v.*	Content.
Excitable	*v.*	Phlegmatic.
Aloof	*v.*	Responsive.
	v.	Social Interests.
Brooding	*v.*	
Sadistic	*v.*	
Suspicious	*v.*	Trustful.

Clinically, this factor seems to correspond to paranoid tendency, and the interpretations of the measurement in terms of social, occupational, and other adjustments can be made accordingly.

The twelve primary personality factors are, as influences, practically, but not entirely, independent.[1] (They have inter-correlations around 0·1 to 0·3.) They account for rather more than half the variance on all personality traits. Although the factors are practically independent, their estimations by means of the above abbreviated trait and questionnaire items will not be so because the same traits reappear in several factors. For instance, A, H, and L will correlate more by this method than by the prolonged mathematical method of true factor estimation.

To those unfamiliar with factor analysis it may seem surprising that two distinct factors can load many of the same traits, as in A and L. In verbal terms this means that the cluster, ' surface trait,' or syndrome constituted by these traits is the result of two (or more) distinct influences or source traits. Indeed, a typical source trait affects most behaviour. Thus it is understandable that the schizoid syndrome, culminating in schizophrenia, is revealed, by mathematical analysis, to require for its fullest manifestation the co-operation of three distinct factors or influences.

3. Objective Tests

As indicated above, few of the objective tests now being experimented upon as tests of the above factors have yet reached a validity or acquired a standardisation justifying their being offered for general use. Consequently the measures here provided will be restricted to the surgency factor F, the cyclothyme-schizothyme factor A, and the dominance-submission factor E, concerning each of which some ten to twenty years of direct research have resulted in fairly stable findings.

[1] See Table III in Cattell, R. B., " The Description of Personality : Principles and Findings in a Factor Analysis," *Amer. J. Psychol.*, lviii, 1945.

F.   SURGENCY-DESURGENCY

(In pathological extremes: Hysteria-Dysthymia)

Three measures have reached appreciable validities in more than one research, and could now promise good validity combined in a single battery.

1. *Goal Discrepancy.* The subject is assigned a task involving dexterity, e.g. as in the pursuit meter, or clerical accuracy at speed, which can be repeated several times. After each performance, when his score is named, he is asked to say what score he will obtain next time. The summed values " goal or aspiration score minus actual score," called the *goal discrepancy*, was found by Eysenck [1] to correlate about 0·5 with dysthymia-hysteria factor and significantly to distinguish hysterics from anxiety neurotics.

2. *Flexibility-Rigidity of Ego-Aspiration.* Using the same type of tests (preferably a battery of three or more) a correlation of about 0·5 is obtainable [1] between hysteria-dysthymia and an *index of flexibility* obtained by subtracting each goal-aspiration score from its successor, adding the difference scores regardless of sign.

3. *Personal Tempo and Fluency.* At least three distinct factors, besides intelligence, enter into quickness of performance in general,[2] viz. : (1) Speed of reaction time ; (2) Ideo-motor speed, in cancellation, etc. ; (3) Fluency or ' f.' (' W ' in Thurstone's terminology.)

The last of these has been shown by Notcutt, the present writer, and others to have a good correlation with surgency, though Eysenck (*op. cit.*) fails to find this in the neurotic extremes (hysteria-dysthymia). The latter finds a significant positive relation, however, between the second speed factor and hysteria. He finds a still better relation with speed divided by accuracy. Since the fluency correlations have in the past been with a *surface trait* of surgency, involving the cyclothyme factor H as well as the

---

[1] Eysenck, H. J., *Dimensions of Personality*, London, 1947. (See page 128 for details.)

[2] Cattell, R. B., *The Description and Measurement of Personality*. World Book Co., New York, 1946.

inverse (C —) of Emotional Maturity—the two factors with which ' f ' also has appreciable positive correlation— we conclude that the correlations with pure surgency, at least in adults and neurotic adults, are not as good as was supposed.   Until further research, the test should be used only as part of a battery.

The following ' f ' test (regular printed forms for which may be obtained in batches of 50 from the University of London Press) has been standardised on 450 14-year-old children, 100 11- and 12-year-olds, 50 9- and 10-year-olds, and 50 adults.

About 20 minutes is required for testing (15 minutes' actual testing time), and the test can be given either as a group or individual test to children over 10 and adults, but only as an individual test to children below that age. Since, as in most temperament, interest, or character tests, a correction has to be made for intelligence when the fullest accuracy is to be achieved, this test should be preceded by at any rate a rough test of ' g.'

Instructions for Administering

There are five sub-tests, each of 3 minutes:
1. Pictures, 3 periods of 1 minute.
2. Word Series, 3 periods of 1 minute.
3. Completing Forms, 3 periods of 1 minute.
4. Topics, 6 periods of $\frac{1}{2}$ minute.
5. Ink Blots, 3 periods of 1 minute.

Pictures

Three pictures (Tree, Street Corner, and Library), see pp. 179–183.   Pictures to be face downwards on the desk with (1) uppermost.

Instructions to Subject.

Turn over the top picture, and you will see a picture of a tree with a cross marked underneath it.

I want you to think of as many *different* things as you can that might be drawn under the tree somewhere about where the cross

PICTURE 1.

FIG. 48.

PICTURE 2.

FIG. 49.

PICTURE 3.

FIG. 50.

is. You might not be able to put them all in the same picture together, of course. Write down anything you can think of as quickly as you can.

With children of *10 years and under* the examiner says, " Tell me anything you can think of," and writes down the things given.

"Are you ready? Go." (One minute)
Repeat for two other pictures.

Scoring.—One point for each idea, e.g. " a cat looking up at a bird," three points in all, for *cat, looking at,* and *bird*.

Word Series

Material.—Pencil and paper.

Instructions to Subject.

(*a*) I am going to give you a minute, and I want you to write down (or tell me) as many things as you can think of that are ' round ' or could be round. A penny would do. Give me as many as you can.

"Ready? Go."

(*b*) Now write a list of things we can ' eat.'

(*c*) Now write as many words as you can, beginning with ' s ' —any words you like.

With children of 10 years and under, the examiner says, " Tell me all the things you can think of," and then writes them down.

One minute allowed for each set.

Scoring.—Number of words (things).

Completing Forms

Materials.—Three foolscap sheets each having a simple figure, repeated as shown in Fig. 51 below.

Examiner demonstrates on first sheet or on an enlarged copy of it on the blackboard.

" You have some lines on your papers like this " (points to blackboard). " I want you to add a few lines to each one of them to turn them into something."

E.g. " This looks rather like the top of a flag, so you might draw a few lines to show where the rest of the flag would come—the flag might look like this."

(Examiner demonstrates.)

" Make each one into something different. It doesn't matter a bit what the drawing is like—it is just to see how many different things you can think of. Don't spend a lot of time finishing each drawing. As long as I can see what it is meant to be, that is enough."

After subjects have finished the first sheet (example), examiner looks at it to make sure instructions are understood.

Scoring.—Number of intelligible drawings on all three sheets (excluding flag drawn as an example).

FIG. 51.

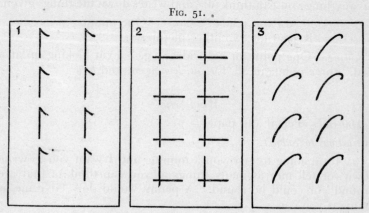

(Three Test Sheets.   Allow 1 minute for each sheet.)

Topics

" I'm going to give you a subject, and I want you to say as many things as you can about it—e.g. suppose I say ' a bad cough,' you say as many things as you can think of about a bad cough—either disconnected things like, ' A bad cough is not often serious '; ' It's annoying when you hear someone with a bad cough in church '; ' I had a bad cough last week, and had to stay in bed for a few days '; ' I felt shaky when I got up, but this fine weather has quite cured it.'

" It doesn't matter a bit whether you go rambling on about one thing, or if you say all sorts of disconnected things. Just do whichever is easier.   I want you to say as many things as possible. Quantity, not quality, counts in this test.

" Try this one—' A man going up a ladder.'—Now, just say as many things as you can think of about a man going up a ladder."

List of Topics to be given:

(1) A man going up a ladder. ⎫
(2) A dog barking. |
(3) A house on fire.   ⎬ 30 seconds each.
(4) A train journey. |
(5) A parcel. |
(6) A poor boy.   ⎭

Scoring.—Number of significant words—i.e. omitting a, the, and, but counting the subject (man going up ladder, dog barking) where repeated.

Ink Blots

Material.—Three ink blots as shown (modelling within the blots should be discernible), preferably individual copies, but a possible method is to have a large sheet on the blackboard for whole class to see.

Instructions.—Examiner arranges for first blot to be exposed and says:

" Now, this is just a blot of ink; try to think of something it looks like.   See how many things you can see in it, just as you see things in clouds or in the fire.   It isn't exactly like anything, of course, but try to think of as many things as you can that it looks rather like.

" You may think of it as turned round or look at it sideways or upside down if you like.

" Write down on your paper all the things you can think of."

Children of 10 or under *tell* one the things they can see.

Time allowed.—One minute for each blot.

Scoring.—Number of items conceived.

Total Score on Fluency Tests.—To compute total score first multiply the score on the third test by three, halve the score on the fourth test (count a half as one), and double the score on the last test.   This procedure is necessary in order to equalise the weights of the constituent tests in the total.

Apparatus Needed.—Three form completion papers, three ink blots, three pictures; stop-watch.   Pictures and completion forms may be reproduced from models shown here.   Ink-blots photo may be obtained from the author.

Evaluating the Score.—' f ' score correlates about ·3 with ' g.' Because of this, the following correction for I.Q. (empirically obtained) is required.

At 10 and 11 years.   Add 1 to ' f ' score for each point of I.Q. below 100.

Subtract ·25 point from ' f ' score for each point I.Q. above 100.

At 12 years.   Add 1 point from ' f ' score for each point I.Q. below 100.

Subtract ·5 point from ' f ' score for each point I.Q. above 100.

At 13 years.   Add 1 point from ' f ' score for each point I.Q. below 100.

Subtract ·75 point from ' f ' score for each point I.Q. above 100.

At 14 years. Add 1 point from 'f' score for each point I.Q. below 100.

Subtract 1 point from 'f' score for each point I.Q. above 100.

These are round figures obtained from averaged 'f' scores of three 'g' groups.

The results thus corrected can be converted finally to decile scores by the following table. Example of working: a child of 12 with a raw score (corrected for I.Q.) of 91 has a decile score of 2, i.e. 8 out of 10 are above him and 1 below. He would therefore be of a markedly desurgent (introvert) temperament.

FIG. 55.—Decile norms for 'f' scores.

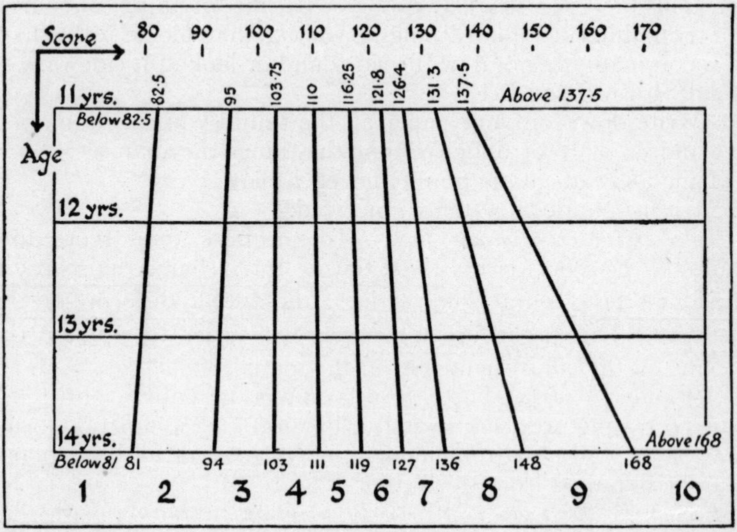

Instructions.—After correcting the 'f' score for I.Q. as described above, drop a perpendicular from the 'f' score position on the scale at the top to the year level concerned and note into which of the ten decile divisions the score falls.

In the research in which the correlations of fluency with surgency were first discovered [1] an agreement of 0·6 ± ·07 was found, but this, as explained on p. 176, was with a surface trait, composed of factors F, H and C —. In view of the failure to get such correlations with pure F ratings in certain groups, notably adult neurotics, the possibility must be considered that special conditions of the group or comparatively slight differences of the test

[1] " Temperament Tests," II, by R. B. Cattell, *loc. cit.*

BLOT I

FIG. 52.

BLOT II

FIG. 53.

Blot III

Fig. 54.

situation eliminate the correlation with F, if not with H and C —.

Thus, although Eysenck found no correlation of ' f ' and F in adult neurotics (hysterics-dysthymics), Studman found ' f ' distinguishing manics and hysterics from depressives, i.e. high from low F. The latter found the correlation better if sheer speed of writing, etc., were cancelled out, but the former found sheer speed of performance (accuracy constant) related to high F. In so far as fluency tests are given, as designed here, to favour careless speed, it would seem that in most situations they can be regarded as contributory to a battery to measure F.

The present writer has always obtained significant correlations among children—0·65 ± 0·07 for 10-year-old children and 0·60 ± 0·07 for 14-year-olds, with consistency coefficient of 0·78 ± 0·07—but not always for adults. Research now in progress, to be published in 1947, may clear up this issue.

A. CYCLOTHYMIA-SCHIZOTHYMIA

The researches of Kretschmer [1] and his school indicate the following test performances to be tied up with the cyclothyme-schizothyme distinction. Since there has been very little attempt to confirm these findings in English and American research, it is uncertain how high the correlations would stand in terms of the methods and populations used here.

(1) When compound material (involving colour, forms, meaning, movement, etc.) is exposed, with the usual brief exposure in a tachistoscope,[2] the schizothyme makes better scores than the cyclothyme if asked to abstract one particular aspect, e.g. to note colour only or form only.[1]

The C's, on the other hand, observe more things than they are asked to observe.

[1] *Korperbau und Charakter*, by Kretschmer, especially p. 180, reporting Kibler's research.

[2] An apparatus for permitting controlled, instantaneous exposures of pictures, printed words, etc.

(2) When reaction times are measured under conditions of distraction (choice reactions to two or more coloured lights in which yet another distracting light may at any moment be switched on), the C's are more disturbed.

The fraction[1] $\dfrac{\text{Reaction time under distraction}}{\text{Reaction time under simple conditions}}$ is significantly higher for C's; but more errors are made by S's.

(3) In tachistoscopic exposure of letters, the span (number of letters perceived) is greater for C's than S's.[2]

(4) The curve of pressure in writing (Kraepelin's writing-table) is more sudden and irregular with S's.[2]

(5) Perseveration, by Wiersma's disc (see p. 234 for ' p ' measurement), is greater for S's.[2]

(6) Speed of finger tapping (natural tempo) is greater for S's.[2] The present writer's investigations, however, do not bear this out.[3]

(7) When left to observe, without specific instructions, coloured objects in a tachistoscope, C's (or integrates) pay more attention to colour and S's to form. [2][4]

(8) This difference, as also differences in the subjectivity of associations, reveals itself in Rorschach's coloured blot tests, which may therefore be used as a temperament test.

(9) Fluency, as indicated on p. 176, is probably significantly higher for C's.

4. Disposition and Dynamic 'Needs'

That aspect of an individual's personality which is called his ' disposition ' has long been considered an important one for occupational and social prognosis. As McDougall pointed out, the classification of dispositions is essentially the same as that of propensities, drives,

---

[1] *Korperbau und Charakter*, by Kretschmer, p. 179.
[2] Kretschmer, *op. cit.*
[3] *Op. cit.*, R. B. Cattell.
[4] O. Oeser, " Some Experiments on the Abstraction of Form and Colour," I, *Brit. J. Psychol.*, xxii, 1932 ; II, *Brit. J. Psychol.*, xxii, 1932.

needs, or ergs.[1] The individual's disposition is defined by those needs or ergs which he has in a high degree. Thus the ergs of escape, pugnacity, sex, or protectiveness give us respectively the dispositions of timidity, irascibility, amorousness, and kindliness. Renewed attention to measuring disposition has arisen recently as a result of the clinical work of H. A. Murray,[2] whose list of ' needs ' represents a further subdividing of McDougall's propensities.

Measuring disposition amounts to measuring the strength of the primary, massive, dynamic traits. Dynamic traits fall into two groups—ergs and metanergs. Ergs manifest themselves largely through the culturally imposed channels of metanergs. The strength of an erg—say, of gregariousness—can only be inferred from a well-distributed sampling of all its metanergic manifestations. Similarly, a person's self-assertiveness is measured as an averaging of his behaviour in all those situations in which self-assertion normally manifests itself. Questions remain to be answered here concerning whether one is measuring solely differences in biological endowment or such differences along with differences in degree of overt (conscious, ego-linked) manifestation. Also there are questions about aim-inhibited drive, about the extent to which the power of these major dynamic traits may change through experience, and about their possibly drawing upon a common ergic source.

The researches so far made—from those of Galton on twins to those of Heymans and Wiersma on whole families —indicate a certain degree of inheritance of disposition, but these researches are based only on estimates of personality (not always adequately checked), and are, moreover, not capable of distinguishing between true inheritance and

[1] The term ' erg ' was introduced by the present writer (" Sentiment or attitude ? The core of a terminological problem in personality research," Char. and Personality, ix, 6–17, 1940) to define more precisely, operationally, and with greater verbal convenience what McDougall had called a propensity. It defines preferred ways of reaction and relative facility in learning brought about by the structure of the nervous system. (See definition in General Psychology, 1941.)

[2] Murray, H. A., et al., Explorations in Personality, Harvard University Press.

the effects of early imitation through primitive passive sympathy.

Certainly many instances are known in clinical work of marked changes of disposition occurring even up to middle life, and the influence of health condition and of drugs is proverbial.

If we regard the instincts as drawing upon a common fund of libido, it follows that the strong development of one instinct (in frequency and intensity of functioning) must impoverish the remainder. Thus, e.g. the assertive and irascible man would have less energy for curiosity, amorousness, and sociability, etc., and vice versa. The defining of a person's disposition, therefore, is a matter of determining which instincts are most developed.[1] Some kinds of disposition, e.g. assertive and submissive, are in practice more important than others, notably in vocational guidance analysis. In any case, no scheme or test assessing all the dispositions yet exists—nor would it be wise to work on one until more is known about disposition structure.[2]

5. Available Tests : Direct and Ego Defence Mechanism

Dynamic trait strength can at present be assessed like endowment in personality factors, interests, and temperament traits by means of ' direct ' questionnaire items or indirectly by objective tests. The objective tests, except for the use of the psycho-galvanometer and similar measures of dynamic, orectic response to stimuli (see

[1] The notion of ' strength of instinct ' is one which raises many theoretical difficulties, mainly because of the mutability of instinct energy described by Freud, and also because of the marked deflections and sublimations which the expression of any instinct can undergo. Nevertheless, in a rough practical way the notion has been very helpful, and attempts at measurement have not been unsuccessful. See e.g. Colman and McCrae, " An Attempt to Measure the Strength of Instincts," Forum Educ., iii, November 1927.

[2] Professor Burt, in discussing the nature of ' general emotionality,' has mooted the question as to whether group factors exist within it. Preliminary statistical work by this writer on a large number of observations of emotional outbursts by young children suggests that at least two such group factors exist : those who are prone to self-assertion being also more pugnacious and gregarious, whilst those who are timid are also more affectionate, submissive, and protective. Disposition, therefore, may be more adequately described as the predominance of a group of instincts rather than, as McDougall suggests, of a single instinct.

Interests), have mainly been of a 'projective' type. Recently the present writer has pointed out that projection tests are only a particular variety of a possible whole class of measuring devices which may be called ego defence mechanism tests. Few finished tests, and certainly no standardised tests, are yet available here, either in the general area of ego defence or in the specific area of projection ; for even in projection less than ten years of research has occurred and major theoretical questions are still unanswered.

However, some complete projection tests are published below, while examples of other tests are provided to enable the psychologist to expand them into items suitable for his own purposes. Otherwise the two chief projection tests are the Rorschach and the Thematic Apperception Tests (by H. A. Murray, published by Harvard University Press). As pointed out elsewhere, the former expresses its results in terms of psychological variables, the existence of which as unitary traits has never been substantiated, while its validities are distinctly poor compared with those of most of the tests recommended in this volume. The Thematic Apperception test is not a pure projection test, for it uses also the mechanism of phantasy, and it is not designed for objective, i.e. selective answer, scoring ; but it has considerable value in clinical work or, in the hands of skilled psychometrists, in providing measures of strengths of needs as research data.

Ego defence mechanism tests are based on the theory that the strength of various drives in the individual's unconscious make-up may be inferred from their appearance in his ego defence mechanisms. Since the individual is normally unaware of these defences the test is objective in that it does not presuppose or require judgments on the subject made by himself, as in questionnaires. The person's total behaviour—i.e. his observed personality—however, is the result both of his conscious and his unconscious dynamic expression. Consequently, until further research is done it is questionable how far and in what manner the results of ego defence mechanism test measurement need to be added to in interpreting the total personality.

The most practicable ego defence mechanisms for test use seem to be :

1. Projection.
2. Phantasy.
3. Rationalisation.
4. Reaction Formation.

An example of each device in measuring the dynamic trait of self-assertion or dominance (as opposed to self-submission) is given with explanations below. In each the subject is instructed to complete the sentence with that one of the four possible alternatives which seems to him to make the best psychological sense, i.e. to be most likely.

1. The man turned up to address the group, having brought with him his superior officer, because

——— he wanted some moral support.
——— he was determined to make them come to his point of view.
——— he admired his superior a great deal.
——— he enjoyed impressing people with his own importance.

In responses one and three the subject *projects* self-abasement, in four he *projects* excessive self-assertion, and this response would be scored positive for self-assertion.

2. Which of the following dramatised stories would you most enjoy as a film ?

——— The life of Napoleon.
——— The life of St. Francis of Assisi.
——— Romeo and Juliet.
——— Huckleberry Finn.

Here the first alternative would be scored as indicating pleasure in *phantasy* of a dominance variety. Actual item analysis might show that the second could be given negative weight in scoring, i.e. self-submission.

3. To lose one's temper with, or to use biting sarcasm on, an assistant is

———— generally a mistake.
———— sometimes necessary when people are lazy.
———— bad manners.
———— often effective.

Here responses two and four are likely to be given by the individual wishing to *rationalise* a naturally assertive or pugnacious disposition.

4. A good teacher should give more attention than is now given to overcoming the shyness of children and encouraging them to be talkative and aggressive.

———— strongly agree.
———— agree to some extent.
———— doubt the wisdom of this.
———— disagree entirely.

A naturally very shy person may develop as a *reaction formation* or over-compensation a talkative and aggressive manner. His response, on this theory, is likely to be that of approving and emphasising the need for acquiring the behaviour contrary to his natural disposition.

This theory of test construction is put forward tentatively. The problem is complex—for instance, rationalisation and reaction formation sometimes operate in opposite directions at different levels—and test items should only be finally included in a sub-test after empirical validation. A more intensive examination of these test methods has been reported elsewhere.[1]

[1] Cattell, R. B., " Projection and the Design of Projective Tests of Personality," *Char. and Personality*, March 1944.
Sears, R. R., " Experimental Studies of Projection—I, Attribution of Traits," *J. Soc. Psychol.*, 1936, vii, 151–163.
Sears, R. R., " Experimental Studies of Projection—II, Ideas of Reference." *J. Soc. Psychol.*, 1937, viii, 389–401.

PROJECTION TEST OF DISPOSITION [1]

The following is a tentative test, using the above principles, employing projection only, and aimed at measuring the following important dispositions. It has been found practicable with children of 12 years of age on up to adults. As only twelve items are given the reliabilities will not be very adequate unless the test is extended. It is desirable to give the test under some such heading as ' Judgment of Reason Test,' or ' Social Situations Test,' and to intermix the disposition items in irregular order ; for with more intelligent subjects the intention of the projection-type test is sometimes divined if it is too baldly presented.

1. Assertiveness-Submissiveness of Disposition.
2. Acquisitiveness of Disposition.
3. Gregariousness of Disposition.
4. Timidity of Disposition.
5. Curiousness of Disposition.
6. Dependency of Disposition.

SET I

Instructions.—" In each of the following statements you have to underline *one* of the alternatives given. There is often little to choose between the alternatives, but always choose that which seems to you the most common-sense motive or reason. If a person, e.g. John, is described, assume that he is of the same age as yourself unless otherwise stated.

" You will be given a very limited time for each item, so that you must underline one alternative *immediately* you have read them through. If you have not already done this when ' Next ! ' is called, you must do so instantly."

Twelve seconds is allowed for reading and underlining each item. This means that the test must be done hur-

---

[1] A recent review of the progress of projection tests and a discussion of their theory will be found in Cattell, R. B., " Projection and the Design of Projective Tests of Personality," *Char. and Personality*, xii, 1944, 177–194.

riedly. According to our preliminary experiments, the revelation of temperament is more marked when time for second thoughts is not given.

Assertive, Submissive Disposition

(Instincts of Self-assertion (Display) and Self-submission)

The numbers on the left indicate the order in which the questions should occur in the combined presentation, i.e. with the other two dispositions.

1. (1) John strained every nerve to beat the others
   because
   ⎧ he was determined to be top. 2
   ⎨ his father wished him to succeed. 1
   ⎩ he needed the scholarship. 0

4. (2) A good deal of the trouble in life arises from
   too much
   ⎧ love of pleasure. 0
   ⎨ love of power. 2
   ⎩ quarrelsomeness. 1

7. (3) At tea the admiral was the most important
   person present and John
   ⎧ tried 1
   ⎨ soon managed 2 ⎬ to go
   ⎩ was scared 0
   up and speak to him.

10. (4) The food brought by the waiter was so bad that, although everyone was looking at him,
    John said
    ⎧ " Take it back, and send the manager to me." 2
    ⎨ " I can't eat it." 0
    ⎩ " I'll have something different." 1

13. (5) A man sometimes makes witty remarks in company because he
    ⎧ feels in a playful mood. 0
    ⎨ thinks the company is dull. 1
    ⎩ wants to show off. 2

16. (6) The new-comer pushed ahead of him in the queue, but because he was a reasonable man he merely
   { gave him a contemptuous glance. 1
   said " That's hardly fair." 2
   took it quietly. 0

19. (7) When arguing with an older and more experienced person to insist that you are right when you know that you are right is
   { rather conceited. 1
   natural. 2
   rather inconsiderate. 0

22. (8) When John found that he had to walk between rows of staring people in his new carnival dress he
   { enjoyed it immensely. 2
   was rather embarrassed. 1
   felt hot all over. 0

25. (9) To try to force one's opinion on others is sometimes
   { necessary. 2
   rude. 0
   a brave action. 1

28. (10) After the Head Master corrected him for keeping the ball to himself, he ceased to speak to anyone, feeling very
   { ashamed. 0
   insulted. 2
   ' fed up.' 1

31. (11) The good business man is he who knows how to keep his assistants
   { in their proper place. 2
   with their noses to the grindstone. 1
   doing work they like. 0

34. (12) A man who doesn't like being contradicted is usually
   { very sensitive. 0
   careful what he says. 1
   obstinate. 2

Acquisitive Disposition
(Collecting Instinct)

2.   (1) One of the keenest pleasures of childhood
is in
    { fighting. 0
      collecting things. 2
      physical exercise. 1

5.   (2) Perhaps the most pleasurable feature of much
Gothic architecture is
    { richness of the decoration. 2
      human and animal forms. 1
      slender aspiring lines. 0

8.   (3) John was quite a nice lad, but he would never
allow anyone to
    { laugh at him. 0
      borrow his butterfly collection. 2
      waste his time. 1

11.   (4) People who have a little more money than
others generally have
    { worked for it. 1
      saved very carefully. 2
      no need for it. 0

14.   (5) John liked playing banker with counters because he loved
    { the luck of the game. 1
      competing with others. 0
      feeling his hoard of counters
       getting bigger. 2

17.   (6) Perhaps the greatest satisfaction in photography is in
    { snapping groups of friends. 0
      looking over the collections one
       has made. 2
      making something artistic. 1

20.   (7) Mr. Smith's desk was always full of papers because he
$$\begin{cases} \text{was naturally untidy. o} \\ \text{hated throwing anything away. 2} \\ \text{liked to look busy. 1} \end{cases}$$

23.   (8) Many a man goes on and on in business because he is at heart
$$\begin{cases} \text{uninterested in anything else. o} \\ \text{a miser. 2} \\ \text{a fighter. 1} \end{cases}$$

26.   (9) Which is the truest proverb?
$$\begin{cases} \text{A bird in the hand is worth two in the bush. 2} \\ \text{More haste less speed. o} \\ \text{A stitch in time saves nine. 1} \end{cases}$$

29.   (10) One of the greatest causes of crime is the desire to have
$$\begin{cases} \text{a good time. o} \\ \text{what belongs to someone else. 2} \\ \text{one's own way constantly. 1} \end{cases}$$

32.   (11) Although John was fond of the cinema he didn't go very often because he
$$\begin{cases} \text{had no one to go with. 1} \\ \text{hated the stuffy atmosphere. o} \\ \text{wanted to save his money. 2} \end{cases}$$

35.   (12) Nothing is quite so irritating to watch as
$$\begin{cases} \text{unnecessary waste. 2} \\ \text{work badly done. 1} \\ \text{unfair play. o} \end{cases}$$

Gregarious Disposition

3.   (1) Solitude is good
$$\begin{cases} \text{for nobody. 2} \\ \text{as a punishment. 1} \\ \text{for everybody. o} \end{cases}$$

6. (2) To say that a good film or football match is not so enjoyable if there are only a few people present is

    { only common sense. 2
    { a popular delusion. 0
    { reasonable. 1

9. (3) When Mary was ill she missed most of all

    { the company of her friends. 2
    { her long country walks. 0
    { her visits to the cinema. 1

12. (4) As the party grew noisier and jollier still John's one wish was to

    { have all his friends there. 2
    { leave at once. 0
    { find a quiet corner. 1

15. (5) We live in a busy age, but most people want to spend at least one of their free evenings a week

    { at a cinema or dance. 2
    { at a lecture. 1
    { with a book or making something. 0

18. (6) John was glad to get back to school because holidays on the farm were so

    { lonely. 2
    { smelly and muddy. 0
    { lacking in interest. 1

21. (7) A dog may be said to be more human than a cat, because it is more

    { clever. 0
    { sociable. 2
    { dependent. 1

24. (8) To hold opinions different from those of one's friends shows that at any rate one has

    { character. 2
    { thought intelligently. 1
    { originality. 0

27. (9) Boarding schools are better than day schools in this respect; that they

$$\begin{cases} \text{make one sociable. 2} \\ \text{supervise one's ' homework.' o} \\ \text{are generally in the country. 1} \end{cases}$$

30. (10) John at length went out into the next room to read because he wanted to

$$\begin{cases} \text{be quiet. o} \\ \text{show people what he had drawn. 1} \\ \text{have some cheerful company. 2} \end{cases}$$

33. (11) A person who doesn't belong to some club or circle of companions is

$$\begin{cases} \text{wasting his life. 1} \\ \text{missing recreation. 2} \\ \text{generally doing useful work} \\ \quad \text{elsewhere. o} \end{cases}$$

36. (12) The thing that hurt John more than anything else was that

$$\begin{cases} \text{they stopped his pocket money. o} \\ \text{he was called an ' outsider.' 2} \\ \text{Harry wouldn't speak to him. 1} \end{cases}$$

SET 2

Cautious or Bold Disposition

Numbers on left indicate order in combined presentation of Set 2 disposition tests.

1. (1) The leader said it was too late to climb the mountain wall, but really he was

$$\begin{cases} \text{thinking of his tired followers. o} \\ \text{nervous about it. 2} \\ \text{feeling giddy. 1} \end{cases}$$

4. (2) Intelligent people sometimes stay away from a circus because they are afraid that the wild animals will

$$\begin{cases} \text{be cruelly treated. o} \\ \text{escape into the audience. 2} \\ \text{hurt their trainers. 1} \end{cases}$$

7.   (3) John $\begin{Bmatrix} (a)\ \text{loved)} \\ (b)\ \text{hated)} \end{Bmatrix}$ to be in the midst of thunder

and lightning because it

was $\begin{cases} (c)\ \text{so difficult to find safe cover.} \\ (d)\ \text{grand.} \end{cases}$

$a + d = 0.$

$a + c = 1.$

$b + c = 2.$

10.   (4) To admire a person who will never take a risk

unnecessarily is $\begin{cases} \text{very sound. 2} \\ \text{ridiculous. 1} \\ \text{unusual. 0} \end{cases}$

13.   (5) It is wise to approach a strange dog

$\begin{cases} \text{only when you can't avoid it. 2} \\ \text{cautiously. 1} \\ \text{in a determined way. 0} \end{cases}$

16.   (6) John thought ghost stories

were $\begin{Bmatrix} (a)\ \text{thrilling} \\ (b)\ \text{silly} \end{Bmatrix}$ but he preferred

reading them $\begin{cases} (c)\ \text{to crime stories.} \\ (d)\ \text{not late at night.} \end{cases}$

$$\begin{bmatrix} a + d = 2. \\ b + d = 1. \\ c + b = 0. \end{bmatrix}$$

19.   (7) It seems true to say that the lives of most wild

animals are governed by $\begin{cases} \text{food supply. 0} \\ \text{fear. 2} \\ \text{aggression. 1} \end{cases}$

22.   (8) John preferred to travel by aeroplane because

he said it was really $\begin{cases} \text{quite safe. 1} \\ \text{most exciting. 2} \\ \text{full of interest. 0} \end{cases}$

25.   (9) To explore a strange cave or ruined building

in a very lonely spot may be adventurous,

but it is also $\begin{cases} \text{dangerous. 2} \\ \text{interesting. 0} \\ \text{instructive. 1} \end{cases}$

28.   (10) John thought he was going to die, but he managed to put away all

$$\left\{\begin{array}{l}\text{anxiety. 2}\\ \text{self pity. 0}\\ \text{thoughts of death. 1}\end{array}\right.$$

31.   (11) In many remote foreign countries it is still advisable and necessary to go about

$$\left\{\begin{array}{l}\text{with a guide. 1}\\ \text{armed. 2}\\ \text{prepared to sleep in the open. 0}\end{array}\right.$$

34.   (12) John became a very enterprising and 'go ahead' young man, though as a child he had always been rather

$$\left\{\begin{array}{l}\text{stupid. 1}\\ \text{timid. 2}\\ \text{dependent. 0}\end{array}\right.$$

37.   (13) As speed in traffic or machinery increases life is bound to become more

$$\left\{\begin{array}{l}\text{exciting. 1}\\ \text{wearisome. 0}\\ \text{dangerous. 2}\end{array}\right.$$

40.   (14) To walk past a notice that says 'Trespassers will be Prosecuted' is

$$\left\{\begin{array}{l}\text{asking for trouble. 1}\\ \text{sometimes permissible. 0}\\ \text{foolhardy. 2}\end{array}\right.$$

Inquisitive Disposition (Set 2, continued)
(Instinct of Curiosity)

2.   (1) The Head Master never punished boys for smoking their first cigarettes because, he said, they are

$$\left\{\begin{array}{l}\text{only curious to see what it is like. 2}\\ \text{sure to be sick. 0}\\ \text{only trying to be grown-up. 1}\end{array}\right.$$

5.   (2) The letters which interested the office boy most of all were those marked

$$\left\{\begin{array}{l}\text{" strictly private." 2}\\ \text{with foreign postmarks. 0}\\ \text{" twopence to pay." 1}\end{array}\right.$$

8. (3) The normal child gets most happiness in life

from his $\begin{cases} \text{eating. } 1 \\ \text{sense of wonder. } 2 \\ \text{games of make-believe. } 0 \end{cases}$

11. (4) John stayed behind to play with the steam engine because he

$\begin{cases} \text{was afraid his brother would steal it. } 1 \\ \text{didn't want to go to bed. } 0 \\ \text{wanted to find out how it worked. } 2 \end{cases}$

14. (5) Few things are more annoying in the telling of

a story than $\begin{cases} \text{not to be told the end. } 2 \\ \text{constant hesitation. } 1 \\ \text{boasting and exaggeration. } 0 \end{cases}$

17. (6) When John stayed at the farmhouse the one room that he longed to enter was the one

with $\begin{cases} \text{the locked door. } 2 \\ \text{apples stored in it. } 0 \\ \text{mice in it. } 1 \end{cases}$

20. (7) The man who reads an encyclopædia in preference to a novel is

$\begin{cases} \text{a little peculiar. } 0 \\ \text{aware of real enjoyment. } 1 \\ \text{likely to thank himself afterwards. } 2 \end{cases}$

23. (8) John saw the crowd gathering at the end of the street and he hurried thither because he

$\begin{cases} \text{thought it was a cheap-jack giving} \\ \quad \text{away presents. } 0 \\ \text{thought it was a house on fire. } 1 \\ \text{couldn't make out what it was. } 2 \end{cases}$

26. (9) It is better to be thought unsociable

than $\begin{cases} \text{over friendly. } 0 \\ \text{talkative. } 1 \\ \text{inquisitive. } 2 \end{cases}$

29. (10) John loved peering through a microscope be-

cause $\begin{cases} \text{he wanted to become a scientist. } 1 \\ \text{he wanted to know what things} \\ \quad \text{were like. } 2 \\ \text{things looked so lovely under it. } 0 \end{cases}$

32.   (11) The Brown family were not much liked in
      Littleton because they

$$\left\{\begin{array}{l}\text{refused to tell anything about them-}\\ \quad\text{selves. 2}\\ \text{kept several dogs. 0}\\ \text{came from another county. 1}\end{array}\right.$$

35.   (12) When John had an evening alone he liked

best of all to $\left\{\begin{array}{l}\text{read a mystery story. 2}\\ \text{paint pictures. 0}\\ \text{take his bicycle to pieces. 1}\end{array}\right.$

Dependent, Plaintive, Disposition (Set 2, continued)

(Instinct of Appeal)

3.   (1) To ask advice of other people instead of trying
      to do something yourself is

$$\left\{\begin{array}{l}\text{natural. 2}\\ \text{generally sensible. 1}\\ \text{generally just weakness. 0}\end{array}\right.$$

6.   (2) If a small boy waits for his big brother to go
      home with him it is usually because he

wants $\left\{\begin{array}{l}\text{someone to talk to. 1}\\ \text{his protection. 2}\\ \text{to show off his big brother. 0}\end{array}\right.$

9.   (3) John was very near tears because

$$\left\{\begin{array}{l}\text{he saw his mother going away. 2}\\ \text{he felt sorry for the dying bird. 0}\\ \text{his broken leg was so painful. 1}\end{array}\right.$$

12.   (4) Many a child likes better to go out with
      grown-up people because boys and girls

$$\left\{\begin{array}{l}\text{don't talk so interestingly. 0}\\ \text{do so much teasing and bullying. 2}\\ \text{can't help one across streets, etc. 1}\end{array}\right.$$

15.   (5) John lost his way completely in the dark and, thinking he would never get home that night, he was overcome with

$$\left\{\begin{array}{l} \text{a sense of his own stupidity. 0} \\ \text{temper. 1} \\ \text{despair. 2} \end{array}\right.$$

18.   (6) One of the most beautiful conceptions of God is that He is a person

$$\left\{\begin{array}{l} \text{to whom one can turn in trouble. 2} \\ \text{of infinite wisdom. 1} \\ \text{who created the universe. 0} \end{array}\right.$$

21. - (7) A sensible child plays $\left\{\begin{array}{ll}(a) & \text{near} \\ (b) & \text{away from}\end{array}\right\}$ home,

so that he is $\left\{\begin{array}{ll}(c) & \text{never far from help} \\ & \quad \text{if hurt.} \\ (d) & \text{able to play on his} \\ & \quad \text{own.}\end{array}\right.$

$$\begin{bmatrix} & & a + c = 2 \\ \text{In} & & b + d = 0 \\ \text{scoring} & & a + d = 1 \end{bmatrix}$$

24.   (8) When John was hurt, he always wanted to $\left\{\begin{array}{l} \text{cry. 1} \\ \text{be left alone. 0} \\ \text{run to his parents. 2} \end{array}\right.$

27.   (9) The child who brings his complaints to the teacher is really more sensible than one who $\left\{\begin{array}{l} \text{defends his rights with his fists. 2} \\ \text{cries to himself. 0} \\ \text{gives in quietly to bullies. 1} \end{array}\right.$

30.   (10) When John found himself in the desert he was pleased to see

$$\left\{\begin{array}{l} \text{a guard of British soldiers. 2} \\ \text{an oasis, with tents. 1} \\ \text{signs of the people he was tracking. 0} \end{array}\right.$$

33.   (11) To call a doctor in, even though he does nothing is $\left\{\begin{array}{l} \text{better than waiting. 0} \\ \text{reassuring. 2} \\ \text{becoming more usual. 1} \end{array}\right.$

36.   (12) The part of the play which affected John most
            uncomfortably was where a young man
    was
    ⎰ drowning miles from shore. 1
    ⎱ fighting against odds. 2
      stealing his father's money. 0

Afterwards the test may be scored for any one disposition by taking the 1st, 4th, 7th items, etc., or for each of the
three dispositions by separating out the three sets of items
after scoring. The score on each item may be 0, 1, or 2
points, and is indicated by the numbers on the right.
In some instances, though one alternative definitely
implies strong projection of a certain motive (scored
2) and one does not (scored 0), the third alternative (middle
value, scored 1) cannot be devised to be with certainty a
weaker projection of the same motive. For reasons of
uniformity these have to be overlooked: every question has
a middle value (score 1) alternative.

The decision regarding the particular alternatives which
shall score highly is not given arbitrarily by the designer
of the tests, but is worked out on an item analysis as
follows. On the basis of the original *a priori* decision as to
the alternatives to be weighed, a group of 90 persons was
divided into a high, a middle, and a low-scoring group (on
all twelve items of the disposition in question). Where
there was any doubt as to the high-scoring alternative (and
ultimately on every item) a decision was arrived at by
referring to the choice made on that item by the high and
low scorers on the test as a whole.

The self-consistency of each of these six disposition tests
is satisfactory, both with adults and children, but the
validity is poor. They will not, therefore, be standardised
until further experiment has revealed ways of increasing
their diagnostic dependability, and they are published
here in the hope that other research workers will be stimulated to inquire into the usefulness of this type of test in
many different types of situation.

E. DOMINANCE-SUBMISSION

The first test mentioned is strictly a questionnaire, but the form of its questions, which deal with specific behavioural situations, put it on a more objective footing than most questionnaires.

Allport's Ascendance-Submission Test. (*A-5 Reaction Study.*) —A series of thirty-five questions covering most of the situations in which assertiveness and submission readily show themselves, and requiring the subject to reply honestly (concerning his habitual response) by underlining one of three responses. One form for men ; one form for women. About half an hour required.

Consistency coefficient for students about ·75.[1] Thirty items seemed more significant than the others and correlated ·97 with the total test.[2] Validity on basis of ratings (college students) varies from ·29 to ·79. Those indicated as ' submissive ' by test tend to do less well in academic performance.[3]

Rosenzweig's P-F. Study. Prepared by S. Rosenzweig and obtainable from the Psychological Laboratory, Western State Psychiatric Hospital, Pittsburgh 13, Pennsylvania, U.S.A.

This is again a ' picture interpretation ' test, depending similarly upon the mechanism of projection.[4] But it concentrates on a relatively circumscribed aspect of personality, namely, the reaction to situations of frustration.

The author classifies and scores the written responses as ' extra-punitive,' i.e. blaming others, ' intro-punitive,' i.e. blaming self, and ' impunitive,' i.e. blaming no one. Logically and psycho-analytically this is a useful classification, but the empirical factor analytic evidence so far indicates clearly that extra-punitive behaviour is specific-

---

[1] G. W. Allport, " A Test for Ascendance-Submission," *J. Abn. and Soc. Psychol.*, xxiii, 1928.

[2] Wang, *J. Abn. and Soc. Psychol.*, 1931.

[3] M. E. Broom, " A Study of a Test of Ascendance-Submission," *J. Appl. Psychol.*, xiv, 1930.

[4] See Rosenzweig, S., " A Test for Types of Reaction to Frustration." In Murray, H. A., *Exploration in Personality.* Oxford Univ. Press, 1938.

ally a manifestation of the dominance syndrome and that the other two responses can be thrown together as scores at the low end of dominance. Presumably they are low dominance responses differentiated by the intrusion of an independent personality factor, perhaps G. This test, scored in the way indicated, is at any rate one of the best available tests for inclusion in an objective battery to measure the Dominance factor, E.

There is some evidence, at present more extensive than direct,[1][2] that perseveration tests, in the form described in a later section, correlate with a *second-order* personality factor, contingently labelled SS, which loads most highly dominance, will-character, and surgency. (It has been called by some experimenters ' forcefulness.' The label SS indicates that it has been found closely associated with social status.) Some popular conceptions of dominance evidently coincide with this second-order factor, though what we mean by dominance is strictly the first-order factor, E. (See p. 171.) Since the second-order factor is involved in E to the extent of about ·6, however, a disposition rigidity (perseveration) test (p. 232) should certainly be included even in a battery directed to measuring pure dominance.

[1] Cattell, R. B., "The Riddle of Perseveration—I, The Nature of Disposition Rigidity," *J. of Person.*, 1946, xiv, 1–20.
[2] Cattell, R. B., "The Riddle of Perseveration—II, Disposition Rigidity and Personality," *J. of Person.*, 1946, xiv, 21–47.

CHAPTER VI

MEASURES OF CHARACTER FACTORS AND PROBES OF EMOTIONAL ADJUSTMENT

1. The Present Organisation of Character Investigation

IN this chapter the primary personality factors C, G, I, J, and K (which may be called character factors, because they have to do with dependability, dynamic integration, and moral standards) are examined. Attention is also given to means of exploring dynamic, emotional adjustment in more specific and individual aspects than are shown in the primary personality factors, and notably with respect to those defects of personality integration known as the psychoneuroses.

Throughout this book runs the assumption that the reader is a psychologist familiar with the psychological principles and facts required for proper interpretation and use of the measurements made. Some tests, notably those of ability and attainment, can be given by teachers or psychometrists without extensive psychological training—though even here the interpretation is bound to be less enlightened and far-reaching than it might be. But in the field of temperament, character, and emotional adjustment, the measurements can have their true significance only for the fully trained psychologist, familiar alike with general psychology, psychotherapy, and those recent research advances which bear on the meaning of the concepts used. Consequently, the brief exposition of theoretical background, which is all that space permits in a book of this kind, and which suffices tolerably in respect to attainment and ability measures, must not be regarded as in itself in any degree sufficient for the full use of the measures about to be discussed in this section (or, indeed, in Chapter V).

The presentation will be divided into three parts:

1. Rating and questionnaire assessment of general character factors. 2. Objective test measures of these factors. 3. Quantitative and qualitative means of investigating specific emotional adjustments, including neurotic and abnormal traits.

2. Rating and Questionnaire Assessments of Factors

FACTOR C. EMOTIONALLY STABLE CHARACTER *v.* DEMORALISED GENERAL EMOTIONALITY

Observer's Rating on :

Realistic, practical	*v.*	Evasive, day-dreaming.
Persevering (in face of obstacles)	*v.*	Quitting.
Facing life's problems	*v.*	Subjective, seeing things distorted by one's own wishes.
Emotionally stable	*v.*	Changeable, moody.
Self-respecting	*v.*	Demoralised.
Self-controlled	*v.*	Impulsive.
Unemotional	*v.*	Emotional.
Loyal	*v.*	Fickle.
Honest	*v.*	Dishonest.
Emotionally mature	*v.*	Infantile, self-pitying.

For an estimate less correlated with other factors :

C +		C −
Realistic, practical	*v.*	Unrealistic, autistic.
Persevering	*v.*	Quitting before obstacles.
Facing life	*v.*	Evasive.
Reserved	*v.*	Intrusive.
Deliberate	*v.*	Impulsive.
	v.	Hypochondriacal.
	v.	Self-deceiving.
	v.	Nervous, ' neurotic ' behaviour.
Content	*v.*	Dissatisfied.
Phlegmatic	*v.*	Excitable.
Unemotional	*v.*	Emotional.

Questionnaire : 20 items marked C.

This is the core of emotional integration underlying 'character.' Presumably it arises from the character development of the earliest years, or from constitutional degree of emotionality. It is the most important single character factor, i.e. it contributes most to the variance of the traits list. It may be the same as the factor of General Emotionality, the importance of which, in child development, has been discussed by Burt.[1] Questionnaire measurements of this factor show that it is most important in distinguishing delinquents from non-delinquents, while Eysenck finds it as the largest general factor (reversed) in neuroticism.

FACTOR G.   POSITIVE CHARACTER INTEGRATION *v.* IMMATURE, DEPENDENT CHARACTER

Observer's Rating on :

Independent	*v.*	Emotionally dependent.
Reliable	*v.*	Undependable.
Mature	*v.*	Emotionally immature.
Persevering	*v.*	Quitting.
Painstaking	*v.*	Slipshod.
Conscientious	*v.*	Not guided by principle.
Realistic, practical	*v.*	Evasive, day-dreaming.
Balanced	*v.*	Neurotic, irritable, unpredictable.
Honest	*v.*	Dishonest.
Thoughtful	*v.*	Unreflective.

Estimate of less correlated factor from :

G +		G —
Independent	*v.*	Emotionally dependent.
Reliable	*v.*	Undependable.
Mature	*v.*	Emotionally immature.
Persevering	*v.*	Quitting.
Painstaking	*v.*	Slipshod.
Conscientious	*v.*	Not guided by principle.
Energetic	*v.*	Languid.

[1] Burt, C. L., *The Young Delinquent*, University of London Press.

G +		G −
Self-confident	v.	Self-distrustful.
Unemotional	v.	Emotional.

This may be the 'environmental mould' character integration, complementary to the constitutional C factor of emotional stability. It resembles the 'will-character' factor of Webb,[1] which, however, is probably the sum effects of C and G—indeed, many researches extract C and G as a single character factor. Pending further research, G may be considered a positive character integration due to training and the development in youth of a well-defined self-regarding sentiment and will-power. It is a narrower factor than C, affecting less of the total personality.

FACTOR I. SENSITIVE, IMAGINATIVE, ANXIOUS EMOTIONALITY v. RIGID, TOUGH POISE

Observer's Rating on :

Grateful	v.	Thankless.
Soft-hearted	v.	Hard-hearted.
Imaginative	v.	Habit-bound.
Intuitive	v.	Logical, heavily precise.
Careless of material things	v.	
Infantile	v.	Emotionally mature.
Self-pitying	v.	
Exhibitionistic	v.	Self-effacing.
Hypochondriacal	v.	
Anxiety and nervous symptoms	v.	

Somewhat less inter-factor correlation from :

I +		I −
Soft-hearted	v.	Hard-hearted.
Friendly	v.	Hostile.
Hypochondriacal	v.	
Nervous, anxious	v.	

[1] Webb, E., " Character and Intelligence," *Brit. J. Psychol. Monog.*, Supplem., **I**, No. 3, 1918.

I +		I −
Emotional	*v.*	Unemotional.
Dissatisfied	*v.*	Content.
Excitable	*v.*	Phlegmatic.
Intuitive	*v.*	Logical, precise.
Labile	*v.*	Habit-bound.

Questionnaire : 20 items marked I.

Further research can alone show whether this factor is better classified with the dynamic integration factors of the present chapter than with the temperament factors of the preceding chapter. It has obvious resemblances to one of the largest factors found in questionnaire items on " neuroticism." Actually (in its extreme loadings), it seems to resemble one particular group of neuroses only— the anxiety neuroses. Some resemblance has also been pointed out to ' femininity ' on the masculinity-femininity of, say, the Terman-Miles Interest Attitude Test. Since it is found in factor analyses of purely masculine groups also, it may be a function of the œstrogen-androgen hormone balance. The individual with high endowment in I is timid, ' jumpy,' excitable, gentle, quick. At present it would be a mistake to call this syndrome of ' nervousness ' a measure of neuroticism as such, but it may be a general associated or favourable condition. Scales for the specific neurotic syndrome groups as such are set out at the end of this chapter.

FACTOR J.   NEURASTHENIA *v.* VIGOROUS, OBSESSIONAL,
DETERMINED CHARACTER

Observer's Rating on :

Slipshod	*v.*	Painstaking.
Quitting	*v.*	Persevering.
Submissive	*v.*	Accentive.
Emotionally dependent	*v.*	Independent
Undependable	*v.*	Reliable.
Immature, irresponsible	*v.*	Emotionally mature.

Observer's Rating on :

Absent-minded	*v.*	Alert.
Languid	*v.*	Energetic, spirited.
Slow	*v.*	Quick.
Incoherent, vague	*v.*	Clear-thinking.

Less inter-correlation from assessment on :

J +		J −
Slipshod	*v.*	Painstaking.
Quitting	*v.*	Persevering.
Unreflective	*v.*	Thoughtful.
Deficient interests	*v.*	Wide interests.
	v.	Analytical.
Languid	*v.*	Energetic, spirited.
Self-distrustful	*v.*	Self-confident.
Inhibited	*v.*	
Unenquiring	*v.*	Curious.
Hypochondriacal	*v.*	
Worrying	*v.*	Placid.
Simple	*v.*	Sophisticated.
Submissive	*v.*	Assertive.

This indicates at one extreme a neurasthenic condition (see also Neurosis Questionnaire below on Neurasthenia), and at the other the type of ' obsessionally ' energetic and precise will-power which has been shown to occur frequently among successful executives (see objective test references below). Otherwise the associations of this source trait have not yet been clarified.

FACTOR K.   TRAINED, SOCIALISED, CULTURED MIND *v.* BOORISHNESS

Observers Rating on :

Thoughtful and analytically minded	*v.*	Unreflective.
Wide interests and knowledge	*v.*	Narrow interests.
Conscientious	*v.*	Not bothering.
Persevering	*v.*	Quitting.

Observer's Rating on :

Intelligent	*v.*	Stupid.
Assertive	*v.*	Submissive.
General æsthetic interests	*v.*	Lack of same.
Musical interests	*v.*	Lack of same.
Idealistic	*v.*	Cynical.
Co-operative	*v.*	Obstructive.

Less factor inter-correlation when assessed on :

K +		K −
Thoughtful	*v.*	Unreflective.
Intelligent	*v.*	Stupid.
Analytical	*v.*	
Wide interests and knowledge	*v.*	
Idealistic	*v.*	Cynical.
Co-operative	*v.*	Obstructive.
Adventurous	*v.*	Timid, withdrawn.
Optimistic	*v.*	Pessimistic.
Enthusiastic	*v.*	Apathetic.
Alert	*v.*	Absent.
Energetic, spirited	*v.*	Languid.
Introspective	*v.*	
Sensitive	*v.*	Tough.
Hurried	*v.*	Lethargic.
Sophisticated	*v.*	Simple.

Questionnaire : 20 items marked K.

This seems to be an 'environmental mould' factor, expressing the effect on the personality of good general education and background. It has indications, however, of more temperamental, constitutional sensitivity. Its central characteristic is thoughtfulness, intellectual interests, and a disciplined mind. If this is correct, the factor, like factor B, can be most economically estimated through an objective test, namely, a test of general knowledge and width of interests (see below).

FACTOR B.   GENERAL INTELLIGENCE IN PERSONALITY

Little has been said about factor B rating, because intelligence can so much better be assessed by test (see also questionnaire in appendix) ; but it should be borne in mind that many ' characterial ' personality traits are strongly loaded with B rating, i.e. an intelligence test is also, in our cultural setting, likely to predict certain character qualities, as follows :

B +		B −
Clear-thinking	v.	Confused.
Intelligent	v.	Stupid.
Clever	v.	
Independent	v.	Emotionally dependent.
Reliable	v.	Undependable.
Thoughtful	v.	Unreflective.
Analytical	v.	
Wide interests	v.	Narrow, defective interests.
Persevering	v.	Quitting.
Painstaking	v.	Slipshod.
Conscientious	v.	Unprincipled.

Questionnaire : 20 items in questionnaire are given to measuring intelligence, marked B or ' g.'

Several of the temperament and character factors described in this and the previous chapter can be assessed at the questionnaire level by means of the *Guilford* and the *Guilford-Martin* Inventories for factors S, T, D, CR, and G, A, M, I, N, respectively. (Obtainable Sheridan Supply Co., Beverly Hills, California.) These have between 100 and 300 questions, require about an hour to administer, and are standardised for student populations. The Guilford index letters are not the same as those used in these chapters, but can be translated by inspection of the factor items, or by reference to the matching set out elsewhere.[1]

[1] Cattell, R. B., *The Description and Measurement of Personality*, World Book Co., New York, 1946.

3. A Note on Rating Procedures

Much difference of opinion exists among psychologists as to the validity of rating methods. This is not surprising, for in different circumstances the accuracy of ratings varies all the way from complete uselessness to very high degrees of precision. The reader will find a discussion of research and opinions on ratings in P. E. Vernon's "The Assessment of Psychological Qualities by Verbal Methods," *Indust. Health Res. Council Rep. No. 83*, London : H.M.S.O., 1938, and in P. J. Symonds' *Diagnosing Personality and Conduct*, New York : Century, 1931.

Direct rating, i.e. that in which the judge assigns a number or letter grade directly to the subject, has several weaknesses. In the first place it is notoriously difficult to get raters to assign grades with a normal distribution. For instance, if given a five-point scale, A, B, C, D, and E, they generally tend to make the average fall at B rather than at C. Secondly, if a single subject is rated on all his personality variables at the same time, there is a tendency to get a ' halo effect.' The estimate of each individual trait is tinged with the judge's general approval or disapproval of the subject. Thirdly, if the judge is a person who stands in a particular relation to the subject, e.g. teacher, foreman, he is likely to see only one side of the subject's personality, or to see him only in one setting, and to misjudge accordingly. Under such conditions the reliability co-efficient, i.e. the correlation of ratings by different raters, may fall as low as zero and is commonly around ·5. But with the precautions described below ratings can be made extremely reliable and, indeed, more dependable than any test (where personality rather than ability is concerned). Experience has shown that the procedure of ' time sampling ' yields reliabilities comparable with those of tests. In ' time sampling ' the behaviour of the subject is not observed randomly, as in most rating procedures. Instead, the judge takes, say, half a dozen five-minute intervals in the subject's day, and records during each of those intervals actual behaviour expressive of the trait or traits which he is concerned to rate. All subjects are observed for the same time and under comparable conditions. Agreement between judges or between two sets of observations by the same judge then reaches ·8 or ·9.

Providing the following conditions are observed, rating can be employed as a thoroughly dependable procedure.

1. Define the behaviour manifestations of the trait precisely and in common for all judges. Do not depend on each judge's dictionary interpretation of what the trait means.

2. Do not use judges standing in some strong emotional relationship to the subjects, e.g. parents, probation officers, teachers, subordinates. The best ratings are by the subject's peers, e.g. schoolchildren by schoolchildren.

3. How many judges. The ideal situation is that in which every member of a group—a group not too large for everyone to know everyone—rates every other member, the ratings being averaged. Between two halves of a fraternity group of 40 members the present writer has commonly obtained reliabilities around ·9 on well-defined personality traits.

4. Whenever possible, ask for rankings rather than ratings. Placing individuals in rank order from highest to lowest enforces more definite paired comparisons than in ratings. Ranks may then be converted to ratings on the assumption of a normal distribution—e.g. a group of 32 people may be put on five-point ratings by cutting the rank order in the following sections : 2, 8, 12, 8, 2.

Naturally, there are many situations in applied psychology where reliable rating is definitely precluded by the conditions ; but the lack of validity of rating in industry, etc., must not blind psychologists to the fact that in research work and under controlled conditions the assessment of personality factors by ratings of behaviour yields very valuable, valid measures not obtainable as yet through objective tests.

The above rating scales are for factors established for adolescents and adults. Most of them have appeared with little modification among children ; but as yet we have insufficient confirmation of the patterns among very young children. A useful practical scale with no assumptions about overall syndrome pattern, for use with children, is that of Bridges.

Bridges' Rating Scale for the Social and Emotional Development in Pre-school children—to be found on p. 232 of *Social and Emotional Development of Pre-School Child*, by K. B. Bridges, 1929.—It has fifty rating items, twenty-two on social development, thirteen on personal development, fifteen on emotional development, and there are complete norms for boys and girls from 2 to 5 years. Choice of rating items, for inclusion in these categories, was not decided by a correlation method, but by observation of the traits which develop in close relationship to general maturity and adjustment in children over that age range. Based on a sound observational technique, the correlation of the total character score with Stanford Binet I.Q. varies between ·2 and ·5.

A good deal has been written about the use of the interview in rating personality traits. For lack of any succinct set of conclusions the reader has to be referred to the literature.[1] No agreed technique for increasing the validity of estimates has been worked out ; though if the interviewer starts off with clear ideas of the traits he wants to assess, the reliabilities are better than if he recalls an unstructured interview. Certain forms useful for recording interviews are published, notably that of Tjaden.

Tjaden's Analytical Interview.—A basis for a rating scale, but also for personal history, etc. 34 pages. Mainly for clinical purposes. Comprehensive and too long for many

---

[1] Bingham, W. V., and Moore, B. V., *How to Interview*, Harper & Brothers, 1931. Oldfield, R. C., *The Psychology of the Interview*, Methuen & Co., Ltd., London, 1941

uses, unless restricted according to interviewer's needs. Obtainable from Messrs. Stoelting.

4. Objective Tests of Character Factors

Considerable attention has naturally been given to developing character tests, but since past research has commonly been directed to specific traits such as honesty, or to some composite of constitutional emotional stability and acquired character integration, it is still impossible to offer clear-cut measures of individual factors in this field.

The work of Brogden,[1] which is supported by some less direct researches, indicates a definite unitary factor in objective tests, appearing with the following loadings. There is some indication that this corresponds to the obverse of the constitutional emotional instability factor C rather than to the general character integration factor G.

Resisting suggestion in picture interpretation	·53
Conscientious following of details of test construction	·37
Perseveration test	— ·46
Accuracy in a test of sorting cards .	2
Tendency to stick to a choice when made	2
Persistence on dynamometer or on an insoluble maze	2

A second ' character ' factor is found in objective tests, which *may be* the second factor (G) found in ratings.

Not cheating on co-ordination test .	·63
Not making false book-list statements .	·55
Questionable preferences among fictitious characters	·34

The tests now to be described, abstracted from the above, may therefore be regarded as *measures of factors*

[1] Brogden, H. E., " A Factor Analysis of Forty Character Tests," *Psychol. Monog.* *52*, No. 3, 39–56, 1940.
[2] The loadings for these are lower, but are not set out, because they belong to researches not comparable in population variance to Brogden's.

C and G in some degree of combination, i.e. of the cluster or surface trait labelled ' Sector AA ; Fineness of Character versus Moral Defect, Non-Persistence ' in the list of observed personality clusters.[1]

The factors of general character integration and stability have considerable diagnostic importance, of course, for psychiatric as well as personnel work and guidance. The sub-average scores represent various degrees of that personality disintegration which is re-cognised in neurosis and psychosis, i.e. these factors have bearing on the measurement of the extent of neurosis.

In the measurement of the general ability factor ' g ' (labelled B in its total personality content) one aims, especially with adults of very varied background and training, either to use a culture-free test employing bed-rock, common data or else to throw together a variety of tests, all high in ' g ' saturation, but sampling many different interest investments of ability. Similarly, for a successful measurement of the general character factors it is desirable to take tests of proven saturation but otherwise diverse. For a thorough measurement of the Character Stability *v.* Neuroticism factors (C and G), a battery of the following five varieties of measurement is suggested:

1. Situational tests of persistence and morality.
2. The Cursive Miniature Situation Test.
3. The Fluctuation of Attitudes Test.
4. Perseveration Tests.
5. Tests of Primary Suggestibility (Eysenck, Hull).

1. *Situational Tests.* A number of ingenious tests have been developed, especially in America, in which the subject is placed in a situation wherein his honesty, adher-ence to accepted rules, persistence, etc., can be directly measured. Brief description of a representative sample of these is as follows :

---

[1] " The Principal Trait Clusters for Describing Personality," R. B. Cattell. *Psych. Bull.,* 1945, xlii, 129–161.

Cady's Measure of ' Incorrigibility.'—(1) Dotting circles or tracing mazes with the eyes shut. Temptation and opportunity to ' peep.'

(2) Willingness to cheat in scoring one's own intelligence test by writing in correct responses from key.

(3) Overstatement, as in Raubenheimer (1) and (2) below.

(4) Moral judgment. As (7) on opposite page.

The consistency of these tests (with 150 12–14-year-old boys) was, respectively, ·74, ·58, ·58, ·38. Total, ·75. The agreement with ratings—in a group showing a very wide scatter (delinquent to highly reliable)—was respectively ·40, ·19, ·41, ·20–·31.

For details see V. S. Cady, " The Estimation of Juvenile Incorrigibility," *J. of Delinquency*, Monograph No. 2 (Whittier, Calif.), 1923.

Voelker's Trustworthiness Test.—Ten tests of trustworthiness. Not all can be given to groups. Consistency of whole test, ·75. Agreement with trustworthiness ratings, ·60.

(1) Willingness to accept undeserved credit (overstatement test).

(2) Suggestibility (two tests from Downey Test).

(3) Tending to accept help in problems after promising to work alone.

(4) Conscientiousness in returning borrowed property.

(5) Dishonesty in accepting overchange.

(6) Willingness to accept a tip for a trifling courtesy.

(7) Trustworthiness in performing a routine task under temptation to neglect it. Also test (7) in new circumstances, and tests (1) and (2) of Cady above.

For details see P. F. Voelker, *The Functions of Ideals and Attitudes in Social Education*, Teachers' College Bureau of Publications, N.Y., 1921.

Raubenheimer's Tests.—An improvement on the original tests of Voelker, Cady, Knight, and others, from which they are derived.

(1) *Overstatement A.* (After Franzen.)—Fifty book titles, twenty of which are fictitious. " We want to see who has

read the most books." Score on number of fictitious titles underlined.

(2) *Overstatement B.* (After Voelker.)—Part I, a statement of knowledge, e.g. " Do you know how to find the square root of decimals ? " Very well, fairly well, not at all. Part II, a test of actual information on these matters. Score is per cent. of over- or under-statement.

(3) *Questionable Reading Preferences.*—A variety of book titles, e.g. " The Boy Inventor," " Roy Black," " The Master Thief," to be arranged according to reading preference. Score sum of squares of deviations from ' correct ' order (desirable according to ethical standards).

(4) *Questionable Character Preferences.*—Eight boys described briefly, e.g. " Ray Stevens is at a school now, but he is anxious to get out. He wants to become a taxi-driver. Ray says that taxi-drivers have an easy time," etc. Asked to place them in order of desirability as chums. Score as for (3).

(5) *Social Attitudes.*—Underlining attitudes to each of twenty-four things or ideas, e.g.

> *chums.*—It is hard to go without them.
> You cannot always trust them.
> They sometimes squeal on you.
> It is best to have them in your gang.

Score equals number of questionable statements.

(6) *Activity Preferences*, e.g. Go camping with the Boy Scouts. Go around seeing the country, getting lifts as you go. Quit school and go with the circus.

(7) *Rating the Seriousness of Offences*, e.g. Sam set fire to the public school which he attended. Ted played hookey to go to a circus. Joe entered the house of the people next door and took $2.50.

Situational Tests of Persistence or Accuracy.—The factor analyses of Brogden, Eysenck, the present writer and others show that simple tests of persistence, e.g. time holding the leg out straight when sitting on a chair, or accuracy (e.g. sorting, cancelling), correlate about ·5 with the character stability *v.* neuroticism factor.

2. *The Cursive Miniature Situation or C.M.S. Test.* In this test the subject sets out to make a high score by marking certain lines on a moving strip of paper, one inch wide, passing a small square window in a box. The continuous onslaught of problem situations simulates everyday life in demanding sound decisions, patience, resource, foresight, and self-control. The strip may be run at a normal or a fast speed, but some degree of speeding is always involved, for it is part of the design to bring out basic reactions of the subject under conditions of speed.

The full test consists of an instruction strip and eight equivalent strips (equivalent in difficulty and in having decisions, surprises, etc., forced upon the subject at equivalent points). Each strip requires two minutes and the whole test therefore about twenty minutes. However, since the test has a reliability [1] co-efficient of ·92, and since any one strip correlates with the total of eight from ·80 to ·96, it has been found practicable to cut the test down to two or three strips in most situations. This reduction is a considerable gain because the test has to be given as an individual test and because the marking of the responses on the strip takes more time than actually running the test. The correlation with age, I.Q., and education are negligible (below ·20).

The validation of the test has been as follows : The score on the test is expressible (*a*) as a total score for the whole strip or strips, (*b*) as a series of analytical scores on decision items, foresight items, resource items, etc.

The total score differentiates psychotics from normals with a critical ratio of difference between 8 and 10, so that there is negligible overlap between the groups. The score on *breaking rules* items (crossing slanting lines) differentiates controls from delinquents with a critical ratio of 7·4. Score on *decision items* correlates about ·4 separately with conscientiousness, foresight, and obsessional character, and therefore above ·4 with our char-

---

[1] Cattell, R. B., " An Objective Test of Character Temperament—I," *J. of Gen. Psychol.*, 1941, xxv, 59–73.

acter factor J (neurasthenia *v.* vigorous obsessional character). Certain combinations [1] of responses have been discovered, which predict (1) the rated Character Factor (C and G), (2) Cautiousness, (3) Timidity, and (4) Leadership by correlations respectively of ·6, ·9, and ·8.

Printed strips for the C.M.S. test may be obtained from the author or from the University of London Press. The apparatus itself requires an electric phonograph motor geared down to pull the strip from spool to spool over a polished channel-piece immediately behind the window in the lid of the box. Experiments are being carried out at the University of Illinois to adapt the test to a booklet form, so that apparatus will be unnecessary and that it may be given as a group test.

3. *The Fluctuation of Attitude Test.* Recent research [2] has shown that a comparatively easily obtainable measure of ' fluctuation of attitudes ' provides one of the most valid measures of character stability. Fortunately, practically any attitude test can be used and the time interval between testing and retesting can be from a few hours up to a month or more. (Of course, for any given set of norms for fluctuation the interval must be the same, for the amount, but not the kind, of change becomes greater the longer the interval.) Fluctuation on attitudes connected with deeper sentiments gives better measurements than on attitudes of a more trivial kind.

The practical set-up, therefore, is to take an attitude test of not fewer than fifty items touching basic sentiments, each being susceptible of at least five graded answers, as in the following example :

It is ⎰ the first duty / one duty / a reasonable requirement / not a solemn duty / by no means a duty ⎱ of every man to defend his country.

---

[1] See Cattell, R. B., " An Objective Test of Character Temperament—II," *J. Soc Psychol.*, 1944, xix, 99–114.

[2] Cattell, R. B., " Fluctuation of Sentiments and Attitudes as a Measure of Character Integration and of Temperament," *Amer. J. Psychol.*, lvi, 1943, 195–216.

One administers the test to the subjects as an attitude test, and after, say, 24 hours unexpectedly re-administers the test, asking the subject to answer it as before. On each item the subject can be scored from 0 to 4 points of change, depending on the extent of his fluctuation from his original marking. A total fluctuation score is computed by adding that for all items.

The fluctuation score correlates as follows :

With a cluster of traits (persistence, dependability, perseverance) constituting the general character factor, ·46 (adult) to ·71 (children); with ' Emotionality,' ·30. One study finds a negligible correlation among children for C qualities, but in others, corrected for attenuation, it has reached ·98.

From these findings (notably the correlation with emotionality) it seems likely that the fluctuation score, if it is found to relate itself directly to a single factor, will be found a better measure of the C than the G character factor, i.e. with the factor responsible for most character trait variance.

4. *Perseveration Tests.* Numerous researches [1] have now shown the existence of a general factor of ' perseveration ' or ' disposition rigidity ' and, further, of a relation between perseveration score and various *character* ratings and measures. Most show negative correlations of ·4 to ·5, as in the above factor of Brogden, and some show in addition a tendency for very low and very high perseverators to be defective in character (i.e. the existence of a curvilinear relation).

Such a relationship is found both among people all of relatively good character and among groups containing chronically delinquent and problem children. Very high perseverators are, on the whole, worse than very low perseverators, the relationship of perseveration (' p ') and character ' w ' being as shown below.[2]

---

[1] A complete review of the evidence about the disposition rigidity factor and its relation to personality will be found up to date to 1945 in *The Description and Measurement of Personality*, World Book Co., 1946.

[2] This non-linear relationship actually gives a linear correlation of about − ·3 between ' p ' and ' w.'

Beyond this one steps into regions of unconfirmed researches, and this is particularly true with regard to the differences which distinguish the character weaknesses of high perseverators from those of low. Though character abnormality is associated with extreme ' p ' scores, extreme ' p ' scores are not invariably associated with poor character, and occasionally very low perseverators are pointed out as being of outstanding dependable character. Stephenson[1] and Pinard[2] found extremely low ' p ' scores among ' maniac ' and ' hysteric ' patients in a mental hospital, and extremely high ' p ' scores among melancholiacs and dementia præcox cases (and to some extent with those unduly sensitive, suspicious, paranoid, or obsessional). These tests, therefore, have diagnostic value in determining the nature of such extreme forms of personality disintegration. Stephenson[3] has further shown that among high p-præcox cases the ' p ' score becomes higher with decreasing accessibility and lower in the rarer instances of recovery, thereby acting as a kind of thermometer of præcox condition.

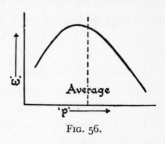

FIG. 56.

The most acceptable theory at the moment about the ultimate nature of disposition rigidity (' p ' measure) is that it represents a second order personality factor SS which[4] loads especially the character factors C and G. The correlation of the test with these first-order factors, therefore, cannot be expected to be raised much by test improvement.

The differences which distinguish the character of

[1] W. Stephenson, " Studies in Experimental Psychiatry—Some Contact of p-factor with Psychiatry," J. Mental Sci., lxviii, 1932.

[2] J. W. Pinard, " Tests of Perseveration—II, Their Relation to Certain Psychopathic Conditions and to Introversion," Brit. J. Psychol., xxiii, 1932.

[3] W. Stephenson, " Studies in Experimental Psychiatry—III, p-score and Inhibition for High p-Præcox Cases," J. Mental Sci., lxxviii, 1932.

[4] A review of the evidence on the psychological and general personality correlates of perseveration will be found in Cattell, R. B., " The Riddle of Perseveration—I and II," J. of Person., 1946-7.

abnormalities of high perseverators from those of low are set out below.   These are derived from three independent researches [1] on normal children and adults, in addition to Stephenson's work with psychotics described above.

The aim of ' p ' tests, therefore, is not merely to measure the level of ' w ' (or C as we would now call the general character factor), but also to indicate the *type* of character integration.

In the present state of our knowledge—which indicates a large part of the variance in disposition rigidity to be due to heredity—' p ' measures must in part be regarded as indicators of temperamental *proneness* to types of integration and adjustment.

CHARACTERISTICS OF [2]

Low Perseverators	*High Perseverators*
Prone to action in dissatisfaction. Masterful ; active.	Resigned, but often seeking expression in tortuous ways—hence sometimes deceitful, cruel, spiteful, unpredictable.
Insistently assertive. High tension. Hence nagging, restless, fussy.	Quiet, slow, more emotional and ' deep ' in general.
Enterprising, self-reliant. Sometimes naïvely individualistic. Tend to be natural leaders.	More sceptical and pessimistic. Conservative in habits.
Not affected by emotional scenes. Inconsiderate, tough.	Sensitive.
Irritable, selfish, silent, and anxious.[3]	Rebellious in outlook, serious, shy and solitary.[3]
Tends to be interested in mechanical, scientific, and mathematical matters.	Tends to be interested in history, languages, and humanities.

---

[1] R. B. Cattell, " Temperament Tests—II," *Brit. J. Psychol.*, xxiv, 1933 ; also " Perseveration and Personality—Some Experiments and an Hypothesis," *J. Mental Sci.*, lxxx, 1935 ; J. W. Pinard, " Tests of Perseveration—I, Their Relation to Character," *Brit. J. Psychol.*, xxiii, 1932.

[2] A review of the evidence on the psychological and general personality correlates of perseveration will be found in Cattell, R. B., " The Riddle of Perseveration—I and II," *J. of Person.*, 1946–7.

[3] This distinction from J. W. Pinard's work in " Tests of Perseveration—I, Their Relation to Certain Psychopathic Conditions and to Introversion," *Brit. J. Psychol.*, xxiii, 1932 ; the others from sources given above.

Low Perseverators	*High Perseverators*
Decisive and impetuous. Ability to grasp situations whole. Good taste and definite style in dress, voice, music, etc.	Absent-minded. Impressed by one thing at a time. Drifting to decisions. Dreamy. Sentimental. Careless of detail. Slovenly in dress.
Dreams very little.	Greater tendency to dreaming (in sleep).
Liable to short periods of acute restlessness and crises of intense emotional dissatisfaction.	Liable to long periods of depression or gentle melancholy.
More interested in scientific, business, and practical matters.	More interested in religious, historical, and language subjects. Neurotic symptoms of a general nature more prevalent.
Makes good use of relatively low I.Q. (In social status, responsibility of occupation, etc.)	Fails to make good use of intelligence in any ordinary sense.
In general character is defective because of 'immaturity' *naïveté* and lack of adequate inhibition.	In general character is defective because of excessive deep inhibition with general discouragement and lack of integrated driving power.

To get the most from ' p ' tests it is necessary at present to be familiar with research trends. In the first place one must give due regard to the above hereditary influence—shown by the greater similarity of identical twins, the correlations of ·3–·4 between siblings and the indications of racial differences—the darker Mediterranean and Jewish groups being higher in perseveration than typical Nordics and Anglo-Saxons.[1] Hence perseveration must be to some extent interpreted relative to the average for the racial type.

On the other hand, some part of ' p ' score must be regarded as indicative of a temporary state rather than a permanent element of personality. Such variation probably accounts for some of the apparent low consistency of ' p ' tests. The present writer finds that delinquent chil-

[1] R. B. Cattell, "The Riddle of Perseveration—II, Disposition Rigidity and Personality," *J. of Person.*, 1946, xiv, 21–47.

dren having very high ' p ' scores when first referred come to have moderately low 'p' scores after successful emotional adjustment has been brought about. ' p '-score, more-over, increases in states of illness and fatigue.[1]

High perseveration is also associated with the following history : (1) frequency of illness and delicacy in early childhood ; (2) being spoilt or brought up very laxly ; (3) being the youngest child of a family ; (4) being brought up in poorer families.[2]

Perseveration, as measured by sensori-motor tests—the ' p ' factor—is not necessarily connected with all forms of observed and introspected psychiatric ' perseveration ' (e.g. of ideas, melodies, intentions, feelings). Most forms of perseveration, persistence of sensations, melodies, moods, and all forms of absent-mindedness are connected with high ' p ' score, but all ' perseverations ' associated with intention, e.g. inability to drop a conversation or turn to new tasks, seem to be associated with high ' w ' and with moderate ' p ' (see p. 229 and footnote 2), rather than with high ' p ' score, whilst other perseveration (e.g. echolalia in imbeciles) is a matter of low ' g.'

Technique of Testing.—Because of the fatigue effect mentioned above, it is desirable to test subjects always at about the same time of day. The norms below are for the late morning session (say 10.30–1 p.m.). The main problem in designing ' p ' tests has been to eliminate correlations with intelligence (dull persons tending to high perseveration when their perseveration was in fact normal) and with speed. The following tests [1] and their manner of scoring eliminate these correlations almost completely.

It has been pointed out [1] by the writer that most perseveration tests in use employ one of two distinct notions of perseveration, as follows : (1) in what may be called ' creative effort ' tests the measurement concerns the ability to reassemble elements of an old habit in a new

[1] R. B. Cattell, " On the Measurement of Perseveration," *Brit. J. Educ. Psychol.*, v, 1, 1935.
[2] R. B. Cattell, " Perseveration and Personality," *op. cit.*

way, i.e. to modify the natural rigidity of mental dispositions ; (2) in what may be called ' alternation ' tests the
measurement is of ' mental inertia,' i.e. of ability to
switch over rapidly mental processes actually operating
and having, as it were, ' momentum.'

Walker, Staines, and Kenna [1] have followed up this
distinction experimentally and shown very clearly that
the general factor of perseveration really resides in disposition rigidity rather than in mental inertia. Consequently the earlier batteries of perseveration tests, due
to Stephenson and the present writer, which were mixtures
of creative effort and alternation tests, have been omitted
from the present edition of this book. The improved
tests now given unfortunately still lack norms. If it is
essential to employ a test with norms, the reader is advised
to return to the first edition of this book. Although the
tests there presented are diluted by what we now know
to be ineffective items, there are sufficient creative effort
tests to give a measure of moderate reliability.

Procedure.—In the following tests the score is obtained
by dividing the old, unimpeded activity speed, X, by the
speed on the novel, adapted performance, Y. Owing to
the brevity of the sub-tests—they are rarely a fourth as
long as an intelligence test sub-test—the constituent parts
of a ' p ' battery rarely correlate mutually more than
·3 or ·4. The rather ' exasperating ' character of the
test—a necessary aspect of its personality testing—precludes making the test longer. In general, ' p ' testing
requires considerably more skill and precision in the
psychometrist than does intelligence testing, and it is not
unusual to find poor validities when they are administered
by individuals lacking psychometric experience. It is
necessary to insist that the subjects work to the limit of
their will-power, at top speed.

The subjects should be perfectly clear regarding what
they have to do before the test starts. Understanding is

[1] K. Walker, R. Staines, and J. Kenna, *Character and Personality*, xii, 32-45, 1943.
See also B. Notcutt, " Perseveration and Fluency," *Brit. J. Psychol.*, xxxiii, 200-208,
1943.

not part of the test performance, as in many psychological tests, and some slight rehearsal is frequently advantageous. The important thing is that the subject should know exactly what to do before he starts, so that he may respond correctly to instructions at speed without failure. For this reason the ' lay-out ' of the test booklet should include some ' reminders ' at the various starting-points, as follows :

Adult Tests of ' p ' or Disposition Rigidity

The following sets out the test forms : the examiner's instructions follow.

Sub-test I

1. Write : *ready ready*

_____

_____

_____

_____

_____

_____

_____

_____

2. Write backwards : [*ready* ⟵ BEGIN HERE]

_____

_____

_____

_____

Sub-test 2
  1. Write : *The sky is deep blue*

_____

_____

_____

_____

_____

_____

_____

  2. Write : THE SKY IS DEEP BLUE

_____

_____

_____

_____

  3. Write : THE sKy Is DeEp BlUe

_____

_____

_____

4. Write :

Iththee sskkyy iiss ddeeeepp bbllnnee

_____

_____

_____

_____

_____

_____

Sub-test 3

1. Begin reading here :

It will be many years before Dr. Crippen, whose trial was the great criminal sensation of 1910, will be forgotten. His crime was remarkable in many ways. It seemed incredible that the little insignificant man should have been capable of such an unusually callous, calculated, and cold-blooded murder. It is not very surprising to find him using hyoscine, a poison new to the annals of crime, for he was a medical man. But the systematic mutilation of the body rendered the crime particularly beastly, and it is a curious circumstance that both Crippen and Mahon managed to dispose of the main organs, though one organ, the head, is particularly difficult to destroy. The method of mutilation and destruction shows that Crippen was skilful, but that Mahon was a miscalculator. Unlike the medical man, the latter had no conception of the magnitude of his task.

The most surprising feature of Crippen's case is that but for his senseless flight the crime might never have come to light, and it would have been told of some other criminal that in his case for the first time wireless telegraphy was employed in the apprehension of a fugitive.

The telegraph was first used to secure the apprehension of a criminal when a man named Tawell, who had committed a murder near Slough, succeeded in boarding a train for Paddington. Before the telegraph system had been installed he would have vanished in the crowd, but unknown to him the police at Slough were able to telegraph his description to Paddington, and on the train's arrival he was arrested. Thus the invention of railways, which facilitated the criminal's escape, was countered by the telegraph, which outstripped him in his flight. The submarine cable was first used in 1864 to capture a murderer named Franz Muller, who had shipped on a steamer bound for America before his guilt was discovered. As in Crippen's case, the police were able, by taking a fast liner, to outsail the vessel he was on and to meet and arrest him on his arrival. It may also be remembered that a year or two ago a man, who was afterwards acquitted, was arrested at Croydon aerodrome just as he was on the point of leaving England by aeroplane. Bevan got away by aeroplane and eluded capture for months until he was run to earth at Vienna.

My own part in the proceedings had nothing to do with Crippen. I was retained to defend his unfortunate companion, Ethel Le Neve, who was charged with complicity in his crime. In order to give a clear idea of her trial and of her acquittal it is, however, necessary to tell the story of Crippen's crime.

It was the outcome of the old familiar matrimonial tragedy.

The little man was nearly fifty. He had qualified in medicine in the States, and in 1900 had come to London to assist a firm of patent medicine vendors. During the ten years that followed he made the round of the patent medicine firms, one of which, the Drouet Institute, had in their employment a young girl, Ethel Le Neve, as a typist. She was under Crippen's orders, and their association continued even when they were not in the same employment.

Crippen was a married man living with his second wife, whom he had married in America. She was half German, half Pole, whose maiden name was Kunegunda Matamotski, though she preferred to be known as Cora Turner at the time of her marriage, and afterwards called herself Belle Elmore.

Answer the following questions based on the passage you have just read :

(1) Which of the criminals was a medical man ?
         Crippen.
         Mahon.

(2) The telegraph was first employed to catch a criminal at : Paddington.
    Dublin.

(3) How old was Crippen ?   _____

2. Start at the bottom of the page.

                          .cebeuQ rof esortnoM
.s.s eht ni delias yeht hto2 eht nO   .nos dna rehtaf
sa gnissap ,nosniboR fo eman eht rednu prewtnA dna
madrettoR ot enog ,tcaf ni ,dah yehT .wonk ton did
eh erehw tub ,yawa enog dah dna yob a sa eveN eL ssiM
desiugsid dah neppirC ,yluJ ht9 no taht wenk weD
            .srepapswen eht dellif noitasnes taerg a
dna detalucric saw noitpircsed riehT ? sevitiguf eht erew
erehW : noitseuq eht emac neht dna ,ht61 eht no deussi
saw hcihw ,tnarraw a rof esac a deraperp ecno ta eH
             .rallec eht fo roolf kcirb eht rednu
deirub eromlE elbaresim eht fo sniamer eht eb ot devorp
tahw derevocsid neht dna ,dehcraes eh syad owt roF
,detsered ti dnuof dna ,esuoh eht ot tnew He .denekawa
-er snoicipsus siH .nwolf drib eht dnuof dna yriuqne
gnilfirt a ekam ot eciffo eht ot tnew weD ,yluJ ht11 nO
                            ↑

                        BEGIN HERE.

Answer the following question based on the passage just read.

(1) Where did Crippen say his wife had gone ? _____

Sub-test 4

Present two mazes, (*a*) and (*b*).
(See pages 240 and 241.)

Sub-test 5

1. Write your *own* name, e.g.   *John Smith*

_____

_____

_____

_____

_____

_____

_____

2. Write your *own* name backwards, e.g.

[*John Smith* ← BEGIN HERE]

_____

_____

_____

_____

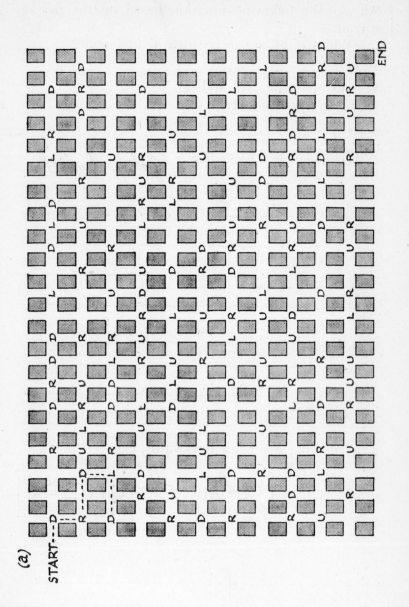

(a)

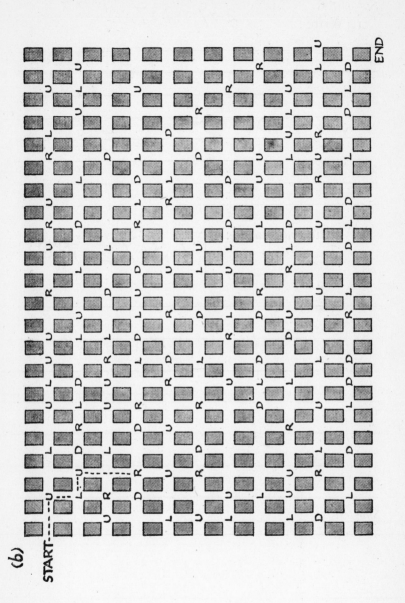

(b)

Sub-test 6

1. Write : *237   237*

---

2. Write backwards : [2 3 7 ← BEGIN HERE]

Sub-test 7

1. Samples : $2 \times 2 \times 5 = 20$
$3 \times 1 \times 4 = 12$

$3 \times 2 \times 2 =$	$4 \times 1 \times 2 =$	$2 \times 2 \times 2 =$
$2 \times 1 \times 4 =$	$1 \times 3 \times 5 =$	$3 \times 4 \times 3 =$
$2 \times 2 \times 1 =$	$5 \times 2 \times 3 =$	$4 \times 5 \times 5 =$
$7 \times 1 \times 2 =$	$4 \times 4 \times 1 =$	$2 \times 2 \times 1 =$
$5 \times 3 \times 2 =$	$3 \times 5 \times 2 =$	$1 \times 3 \times 3 =$
$4 \times 1 \times 1 =$	$6 \times 3 \times 2 =$	$1 \times 2 \times 3 =$
$2 \times 3 \times 2 =$	$2 \times 3 \times 5 =$	$1 \times 4 \times 1 =$
$3 \times 6 \times 2 =$	$1 \times 6 \times 3 =$	$2 \times 3 \times 1 =$

Sub-test 7—contd.

$6 \times 1 \times 2 =$	$1 \times 2 \times 7 =$	$2 \times 3 \times 2 =$
$2 \times 2 \times 3 =$	$2 \times 1 \times 2 =$	$3 \times 2 \times 1 =$
$5 \times 4 \times 1 =$	$5 \times 2 \times 1 =$	$2 \times 7 \times 2 =$
$2 \times 4 \times 1 =$	$3 \times 2 \times 2 =$	$3 \times 4 \times 2 =$
$1 \times 3 \times 3 =$	$1 \times 4 \times 3 =$	$3 \times 2 \times 5 =$
$2 \times 3 \times 2 =$	$1 \times 1 \times 7 =$	$4 \times 3 \times 3 =$
$2 \times 6 \times 1 =$	$4 \times 3 \times 2 =$	$3 \times 1 \times 6 =$
$3 \times 3 \times 1 =$	$2 \times 4 \times 1 =$	$3 \times 2 \times 1 =$
$4 \times 1 \times 4 =$	$5 \times 3 \times 2 =$	$4 \times 1 \times 2 =$
$1 \times 5 \times 1 =$	$4 \times 4 \times 2 =$	$6 \times 2 \times 6 =$

2. Example :

$2 \times 3 = 7$	$3 \times 2 = 7$	$3 \times 1 \times 2 = 7$
$1 \times 4 = 3$	$4 \times 1 = 3$	$4 \times 1 \times 1 = 3$

Samples :

$2 \times 3 \times 4 = 28$
$1 \times 4 \times 2 = 6$

$2 \times 3 \times 1 =$	$2 \times 3 \times 3 =$	$5 \times 4 \times 1 =$
$3 \times 2 \times 2 =$	$2 \times 3 \times 5 =$	$3 \times 5 \times 2 =$
$1 \times 4 \times 1 =$	$4 \times 3 \times 2 =$	$2 \times 3 \times 2 =$
$1 \times 3 \times 3 =$	$1 \times 4 \times 2 =$	$3 \times 3 \times 2 =$
$1 \times 4 \times 3 =$	$3 \times 4 \times 2 =$	$5 \times 1 \times 4 =$
$4 \times 1 \times 2 =$	$2 \times 3 \times 6 =$	$1 \times 2 \times 7 =$
$5 \times 1 \times 4 =$	$2 \times 4 \times 1 =$	$2 \times 6 \times 1 =$
$2 \times 2 \times 3 =$	$4 \times 1 \times 4 =$	$3 \times 2 \times 6 =$
$2 \times 3 \times 7 =$	$2 \times 3 \times 7 =$	$3 \times 2 \times 1 =$
$4 \times 1 \times 4 =$	$5 \times 3 \times 2 =$	$4 \times 1 \times 2 =$
$3 \times 3 \times 1 =$	$2 \times 6 \times 3 =$	$1 \times 4 \times 2 =$

3. Samples :

$E \times C = 12$
$A \times C = 6$

$A \times C =$	$3 \times C \times A =$	$5 \times A \times C =$
$C \times E =$	$2 \times E \times C =$	$A \times E \times C =$
$A \times E \times 2 =$	$E \times 3 \times A =$	$A \times 7 \times E =$
$C \times A \times E =$	$A \times E \times 3 =$	$E \times A \times 2 =$
$C \times E \times 3 =$	$C \times A \times 4 =$	$6 \times E \times C =$
$4 \times A \times C =$	$E \times A \times 5 =$	$C \times 4 \times E =$
$C \times E \times 1 =$	$2 \times A \times C =$	$A \times 5 \times 1 =$
$1 \times C \times A =$	$E \times C \times A =$	$A \times C \times 7 =$
$5 \times A \times C =$	$A \times E \times 1 =$	$4 \times C \times 2 =$
$E \times A \times 6 =$	$6 \times C \times E =$	$2 \times E \times C =$

The whole battery takes 20 minutes (not including instructions). It is designed to be split if necessary into two sections : 1, 2, 3, and 4 on the one hand (12 minutes), and 5, 6, and 7 on the other (7 minutes).

Instructions for administration are as follows:

Write your name on the cover where indicated.

These are tests of speed and, therefore, it is necessary for you to work just as fast as you can throughout the entire test. They are in no sense tests of intelligence, only tests of speed. When I say " *Go*," you are to begin at once without wasting any time. When I say " *Stop*," you are to put your pencil down at once regardless of where you are in the test.

Sub-test 1

Open your booklet to test 1. This test depends on your speed of writing. You are to write the word ' ready,' (spell out) r-e-a-d-y, as many times as you can before I tell you to stop. You will have one minute. When I say " *Go*," start at 1 and go on writing the word ' ready ' after the two samples that have already been written in. Keep your writing clear and controlled. Remember, write as fast as you can.

" Ready ?   *Go !* "

At the end of *exactly* one minute, say :

" *Stop !*   Put your pencil down and look up."

Make sure that everyone stops immediately, puts his pencil down, and looks up.

Now I want you to write the same word as often as you can in one minute, but this time you must start at the tail of the letter ' y ' and work back to the letter ' r.' Look at 2. The arrows on the large word in brackets will show you how your pencil is to move. You will receive no credit if you do not write the word backwards. Start at the end of the word and write backwards. Although the words themselves are written backwards, you start with the left-hand word on each line. Work as fast as you can.

Make sure that everyone understands what he is to do. Answer any questions concerning procedure, then say :

" Ready ?   *Go !* "

At the end of *exactly* one minute, say :

" *Stop !*   Put your pencil down and look up."

Sub-test 2

Turn to test 2. This time you are to write the whole sentence, ' The sky is deep blue.' Look at 1 where it is written. You are to write the sentence as many times as you can in the time allowed, keeping your writing clear and controlled. You will have one minute. Write as fast as you can.

" Ready ?   *Go !* "

At the end of *exactly* one minute, say :

" *Stop !*   Put your pencil down and look up."

Make sure that everyone stops as soon as the command " Stop " is given.

Now look at 2.   Here the same sentence is printed in block capital letters.   In your usual style of printing block capitals, you are to print the sentence as many times as you can in one minute.

Make sure that everyone understands what he is to do and answer the necessary questions.

" Ready ?   *Go !* "

At the end of *exactly* one minute, say :

" *Stop !*   Put your pencil down and look up."

Look at 3 in test 2.   You are to write the same sentence, this time alternating block capital and small written letters.   The first letter should be a printed capital letter ;   the second, a small written letter ;   the third, a capital, etc.   If you make an error, correct it before you go on.   Remember, write as fast as you can.   Are there any questions ?

Answer any questions concerning procedure to be followed, then say :

" Ready ?   *Go !* "

At the end of *exactly* one minute, say :

" *Stop !*   Put your pencil down and look up."

Look at 4.   The same sentence has been written, only this time each letter is doubled in every word.   You are to write the sentence, writing every letter twice.   Write as quickly as you can.

" Ready ?   *Go !* "

At the end of *exactly* one minute, say :

" *Stop !*   Put your pencil down and look up."

Sub-test 3

This next test consists of a passage which you are to read and then answer questions based on it.   When I tell you to start, you are to read the passage as fast as you can.

But remember that you will be asked questions on it, so read it carefully. When you finish the first page, go right on to the next until I tell you to stop. When I tell you to stop, you are to stop at once and underline the last word that you finished reading, even though it may be in the middle of a sentence. Are there any questions?

Answer any questions concerning procedure to be followed, then say :

" Ready ? *Go !* "

At the end of *exactly* one minute, say :

" *Stop !* Put your pencil down and look up."

On the next page there are three questions based on the passage that you have just read. Try to answer the questions on as much of the story as you were able to read. Write or underline your answer by the right side of each question. Now turn to the next page and answer the questions.

Allow no more than half a minute. Then say :

Look at the next page. You are to read as much of this passage as you can in the time allowed. You will then be asked a question on it. The passage and the individual words are this time printed backwards and must be read from the bottom of the page up to the top, and from the right to the left. Read it as carefully and as fast as you can. When I tell you to stop, underline the last word that you finished reading. Remember to start at the bottom of the page and to read up. Are there any questions ?

Answer any necessary questions, then say :

" Ready ? *Go !* "

At the end of *exactly* one minute, say :

" *Stop !* Put your pencil down and look up."

On the next page is a question based on the passage that you have just read. Write your answer on the line to the right of the question. Now turn to the next page and answer the question.

Allow no more than half a minute, then say :

" *Stop !* Put your pencil down and look up."

Sub-test 4

Look at test 4. In this test you are to follow a course with your pencil through a map of city streets. Start at the left where indicated and draw a continuous pencil line to show where you go. The letters in the path show you where to go. R means move to the right, L means move to the left. U means move up toward the top of the map, and D means move down toward the bottom of the map. Continue straight until you meet a letter, then go in the direction it tells you till you meet another letter. The dotted line at the start is to show you how to follow the map and help you to get started. If you make a wrong turning, go back to where you made the error and continue on the right path. When I tell you to start, begin at the word ' start ' before the dotted line and see how far you can go before I tell you to stop.

See that everyone knows what he is to do, then say :

" Ready ? *Go !* "

At the end of *exactly* one minute, say :

" *Stop !* Put your pencil down and look up."

Turn to the next page. This map is similar to the one before, and you are again to follow the course through it. This time, however, it is very different in one important way. You are to do the direct opposite of what the letters tell you. R will then mean left, L will mean right, U will mean down, and D will mean up. Always correct your errors by coming back to the point where you went wrong. When I tell you to start, begin at the word ' start ' before the dotted line and see how far you can go before I tell you to stop. Remember to do the opposite of what the direction letters tell you to do. Are there any questions ?

See that everyone knows what he is to do, then say :

" Ready ? *Go !* "

At the end of *exactly* two minutes, say :

" *Stop !* Put your pencil down and look up."

Sub-test 5

Turn to the next page. This test depends on your speed of writing your own name. You are to write your own name after the sample name 'John Smith' as many times as you can in the time allowed. Write your *own* name, first and last names only, in your usual style. You will have one minute. Write as fast as you can, keeping your writing clear.

"Ready? *Go!*"

At the end of *exactly* one minute, say :

"*Stop!* Put your pencil down and look up."

Now look at 2. Here 'John Smith' has been written backwards, starting at the letter 'h' and ending at the letter 'J.' The arrows on the large 'John Smith' show you how it is written. You are to write your own name backwards. You are to start at the last letter in your own last name and end at the first letter of your own first name. In writing your name from the right hand, you should start near the right-hand side of each line. Start writing your name backwards after the sample name 'John Smith' and write it as many times as you can before I tell you to stop. You will receive no credit if you do not write backwards.

Make sure that everyone understands what he is to do. Answer any questions concerning procedure, then say :

"Ready? *Go!*"

At the end of *exactly* one minute, say :

"*Stop!* Put your pencil down and look up."

Sub-test 6

Turn to test 6. Here you are to write the number '237' as many times as you can in one minute. Look at 1. The number has already been written twice for you. At the signal, continue writing it as fast as you can until I tell you to stop.

"Ready? *Go!*"

At the end of *exactly* one minute, say :

"*Stop!* Put your pencil down and look up."

Now you are to write '237' in the same order, but this time you are to write it beginning at the end of the

number.   Start at the bottom of the 7 and end at the top
of the 2.   Look at 2.   The arrows on the large 237 show
you what you are to do.   You will receive no credit if
you do not write the number backwards.   Work as fast
as you can.

"Ready?   *Go!*"

At the end of *exactly* one minute, say :

"*Stop!*   Put your pencil down and look up."

Sub-test 7

Turn to test 7.   Work out the multiplication problems
as quickly as possible.   Do all of the left-hand column
before you go on to the next one.   The first two examples
are done for you.   Check them and go on as carefully and
quickly as you can until you are told to stop.   You will
have one minute.

"Ready?   *Go!*"

At the end of *exactly* one minute, say :

"*Stop!*   Put your pencil down and look up."

Now look at 2 on the next page.   These are some more
numbers to be multiplied.   This time we will use two
made-up rules.   Whenever 2 and 3 appear in the same
line to be multiplied, their product will be considered 7.
Whenever 1 and 4 are multiplied, the answer is to be
considered 3.   These special cases are at the top to remind
you, and the first two examples are done.   Do all the left-
hand column before going on to the next one.   Read the
examples now.   (Pause.)   All the other numbers are
multiplied in the usual way.   Work as fast as you can.
Are there any questions?

Answer any necessary questions, then say :

"Now go on with the rest of the problem.   Ready?
Go!"

At the end of *exactly* one minute, say :

"*Stop!*   Put your pencil down and look up."

In the third part of this sub-test you will have some
letters to multiply.   Each letter stands for a number.
A is equal to 2, C is equal to 3, and E is equal to 4.   Do all

of the left-hand column before you go on to the next one. The first two examples are done for you. Work as fast as you can until you are told to stop. Look at the samples. (Pause.) Remember that A is equal to 2, C is equal to 3, and E is equal to 4.

Answer any necessary questions, but once the test starts, the numerical equivalents of the letters may not be given. Then, say :

" Ready ? *Go !* "

At the end of *exactly* one minute, say :

" *Stop !* Put your pencil down and close your test booklet."

Collect the test materials.

The instructions for scoring are as follows :

Sub-test 1

$X =$ Number of letters correctly written in ' ready, ready.'

$Y =$ Number of letters correctly written in words ' ready, ready,' when written backwards. Cancel any unintelligible, badly written letter.

Total score (Perseveration, Motor, 1) : Divide X by Y.

Sub-test 2

$X' =$ Number of letters correctly written in ' The sky is deep blue.'

$X'' =$ Number of letters correctly written in ' THE SKY, etc.'

$Y =$ Number of letters correctly written in ' ThE sKy, etc.' Cancel any misformed letter or extra letter and take off one for any letter missed out.

$Z =$ Number of letters correctly written in ' Tthhee sskkyy, etc.' Cancel similarly.

Total score (Perseveration, Motor, 2) : Divide sum of X' and X'' by Y.

Total score (Perseveration, Motor, 3) : Divide X' by Z.

Sub-test 3

 X = Number of words to point at which subject indicated he stopped reading.

 Y = Number of words (from bottom) to point at which subject stopped reading.

 Total score (Perseveration Reading) : Divide X by Y.

 (*Note.*—There is no score for answering the questions on reading. They are introduced only to produce a correct attitude in the reading.)

Sub-test 4

 X = Number of letter-corners correctly passed (not necessarily continuously). (Fix stencil and make sure that no loop is left out. Omit from score if it is.)

 Y = Number of letter-corners correctly passed (as above).

 Total score (Perseveration of Direction Habit) : Divide X by Y.

Sub-test 5

 X = Number of letters correctly written (John Smith).

 Y = Number of letters correctly written backwards. Cancel any unintelligible, badly written, or forward written letter.

 Total score (Perseveration, Motor, 4) : Divide X by Y.

Sub-test 6

 X = Number of numbers correctly written at 1.

 Y = Number of numbers correctly written at 2. Cancel any very badly formed.

 Total score (Perseveration, Motor, 5) : Divide X by Y.

Sub-test 7

 X = Number of calculation items correctly done at 1.

 Y = Number of calculation items in 2 correctly done.

 Z = Number of calculation items in 3 correctly done.

Total score (Calculation Perseveration, 1) : Divide X by Y.

Total score (Calculation Perseveration, 2) : Divide X by Z.

A preliminary factorisation of the above battery administered to 120 undergraduate men and women shows the intercorrelations to be accounted for by two general factors, the larger of which is ' perseveration ' or disposition rigidity. (The second, decidedly smaller, factor may be intelligence.) The disposition rigidity factor loads the seven scores from the first six sub-tests as follows : ·76, ·38, ·33, ·32, ·46, ·79.

Since the standard deviations of the raw scores of these sub-tests are markedly different—and not in the direction of the weighting suggested by the factorisation—more accurate total scores will be obtained by transforming the sub-test scores into standard scores, or at least into a ten-point scale covering the range, before adding them to give the total score.

' P ' Tests for Children

A shorter battery of four tests on the same principles has been designed for children (6–16 years).

In these tests everything possible (short of rehearsing the whole test) should be done to make the child *perfectly clear* as to what he has to do. This may be done by clear instruction, use of model (see below), and use of prepared, standard test blanks, with lines and reminders at the beginnings of lines for the actual writing. It is a test of pure speed, not of understanding. The child should be allowed to make one of each kind of shape (X activity and Y activity) before commencing.

Particulars of Tests

1. *A, B, C.*—I want you to write abc as quickly as you can. Start when I say " Go," and stop as soon as I say " Stop." After that I want you to write capitals as quickly as you can, like that (point to a model). Then we'll do

both again (model).   After that I want you to write little
a, big A, like this (model) as quickly as you can.

Let the child write one set: aAbBcC.   Then remind him
to go *as quickly as possible*.   Say " Ready—Go!" sharply,
and " Stop!" at end of 15 seconds.

Model in front: (1) abc   .   .   . 15 seconds
                 (2) ABC   .   .   . 15 seconds
                 (3) abc   .   .   . 15 seconds
                 (4) ABC   .   .   . 15 seconds
                 (5) aAbBcC   .   . 15 seconds
                 (6) aAbBcC   .   . 15 seconds

Allow about 7 seconds between "Stop" and the next
"Go" (for avoidance of fatigue), and in this interval remind the subject what has to come next.

$$\text{`P' score} = \frac{1 + 2 + 3 + 4}{2(5 + 6)}$$

2. *Triangles.*—I want you to do a row of triangles with
the points upwards.   (Draw triangles, making strokes very
clearly and always in the same way.)   Then a row with the
points downwards. Repeat both. Then a row mixed,
like this (model). As quickly as possible all the time.
" Ready—Go! "

                 (1) 15 seconds
                 (2) 15 seconds
                 (3) 15 seconds
                 (4) 15 seconds
                 (5) 15 seconds
                 (6) 15 seconds

$$\text{P score} = \frac{1 + 2 + 3 + 4}{2(5 + 6)}$$

3. *W's.*—Write me a row of W's like that (model) (the
usual way of writing W's to which the child is accustomed).
Good! Ascertain if child is left-handed and make note on
his paper if he is.   Now I want you to write me a row of
W's backwards like this, beginning at the opposite end of

the letter. (Draw four, with reverse stroke, thus:

instead of   Let child do four.)

As quickly as possible. (Remind child of this at frequent intervals. The whole thing *must* be done under pressure of speed.)

    (1) 15 seconds Forwards (ordinary way)
    (2) 15 seconds Forwards (ordinary way)
    (3) 15 seconds Backwards
    (4) 15 seconds Forwards (ordinary way)
    (5) 15 seconds Backwards

$$\text{P score} = \frac{2+4}{3+5}$$

4. *Colours.*—You have to pick out the reds and the blues in these rows of colours, pointing to them with the pencil and calling out the names, like this: " red, blue, red, red, blue," etc.

When you've done that twice, I want you to pick out the same colours again, but call the red ' blue ' and blue ' red.' As quickly as possible each time. If you make a slip you must correct it before you go on.

Count number of colours named according to instructions, omitting errors or spots passed over.

    (1) Normal, 15 seconds
    (2) Normal, 15 seconds
    (3) Reversed naming, 15 seconds
    (4) Normal, 15 seconds
    (5) Reversed naming, 15 seconds

$$\text{P score} = \frac{2+4}{3+5}$$

In general, when scoring, first cross out each error, i.e. errors do not penalise, they merely are not allowed to count in the total.

The total score is the sum of the four scores. Since this test battery is so short—only $5\frac{1}{2}$ minutes of actual testing time—it is advisable, if a reliable measurement is to be obtained, that it should be given twice (an intelligence test can conveniently be sandwiched between the repetitions), especially since the inter-correlations are low on a single administration.[1]

Norms.—Since this particular battery has been shown [1] to be independent of ' g,' there is no need to make any correction for intelligence, but each year of age has a slightly different score.   The deciles on the graph overleaf are based on measurements on 300 boys and girls of 10–14 years of age, but until these norms are extended empirically above and below, the decile scores for younger and older children can best be obtained by continuing the decile lines upwards and downwards in the directions indicated.

The mean score for boys is about ·5 higher than for girls at 14 years of age and about ·25 higher at 10 years. These norms are for boys and girls together, so a rough correction may be made for, say, 14-year-old children by subtracting ·25 from individual boys' scores and adding ·25 to girls' scores.

When the test is given for a second time in quick succession (to provide two measurements, for greater reliability, as recommended above), ·1 should be added to this second score before reading off the decile position, since there is on an average about ·1 decrease in score resulting from practice (see Fig. 59, p. 256).

5. *Primary Suggestibility Test.*—The work of Eysenck [2] has demonstrated clearly that in the realm of responses to suggestion two major factors (apart from intelligence) are operative, as follows: (1) Primary or Direct Suggestibility —the ideo-motor tendency to put into action ideas dwelt upon personally or propounded by a suggestor. (2) Secondary or Indirect Suggestibility, as occurs, for example, in the Binet Progressive Lines test.   There *may* also be a third factor, of prestige suggestion, most clearly demonstrated in the heat illusion test (see p. 260).

Primary suggestibility is now known to be highly correlated with hypnotisability, whereas secondary suggestibility is not.   The heat illusion test measures seem to account for that lesser part of the variance in hypnotisability not

---

[1] R. B. Cattell, " On the Measurement of Perseveration," *Brit. J. Educ. Psychol.*, v, 1, 1935.
[2] Eysenck, H. J., *Dimensions of Personality.* London : Kegan Paul, 1947.

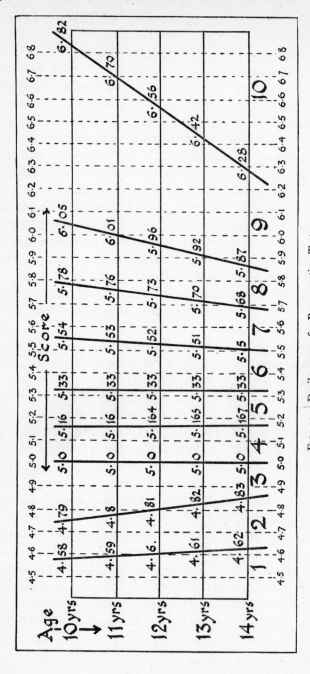

FIG. 59.—Decile norms for Perseveration Tests.

Instructions.—Find the score on the scale at the top and drop a perpendicular to the year concerned.   Then note the decile section (large numbers at base) in which the score falls.

accounted for by primary suggestibility.   Further, Eysenck has shown that high endowment in ' hypnotisability-suggestibility' does *not* distinguish hysterics from other neurotics, as many psychiatrists have supposed, but instead strongly distinguishes neurotics from normals.   That is to say, primary suggestibility correlates very well—about ·7—with the general factor of neuroticism, the inverse of our C (or C + G) factor.   (Within the neurotic group it correlated particularly with such items as: unable to hold steady job, invalided from army, effort intolerance, abnormality in family, dyspepsia, tremor, apathy.)

The best single measure of primary suggestibility is the Body Sway test, though the Chevreul Pendulum, the Press-Release, and a straight measure of ataxia (sway when standing) also have good loadings with this factor.   Instructions for administering the Body Sway test are given on p. 261.

Summary on the Measurement of the Character Stability v. *Neuroticism Factor.*

In the present state of our knowledge the C (or C + G) factor is best measured by a battery containing a test from each of the above five fields (possibly with an extra test from the first).   Two of these—the C.M.S. and the Body Sway—have to be given as individual tests, and for none of the tests is there a wide standardisation available.   But in spite of these difficulties and disadvantages, the measurement of this source trait is of such importance for so many fields of diagnosis and prediction that its measurement cannot be neglected.

The Measurement of Character Factor J.—The following objective test situation scores, according to recent research, are likely to be measures of the vigorous ' obsessional' character factor (obverse of ' neurasthenia ') with the saturations shown :

Strength or time of holding a constant dynamometer grip	·55 to ·79
Time subject will endure a painful pressure or electric shock . . .	·62 to ·69
Tending in vocabulary test to translate slang terms into precise English rather than into other slang terms . .	·55
Score on Allport A-S Test . . .	·44

A significant correlation with obsessional tendencies is also found on the C.M.S. test (see above), and the spot-dotting test (which is a very similar situation). Culpin and Smith,[1] investigating nervous symptoms among office and factory workers, first make the discovery that unusually high scores on the McDougall-Schuster spot-dotting apparatus were made by subjects of obsessional make-up, whereas unduly poor scores were made by those with anxiety hysteria symptoms and nervousness.

These two important nervous types, as described by these research workers, need to be briefly defined as follows, since they do not correspond exactly with the conceptions of obsessional and anxiety neuroses to be found in some psycho-analytic literature.

Obsessional ' Neurotic.'—Symptoms characterised in consciousness by unreasonable drive. ' Gnawing, craving, urgency' to think certain thoughts, or carry out certain actions (which may appear to the subject futile or irrational). The subject's sentiments cause him to believe strongly in the power and importance of self-control. He is generally over-conscientious, very thorough, and inclined to overwork. Such persons are frequently found among the intellectually superior, and tend to occupy superior positions of responsibility and control.

Anxiety ' Neurotic.'—Symptoms have recognisable emotional form—indeed, emotion is the main cause of discomfort. Fear of small rooms, of the dark, of being watched, etc. In positions of responsibility and authority show strain and are irritable, erratic, and unreliable with subordinates, often nagging. Prone to irrational worries. These types should be related to those described in the rating scales on pp. 265 and 267.

Probably (in the present state of our knowledge we cannot say ' certainly ') the obsessional type is one with high G, or low J, but not low F. This is implied in the above description. It is deducible also from the fact that certain forms of perseveration described in the section

---

[1] *The Nervous Temperament*, by M. Culpin and M. Smith (H.M.S.O., 1930).

above, which are in fact not ' p ' but typical obsessional symptoms, are associated with high ' w ' (G) rather than high perseveration. It follows again, from the observations of the present writer, agreeing with those of most clinical workers, that children of high G tend to score more highly on performance tests (e.g. the Goddard Board) than their intelligence would lead one to expect—and spot dotting is, after all, a kind of performance test.

Technique.—The apparatus is a disc revolving at uniform speed, carrying a spiral trail of irregularly arranged dots. The test takes only a few minutes, during which time the actual transit speed of the dots (at which objects the subject has to aim with a pencil) increases to a degree at which failure to continue the performance occurs.

The score can be either : (1) total number of circles correctly marked ; (2) number aimed at before breakdown (arbitrarily fixed at five misses in succession) ; (3) number correctly hit before breakdown. The correlation between these is from ·93 to ·96, so that any one is equally sound ; (2) being the easiest to mark, is therefore accepted as the best for practical purposes.

Norms.—On this basis, among clerical workers and factory workers, the median score for obsessionals is about 190 (number aimed at before breakdown) ; for normal, non-nervous individuals 135 ; and for those with anxiety symptoms 123. About 30 per cent. of those with obsessional symptoms score above 240, and practically none below 120, whereas normals and anxiety types give 3 or 4 per cent. above 240 and at least 20 per cent. below 120.

The test, therefore, has by no means perfect validity, but as an adjunct to other character tests is definitely helpful.

There is no correlation of spot-dotting speed with age among adults, but some correlation with dexterity, absence of eye defects, and ' g ' ; so that these, especially the second, should be taken into consideration.

5. Some Measures of Specific, Restricted Personality Traits

The testing of single aspects of character is sometimes necessary for special purposes, notably in vocational selection. Various tests on ' miniature situation ' lines have been devised, but they have rather less validity than those described above for soundness of character as a whole. This is partly because preliminary research as to whether a single trait or ' confact ' really exists, and if so within what limits, has not been made. Useful as such tests would be, one can at present only point to the following tentative tests and suggestions.

Aggressiveness, tested by ability to gaze fixedly at an experimenter while doing difficult mental work. (This has been shown to correlate well with aggression on ratings.[1])

Conceit Index.—Suggested by Allport from a contrast of self-estimates on desirable qualities with those of independent raters.

Confidence.—A variety of tests of confidence, in judging lines, making moral judgments, etc., have been tried out by Trow, who did not find, however, much inter-correlation of the different situations.[2]

Endurance Test.—(Fernald.)—Ability to endure prolonged discomforts or pain (e.g. electric shocks ; the holding up of a column of mercury as long as possible with the breath ; standing on one leg).

Helpfulness, by reactions of subject to a second subject to whom he is instructed to give a complex test requiring much explanation.

Minnesota Scale for Measuring Inferiority Attitudes (fair consistency and validity).

Suggestibility.—This much-overworked concept in psychology has included such diverse notions as low intelligence, ignorance, prejudice, primitive passive sympathy, herd suggestibility, cognitive imitation, habits of deferring to prestige authority (partly submissive disposition), emo-

[1] Moore and Gilliland, " The Measurement of Aggressiveness," *J. Appl. Psychol.*, v, 1921.
[2] Trow, " An Experimental Study of Confidence," *Amer. J. Psychol.*

tional dependence on the father image, susceptibility to dissociation, etc.   It is not surprising, therefore, that Otis,[1] Brown,[2] Estabrooks, and others found little agreement between various tests of so-called suggestibility.

On the other hand, Aveling,[3] Hull, and, recently, Eysenck have found unitary functional tendencies in the tests used, as indicated on p. 255.   Eysenck found the primary suggestibility factor strongly correlated with neuroticism, while Aveling found prestige suggestibility correlating negatively with ratings of common sense, intelligence being constant.

The Body Sway Test of Primary Suggestibility is administered as follows.   The subject (with closed eyes) is told to stand quite still and relaxed.   A thread is attached to a firm part of the clothing about 4 feet above the ground and is led over a pulley in the wall a yard away to a (hidden) indicator of level on the wall.   The experimenter (or, better, a standard phonograph record) says to him: " You are beginning to fall forward, you are falling forward now, forward . . . etc." for one minute.   The sway is measured in inches, also with backward suggestion, an average being taken.

6. Probes of Complex Formations and Patterns of Emotional Adjustment

(A) ASSESSING DEGREE OF NEUROSIS

Two kinds of measurement are described here : (1) Estimating the degree of neurosis in terms of certain specific neurotic syndromes, and (2) Measuring and exploring particular emotional attachments and fulcra of conflict.   This section deals with the first, i.e. rating and questionnaire scales of neurotic syndromes.

The extent of agreement among psychotherapists on neurotic syndromes is not as complete as on psychotic syndromes.   Freud distinguished three true neuroses (i.e.

---

[1] M. A. Otis, " A Study of Suggestibility in Children," *Arch. of Psychol.*, xi, 1924.
[2] W. W. Brown, *Individual and Sex Differences in Suggestibility*, University of Calif., Publ. 11, 1916.
[3] F. Aveling and H. L. Hargreaves, " Suggestibility with and without Prestige in Children," *Brit. J. Psychol.*, xii, 1921.

physiological disorders of the nervous system)—neurasthenia, anxiety neurosis, and hypochondria—and four
psychoneuroses—conversion (classical) hysteria, fixation
hysteria, anxiety hysteria (including phobia), and obsessional neurosis. Along with most psychotherapists we
have adopted a syndrome classification on these lines,
but slightly simplified. The recent factor analytic studies
of hospital neurotics (i.e. studies not based merely on
neurotic questionnaire responses by students) by Eysenck [1]
reveal some four factors. One of these is a neurasthenia-
hypochondria factor with emphasis on psychosomatic
disturbance. Another suggests that conversion and anxiety-
hysteria are reactions to emotional conflict resulting from
opposite extremes of temperamental constitution ; for this
factor loads conversion symptoms in its positive extreme
and anxiety-depression in its negative extreme. It has been
suggested [2] that these are the pathological extremes of the
surgency v. desurgent melancholy temperament factor F in
Chapter V above. However, though this patterning adds
support to the choice of clinical syndromes adopted here our
assessments made are actually of *syndromes*, not of factors.

Naturally the psychiatrist looks at the functional side
and considers that a neurosis is more than a symptom or
collection of symptoms. Consequently the completion of
a rating scale or inventory is of little or no value in deciding the course of treatment. Its value lies in (1) diagnostic
assistance, especially with regard to degree of neurosis ;
(2) statistical treatment of results from whole groups, e.g.
extent of neurotic difficulties among certain groups of
children, students, or workpeople ; frequency of neurotic
traits among relatives of the insane (such surveys have in
the past often given most conflicting results owing to the
absence of standards of neurotic conditions) ; (3) deter-
mination of general type of character among ' normal ' people. It is probable (*vide* McDougall, *Abnormal Psychology*)

---

[1] Eysenck, H. J., " Types of Personality : A Factorial Study of Seven Hundred
Neurotics," *J. Ment. Sci.*, 1944, xc, 851–861.

[2] Cattell, R. B., " The Diagnosis of Neurotic Conditions : A re-interpretation of
Eysenck's Factor," *J. of Nervous and Mental Diseases*, 1946, cii, 576–90.

that the type of disorder to which a person is prone under stress is determined by the general character-temperament constitution. Or, looking at the matter from the psycho-analytic point of view, the general observed character-temperament make-up is a product of the particular type of fixation, repression, and conflict from which each person suffers. Whichever way the causality lies (and it may well be partly in both directions), a connection exists and, in assessing character among normal people, a measure of the tendency to one or another of the neurotic syndromes is of far-reaching importance for vocational guidance and selection, analysis of scholastic difficulties, or treatment of problem behaviour.

The following rating scales, each with a corresponding self-inventory cover six types [1] and are scored separately, but the total score on all may also have some value as a measure of total 'neurotic personality' tendency (C factor), as is done in Woodworth's questionnaire (see Vernon, p. 219). For, as we have seen on p. 212, there is evidence[2] of a 'general neurotic factor' or neuropathic constitution apart from the special and definite types clinically separated. Finally, one must bear in mind that, though according to clinical evidence most psycho-neurotics tend to fall into one or another of three types (i.e. for a syndrome to exist), transitional and mixed 'types' are found with some frequency. Moreover, as Freud, for example, has pointed out, the neurotic patterns are developmentally interrelated; for instance, an obsessional-compulsive act may arise as a solution of the anxiety (or reproach) in anxiety hysteria. Nevertheless, it seems most probable that such a solution, replacing anxiety, takes place only when a particular constitutional trend (obsessional make-up) exists or with those having a fixation at a particular level (active anal-erotic).

[1] The items included in these symptom complexes are those described by Rivers, Freud, Henderson and Gillespie, Jones, Stoddard, Hollingworth, White, and McDougall.
[2] The evidence was formerly the impressionistic evidence of clinical psychologists, notably expressed by Rosanoff (' neuropathic inheritance '), Freud (' psycho-sexual constitution '), Babinski, and others, while some, e.g. Hollingworth (*Abnormal Psychology*), found no objective evidence of the existence or nature of this generalised psycho-neurotic tendency.

An 'epileptic' and a 'paranoid' type have been included in the rating scales, since, although these conceptions belong to the realm of psychosis, the 'epileptic character' may be more widely distributed and its diagnosis may be of importance even when typical fits are not present; whilst the 'paranoid constitution' is far more widespread than paranoia and gives at once a picture of a definite character type. The cyclothyme and schizothyme types of the last chapter (p. 169), for that matter, constitute equally attenuated forms of the remaining important psychosis syndromes.

Three modes of assessment of each type are provided below:

(1) A Rating Scale for 'Observers,' which may be filled in by acquaintances familiar only with the observed behaviour and ordinary conversation of the subjects to be rated (as e.g. teachers assessing children, students assessing fellow students).

(2) A Rating Scale for 'Consultants,' who have special 'rapport' with the subject and training in expert psychological enquiry, and who are in a position to take into account information given confidentially by the subject.

(3) A self-inventory questionnaire, in which the subject answers particular questions (necessarily more numerous in most cases than the traits to be rated, because each trait may need to be approached in several ways), and in which the scoring is made by another person. Such self-inventories are subject to all the criticisms mentioned on p. 202, but they give reliable results under particular conditions of research (namely, with honest and intelligent subject, trained in estimates), and can also be improved slightly by a more indirect style of question than that commonly used.

Norms for these scales have not yet been formed. The writer would be much indebted to psychologists using them for any norms, validities, and consistencies found in particular researches.

(i) Rating Scales (' Observer's ' and ' Consultant's ')

1. *Rating Scale on Neurasthenic Tendency (closely similar to Kraepelin's ' Chronic Nervous Exhaustion ')*

Underline 0, 1, or 2: 0 meaning completely absent.
2 meaning present in marked degree.

(1) Gets tired very easily physically [1]	. . . . .	0 1 2
(2) Gets tired very easily mentally [1]	. . . .	0 1 2
(3) Unable to make any effort, trembles at thought of any task	. .	0 1 2
(4) Unable to concentrate; attention easily distracted	. .	0 1 2
(5) Memory poor	. .	0 1 2
(6) Interest lacking or quickly disappearing	. . .	0 1 2
(7) Sense of pressure on head, pain at occiput and back of neck, irritable spine	. . . .	0 1 2
(8) General malaise, aches and pains, leg heavy	. . .	0 1 2
(9) Irritability, aggressive temper	. . . .	0 1 2
(10) Moodiness	. . .	0 1 2
(11) Depression, tearful or dull	. . . .	0 1 2
(12) Flatulent dyspepsia and disturbances of appetite	. . .	0 1 2
(13) Constipation	. . .	0 1 2
(14) Exaggerated (deep) reflexes	. . . .	0 1 2
(15) Poor sleep at night, difficulty in waking in morning	. .	0 1 2
(16) Hypersensitiveness to bright light, to noise, and to cold	. .	0 1 2
(17) Sweating of skin and palms of hands	. . . .	0 1 2
(18) Nocturnal emissions (and ejaculatio præcox impotence)	. .	0 1 2

Total Rating Score . . .

For rating by observers, without interview and questioning of the subject, a ten-item scale is used (namely, items 1, 2, 3, 4, 5, 6, 9, 10, 11, and 16), but with the evidence of the subject himself (consultant's rating), the scale is used on all eighteen items. Norms for these should be distinct.

2. *Rating Scale on Anxiety Neurosis Tendency*

(1) Morbid, excessive feeling of anxiety or dread	. . .	0 1 2
(2) Occasional ' fits ' (loss of consciousness, without convulsions) .	.	0 1 2
(3) Rapid heartbeat	. . .	0 1 2
(4) Palpitation, anginal pain (pseudo-angina)	. . .	0 1 2
(5) Tremor, twitching of muscles	. . .	0 1 2
(6) Sweating of hands and feet, nocturnal perspiration	. .	0 1 2
(7) Lack of appetite, dryness of mouth, flatulence, fullness in stomach, nausea	. . . .	0 1 2
(8) Breathlessness, sense of suffocation or breathing oppression, asthma .		0 1 2
(9) Constipation and diarrhœa co-existing	. . .	0 1 2
(10) Sleeplessness	. . .	0 1 2
(11) Hypersensitiveness to light, sound, etc., ' jumpy ' nerves	. .	0 1 2
(12) Depression, irritability, and excitability	. . .	0 1 2
(13) Restlessness and inability to concentrate	. . .	0 1 2
(14) Vasomotor constriction, coldness and blueness of extremities .	.	0 1 2
(15) Weakness of limbs and blurring of vision	. . .	0 1 2
(16) Frequency of micturition (and of seminal emissions)	. .	0 1 2

Total Rating Score . . .

[1] This is observable at once by the way in which the work curve on the ergograph or adding sheets declines from the beginning. Also in eye fatigue in reading and in restriction of visual field (perimeter).

Not all psychologists are agreed that the last five items are rightly included. An ' Observer's ' rating can be made on 1, 2, 5, 7, 11, 12, 13, and 14; a ' Consultant's ' on all sixteen items.

3. *Rating Scale on Anxiety Hysteria Tendency (Phobias)*

Some psychologists include this and the anxiety neurosis in one syndrome under the term ' psycho-neurotic anxiety state.' It seems better, however, to regard the anxiety neurosis as a syndrome which may exist alone or, with additional features, as an anxiety hysteria, since, after dissolution of the latter by psycho-therapy, a core of physical symptoms—the anxiety neurosis—may persist.

A rating on this tendency should therefore include the sixteen items of (2) above, *plus* the following:

(17) Anxiety, fear or anguish in closed spaces, railway carriages . . o 1 2
(18) Anxiety, fear or anguish in large gatherings or open spaces . . o 1 2
(19) Fear of insanity or of recurrence of hysterical fit . . . o 1 2
(20) Fear of bodily illness or disease . . . . . o 1 2
(21) Exaggerated fear of heights . . . . . o 1 2
(22) Any particular 'irrational' fear (fire, cats, opening letters, insects, thunder) . . . . o 1 2
(23) Night terrors (nightmare) . . . . . o 1 2

Total Rating Score . . .

Though the deduction of these from behaviour may make possible an ' Observer's ' rating, the phobias are often so well concealed, even from close friends, that only a 'Consultant's ' rating can be made.

4. *Rating Scale on Conversion (Classical) Hysteria Tendency*

(1) Presence of non-organic paralysis (of co-ordinated muscles) . . o 1 2
(2) Presence of non-organic anæsthesia (glove and stocking type) . . o 1 2
(3) Fits, occurring only in presence of others, with trivial self-injury . o 1 2
(4) Presence of tics, contractures, or convulsions . . . o 1 2
(5) Other physical conversion symptoms, pains, headaches, migraine, dermatographies,[1] globus hystericus [2] . . . . o 1 2
(6) Peculiarities over food, occasionally excessive eating, more commonly inadequate eating and loss of appetite. Cyclic vomiting . o 1 2
(7) Splitting of personality, variation of two or more personalities . o 1 2
(8) Somnambulism or excessive sleep talking . . . o 1 2
(9) Episodic dream states, fugues . . . . o 1 2
(10) Stuttering, inability to speak, loss of voice . . . o 1 2
(11) Complete forgetting of certain (important) incidents and remarks (sometimes over a few days only) . . . . o 1 2
(12) Susceptibility to hypnosis and suggestion . . . o 1 2

[1] Markings, blisters, etc., appearing on the skin without apparent cause.
[2] A feeling of fullness in the throat and sense of suffocation.

(13) Combination of emotionality (especially erotic) and excitability, with primness and reserve . . . .   o I 2
(14) Shallow feelings, but excessive expression. Theatricality . .   o I 2
(15) Lack of persistence of feelings and of efforts . . . . .   o I 2
(16) Vanity, desire to impress and gain attention . . . . .   o I 2
(17) Craving and seeking sympathy (with avoidance of responsibilities) .   o I 2
(18) Emotional instability. Rapid variation and unpredictability (crying and giggling, kiss and slap) . . . .   o I 2
(19) Elation or offence at trivialities, outbursts of excitement, anger, and sullenness . . . .   o I 2
(20) Simulated foolishness and childishness, inept funniness . . .   o I 2
(21) Vivid compensatory day-dreaming, leading to fabrication of half-believed stories . . . .   o I 2
(22) Essentially calm mental attitude, Janet's 'belle indifférence' to grave personal problems, except for short periods of stress . .   o I 2
(23) Sleeplessness . . . .   o I 2
(24) Vasomotor disturbances, flushing, trembling, blanching . . .   o I 2

Total Rating Score .   .   .

Suggested 'Observer's' scale: Nos. 1, 2, 4, 6, 7, 10, 11, 13, 14, 15, 16, 17, 18, 19, 20, 21, 22, 24.
'Consultant's' scale: All numbers.

5. *Rating Scale on Obsessional-Compulsive Tendency (Janet's 'Psychasthenia')*

(1) Constant preoccupation with a single topic (usually trivial and felt by the subject to be so) . . . .   o I 2
(2) Obsessive rumination (*folie de doute*), e.g. speculations about small religious points or 'Why must I breathe?' 'What was the first cause?' . . . .   o I 2
(3) Scrupulous compulsions to carry out trivial tasks, e.g. to read notices, to fold up clothes in a particular fashion . . . . .   o I 2
(4) Compulsions to totally unnecessary acts, e.g. to count windows, to utter rhymes or phrases, to touch or step over objects, to wash too frequently . . . .   o I 2
(5) Fear of compulsion to carry out dangerous, immoral, or destructive acts, e.g. to stab someone, to set fire to something, to mutilate animals, to swear in church, etc. . . . .   o I 2
(6) Obsessive fear of some unlikely danger or of no danger, e.g. of destroying something valuable, of blushing, of dust, of fire . . .   o I 2
(7) Obstinacy. Assertive character with insistence on the power of the will, aggressiveness . . . .   o I 2
(8) Orderliness. Over-conscientiousness and exaggerated detailed thoroughness in general work . . . .   o I 2
(9) Insomnia (not invariable) . . . .   o I 2
(10) Parsimony . . . .   o I 2

Total Rating Score .   .   .

Assessment on practically all of this scale requires the co-operation of the subject, since compulsions are generally effectively disguised or hidden from acquaintances.

6. *Rating for Epileptoid Character*

It is generally agreed to-day that the epileptic character is not secondary to the disease; that it may be present in some degree in those not subject to discernible fits, and that the diagnosis of epileptic personality is important in deciding whether or not fits are of an epileptic nature.

(1)	Presence of fits (grand mal, petit mal, or trance state) . . .	0	1	2
(2)	Egocentricity (undue importance attached to own activities, however trivial and childish they may be)	0	1	2
(3)	Vain,[1] susceptible to flattery ; will work for praise but not for love .	0	1	2
(4)	Matters of personal interest remembered (especially bodily illness) ; all matters of general interest forgotten	0	1	2
(5)	Inattention and loss of interest in what is happening around him .	0	1	2
(6)	Memory poor both for recent and remote events	0	1	2
(7)	Poverty and restriction of ideas, words brought out and used with increasing difficulty (low ' f ')	0	1	2
(8)	Sluggishness, speech, and thinking slow; slow to grasp new ideas (hence misunderstandings)	0	1	2
(9)	Perseveration, pedantically elaborates ideas with stilted and hackneyed phrases and composition	0	1	2
(10)	Constantly busily engaged, yet essentially lazy and avoids effort .	0	1	2
(11)	Irritable, sensitive, quickly in a rage, not subservient to discipline .	0	1	2
(12)	Brutal and ferocious—disproportionate violence	0	1	2
(13)	Prone to sexual perversions, especially auto-erotism (infantile, polymorphous perverse)	0	1	2
(14)	Deliberate, ' plateaux '[2] speech	0	1	2
(15)	Taciturnity alternating with over-friendliness	0	1	2
(16)	Selfish kind of religious devotedness (father dependence ?) and shallow professions of interest in others	0	1	2

Total Rating Score . . .

In this case the ' Observer's ' rating scale corresponds with the ' Consultant's '—sixteen items in each.

Rating Scale on Paranoid Constitution—Syndrome 7

Paranoia—the tendency to systematised delusions without disturbance of emotional constitution—has a considerable hereditary element. A greater or lesser tendency to paranoid reactions is often evident, therefore, when no development of the disease has taken place. In contrast with all other psychotics, paranoiacs rank high on ' w ' estimates, and do not have a ' p ' score differing in any way from that of normal people (see p. 230).

(1)	Systematised delusions of a megalomanic, persecutory, amorous, jealous, litigious, religious, or hypochondriacal type . . .	0	1	2
(2)	Addiction to fads, garrulity on special topics, writing to the newspapers, etc.	0	1	2
(3)	Sensitive, brooding, uneasy mind	0	1	2
(4)	Inability to correct and modify ideas once adopted or to make practical concessions	0	1	2

[1] But not necessarily caring about the personal appearance.
[2] Speech with a monotonous tone, lacking flexibility, discernible by plateau form of voice-curve tracing.

(5) Self-willed obstinacy	.	.	.	.	.	.	.	o	1	2
(6) Egotism (but not selfishness in other senses), seeing first and last the reference of any happening to the self	.	.	.	.	.	o	1	2
(7) Suspiciousness and distrust, leading to misinterpretation of events and intentions and to re-interpretation of events in memory .	.	o	1	2
(8) Retiring, solitary	.	.	.	.	.	.	.	o	1	2
(9) Shame and uncertainty in relation to others, morbid, introspectiveness as to standing in others' opinions	.	.	.	.	o	1	2
(10) Irritability	.	.	.	.	.	.	.	o	1	2
(11) Passionate excitability, sometimes leading to rough and violent behaviour	.	.	.	.	.	.	.	o	1	2
(12) Ill-balanced aims, unduly lofty or expansive projects	.	.	o	1	2
(13) Exaggerated pride and self-esteem	.	.	.	.	o	1	2
(14) Easily fatigued by work or emotion, inability to perform steady work	o	1	2
(15) Insomnia and sense of worry	.	.	.	.	.	o	1	2
(16) Unsteadiness of gaze	.	.	.	.	.	.	o	1	2

Total Rating Score   .   .   .

All of these (with the possible exception of (15)) are equally suitable for observers' or consultants' rating, but most incipient paranoid reactions are so well disguised that a ' Consultant ' type of estimate is alone reliable.

(ii) *Personal Questionnaires, Corresponding to above Rating Scales*

The following questionnaires imply a certain amount of self-rating, but are as far as possible indirect—to the extent of demanding information about behaviour, mental habits, and judgments on others instead of direct assessments of the self on personality features.

Each questionnaire agrees very closely in its items with the corresponding Rating Scale above. (There is, however, none corresponding with Epileptoid personality.)

No title (other than Syndrome 1, etc.) is given at the head of the questionnaire, because it is meant to be presented exactly as it stands. Subjects should be given a preliminary talk on the confidential nature of the results and the need for being entirely frank. The system of underlining one of three alternatives after each item should be explained. No time limit is applied.

The Minnesota Multiphasic Test is a well standardised questionnaire which may be considered an alternative or supplement to the present test, aiming at assessments of essentially the same syndromes, but intended to range over both normal and clinical, abnormal populations.

All the Cattell questionnaires together (less the epileptoid character) add up to a rating on general neurotic traits covering practically the same ground as the Woodworth Personal Data Sheet. For this purpose the experimenter must arrange the six syndromes to run consecutively, forming 120 [1] questions in all.

Personal Questionnaire—Group I Syndrome

1. Do you find yourself getting physically tired very easily and wanting to lie down?
   - 0. No.
   - 1. Occasionally.
   - 2. Often.

2. Do you get tired mentally very easily and feel tired most of the time?
   - 0. No.
   - 1. Occasionally.
   - 2. Often.

3. Do you get very worried, tremble, and perspire at the thought of a difficult task before you?
   - 0. No.
   - 1. Occasionally.
   - 2. Often.

4. Are there times when you are unable to concentrate, when your mind wanders, and the slightest thing distracts you?
   - 0. No.
   - 1. Occasionally.
   - 2. Often.

5. Do you have much trouble in making up your mind, e.g. as to what you will do next?
   - 0. No.
   - 1. Occasionally.
   - 2. Often.

6. Do you find your memory very poor and letting you down on important matters?
   - 0. No.
   - 1. Occasionally.
   - 2. Often.

7. Do you feel a lack of interest in things that used to interest you and find yourself quickly getting tired of friends, amusements, etc.?
   - 0. No.
   - 1. Occasionally.
   - 2. Often.

8. Do you sometimes get a dragging sense of pressure on top of your head or the back of your neck?
   - 0. No.
   - 1. Occasionally.
   - 2. Often.

9. Have you frequently a kind of backache, heaviness of the limbs, and a sense of general unfitness?
   - 0. Not at all.
   - 1. In a slight degree.
   - 2. Very much.

[1] The insomnia item occurs more than once; it should therefore be omitted on its second occurrence.

10. Do you find yourself getting irritable and aggressive without cause, snapping at people for trifles?

   0. No.
   1. Occasionally.
   2. Very much.

11. Are you troubled by moods of ' fed upness,' grouchiness, lowness of spirits, and feelings of despair?

   0. No.
   1. Occasionally.
   2. Very much.

12. Do these moods keep coming and going without any particular reason for them?

   0. No.
   1. Occasionally.
   2. Often.

13. Do you suffer from indigestion, so that your appetite is ' finnicky ' and uncertain?

   0. No.
   1. Occasionally.
   2. Often.

14. Are you constantly troubled by constipation?

   0. No.
   1. Occasionally.
   2. Often.

15. Do you find yourself unable to sleep well?

   0. No.
   1. Occasionally.
   2. Often.

16. Do you have difficulty in waking in the morning and feel not well rested after sleep?

   0. No.
   1. Occasionally.
   2. Often.

17. Are you ' jumpy,' e.g. do you find it hard to work where there are bright lights or sudden noises?

   0. No.
   1. Occasionally.
   2. Often.

18. Are you very sensitive to pressure of boots, clothes, etc., or unable to tolerate rough material next to your skin?

   0. No.
   1. Occasionally.
   2. Often.

19. Are you troubled by sweating of the skin, generally and especially of the palms of the hands?

   0. No.
   1. A little.
   2. Very much.

20. As a child, did you have the habit of bed-wetting or, as an adult, are you troubled by excessive nocturnal sexual emissions?

   0. No.
   1. Occasionally.
   2. Often.

Personal Questionnaire—Groups II (1 *to* 18 *inclusive*) *and III*
(1 *to* 28 *inclusive*)

1. Do you ever have a queer excessive   0. No.
   feeling of anxiety or dread with-   1. Occasionally.
   out any reason?   2. Often.

2. Have you ever had a ' fit ' of dread   0. No.
   (without obvious cause) which   1. Occasionally.
   has caused you to faint or col-   2. Often.
   lapse?

3. Does your heart beat too quickly at   0. No.
   times or thump in your ears so   1. Occasionally.
   that you cannot sleep?   2. Often.

4. Are you bothered by fluttering or   0. No.
   palpitating heart (seeming to miss   1. Occasionally.
   a beat) or by cramp pains in the   2. Often.
   heart region?

5. Have you tremors of the hand   0 No.
   (feeling shaky) or incessant   1. Occasionally.
   twitching of certain muscles?   2. Often.

6. Are you bothered by excessive   0. No.
   sweating of hands and feet, and   1. Occasionally.
   have you awakened in the night   2. Often.
   covered with perspiration?

7. Do you suffer from indigestion and   0. No.
   impaired appetite?   1. A little.
      2. Very much.

8 Do you ever have feelings of fullness   0. No.
   in the stomach, of dizziness and   1. Occasionally.
   sickness without apparent cause?   2. Often.

9. Have you ever had feelings of suf-   0. No.
   focation; of inability to get suf-   1. Occasionally.
   ficient air and oppression of   2. Often.
   breathing?

10. Have you suffered from prolonged   0. No.
    intestinal disturbance with alter-   1. Slightly.
    nating constipation and diar-   2. Very much.
    rhœa?

11. Do you sleep badly, waking after a few hours' sleep, etc.?
   0. No.
   1. Occasionally.
   2. Often.

12. Do you 'jump' badly at sudden lights, sounds, or touches?
   0. No.
   1. Occasionally.
   2. Often.

13. Do you find yourself having moods of undue excitability, depression, or irritability?
   0. No.
   1. Occasionally.
   2. Often.

14. Are there times when you feel very restless, unable to settle down or to concentrate on anything?
   0. No.
   1. Occasionally.
   2. Often.

15. Are you bothered by cold feet and hands, going blue even in moderate cold?
   0. No.
   1. Very slightly.
   2. Very much.

16. Does the power ever go out of your limbs so that you have to lean against something?
   0. No.
   1. Occasionally.
   2. Often.

17. Do things ever swim before your eyes, or go blurred or misty?
   0. No.
   1. Occasionally.
   2. Often.

18. Are you troubled by having to pass urine with undue frequency?
   0. No.
   1. Occasionally.
   2. Often.

19. Are you troubled by fear of being crushed in a crowd?
   0. No.
   1. Occasionally.
   2. Often.

20. Are you apprehensive when shut in small closed spaces, e.g. railway carriages, tunnels, cellars?
   0. No.
   1. Occasionally.
   2. Often.

21. Does it make you uneasy to cross a bridge, or a wide street or open square?
   0. No.
   1. Slightly.
   2. Very.

22. Have you ever been afraid of going insane?
   0. No.
   1. Occasionally.
   2. Often.

23. Have you ever feared that you are a   0. No.
    victim to heart trouble or to some   1. Occasionally.
    constitutional disease?   2. Often.

24. Are you afraid that you may jump   0. No.
    off or step over when you are on a   1. Occasionally.
    high place?   2. Often.

25. Do you have fears and worries about   0. No.
    things without sufficient cause?   1. Occasionally.
                                          2. Often.

26. Have you a particular dislike of any 0. No.
    one of these, so that you cannot   1. A little.
    contemplate it without a shud-   2. Very much.
    der? Thunder, spiders, moths,
    the dark, cats, blood.

27. Have you any particular dread not   0. No.
    mentioned above, and are you   1. Occasionally.
    much worried by it?   2. Often.

28. Do you have nightmares or wake up   0. No.
    frightened in the middle of the   1. Occasionally.
    night?   2. Often.

Personal Questionnaire—Group IV Syndrome

1. Have you ever had an arm or leg or   0. No.
   face muscle paralysed?   1. Once.
                                          2. Several
                                             times.

2. Have you ever gone temporarily   0. No.
   blind, half-blind or deaf, or lost   1. Occasionally.
   sensation?   2. Often.

3. Have you ever had fits or convul-   0. No.
   sions?   1. Occasionally.
                                          2. Often.

4. Have you ever had the habit of   0. No.
   twitching your face, neck, or   1. Slightly.
   shoulders involuntarily?   2. Very
                                             occasionally.

5. Are you troubled by severe headaches of a neuralgic kind?

0. No.
1. Occasionally.
2. Often.

6. Have you at times had a dislike for
all food, or a feeling that you
would be sick at the thought of it?

0. No.
1. Occasionally.
2. Often.

7. Do you at some times feel a totally
different person from what you
are at other times, and find yourself contradicting your other
point of view?

0. No.
1. Occasionally.
2. Often.

8. Do you walk in your sleep?

0. No.
1. Occasionally.
2. Often.

9. Do people tell you that you talk in
your sleep?

0. No.
1. Occasionally.
2. Often.

10. Do you ever do things in a dream-
like state without remembering
afterwards what you have done?

0. No.
1. Occasionally.
2. Often.

11. Have you ever been a stutterer?

0. No.
1. Slightly.
2. Very much.

12. Have you ever been temporarily
dumb, or lost your voice (except
from a cold)?

0. No.
1. Occasionally.
2. Often.

13. Do you ever find that you have forgotten periods of your life completely (since infancy)?

0. No.
1. Possibly.
2. Yes.

14. Have you ever been in an hypnotic
state?

0. No.
1. Occasionally.
2. Often.

15. Do you think that most people hide
a good deal of their emotion?

0. To a slight
extent.
1. To some ex-
tent.
2. To a high
degree.

16. Do you like acting and theatrical activities?

    0. No.
    1. A little.
    2. Very much.

17. Would you choose to have constant change and variety of excitement if you could?

    0. No.
    1. In moderation.
    2. A good deal.

18. Do you admire a person who can make a great impression in company and evoke general attention?

    0. No.
    1. Occasionally.
    2. Often.

19. Have you ever been the victim of cold and unsympathetic treatment, e.g. by parents, teachers, friends, or employers?

    0. No.
    1. Occasionally.
    2. Often.

20. Do you sometimes have emotions that you hardly know how to express, so that people don't understand you?

    0. No.
    1. Occasionally.
    2. Often.

21. Do you sometimes have cause to regret having been unduly angry, sulky, or excited in disagreements over trivial matters with friends?

    0. No.
    1. Occasionally.
    2. Often.

22. Do you find it a relief at times to throw off your responsibilities and indulge in childish amusements, have a lark, and be generally foolish?

    0. No.
    1. Occasionally.
    2. Often.

23. Have you ever had vivid day-dreams (since infancy) in which you could almost believe the happenings to be true?

    0. No.
    1. Occasionally.
    2. Often.

24. Are you capable of shutting out of your mind completely for a time things that might worry or disturb you so that you can be happy even in difficulties?

    0. No.
    1. Occasionally.
    2. Generally.

25. Do you suffer from disinclination to sleep and periods of wakefulness at nights?

0. No.
1. Occasionally.
2. Often.

26. Are you inconvenienced by uncontrollable blushing, trembling, or blanching?

0. No.
1. Slightly.
2. Very much.

Personal Questionnaire—Group V Syndrome

1. Are you aware of being bothered by trivial, useless thoughts or ideas that keep coming into your mind, e.g. a tune or a saying?

0. No.
1. Slightly.
2. Very much.

2. Do you sometimes think over some small problems again and again until you find you can't leave them alone?

0. No.
1. Occasionally.
2. Often.

3. Are you ever impelled to carry out trivial tasks with undue scrupulousness; e.g. folding up clothes, reading notices, cleaning things?

0. No.
1. Occasionally.
2. Often.

4. Do you sometimes get satisfaction from doing quite useless acts, e.g. counting windows, uttering rhymes or phrases, tapping lamp-posts?

0. No.
1. Occasionally.
2. Often.

5. Have you ever been afraid that you might strike or stab somebody, or set fire to something, or steal, in spite of your will?

0. No.
1. Occasionally.
2. Often.

6. Were you ever haunted by a fear of some unlikely or trivial happening, e.g. destroying valuable papers, being spied upon, blushing?

0. No.
1. Occasionally.
2. Often.

7. Do you regard strong will power as one of the most important virtues?

0. No.
1. Occasionally.
2. Often.

8. Do you think it right to insist on orderliness and thoroughness in everything that a person does?

0. No.
1. Moderately.
2. Yes. Decidedly.

9. Are you troubled by sleeplessness through ideas running on and on in your head?

0. No.
1. Occasionally.
2. Often.

10. Have you ever had a strong desire to commit suicide?

0. No.
1. Occasionally.
2. Often.

11. Were you brought up to feel that thrift is one of the most important virtues?

0. No.
1. To some extent.
2. Very definitely.

12. Did you ever have the habit of biting your finger-nails or gnawing the end of your pencil?

0. No.
1. Occasionally.
2. Often.

Personal Questionnaire—Group VI Syndrome

A self-rating on the epileptic character is not possible by a direct questionnaire, since the features are not introspectible happenings, but traits of personality, which could be reliably assessed only by projection tests or some other indirect technique.

The following questionnaire on paranoid reactions / depends for the assessment of milder symptoms on frank self-introspection. But owing to the impregnable self-opinionatedness of the paranoiac, no indication of graver symptoms could be obtained in this way. Consequently, the questionnaire attempts to approach these indirectly, with what success remains to be seen.

In evaluating results it must not be overlooked that such a constitution is not, in a sense, abnormal; that many valuable reforms and inventions have been carried through by paranoid types, etc., and that only certain forms of paranoia find their way into mental hospitals.

Personal Questionnaire—Group VII Syndrome

1. Do you hold a number of views on important matters which differ radically from those of the average man and concerning which you think the general viewpoint is entirely wrong?

   0. None of importance.
   1. A few points.
   2. Many points.

2. Do you know of any people who are trying to do you harm?

   0. No.
   1. One or two.
   2. Many.

3. Looking back at your school days, do you think that parents or teachers found fault with you perhaps more than you deserved?

   0. No.
   1. Occasionally.
   2. Often.

4. Do you feel upset when friends fail to see you and ' Cut you dead ' in the street (presumably by accident)?

   0. No.
   1. Slightly.
   2. Very much.

5. If you have a difference of opinion with people, does it disturb you inwardly, rankle, or make you feel uneasy for a long time?

   0. No.
   1. In a slight degree.
   2. Very much.

6. Have you ever been troubled when walking in the street by the feeling that many people are watching you?

   0. Never.
   1. Occasionally.
   2. Often.

7. Have you ever had an unaccountable feeling that people can read your thoughts and make you do things against your will (by a kind of hypnotism)?

   0. Never.
   1. Occasionally.
   2. Often.

8. If you have entered on a course of action with a certain plan in mind, do you prefer to carry on with it in spite of discomforts instead of modifying it all the time in response to suggestions?

   0. No.
   1. Occasionally.
   2. Often.

9. Can you be ' self-willed ' and ' ob-   0. Never.
   stinate ' when a principle is con-   1. Sometimes.
   cerned?   2. In a high de-
                gree.

10. When you have heard a story but   0. Never.
    are later told some new facts   1. Rarely.
    which modify it, do you ever find   2. Fairly often.
    yourself absent-mindedly sticking
    to the original?

11. Do you feel that people take an un-   0. No.
    necessarily long time to recognise   1. In some
    the value of your work?   things.
                                         2. Often.

12. Have you ever been accused of be-   0. Never.
    ing too cold, proud, and ' stuck   1. Occasionally.
    up '?   2. Often.

13. Have you ever had cause to suspect   0. Never.
    that someone has been trying to   1. Occasionally.
    poison you or make you ill?   2. Often.

14. Do you think that most people spend   0. No.
    too much time in social life and   1. To some ex-
    have insufficient time to think in   tent.
    solitude?   2. Decidedly.

15. Are you shy and uncertain of your-   0. No.
    self in your relations with others   1. In a slight
    (particularly inferiors and super-   degree.
    iors), and are you troubled a lot   2. Very much.
    by thoughts about what others
    are thinking of you?

16. Do you sometimes unjustly accuse   0. No.
    yourself of disagreeableness and   1. Occasionally.
    find later that the fault was in fact   2. Often.
    with the other people?

17. Are you the sort of person who is   0. No.
    normally calm, but who can be   1. In a mild de-
    moved passionately to action by   gree.
    injustice or for the sake of a prin-   2. Very much so.
    ciple?

18. Have you ever taken violent action   0. Never.
     against a persistently evil person   1. Occasionally.
     for the above reasons (17)?   2. Often.

19. Do you find yourself getting tired   0. No.
     easily by work or emotional stress,   1. Occasionally.
     so that you can't apply yourself   2. Often.
     as you would wish?

20. Do you find ideas about some parti-   0. No.
     cular thing going on and on in   1. Occasionally.
     your mind so that you are unable   2. Often.
     to sleep?

No norms for these questionnaires among normal and abnormal persons have yet been built up. They should be built up on a percentile basis for the groups with which each experimenter is concerned. The author will be pleased to receive contributions towards such norms from authenticated research sources.

(B) MEANS OF EXPLORATION OF CONFLICT AREAS

(i) *Word Association*

Few techniques have proved their value so definitely as Jung's cleverly-worked-out Word Association method, first propounded forty years ago.[1] The method consists in instructing the subject to respond to the word which is called out to him with the first word that comes into his mind, as quickly as possible and without regard to the apparent relevance or propriety of the response word. A carefully prepared series of stimulus words is read out, the response word is noted, and the time elapsing between the utterance of the stimulus word and the response is recorded by a reaction time apparatus (lip key is best) or stop-watch reading to fifths of a second.

Immediately afterwards the stimulus words are read out to the subject again, and he is asked to reproduce the words he gave as responses on the first occasion (he is not forewarned that this will happen). His ability to do so, or, failing that, the substitute words he presents, are recorded.

---

[1] *Diagnostische Assoziationstudien*, Leipzig, vol. i, 1906 ; vol. ii, 1910.

Jung's list of 100 words for adult analyses is given below. Both the original[1] and the modified series are given, the original being in brackets where the words differ from the later version.

	1. head		35. mountain			68. paint
	2. green	(to die)	36. play			69. part
	3. water		37. salt			70. old
(to sing)	4. stick		38. new			71. flower
(dead)	5. angel		39. custom	(to beat)	72. strike
	6. long	(to pray)	40. ride	(box)	73. chest
(ship)	7. boat	(money)	41. wall	(wild)	74. savage
(to pay)	8. plow	(foolish)	42. stupid		75. family
(window)	9. wool	(pamphlet)	43. handle		76. wash
	10. friendly		44. despise		77. cow
(to cook)	11. table	(finger)	45. tooth	(friend)	78. strange
	12. ask	(expensive)	46. right		79. luck
(cold)	13. state	(bird)	47. folk	(lie)	80. tell
(stem)	14. defiant	(to fall)	48. stink	(deportment)81. decorum
(to dance)	15. stalk		49. book		82. narrow
(village)	16. dance		50. unjust		83. brother
(lake)	17. sea		51. frog	(to fear)	84. injury
	18. sick	(to part)	52. divide		85. stork
(bride)	19. pride		53. hunger		86. false
	20. cook		54. white	(anxiety)	87. decorum
	21. ink	(child)	55. ox		88. kiss
(angry)	22. bad	(to take care)56. attend	(bride)	89. fire
	23. needle	(lead pencil) 57. pencil	(pure)	90. dirty
	24. swim		58. sad		91. door
(voyage)	25. journey		59. plum		92. choose
	26. blue	(to marry)	60. meet		93. hay
(lamp)	27. bread	(house)	61. law	(contented)	94. steep
(to sin)	28. threaten	(dear)	62. love	(ridicule)	95. derision
(bread)	29. lamp		63. glass		96. sleep
	30. rich	(to quarrel)	64. fight	(mice)	97. month
	31. tree	(far)	65. traits		98. coloured
(to prick)	32. sing	(great)	66. great	(woman)	99. dog
	33. pity	(carrot)	67. potato	(to abuse)	100. speak
	34. yellow				

The list which the author finds most useful with children and adolescents is given on pp. 284-5. Most of these words are likely to be of significance with ' problem ' cases. They are arranged in alphabetical order so that the subject may not be led to ponder unduly on the selection and arrangement of words, and so that the experimenter may be assisted to refer quickly to the result on any word that particularly interests him. Banal words lacking in possible significance have been inserted as a buffer between words likely to have emotional value, in order that

[1] Jung, " The Association Method," *Amer. J. Psychol.*, 1910.

perseveration effects from any given word (see p. 286) may be more clearly revealed.

Explain to the subject that he must respond *as quickly as possible*. With children it is necessary to insist on this afresh from time to time. Give four practice words (dog, pen, etc.) before the 100 significant words begin. Proceed at an even rate, calling words very clearly and timing from the last syllable of the uttered word to the first sound of response. Make no comment on responses—this would upset reproduction by modifying the carry-over effect from one word to another. Facilitate recording by having the words printed in the manner shown; the time can be indicated by a tick in the appropriate column, if less than 4 seconds (fractions of a second are not important) and by a number if 4 seconds or more. Similarly, physical signs of embarrassment can be recorded by a tick. When working through the reproductions, try to proceed with a smooth, even rhythm, ticking where correct, writing down quickly where different. Afterwards write in the space below the list the words and responses which have been selected as significant according to the criteria listed below.

Complex Indicators and Criteria of Significant Associations

The following list includes those suggested by Jung, those confirmed by later workers, and some items observed in the work of the present writer.

A. *Concerning the Manner of the Responses*

(1) Unduly long reaction time (also, rarely, abnormally rapid).

(2) Unduly long reaction time to the stimulus immediately following. Very rarely this may arise from intellectual difficulties, e.g. absence of a synonym or an opposite when the subject is set to give each.

(3) Hesitation and correction of barely uttered word.

(4) Physical signs of embarrassment, twitching, blushing, expressive gesture, drumming with the fingers, etc., with apparatus, also, breathing curve (effort sign); increase of pulse rate; psychogalvanic reflexes (see p. 296).

FIG. 61.—STANDARD ASSOCIATION-WORD CARD.

List of one hundred association words arranged especially for use with children.

Stimulus Word.	Time. (in seconds)						Response.	Reproduction.
	½	1	2	3	More than 3	Standard Time.		
Practice Words.								
DOG								
PEN								
CLEVER								
JUMP								
afraid*				√		6½	Against	√
ask		√				3	question	√
ashamed*					7	6	dishonest	deceitful
baby			√			3½	small	√
bed			√			2	rest	√
be careful		√				4½	warning	√
boys					8	2	human beings	friends
blushing		√				2½	colour	√
brother	√					2	in family	√
bully	√					2½	enemy	afraid
burglar			√			3	thief	√
can't do it	√					4	afraid	√
clumsy	√					3½	careless	√
cocoa			√			1½	liquid	√
cruel					4	2½	coward	hard
cradle			√			2½	rest	√
coward*			√			4½	afraid	against
chase	√					2	run	√
Daddy			√			1	parent	√
dark		√				2	colour	√
dash		√				2	make haste	√
death		√				3	asleep	√
desk			√			1½	sitting	√
deceitful*	√					4	sly	√
dirty					4	2	unclean	√
disobey*					5	5½	untrustful	unfaithful
do-your-best	√					4½	faithful	√
dreaming		√				2½	sleeping	√
eating sweets		√				2½	chewing	√
enemy	√					4	against	√
fainting		√				4	sleeping	√
fool			√			3½	silly	√
forget*			√			3	thoughtless	√
far away			√			2	miles	√
friends			√			3½	company	√
goodhiding		√				4	disobey	√
girls					4	2	family	√
guilty					6	4	treason	unfaithful
grown-up-people		√				1½	adults	√
happy*	√					2½	joyful	√
helpless	√					6	weak	√
hate			√			3	enemy	√
hospital	√					2	place	√
hurry up	√					1½	quick	√
intelligent*	√					4	sense	√
jealous*	√					4½	against	√
kind	√					2	enemy	√
kiss	√					4	love	√
lamb	√					1½	sheep	√
laugh		√				2½	happy	√
laziness	√					2	ungrateful	weak
lavatory					7	6	article	√
little	√					1	small	√
liar	√					2	deceitful	√

Stimulus Word.	Time.						Response.	Reproduction.
	½	1	2	3	More than 3	Standard Time.		
love*		✓				3	kind	✓
manners		✓				3½	polite	✓
marry	✓					2½	love	✓
mother					4	1½	parent	home
money				✓		2	spend	✓
mischievous		✓				3	sly	✓
mother's boy (or girl)[1]		✓				2	daughter	✓
music		✓				2	joyful	✓
naked	✓					1½	stripped	✓
narrow	✓					2	thin	✓
nasty man*	✓					4	hateful	✓
nest		✓				2	home	✓
nightmare						3	dream	✓
orphan boy (or girl)[1]	✓					2½	homeless	✓
playing	✓					2½	toy	✓
punishment*		✓				3½	disobey	✓
quarrelling*		✓				2	unfriendly	✓
row*		✓				2½	quarrel	✓
romping		✓				2	noise	✓
run away*					4	3½	afraid	stay
school work			✓			2	lesson	✓
selfish		✓				4	unkind	✓
showing-off*		✓				4½	swank	✓
sister	✓					2	friend	✓
shy					4	6	against	afraid
sickness	✓					2	ill	✓
sleep*				✓		2½	sound	✓
stay at home*		✓				2½	away	✓
stealing		✓				1½	thief	✓
stories	✓					2	tales	✓
strict*		✓				3	harsh	✓
strong		✓				2	brave	✓
stubborn*					4	4½	awkward	weak
success			✓			3	powerful	effort
swearing				✓		3½	dirty	✓
teddy bear		✓				2	toy	✓
temper		✓				3½	hard	evil
tickle		✓				2½	toy	silly
top of the class		✓				1½	position	✓
thumb sucking		✓				3	baby	✓
unfair					5	4½	deceitful	unfaithful
won't eat it			✓			2½	unwanted	✓
wet	✓					1	cold	✓
whisper		✓				2	quiet	✓
wicked				✓		1½	nasty	hard
subject's name[2]	✓					3	name	✓

SPACE FOR NOTING SIGNIFICANT WORDS.

ashamed	lavatory
boys	mother
cruel	run away
dirty	shy
disobey	stubborn
guilty	unfair
	wicked

[1] Say ' boy ' for boys and ' girl ' for girls.

* Words which 50 per cent. or over among average children fail to recall.

[2] Say child's name here, e.g. John Smith.

NOTE: The times, response words and reproductions in the above list are those of a particular child (see p. 290) given here as an illustration.

(5) Complete failure of reaction. " Cannot think of anything."

B. *Concerning the Nature of the Response Word*

(6) Misunderstanding stimulus word; interpreting it in an unusual sense in keeping with interests of the emotional complex.

(7) Avoidance by superficial reactions :

(*a*) Naming objects in room, e.g. ink, desk; or reacting with a word prepared before the stimulus arrives (easily detectable).

(*b*) Giving opposites, or synonyms or definitions. ' Too easy ' associations. The former are partly a matter of mental set and of temperament. In the writer's observation schizothymes are particularly liable to adopt a definite set—minds craving order, obsessionals, etc., do the same. Wehrlin found that the tendency to give definitions (especially banal ones) was partly a matter of low intelligence, being very common in imbeciles.

(*c*) Repeating the stimulus word, or the stimulus word slightly modified, or a word given as a response a few moments before.

(*d*) Clang, rhyme, or punning associations or associations avoiding normal sense, e.g. slang on the one hand or foreign translations, and pompous, stilted reactions on the other.

(*e*) Reacts with several words instead of one word, according to the instructions ; names objects in room.

(8) Unusual, far-fetched, or idiosyncratic reactions (these to be investigated later).

(9) Perseverations of an idea. When reactions to subsequent words have evidently little relation to the meaning of these words and instead are clearly perseverations of an idea evoked by the first word.

(10) Failure of Reproduction. (The subject cannot remember the word he gave the first time or gives a word quite different under the impression that it is the right one.)

Discussion on Interpretation

It is well established that some, if not all, of these signs tend to accompany associations which touch powerful emotional roots in the subject. But not all anomalous reactions are associated with complexes in the true restricted meaning of complex. Rather would it be true to say that there are three sources for reactions having these stigma: (1) a true complex or emotional conflict not consciously realised by the subject; (2) an emotional conflict fully in consciousness, but which the subject wishes to hide from the experimenter (or society generally —as in the case of a crime); (3) any idea having strong emotional value, e.g. as part of a sentiment. The delay, etc., in response may therefore be due to unconscious inhibitions, conscious caution, or the upset of cognitive activity due to the presence of emotion.

The test has been used with success by Jung and by others to detect crime—even minor ' crime ' involving little emotional tension. Professor Washburn and Miss Leach,[1] for example, evaluated the above listed criteria with regard to their effectiveness for this purpose. Abnormality of time of response they found most diagnostic, and were able to detect 22 out of 26 cases of deceit by this means alone. Three of the remaining four they diagnosed correctly by time plus nature of association. A *very* long association proved invariably to be connected with the emotional memories in question. Jung picked out the long association times, not by comparing times with the average for 100 words, but by ranking times and taking all those above the middle value (median) established for that particular person. In most people he found the majority of the reactions at little more than $\frac{1}{5}$ second, but with hysterics he found all the reactions (even to the non-significant words) much longer—averaging, in fact, several seconds.

Using a stop-watch (i.e. dispensing with exact reaction time apparatus) the present writer finds, at any rate with

---

[1] *Amer. J. Psychol.*, 1910.

children and adolescents, that most normal reactions are recorded as ½ second or 1 second. There is no loss of effectiveness through this less fine measurement (except in detecting those rare ' very rapid ' reactions—which in any case are generally evident to ordinary observation alone), for the great majority of significant reactions are more than 3 seconds (hence the division of columns at this point in the above record card). Jung's technique may be decidedly improved by allowing for the fact that some words are emotionally toned for all people. The list of 100 words here used contains a great number of emotionally significant words, so that short reactions will be almost the exception. Moreover, the writer's results suggest that children and adolescents are normally distinctly slower in reactions than adults,[1] possibly because their inhibitions have been more recently acquired. The average times on each word for a group of varied mildly neurotic or difficult children and adolescents have been included in the record card above, so that each new subject's times may be put against a standard for comparison. The realisation that even in general there is a long reaction time to such words as ashamed, afraid, lavatory, etc., should save the analyst from many a wild-goose chase.

Undoubtedly long reaction time and failure of reproduction (1 and 10 above) are the most important indications of emotional conflict and of resistance. Avoidance by superficial reaction (7) is only adopted by certain types, and in any case, the use of opposites and synonyms (7b) occurs with practically everyone in response to many stimuli having no emotional significance.

When the significant words have been selected (usually about a dozen) they can be used as the basis for free association at a later sitting, when the reasons for particular responses can be unravelled and the main motives revealed.

In addition to the analyses of complexes by the above approach, the experiment offers evidence as to general

[1] This is found in most association experiments.

psychological type. Thus there is the type of person who indulges in adjectives of value, usually exaggerated, describing the subject's personal attitudes, e.g. *to piano*—'*horrible*'; *father*—'*something good, nice, holy*'; or, more personal and less affected, *money*—'*convenient*.' This mentality Jung calls the 'value predicate type,' and it is found chiefly in persons with emotional affectation, over-enthusiasm, etc., hiding an inner lack of true feeling. Fürst found the personal predicate type particularly common in women over 40 and men over 60. In addition to the various predicate types, we may also distinguish: (1) the objective type, with undisturbed reactions: this is the normal, balanced personality; (2) the pedantic definition type, found principally among those of low intelligence (or who wish to hide intelligence), e.g. *apple*—'*a fruit tree*'; *father*—'*chief of the family*'; (3) the type with marked complexes, for the qualitative analysis of which the test was mainly devised.

The full possibilities of the experiment in this direction of type analysis have not yet been worked out. The significance of synonyms, opposites, definitions, etc., as an indication of obsessional types, of long reaction times at all points, together with many-worded responses, as indication of hysterical types, is repeatedly evident in the writer's experience. The test has been used by Rosanoff[1] to distinguish various psychotic conditions, and by Claude and Robin with etherised dementia præcox patients as an aid to prognosis. The results in the latter case were promising, but not of striking value.

The ease with which the child is able to assume the 'free association' attitude, i.e. to act without some definite mental set, is also of value in diagnosing personality. Poverty of ideas, as shown in constant employment of a relatively meagre set of response words, should also be noted (particularly as evidence of amount of Fluency of Association or of general emotional resistance).

Fürst found a marked resemblance in reaction pattern

[1] A. J. Rosanoff, *Manual of Psychiatry*, 1927.

(particularly in the nature of associations) between members of the same family. For mother and child it is greater than for father and child; for parent and child of the same sex than for those of opposite sex.

Finally, one should bear in mind that intelligent subjects of good psychological insight are better able (though never completely able) to disguise complexes. Chronic patients (long-established complexes) also tend to show less obviously the typical signs in this experiment.

Example.—Girl of 13·7. Referred for stealing, lying, and bad language at home. I.Q.90. Fluency of Association, 3rd Decile. Perseveration, 8th Decile, before treatment; 3rd Decile after. Reactions on word association test given in sample record sheet on p. 250. Significant words: ashamed, boys, cruel, dirty, disobey, guilty, lavatory, mother, run away, shy, stubborn, unfair, wicked.

Social worker's report shows child's mother (who had spoilt her) died when she was 5. Since 10 years has been brought up by father and stepmother. Father strict but emotional, and much more attached to stepmother than to daughter.

Free associations, etc., on above significant words, and the responses to them (dishonest, deceitful, hard, unfaithful, etc.) revealed: (1) (ashamed, boys, guilty)—she had lately been seeking affection with boys, and indulging in premature sex play; (2) (lavatory, dirty) an outbreak of fæcal incontinence and enuresis lasting a year, not reported by parents; (3) (disobey, stubborn, unfair, unfaithful) a profound resentment at father preferring stepmother to herself; (4) (cruel, wicked, guilty) the persistence of considerable love for the father (with some fantasies about their relation) alongside hatred (ambivalence). This expressed itself in a masochistic form, inviting cruelty from the father and welcoming a sense of guilt and wickedness. Many anal-erotic elements. Treatment, through direct psycho-therapy with child, together with removal to a stable foster parent (on Children's Court order as ' beyond control ' at home).

Group Test

The Pressey X-O Test, for students and for children, can be used, in one of its aspects, as a guide to emotional abnormalities, worries, and affective associations. It takes rather less than 30 minutes with children. Obtainable from Messrs. Stoelting.

Davis Personal Problems Test.—More direct in its approach. Requires 20 minutes or less. Messrs. Stoelting.

(ii) *Free Association, Play Observation, and Other Psychoanalytic Techniques*

It is somewhat difficult to describe fully the technique of ' free association ' without entering into therapeutic notions in psycho-analysis which lie outside the scope of this book and which have not been subjected to the same degree of examination by scientific method as have the other notions to which we have given space.

To whatever school of psycho-therapy one may belong, however, it is impossible for one to deny the value of free association (and its homologue ' play observation ' in the child) in getting at deeper emotional trends, particularly in the unconscious. Usually the subject is allowed to lie on a comfortable settee or bed in a darkened room, in circumstances which induce a half-asleep, dream-like, or hypnotic state. He is instructed to relax completely, to offer no obstacle to whatever enters his mind, to forget the usual inhibitions and embarrassments, and to describe the ideas and images that float into his mind, without regard to the need for logical connections. The psycho-therapist, out of sight, records these ideas, making particular note of long pauses, complete blanks, and other signs of resistance. It is about these points that the psychotherapist sets the train of association working on later occasions. The subject's attitude in free association is one obtained by most people with difficulty, so that practice is necessary before the procedure is carried out satisfactorily.

Opinions differ as to how far this technique is possible

with children. It is certainly possible with secondary school children of 12 years or more, but, if only because of the artificiality of the procedure when demanded of younger children, it seems advisable to make some modification for them. A useful modification consists in having a darkened box with a hole at one end through which the child peers. He is instructed to imagine things happening within and to report what he sees (" Like seeing things in clouds or in the fire "). Griffiths,[1] in her excellently controlled study of imagination, reports that the fantasies reported under such circumstances have a close connection with the child's actual dreams.

Yet to ask most children of less than 9 years, " What are you thinking about? " or even " What can you see? " (in imagination) is to draw a blank. It is then that one must turn to the observation of play. A range of toys suitable for children of all ages should be exposed to view in the clinic play-room. Teddy bears, dolls of varying mien, constructional toys, steam engines, fire engines, skittles, games of skill may well be included. In the first place, some knowledge of the emotional age of the child is gained from observing his or her preferences. Secondly, one looks for the phantasies which the child works out, often with the aid of monologue, with the toys. The present writer has found most useful in this respect (and also most popular) a variety of figures in lead, soldiers, farmer, farmer's wife, children, animals, redskins, etc., together with houses and fences which may be variously arranged in a large sand tray. Equally important are opportunities to draw and scribble, to build in bricks, and to make patterns in counters. Featureless objects like bricks are especially valuable in being more completely amenable to whatever symbolisation the child wants to give them.

Perhaps the fullest study of the significance of play (though restricted to the psycho-analytic sexual conceptions of motivation) is that made by Klein,[2] who says, " The

---

[1] Griffiths, *Imagination in Early Childhood* (Kegan Paul).
[2] M. Klein, " Personification in the Play of Children," *Internat. J. of Psycho-Analysis*, x, 1929; *The Psycho-analysis of Children*, 1932 (Hogarth Press).

child expresses its phantasies, its wishes, and its actual experiences in a symbolic way through play and games. In doing so it makes use of the same archaic and phylogenetic mode of expression, the same language, as it were, that we are familiar with in dreams; and we can only fully understand this language if we approach it in the way Freud has taught us to approach the language of dreams. Symbolism is only a part of it. The psychologist may well observe some of this play, and most of the games behaviour with other children, from behind a one-way screen, but if he is to make a fuller analysis of play he will need to be by the child's side, to listen to the child's spontaneous comments, to interject questions as certain things are being done or drawn, and, more rarely, to create test situations in play. There is a great deal of deeper probing to be done in play, on the lines of Klein's work, but without necessarily the same pre-conceptions. Even without this, however, it is possible, through play observation, to get a shrewd notion of the main trends of instinct for which the child is seeking expression.

(c) PHYSIOLOGICAL APPROACHES AND METHODS

A valuable ancillary to the above methods of studying emotional tendencies is provided by the techniques that have been developed for recording emotional reactions to particular stimuli through observations of certain accompanying physiological indicators of emotion, etc. Indeed, these are the only methods yet available for measuring quantitatively an emotional response, and we must not forget that a true science of sentiment and complex structure will only be possible when quantitative calculations can be made.

The principal apparatuses and methods available are:

(1) Sphygmograph for recording frequency and amplitude of pulse.

(2) Plethysmograph for studying the changes in volume of blood vessels and arteries.

(3) Sphygmomanometer for recording blood-pressure.

(4) Electro-cardiograph for recording magnitude of the heart's contraction.

(5) Pneumograph for studying the breathing curve.

(6) Psychogalvanic reflex for recording electrical changes in the skin.

(7) Measures of metabolic rate changes through recording oxygen consumption.

The mental changes associated with records on (1), (2), (3), (5), and (6) have up to the present been most studied, so that fairly compact sets of apparatus and a convenient technique for using two or three of these at once have been worked out.[1] Much is gained by recording several changes side by side in this way, but when a choice must be made of one only (because of time, space, or cost), then the psychogalvanometer, which is the most promising, is best used. Consequently, that alone will be described in any detail here.

Brief Account of Indications to be gained and Methods to be used with various Apparatuses

(1), (2), (4). The effects of emotional responses on heart-beat and blood-pressure are well known. Darrow[2] has made the curious observation that disturbing external stimuli lower blood-pressure, whereas disturbing ideational stimuli increase it. Since the former generally give a larger psychogalvanic response than the latter, the combination of the records of these two instruments shows pretty clearly whether an emotion is due to an ideational or a presented stimulus.

(3) The plethysmograph, recording the swelling and contraction of the forearm, is somewhat cumbersome, but by means of a tambour connected to an air residue above the liquid, it can be made accurately self-recording. It has the disadvantage of a big time lag (several seconds) between the emotion and the effect; of absence of response to all but the coarser qualities of emotion, and of being

---

[1] Caster, *J. General Psychol.*, iv, 1930; Darrow, *J. Exp. Psychol.*, xii, 1929; Messerle, "Puls, Elektrokardiogramm, Atmung und Galvanogramm bei Schiess," versuchen. *Z. f. d. ges. Neur. u. Psychiat.*, cviii, 137.

[2] *Op. cit.*

affected by factors other than emotion, e.g. physical exertion, direction of attention to limb, heart peculiarities. Nevertheless, striking results are sometimes obtained.[1]

(5) Pneumographic records, from a tambour attached to bands encircling the body at the thorax and below the diaphragm, are very easily recorded. Although plateaux in the curve, indicating an involuntary arrest of breathing, are of value for detecting moments of attention and effort, and although the speed and depth of breathing correlate with emotional response, the main diagnostic interest lies in the ratio of length of inspiration to expiration in individual waves.

The ratio $\dfrac{\text{Time of inhalation}}{\text{Time of exhalation}}$ and subsequent pause is usually about $\frac{1}{4}$, but may rise to almost 1 in conditions of emotional stress. This fact has been applied with about 80–90 per cent. success to detecting lying in persons not seasoned liars.

(6) Metabolic rate is very little increased by cognitive activity, but with the same cognitive activity under external stress (e.g. noise) or when accompanied by the slightest emotional under-current or worry, the rate increases markedly. This is a promising instrument for further investigation, though at present insufficiently sensitive, since the oxygen consumption of the body, even during resting conditions, is hundreds of times greater than that of the nervous system itself.

(7) *The Pyschogalvanometer.*—The reaction here described (also called the galvanic skin reflex) has been the subject of at least 150 published investigations, the main findings of which are implicit in the following instructions.

Two distinct phenomena are involved:

(1) The T-phenomenon, which is an actual E.M.F. produced in the body by certain mental changes.

(2) The F-phenomenon, which is a change in the electrical resistance of the body, almost entirely in the skin, associated with certain mental experiences.

[1] See, e.g., H. Eng, *The Emotional Life of the Child* (Oxford Univ. Press).

The latter is a much larger effect, and has been almost exclusively used for the purposes of measurement.

The Apparatus (for the F-phenomenon) may be one of two kinds:

(1) The ordinary Wheatstone bridge circuit with resistances approximately as shown below, which has to be balanced before the experiment, and which shows changes of the subject's resistance by movements of the delicate galvanometer.

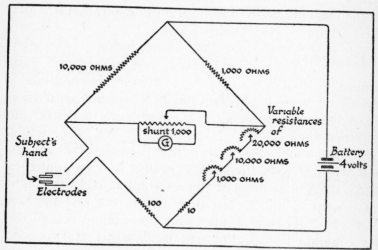

Fig. 62.—Diagram of psychogalvanometer circuit.

(2) The tachogram circuit, in which a current is continuously passing through the subject. Slow continuous changes of resistance are not recorded, but only the sharp sudden deflections. This has the advantage that constant vigilance in 'balancing' by the experimenter is not required, but the disadvantage that (*a*) deflections have to be calculated from the *area* beneath the deflection curve, and (*b*) the slow changes of resistance, not recorded, are nevertheless often of psychological importance.

We shall, therefore, proceed as if the first-named apparatus were being employed.

Three practical difficulties arise: (1) the necessity for avoiding polarisation effects at the electrodes attached to the subject; (2) the need to avoid changes of resistance due to muscular movements at the attached point; (3) the problem of working out the changes of resistance from the observed galvanometer deflections.

(1) and (2) are largely avoided by using flat brass or copper-electrodes of about 1 inch diameter, covered by chamois leather soaked in physiological salt solution and strapped firmly to the palm and back of the hand respectively, the arm being fixed to the chair. The same pad should always be attached to the same face of the hand (the resistance being different in different directions). Liquid non-polarisable electrodes, consisting of small cylinders into which the fingers are placed, have also proved successful.[1]

From this calibration of the apparatus one can construct curves which enable one to read off the fall of resistance in ohms, for any given size of deflection (in cms.) at any particular absolute resistance of the subjects. This value (in ohms), to be made comparable with others, must next be expressed as a percentage (fall) of the absolute resistance of the subject. Even falls expressed as a percentage, however, are found not to be strictly comparable. It has been found that, on an average, the size of deflection (as a percentage fall) decreases slightly with increasing absolute resistance, at the rate of 5 per cent. (of itself) for every 10,000 ohms increase in the total resistance of the subject.[2] Therefore, before making psychological comparisons, every deflection at a resistance above some agreed value (say 10,000 ohms) should be increased to the size which it would have at 10,000 ohms—the standard—by the 5 per cent. correction mentioned above.

(3) is most easily overcome by substituting a P.O. Box or some other controllable resistance for the subject and

[1] See Lauer, " A New Type of Electrode for the Galvanic Skin Reflex," *J. Exp. Psychol.*, xi, 1928.

[2] R. B. Cattell, " Experiments on the Psychical Correlate of the Psycho-galvanic Reflex," *Brit. J. Psychol.*, 1929.

working out empirically the relation of various arranged falls of resistance (at various absolute resistances) to observed deflection.

Deflections also diminish with repeated stimulation,[1] the tenth stimulus (each being fresh to the subject) producing on an average only about half the deflection of the first; here too a correction must be applied.

The galvanometer (moving coil with mirror) deflections can be read off directly on the graduated light screen, but this generally necessitates an assistant being present. A satisfactory alternative arrangement consists in recording the deflections on a moving strip of photographic paper on which a time marking and the movement and duration of the stimulus are also recorded. Further information is then often obtainable from studying the developed tracings at leisure.

Procedure.—The subject's left hand should be washed free of dust or grease and strapped lightly but firmly between the electrodes. The resistance falls rapidly for the first 5 minutes, after which it reaches a stable level.[2] The bridge is then balanced, bringing the spot light of the galvanometer back to zero, and the presentation of stimuli may begin. These may be isolated words, as when the psycho-galvanic apparatus is used with the word association method (p. 281). The deflection resulting from each is noted. The magnitude of this deflection is a more reliable[3] ' complex indicator ' than the length of reaction time, etc., used in Jung's method, but both together provide highly valid indications.

The psycho-galvanic apparatus has also been used in dream analysis, the points at which marked deflections occur while the subject is relating his dream being noted.[4] It has been employed to determine reaction to particular

[1] R. B. Cattell, " Experiments on the Psychical Correlate of the Psycho-galvanic Reflex, "*Brit. J. Psychol.*, 1929.
[2] " The Significance of the Actual Resistances in Psycho-galvanic Experiments," *Brit. J. Psychol.*, xix, 1928.
[3] Whately Smith, *The Measurement of Emotion.*
[4] Ikin, Pear, and Thouless, " The Psycho-galvanic Phenomenon in Dream Analysis," *Brit. J. Psychol.*, xv, 1924.

objects; to differentiate among the insane [1]; to measure the strength of instincts and sentiments (with success), and to distinguish various types of personality [2]—on the basis of each person's average size of deflection to a standard series of stimuli. A recent bibliography, with references to other bibliographies, has been given by the present writer.[3]

Interpretation of Measurements.—The actual (absolute) resistance of the subject, which may vary from about 5,000 to 200,000 ohms, is commonly about 15,000, and itself has significance as indicating the degree of ' awakeness ' of the subject. It rises as a subject settles into a state of boredom or fatigue, and becomes very high in sleep. It is low in a state of excitement, worry, or after a shock.

There is also evidence that this resistance is low in epileptics, nervous temperaments, and those suffering from Basedowism. It is high in hysterics and in the early stages of spinal paralysis. Among normal characters, resistance may be regarded as roughly proportional to the amount of suppression continuously exercised upon himself by the subject.

As regards the actual deflections, these may arise from coughing, sneezing, and laughter, but such deflections are readily distinguishable from the true deflections resulting from psychical causes.

The magnitude of deflection was once thought to be proportional to the amount of emotion, but there is considerable evidence that it corresponds rather to conation and the conative element in emotion. (Greatest deflections occur with Pain, Tension, Fear, Excitement, Will Acts, Impulses and Effort.[4]) Deflections are proportional to the intensity of the experience,[4] whether it be pure conation or emotional toned conation.

Their magnitude is decreased by fatigue, depression,

---

[1] Ikin, Pear, and Thouless,"The Psycho-galvanic Phenomenon in Dream Analysis," *Brit. J. Psychol.*, vol. xv, 1924.

[2] See M. Washburn in R. B. Cattell's summary, *op. cit.*

[3] R. B. Cattell, *op. cit.*

[4] R. B. Cattell, *op. cit.*

alcohol, morphine, chloroform, ether, and during men-
struation. The hypothesis which seems to the present
writer most apt to the facts, is that the deflection is proportional to the act of suppression which the ego finds
it necessary to exercise upon the impulse aroused. The
psychogalvanometer can therefore be used as a measure
of the strength of impulses, of will acts, and of the conflict
between them.

It has a secondary value in discriminating between
various types of personality, according to the size of mean
deflection on a representative collection of stimuli.

Large deflections are found in cheerful as opposed to
depressed temperaments, in subjects of lively and emotional
disposition; those who rank high for quickness of decision,
soundness of bodily constitution, and desire to excel;
those who do well in examinations with only normal intelligence, and those with surgent cyclothyme (H) temperament (p. 173). The correlation with the latter is ·30 to
·60, but it may be higher with some of the other qualities.

Unduly small deflections are found with most psychotics,
but particularly with manic depressives in the depressive
phase, and dementia præcox cases, especially in the
hebephrenic and katatonic forms. Idiots and dements
give very small deflections. Among normals small deflections are indicative of depressed temperament low
emotionality, desurgent temperaments,[1] and a 'run-
down' condition.

*Physiological Measurements and Individual Differences of
Mentality.*—Attempts have been made to relate most of the
above physiological measurements to temperament estimates. One of the most thorough of these [2] shows that
the physiological measurements of basal metabolism,
blood-pressure (both systolic and diastolic) and pulse-rate
have a low positive inter-correlation. A high metabolic
rate was associated (to a significant degree) with ' lively '

---

[1] R. B. Cattell, " Temperament Tests, II," *op. cit.*
[2] Omwake, Dexter, and Lewis, " The Inter-relations of Certain Physiological
Measurements and Aspects of Personality," *Character and Personality*, iii, 1,
1934.

as opposed to ' calm ' temperaments, with high scholastic performance, and possibly with high intelligence (correlation $\cdot24 \pm \cdot076$). The only other finding sufficiently significant to be of any practical use was the association of low pulse-rate with self-sufficiency, dominance, and degree of effective participation in student activities.

The Electro-encephalogram (' E.E.G.'). The electro-encephalographic examination of psychotics, neurotics, delinquents, etc., is at present too complicated, expensive, and time-consuming a procedure for general clinical use ; nor is research sufficiently advanced to justify a review of the present confused and conflicting evidence. However, with the improvement of procedure now taking place and the clarification that is appearing in the significance of results, the instrument should definitely become of value for psychological examinations within the next few years. At present its surest value is in pathological work, in detecting epileptics and potential epileptics and various organic brain defects and lesions. The correlation of high delta rhythm activity with emotional responses and emotional instability give the instrument about the same application as the psychogalvanometer.

CHAPTER VII

THE MEASUREMENT OF INTRA-FAMILIAL ATTITUDES

1. The Attitude Scales Needed in Psychiatric Social Work

In child-guidance clinics, as well as in the routine work of psychiatrists in hospitals, and in the work of psychotherapists generally, the assessment of the emotional structure of the family situation in which the patient lives is often of primary importance for successful diagnosis and treatment.

The task of assessing the psychological forces at work in the family situation is usually left to the skill of the psychiatric social worker, who returns information also on such matters as living conditions, financial status, and family history. Unfortunately the estimation of emotional attitudes between members of the family cannot be nearly so accurate as the estimation of other home conditions. Clinicians who have tried the experiment of allowing two social workers independently to estimate the emotional factors at work in some one family situation have found that the unreliability of personal judgment and impression, despite professional training, may be very great. For even the most skilful and dependable investigators of the home are apt to let their judgment remain too subjective or to be influenced by projection of their own emotional problems or by interpretation in terms of the family-conflict stereotypes with which they are most familiar. In pure research, psychological and sociological, the need for some more objective technique of attitude assessment is even more strongly indicated.

Accordingly, the present writer, in collaboration with Dr. P. S. de Q. Cabot of the Cambridge-Somerville Youth Study, set out first to discover the principal interindividual attitudes regarded as being of importance in child-guidance and similar work, and secondly to provide some more objective scales for measuring these attitudes.

The study of intra-familial attitudes should not confine itself only to parent-child or child-parent attitudes, but should take into account the whole family structure of interpersonal relationships. There are eight standard relations—(1) husband-wife, (2) father-son, (3) father-daughter, (4) mother-son, (5) mother-daughter, (6) sister-sister, (7) sister-brother, (8) brother-brother—and six of these require attitude scales made up for two distinct directions, so that there are *14 family attitude* relations for which attitude scales can be made and standardised. However, if rough total situations only are viewed and sex differences are regarded as of secondary importance, scales might be reduced to only four : (1) Inter-parent, (2) Parent-child, (3) Inter-sibling, and (4) Child-parent.

2. The Varieties of Emotional Continua

The varieties of emotional attitude to be scaled within each and all of these situations need next to be surveyed. Between husband and wife we find the following attitudes most frequently reported upon :

A. SPOUSE RELATIONSHIPS

Affectionate	Indifferent
Dependent	Self-sustained
Hostile	Indifferent
Dominant	Submissive
Jealous of	Confident in relation to
Proud of	Ashamed of
Co-operative	Individualistic
Protective	Indifferent
Trustful	Suspicious
Close to	Withdrawn from
Sexually attracted	Sexually indifferent
Respecting	Being contemptuous of
Observing rights of	Ignoring rights of

If these and other family situation attitudes are to be measured intelligently and economically, the psychologist has to have in mind a clear and correct system of analysis for reducing emotional attitudes to a minimum, basic list. McDougall's, Murray's, or the present writer's analysis of dynamic traits into a basic list of drives, propensities, or ergs [1] would provide such a fundamental reduction ; but by the nature of social conditioning some of the most important attitudes are not primary ergs but metanergs or sentiments. Thus the attitude of ' affection ' could be resolved into primary ergic components, but since this sentiment follows a well-known social mould, there is no point in such artificial analysis and it is best measured as a trait in its own right. Consequently some of the attitudes—e.g. affection, jealousy, comradely co-operative-ness—are metanergs, and others—e.g. sexual attraction, dominance, protectiveness, hostility—are ergs, to be assayed by analysing out from more complex, derived behaviour. It will be noticed that the psychological, dynamic view-point does not permit the merely ' logical ' arrangement of setting, say, Hostility, at the opposite end of the con-tinuum from Affection, in a single-attitude scale. As psychoanalysis readily illustrates, affection and hate can be directed simultaneously to the same object. Psycho-logically, therefore, it is necessary to measure affection and hostility on two distinct scales, each operating between a zero point of indifference or complete lack of interest in the object and an extreme high point of affection or hostility.

The following are the most frequently reported (in social workers' files) as attitudes of parent to child :

B. PARENT-TO-CHILD ATTITUDES

Affectionate	Cold
(Fond, devoted, kind)	(Heartless, uninterested)
Accepting	Rejecting
(Responsible, loyal, having vigorous contact)	(Neglecting, disowning, begrudging, impatient)

[1] Chapter 6. *General Psychology.* Sci.-Art Publishers, Cambridge, Mass.

Hostile-sadistic
(Bullying, severe, censori-
ous, callous)

Lacking aggression

Dominant-nurturant
(Supervisory, imperious,
commanding, coercive)

Submissive
(Self-effacing, lax, diffident)

Jealous of
(Competitive towards, in-
secure in regard to, feeling
frustrated by)

Trusting
(Secure in relation to,
grateful towards, friendly)

Proud of
(Admiring, exhibitionistic
about)

Ashamed of
(Guilty or depressed
about)

Comradely
(Close in emotional rap-
port and sympathy, af-
filiative, seeking social
contact with)

Socially distant
(Out of touch, merely
dutiful or official)

Protective-solicitous
(Succourant, anxious
about, over-careful, sheltering, babying)

Adventurous about
(Allowing child uncon-
sciously to get his own
experience)

Claimant-appealing
(Demanding affection,
emotionally dependent on
child)

Independent

C. CHILD-TO-PARENT ATTITUDES

Affectionate

Cold

Dependent-appealing
(Claimant, identifying)

Confident-adventurous
(Independent, assured)

Hostile-aggressive

Lacking aggression

Fearful-submissive
(Respectful, awe-struck)

Bold towards
(Independent, not respectful to)

Jealous of

Trusting
(Grateful towards, not
rivalrous)

Proud of
(Admiring, worshipping)
Rebellious
(Negativistic, rude to-
wards, disobedient)
Exhibitionistic
(Attention-seeking)
Comradely
(Sociable, confiding, close
emotional rapport)

Ashamed of
(Critical of)
Docile
(Obedient, tractable)

Effacing

Socially distant
(Independent)

D. INTER-SIBLING ATTITUDES

Affectionate

Cold
(Rejecting)

Dependent
(Following, subordinate,
demanding protection)

Independent
(Self-assured)

Hostile-sadistic
(Bullying, destroying,
critical, spiteful)

Indifferent

Dominant
(Ascendant, exploitative,
leading)

Submissive
(Diffident)

Jealous of
(Competitive for affection,
feeling frustrated by)

Trusting
(Grateful and helpful to-
wards)

Proud of
(Admiring, possessive)

Ashamed of
(Guilty about disowning)

Comradely
(Sociable, confiding, constant emotional rapport)

Socially distant
(Withdrawn, lacking in
sympathy and harmony,
isolative)

Protective
(Sheltering, babying, dot-
ing on)

Adventurous, unconcerned

Dutiful about
(Anxious over, responsible
for)

Ignoring any responsibility
about

It will be noticed that the majority of the attitudes in the four familial relationship situations are similar. However, it is probable that research will indicate slight differences in slant even among attitudes which seem equivalent.

Ideally the clinic or the research worker should have scales for all of these attitudes. Only one may be reported as extreme in a given case under inquiry, and generally it may be enough to measure only those which direct observation suggests to be factors in the maladjustment; but if suitably brief measuring instruments could be found, it might well become a regular routine in clinical practice to measure all important attitudes in the dynamic structure of the family.

3. The Available Scales

Scales are provided below only for ten attitudes, as follows:

1. Parent-to-child	Affection	Scale	1
	Hostility	,,	2
	Domination	,,	3
	Over-protection	,,	4
2. Child-to-parent	Affection	,,	5
	Dependence	,,	6
3. Inter-sibling	Affection	,,	7
	Jealousy	,,	8
4. Inter-spouse	Affection	,,	9
	Hostility	,,	10

For each attitude some 24 symptomatic acts are listed. These are the items of behaviour which the experienced social worker looks for in judging the strength of the attitude in question. For example, in judging maternal over-protection the social worker might observe whether the mother helps dress the child when the latter is beyond an age at which a child usually receives help, or whether she interferes to settle minor disagreements between the child and others.

Later, these items may receive special weights after being ranged in order according to their position on the continuum, but at present the practitioner should get his own local norms, simply by adding up the total number of items (one for each) checked off as present in the given case and constructing percentile distributions of case scores.

Obviously such a scale does not completely eliminate subjectivity, since the social worker still has to judge whether each item is present or not ; but it reduces subjectivity and at least records a pattern of behaviour which the psychotherapist can judge for himself. Where age, social status, or other variables condition the score it will probably be best, in the long run, to ignore them in observation, simply recording behaviour, and later interpreting the total score in terms of norms established for different ages, social and cultural groups, etc. It is hoped in due course to translate the items also into questionnaire form, to be submitted to the parent or child whose attitude is to be measured, so that a subject's as well as an observer's rating may be used. By the use of sufficiently oblique, projective, and similarly designed questions this might almost match the observer's rating scale in validity.

SCALE I.   PARENT-TO-CHILD.   AFFECTION—INDIFFERENCE

1. Parent rarely speaks to child without smiling.
2. Parent tries to put himself in child's position when discussing child's behaviour.
3. Parent brings child small presents other than seasonal ones.
4. Parent takes child with him on trips at some personal inconvenience.
5. Parent complains boy is wearing him out and constantly criticises him.   (Negative.)
6. Parent constantly compels child to keep out of the house and out of his way.   (Negative.)

7. Parent does not deliberately plan definite periods of companionship with child. (Negative.)

8. Parent does not kiss or greet child after long absence. (Negative.)

9. Parent fails to reciprocate son's friendly advances, e.g. to sit on parent's knee. (Negative.)

10. Father shares child's creative play activities, e.g. drawing erector sets, school works, favourite reading.

11. Parent romps with child and encourages physical development.

12. Parent does not inquire about child's whereabouts, his needs, or his activities. (Negative.)

13. Parent denies himself—e.g. food, clothing, amusement —in order that child may have equivalent satisfactions instead of himself, e.g. has time to play with friends but plays with child.

14. Parent anticipates child's physical, mental, and emotional needs—e.g. prophylaxis for cold, need for holiday, new hobby, clothing—before child is fully aware of it himself, e.g. planning meals with regard to child's likes and dislikes.

15. Parent ignores and is indifferent to child, despite cries and appeals for something which by the standards of his environment he ought to have. (Negative.)

16. Parent smiles and praises child at latter's successes.

17. Parent resents criticism of child.

18. Parent accepts irksome, aggressive, or anger-provoking behaviour from the child without being ruffled or retaliating.

19. Parent sacrifices energy, time, and money to enable child to have better start in life than he himself had.

20. Parent shows he is ready to listen to child's account of his exploits, hobbies, interests, and friends.

21. Parent sides with and shows favouritism for this particular child in contrast with siblings or others with whom quarrels arise.

22. Parent allows child to use family property without stint, restriction, or inquiry.

23. Parent allows child excessive satisfaction of his impulses, even though detrimental in the parent's opinion, e.g. eating candy to excess, destroying furniture, defacing rooms, disrespect to other people.

24. Parent shows little remorse or feeling when child's property—e.g. favourite doll, book, or toys—are accidentally destroyed. (Negative.)

SCALE 2.   PARENT-TO-CHILD.   HOSTILITY

1. Parent punishes child when punishment is not the best and most effective means to gain the end the parent desires, say, on account of limits of a child's intelligence, physique, and maturity, age, e.g. a first-grader who does not compute with fractions, a frail boy who cannot pull a heavy roller.

2. Parent continually upsets boy by comparing him unfavourably with older or more competent siblings and friends.

3. Parent punishes child for deserved reasons, but with severity disproportionate to the occasion, e.g. whipping for disobedience, solitary confinement for breaking ordinary household objects, forbidding child to play outdoors because of minor lapse in school work.

4. Parent encourages teachers or others in authority to be severe when punishing child.

5. Parent constantly criticises child without adequate reason in a nagging, cruel fashion.

6. When child gets into difficulties parent is more given to blaming him than constructively helping him to avoid them in the future.

7. Parent constantly makes use of threats in dealing with child's activities, e.g. calling in police, sending to reform school, telling school authorities.

8. Parent uses disparaging remarks damaging to the child's self-respect.

9. Parent beats child without first giving an opportunity for child to give reasons for his behaviour.

10. Parent displays irritability as judged by angry remarks, boxing child's ears, pushing him aside when child gets in his way.

11. Parent verbally punishes child by saying, ' I could kill you,' or ' I wish you were dead,' expressing annihilation wishes.

12. Parent never wants to see child, tries to keep him out of his way.

13. Parent damages child's belongings, toys, etc., without compunction if they happen to get in his way.

14. In any dispute with other parents or relatives, parent tends to lay the blame on the child whenever possible.

15. Parent, after scolding child for some trivial fault—e.g. coming in with dirty shoes—doesn't forget it, but keeps telling child how angry he has made her, i.e. blames child for upsetting her.

16. Parent discourages child from bringing his friends home and insults and mistreats them when he does.

17. Parent denies child pleasure and play for no good reason other than to frustrate him (though given a ' moral ' colouring).

18. Parent always tries to send child away for vacations and to spend as little time with him as possible.

19. Parent is inclined to put the worst interpretation upon child's actions. Automatically and unconsciously parent ascribes worse motives and standards than the average onlooker would be inclined to do.

20. Parent readily ' sees in the child ' features of less reputable relatives, and is inclined to adopt a pessimistic view about the child's future.

21. Parent uses expression ' Don't, etc. —— ' with obvious frequency.

22. Parent frequently reminds child that he (the parent) did not have such a good time when he was a child.

23. Parent sets children one against another and encourages older child to punish others.

24. Parent ' docks ' child's pocket money on slightest provocation, or continually forgets to give child his pocket money even when he is in obvious need of it.

SCALE 3.   PARENT-TO-CHILD.   DOMINATION—SUBMISSION

1. Parent insists on child doing chores or school assignments according to an arbitrarily dictated schedule.

2. Parent controls child by adherence to a rigid system of rewards or punishments.

3. Parent demands that child gets permission regarding everything he wants to do, e.g. buying papers with own pocket money, playing in nearby playground, going to movies with friends, taking out toys to play, climbing trees.

4. Parent allows child to adopt own religion or political loyalty.

5. Parent allows child to choose own hobbies, friends.

6. Parent demands that child respect values of parents' generation instead of contemporary values, e.g. interference with school's methods of teaching.

7. At slightest failure on part of child to comply with parental wishes parent is overbearing, threatening, forceful, e.g. lateness for meals prevented by deprivation of food, parent fulminates when child fails to complete chores.

8. Parent tries to dictate to child how he shall think on various issues.

9. Parent decodes child's requests arbitrarily and abruptly, without reasoning with the child or asking further about his needs.

10. Parent more frequently tells child that he cannot do things than that he can.

11. When asked by neighbours or others to control child, parent throws up his hands, saying, ' What can I do? '

12. Parent does not leave child free on day's holiday to go wherever he wants in the neighbourhood.

13. Parent does (or does not) dictate to child how and where he shall spend pocket money or other money allotted to him.

14. If child attempts to show initiative and stand up for his own ideas, parent humiliates him before his playmates and younger siblings by open ridicule.

15. Parent tells tales of child's incorrigibility, or the worthlessness of his word, in order to block child's appeal to other parents or to neighbours from his domination.

16. Parent insists on supervising and knowing nature of correspondence which child has with other children, relatives, etc., and the nature of his reading (to see it is not immoral). Allows no initiative for own interests.

17. Parent requires instant obedience, without reasoning, to any of his commands.

18. Parent supervises, orders about, and disciplines child before guests and visitors, in unnecessarily harsh degree and in humiliating way.

19. Parent has definite ideas about future career of the child, not regarding possibility of child feeling differently on the matter, and without regard to his abilities.

20. Parent gives child additional homework, or chores about the house, not so much because they need to be done, but as an arbitrary exercise of power demonstrating to the child that he has to obey parent's will.

21. Parent demands child shall not associate with strangers or political and social enemies of the parent.

22. Parent teaches child it is bad manners to voice his opinions when not asked for.

23. Parent forces child to keep at study or occupation for which he has no aptitude.

24. Parent tries to keep all children's affections within the family, discourages interests outside, dominates relations within the family.

SCALE. 4. PARENT-TO-CHILD. OVER-PROTECTION

1. Parent very rarely allows child out of sight.
2. Parent encourages child to sleep with her after six years of age, in spite of other sleeping facilities available.
3. Parent allows child to come to him for guidance in making decisions on even the most trivial issues.
4. Parent does not allow child, over six, to run errand, travel by bus, or to wander in nearby streets, unless accompanied by older companion.
5. Parent appeals to teacher not to subject child to strain, despite the absence of medical and psychological evidence for such a precaution.
6. Parent encourages child to take on responsibilities, e.g. dressing, planning the earning and use of pocket money, choice of presents on festive occasions. (Negative.)
7. Parent constantly interferes to settle child's differences, quarrels, and social arrangements with other children.
8. Parent intimidates child by exaggerating dangers of adventurous behaviour.
9. Parent actively discourages child from joining organisations outside family control, e.g. Scouts, Y.M.C.A., Boys' Club, Community Centre, summer camp, gangs, hobby clubs.
10. Parent constantly takes boy's side in any issue regardless of objective evidence.
11. Parent persistently boasts of child's toughness, resource, ' guts,' and initiative. (Negative.)
12. Parent guards child unduly from common physical dangers and discomforts which are no real threat to health, e.g. playing in snow, wetting feet,

climbing trees, collecting junk, playing with dirt, soiling clothes.

13. Parent worries over child's eating, seeing e.g. that it has only food that it likes, ' can digest,' or that is rich in food accessories.

14. Parent stands between child and standards of outside world, e.g. doing child's homework for him, standing between child and school discipline, seeing he is not late for school.

15. Parent selects child's friends, to be of an innocuous, colourless kind.

16. Parent is constantly worried about child's health (unjustified by medical reasons) and takes precautions of an extreme kind, e.g. refuses to allow child to play with other children, even when no medical evidence of contagion possibilities surround him.

17. Parent speaks to older child in terms appropriate to a much earlier level, e.g. baby talk, calls adult ' my big brown baby ' (other than jocosely).

18. Parent consistently shields child from full consequence of self-indulgence or delinquent behaviour, e.g. overlooks delinquent episodes, withholds information from police, lies to neighbours regarding destruction of property.

19. Parent endorses indulgent behaviour, e.g. over-eating.

20. Parent prohibits child from mixing with other children lest he be tempted to behave in a way likely to lead to emotional conflicts.

21. Parent worries over child's sleeping habits.

22. Parents worry over (talk about) possible difficulties child may encounter in sexual development and seeks to shield child from all possible stimuli.

23. Parent worries about child's school progress, wondering if his abilities are being properly developed and if his emotional development is receiving proper attention, etc.

24. Parent never goes to bed without ascertaining that child is in bed and asleep.

SCALE 5. CHILD-TO-PARENT. AFFECTIONATE-TO-COLD

1. Although his mother neglects and punishes him severely, boy says he likes her more than anyone else and, e.g., talks of plans to make a lot of money and live with her.
2. Child occasionally hugs mother spontaneously.
3. Boy makes every opportunity to follow father around house when latter is doing chores and offers to help him.
4. Child hugs parents when he returns from short visits to neighbours, from school, or from vacations.
5. Child always wants to ' buy my mother a present.'
6. Child boasts about father's accomplishments.
7. If child is hurt in play with parent, he may cry, but does not resent it and get angry with parent.
8. Child likes to go to meet parent when latter is returning from a trip.
9. Child climbs over parent when parent is sitting idly and shows desire for physical contact generally.
10. Child imitates parent a good deal, unconsciously, even to slight mannerisms.
11. Child shows genuine concern (not merely for himself) if parent does not return home at expected time.
12. Child expresses frequently the wish, ' I want to be like Daddy (or Mummy) when I grow up.'
13. Child is very careful to avoid disturbing parent by questions or noise when he finds parent is unwell.
14. Child anticipates chores and small tasks for parent before parent asks for them to be done.
15. Child obviously over-estimates, in conversation and action, beauty of mother, intelligence of father, and other desirable attributes of parents.
16. Child usually knows where parent is—keeps in touch with parent's doings as far as possible.
17. Child always wants parent to share with him his happy experiences, e.g. to see new toys, to go to a show, to see things he has discovered.

18. Child shows marked depression and concern if parent is ill.
19. Child knows something about parent's wishes and hopes, e.g. that mother is eagerly looking forward to a new spring hat, or that father wants to make such and such improvements on the car.
20. Child stands loyally and indignantly by parent when other children criticise parent.
21. Child takes especial care to avoid damaging property which he knows parent values.
22. Child is not afraid to be independent of parent in thought or action, but tries to avoid hurting parent's feelings by being tactful when such differences arise.
23. Child follows parent's wishes without coercion of any kind, even in cases where he has definitely expressed his own wishes as being different from those of parent.
24. Child never questions that parent's actions are guided by the best intentions.

SCALE 6. CHILD-TO-PARENT. DEPENDENT ATTITUDE

1. Child stays in house most of the time, likes to sit watching mother. (See 9.)
2. When away from parent, child has frequent thoughts about her, speaks a lot about her, and writes to her appealing letters, etc., even when he doesn't speak about friends, etc., around home.
3. Child readily makes plans to leave home, for vacation, visits, not mentioning parents going with him. (Negative.)
4. Child laughs at parents, ridicules them, and does not seem to be troubled if he loses their esteem, e.g. says they're ignorant and old-fashioned. (Negative.)
5. Child does not constantly make room in his plans for his parents, but goes his own way, e.g. recreations, parties. (Negative.)

6. Child demands his own way and gets it, but then does what he knows his parent wants him to do, even though he doesn't believe it is right.

7. Child hesitates to do even trivial things without parent's consent and consulting parents and getting permission, e.g. choice of what to wear, etc.

8. Child seems over-concerned not to offend parent or to lose parental goodwill, e.g. worries, out of all proportion to overt punishment, over transgressions ; does not show normal aggression toward parent ; does not exercise normal individuality and autonomy and accepts willingly restrictions which other children might resent.

9. Child cannot stay away from parent long without great distress, e.g. runs home from school or from camp.

10. Child truants from home, says he wants to see the world, stays away nights. (Negative.)

11. Child constantly appeals to parent to intercede against other authorities and in other difficulties.

12. Child seems to have no attitudes of his own, independent of those opponent.

13. Child will not speak to strangers or confide in them until parent has O.K.'d his doing so.

14. Child does not dream of questioning correctness of parent's views—e.g. on religion, politics—and accepts them as his own, totally.

15. Child does not readily form attachments to others of same age.

16. In any issue with children, child does not try to settle it among them but always turns to parent or adult authority.

17. If child is away from parents, he quickly attaches himself dependently to teacher or other parent substitute.

18. Child frequently prefaces his assertions with ' Mother says ' or ' Father says ' so-and-so.

19. Child disagrees with parent, if he does disagree, only

in security of home and family ; but when out among strangers, with parent, is usually docile.

20. Child cannot fall asleep at night unless he is sure parents are at home.

21. If child is disobedient on impulse, he shows unusual amount of contrition, obviously ' making up ' to parent.

22. Child is unhappy and resentful if he hears his parents criticised or their knowledge or prestige questioned.

23. Child responds markedly to moods of parent and is obviously distressed and insecure when parent becomes emotionally upset.

24. Child confides more than most children his emotional difficulties, hopes, and fears to the parent and demands parent shall share them.

SCALE 7. INTER-SIBLING. AFFECTIONATE—COLD

1. Child follows sibling around wherever he goes, spends most of time with him.

2. Tears come in child's eyes when he talks of his sibling.

3. Child protects sibling in relations with other children and is ready to fight for him if necessary.

4. Child says kind things about his sibling, praises him.

5. Child intercedes and argues on behalf of sibling when he is in trouble with parents or teachers.

6. Child identifies himself with sibling and shares most interests and recreations.

7. Child protects sibling from physical dangers and deprivations.

8. Child complains of parental favouritism to sibling.

9. Child damages toys and property, reputation, on slightest inconvenience caused by him, e.g. ' She's a pain in the neck ' ; ' He gets in my hair.'

10. Child talks about sibling a great deal, shows he is often in his thoughts.

11. Child runs over to greet and say good-bye to sibling when greeting and parting.

12. Child gets angry with those who say derogatory things about sibling.

13. Child helps sibling in all kinds of ways, e.g. with clothes, making things.

14. Child does not know much about sibling, e.g. his birthday, his hobbies, where he is. (Negative.)

15. Child buys and shares candy, etc., freely with his sibling.

16. Child becomes sad when sibling is in trouble.

17. Child will lie or get into trouble to help save sibling from greater trouble.

18. Child shows affection for sibling by physical closeness, puts arm around his shoulder when walking with him, romps and gambols with him.

19. Child shows marked tendency to imitate sibling in dress, manner, etc.

20. Child usually knows where sibling is, and what he is doing.

21. If hurt in games with sibling, child does not get angry or show resentment.

22. Child over-estimates prowess, goodness, or good looks of sibling.

23. Child frequently makes casual gifts to sibling, or forgets what he is owed in barter exchanges.

24. Child knows what are principal hopes and needs of his sibling.

SCALE 8.   INTER-SIBLING.   JEALOUSY

1. Child constantly seeks for activities in which he can excel and beat his sibling, or finds something in which sibling has failed.

2. Child constantly seeks opportunities to tell tales about his sibling and hurt his standing with others.

3. Child becomes attention-getting when sibling is around, and not at other times, e.g. arranges to sit nearer visitors, gives little presents.

4. Child tries to get more of parent than sibling gets, e.g. arranges to sit next to parent in car.

5. When sibling is praised, child enters objections and contradictory remarks.
6. Child spends time seeking evidence which can be used against sibling, never lets him escape possible punishments.
7. Child is very sensitive to possibility of sibling getting advantages, and is on constant look-out lest these occur unknown to him.
8. Child makes frequent charges of unfairness of treatment in relation to sibling, e.g. ' X gets all the breaks.'
9. When in presence of other sibling, child seems frustrated, resentful, glum, quiet, and lacking in spontaneity.
10. Child tolerates sibling's attention-getting behaviour, not being provoked to similar behaviour or anger. (Negative.)
11. Child avoids family or truants from home, saying it is because of favouritism and discrimination in favour of sibling.
12. Child, when punished by parents, tends to ' take it out ' on sibling, by physical assault, or in other ways if sibling is stronger.
13. Child reacts violently (angrily) to any comparisons with sibling, or normal attempts to get him to emulate sibling.
14. Child gets angry when attention is shown sibling by guests or parents.
15. In dispute between sibling and parents, child always sides with parents.
16. Child seeks parent's attention when no real need to do so, simply to keep sibling from getting nearer parent.
17. Child does special tasks and is especially virtuous—e.g. washes hands, combs hair—before parents when other sibling is by, rivalling in goodness.
18. Child destroys paintings, handwork, etc., of sibling through which the latter would gain attention or admiration from parent.

9. If child discovers anything good, he tends to keep it to himself, guarding the secret carefully.

20. Child seeks companions outside the family and tries to keep sibling from sharing these friends.

21. Child attacks sibling when parents are not about and reports to parents that he was attacked first.

22. Child feigns illness at times when sibling is getting especial attention for some admirable performance.

23. Child tends to make quite trivial issues a basis for serious quarrelling.

24. Child invents objectionable nicknames for sibling and tries to popularise their use.

SCALE 9.   SPOUSE-TO-SPOUSE.   AFFECTIONATE—INDIFFERENT

1. Wife purchases small gifts which she knows husband will enjoy.

2. Wife prepares special dishes that husband is particularly fond of.

3. Wife anticipates little needs which she knows will contribute to husband's comfort and happiness.

4. Wife makes it a point to be at home to greet husband when he returns from work.

5. Husband senses wife's moods and respects them.

6. Wife makes it a point to cultivate and be intelligent on subjects in which husband is interested.

7. Husband and wife share their hopes and dreams together.

8. Wife speaks admiringly of husband in presence of others.

9. Wife expresses her confidence in husband's ability and judgment.

10. Wife encourages husband when he is faced with difficulties or uncertainty.

11. Husband assists wife with household cares.

12. Husband voices appreciation of wife's effort on his behalf.

13. Husband makes personal sacrifices in order to give wife things he knows she desires.

14. Husband forgoes doing what he enjoys so that he may accompany wife to functions that interest her.

15. Husband brings wife small tokens of affection, e.g. flowers, books, music, perfume, pretty clothes, etc.

16. Husband and wife take pleasure in recalling incidents which occurred in the past that they shared and enjoyed together.

17. Husband plans special treats to celebrate anniversaries.

18. Husband or wife does not resent interruptions of work in which (s)he is engaged, by affectionate or friendly advances on the part of the spouse.

19. Husband or wife chooses to wear clothes, etc., which spouse has indicated a preference for, even by a slight hint.

20. Husband or wife makes a definite move to become friendly with and appreciate those people whom spouse introduces as his or her friends.

21. Husband takes more than usual amount of life insurance to provide for the security of his wife.

22. Husband carries wife's picture in pocket book, has it on desk, etc.

23. Husband tends to be depressed or worried if wife is unwell.

24. Husband is content to be with wife alone in his leisure time and does not seem to want parties and other entertainments unless she desires them.

SCALE 10. SPOUSE-TO-SPOUSE. HOSTILITY

1. Husband refuses to inform wife as to true financial status and spends money without telling her what he is spending it on.

2. Husband makes wife ask for spending money.

3. Husband criticises wife's use of money.

4. Husband draws attention to his possessions in contrast to his wife's.

5. Husband avoids wife's company whenever possible ; makes social contacts excluding her.
6. Husband refuses to recount his activities to his wife.
7. Wife belittles husband's opinions and judgment.
8. Wife shuns any physical contact with her husband.
9. Wife draws attention to husband's weak points and failures publicly.
10. Wife refuses to share her thoughts with her husband.
11. Husband contradicts disciplinary injunctions made by wife regarding children.
12. Wife attempts in subtle ways to alienate children's affections from husband.
13. Wife deliberately misinterprets husband's statements.
14. Husband and wife belittle each other before others.
15. Wife expresses distaste over husband's personal habits, i.e. personal cleanliness.
16. Wife does not return husband's manifestations of affection.
17. Husband criticises wife's taste in dress.
18. Husband deliberately upsets domestic routine by tardiness or absence.
19. Husband is hostile to wife's religious views. Refuses to accompany her to church.
20. Husband ignores wife and neglects her at social functions.
21. Husband sits in ' stony silence ' and harbours grievances.
22. Husband imbibes too freely, knowing wife dislikes his drinking.
23. Open hostility shown towards in-laws, e.g. husband ignores mother-in-law when she visits them.
24. Husband belittles wife in front of his mother, e.g. ' She is a poor housekeeper,' etc.

Measurement of attitudes in this manner naturally cannot take into account certain areas of observation. An attitude may express itself by the lift of an eyebrow, an inflection of the voice, or a manner of shutting a door.

These are beyond any simple use of a stop-watch or check tallying. We have, for the present, to confine ourselves to gross and easily describable behaviour, though not necessarily to isolated acts ; for each of the above items tends to be a total pattern, interpreted in the light of the whole configuration.

The above scales are being tried out by the social workers of the Cambridge-Somerville Youth Study ; but due to wartime interruptions it has not yet been possible to arrive at validities, reliabilities, and norms.

CHAPTER VIII

NOTES ON THE SELECTION OF TESTS, INTER-PRETATION OF RESULTS, AND SYNTHESIS OF EVIDENCE

1. Grounds for Selection of Tests

SUCCESSFUL diagnosis, estimation or selection, depends partly on skilful and accurate testing, but even more upon a wise choice of tests having regard to the particular physical or sensory defects, education, and temperamental make-up suspected in the individual to be tested. Age, sex, state of hearing or eyesight, acquaintance with the English language, previous experience of particular tests or of manipulative material similar to performance tests, type of school attended, attitude to teacher, nervous or nonchalant approach to testing, voluntary or compulsory attendance for testing, amount of time available, degree of accuracy required, liability of the subject to fatigue. These are some of the factors which the psychologist needs to consider in the swift preliminary survey on which he is to base his decision as to the selection of test material and the mode of approach.

Always the psychologist should get some conception of the subject's educational background and a rough estimate of his mental age. The order of presentation of tests is also important. Generally speaking, it is best to start with performance tests, which evoke zest, and help to dissolve any feeling of strain or strangeness felt by the subject. Also one should start with easy tests, or at least tests which do not permit the subject to realise how far he is failing. In certain cases, notably when it is inadvisable to let the subject feel that he is being singled out for anything more than an ordinary school examination, it is best to start with attainment tests. In occupational selection, before passing to more purely psychological tests, it is best to present tests obviously bearing on the work to be done, in order to set the tone and purpose of the sitting and call upon the requisite drives.

The technique of calling into play powerful motives has already been discussed in regard to intelligence testing, but it is equally important in every test. Except for special diplomatic reasons, the subject to be tested should be given a full explanation of the purpose of the testing and every effort made to enlist his entire goodwill. (See next section on the general interview.)

Devotees of the Binet test, whilst admitting its deficiency in ' g,' will sometimes argue that it is yet superior to the tests here advocated, in which the subject works for several minutes at a stretch on his own, because of the close 'rapport' between tester and tested. But this 'rapport' is in many cases nothing more than the rather tense atmosphere in which the experimenter is insistently firing questions at a fundamentally unwilling subject. From our knowledge of unconscious mechanisms, we must know that we deceive ourselves if we imagine that we are going to get a sound measure even of intelligence under such conditions. The time spent in getting *true* ' rapport ' is well invested, not merely because it permits one to use what tests one chooses, but because it is in any case essential to the whole of the further course of treatment.

Nevertheless, there are some tests, notably performance tests, attainment tests, and physiological tests (psycho-galvanometer, pneumograph, etc.) which can be given satisfactorily before the subject has reached any very confidential footing with the psychologist, whilst there are others, principally probes of temperament, attitude, character, and ' free association ' which should be given when possible as late as the second or third sitting.

Most psychologists tend to get into a groove in testing, and thus fail to make use of the full resources of test material now available. This restriction is partly on grounds of expense and partly on grounds of portability of apparatus.

Largely, however, it is because each psychologist, in clinic, workshop, or school, finds himself dealing in the main with a narrowly circumscribed type of case.

Provided the psychologist is prepared to draw upon fuller resources when the unusual case comes along, there is no disadvantage—indeed, there are many advantages—in settling down to a particular battery of tests. He gets quick and skilful in the use of those tests, and gains valuable experience in interpretation through constant comparisons. Thus, for all normal ' educational disability ' (i.e. backward or dull) cases in junior and infant schools, the present writer uses invariably the Seguin Form Board, the Dartington Scale O Intelligence Test, and the Midland Attainment Tests (Reading Comprehension and Arithmetic Knowledge only). The performance tests act as an introduction, as a check on the intelligence tests, and as a sidelight on temperament and character. The whole procedure takes less than an hour, and, since half the tests in Scale O can if necessary be given as a group test to four or five children immediately under the psychologist's eye, it is possible, when occasion demands, to test half a dozen children in a morning.

Always the testing programme should be flexible enough to be altered in response to findings appearing in the opening stages of testing. Unexpectedly limited speech vocabulary (as in a case which might prove to be aphasic) may indicate the desirability of calling in a second or third performance test and shifting the emphasis in diagnosis upon them. Oddities in the approach to performance tests may suggest the desirability of adding a test of temperament or perseveration and of making a fuller home study. In a vocational selection undertaking, a change in the calibre of applicants, as, for instance, a rise in the general level of intelligence so that the scores crowd the upper reaches of the test, may necessitate a different type of test or a new manner of combining scores which will give less weight to intelligence (since it is now less a critical issue) and more to the special abilities concerned in the occupation.

Of all factors, that of time is most tyrannical to the psychologist, for the layman, accustomed to the relatively short time required for physical examinations, is prone to begrudge the longer allowance which is absolutely necessary for a reliable psychological testing. Fortunately, the subject's time and the psychologist's time are not always the same thing, for, as is shown by the example below, it is possible for the psychologist, by arranging group testing wherever it is reliable, and by choosing tests which the subject can work with a minimum of supervision, to free himself for a good proportion of the time actually required for examining the subject. And except in certain vocational guidance and employee selection schemes, it is the psychologist's time that is the prime consideration.

Time can most easily be saved by eliminating from the routine test battery those tests which make big demands in administration and scoring. An intelligence test, to be reliable, must be fairly long, but it should be scorable by a stencil key with a ready-reckoner for the I.Q.s. Probably most time is thrown away on excessive use of performance tests, excessive, that is, relative to their real contribution to one's knowledge of the individual. With a few exceptions they measure no known special aptitude, and are rightly used only as a check on an intelligence test or to replace an intelligence test in the exceptional instances of a deaf or a foreign child. Many of them, e.g. Koh's block and the Dearborn Form Board, are as intricate and time-consuming in their method of scoring as they are in administration.

Finally, though there is yet no means of shortening the treatment procedures of the psychological (psychotherapeutic, psychiatric, psychoanalytic) interview by rendering the therapeutic influences more potent, the initial diagnostic approach could be much facilitated, both with children and adults, by the right use of the objective temperament tests and character probes described in Chapters V and VI.

The above recommendations, as well as the detailed testing instructions in the preceding chapters, can best be given point by brief illustration through a few actual cases, mostly from the writer's own practice, showing how the psychologist meets various situations.

Case 1.—A girl, aged 12·5, referred as being backward in school and dull, possibly feeble-minded. Since her mental age is probably between 6 and 10 years, she will be most accurately tested by the Dartington Individual Scale (p. 17). This was preceded by the Seguin-Goddard Form Board (p. 36), which is sufficiently ' g ' saturated over these lower mental ages, and followed by Burt's Attainment Tests in English (Reading Vocabulary) and Arithmetic, since she was educated in London schools for which these tests were standardised.

Total time for testing, 1 hour 15 minutes, which is as much as can usually be afforded for straightforward diag-nostic cases of this kind.

Result: I.Q. 81. Performance, Mental Age 9, i.e. in agreement with intelligence test result. English attain-ment, 10 years, which is quite up to her mental age. Arithmetic attainment, 7 years. Put in a ' C ' class and coached as an Arithmetic disability.

Case 2.—A deaf boy, aged 8·6, not having learnt to speak and suspected of possible feeble-mindedness. Test of hearing shows sensory defect absolute. A testing of intelligence through performance tests, sufficiently long to leave no doubt about mental capacity, is here indicated. Given complete Drever-Collins Scale of Performance Tests (p. 43).

Result: Exactly normal. Sent to Special School for Deaf and Dumb Children, with report to treat as of normal intelligence.

Case 3.—A child, aged 3 years, tested after stay in hospital resulting from a fracture. One hospital sister considered the child ' deficient ' on account of behaviour. Parents stated, on the other hand, that he was far above average.

Observed behaviour in play-room. Questioned and experimented with child, thereby making assessment on Gesell's norms of (1) Adaptation, (2) Motor and Language Development, (3) Personal-Social Behaviour.

On following morning—child now feeling at home in clinic—gave Merrill Palmer Scale. Results: above average on all three of Gesell's norms. Merrill Palmer Scale Mental Age 46 months, giving a percentile rank of 95, agreeing with Gesell's norms for adaptation. Child exceptionally independent and self-reliant for his age on norms of personal-social behaviour, this accounting for his unusual response to adult approaches by adults accustomed to children usually somewhat below average.

Case 4.—Three hundred elementary school children, aged 11, candidates for secondary school scholarships, representing the topmost 60 per cent. (according to English and Arithmetic attainment) of the original entrants. Final selection now to be on basis of intelligence.

Such an important decision in the children's careers should not be based on an intelligence test lasting less than an hour. Enquiries among inspectors reveal that the Otis Test and the N.I.I.P. Test 34 have previously been used in some schools, whilst Cattell Scale IIA has been given to some children individually. The test must cover the 11–14 mental age range, since the point of greatest required discrimination will fall at about 12½ years (Scholarship I.Q.s in areas with the normal percentage of free places, rarely fall below 125) (see p. 33).

Tested with the Moray House Test on the first Scholarship examination; the Simplex test on the second, and the Cattell Scale II Form B (which is much more rarely used than the A form) on the third. Such a continual changing of tests is obviously necessary to avoid temptation and opportunity for coaching.

Case 5.—A scheme of vocational guidance for elementary school leavers in a Midland industrial city. Required not to take more than three hours from the child's school life and to place a minimum of ' rating for character traits ' duty on the teachers.

Intelligence is the basic measurement to be made. With older children it might be measured by Cattell Scale IIIA, since occupational norms have already been obtained by

this test (p. 42).   But both this and the N.I.I.P. Group
Test 33 have a vocabulary too wide for the less intelligent
of the elementary 14-year-olds.   Cattell Scale IIA was
actually given, but the Cattell Culture Free (p. 26) was
given when the former test had already been recently used
in a school.

Attainment by the Midland Attainment Tests, four
sections of English and two Arithmetic (method and
skill) separately recorded (since different callings demand
proficiency in different branches of arithmetic).   Other
school subjects recorded on five-point classification, in each
school independently.

Main occupations are factory work, engineering, clerical,
and shop work.   Special aptitude tests, therefore, chosen as
follows: (a) Mechanical Aptitude—Cox's Test, which will
provide a varied test in 40 minutes and select well among
the more able 14-year-olds (p. 68).   (b) N.I.I.P. Spatial
Relations Test, given to all girls and some boys, with an eye
to dressmaking, cutting, and similar skills in the boot
trade.   (c) Manual Dexterity, entering into many factory
skills (particularly packing and sorting), tested by the Eye
Board Test (p. 65), which appears to be practically the
only satisfactory test of so short duration.   (d) Meier-
Seashore and Cattell-Reynolds Art Tests to a small percentage of boys and girls already considered likely candidates for further art training.   (e) A test of ' clerical
aptitude ' is not given, for reasons explained elsewhere
(p. 61).   Instead, suitability for office work is judged from
attainment tests of English and Arithmetic, I.Q., and the
outcome of the temperament and character tests now to be
described.   To this an assessment of handwriting on the
five-point scale (p. 120) is added.

Temperament and character are assessed partly by
ratings (which, however, are apt to be inaccurate and require too much time from the teacher) and partly by actual
tests.   Ratings on the first three qualities in (a) Surgency
(p. 174) and (b) Will-character (p. 212), together with
certain traits—Initiative and Imagination—not covered by

these two factors. Test of temperament by Fluency of Association (also valuable in itself as a check on rating of ' Imagination '). A Perseveration Test battery, used as a group test (p. 234), gives a rough measure which is a further indication of temperament and an independent measure of stability of character, ' C.'

This testing programme, except for the special tests given to restricted groups of children, and neglecting the Attainment Tests which are given in lieu of the ordinary examination, takes slightly more than three hours. These are naturally not taken consecutively. If a further half-hour is available, the examination can be made still more thorough and complete by adding the Interests Test (p. 134), which offers valuable help in deciding whether the individual is most at home in dealing with people, with material things, or with abstractions.

Results arranged in a profile on cards giving also particulars of home circumstances and physical characteristics.

Case 6.—A public school boy, aged 15. So backward in school that the headmaster advises his leaving. His father, however, is very keen for him to obtain a university degree before being taken into the family business.

Proves to have been much absent with illness, but health now recovered. Attainment Test necessary, partly to decide which intelligence test to use. As youth is dependable and can be trusted to put forth his best efforts on his own, he is given Northumberland Attainment Tests (pp. 95 and 113), which permit psychologist to attend to other work and show less time on the case. Particular backwardness in English is revealed, which suggests that performance-test evidence must be made fairly ample. Given Passalong (p. 43) and Ferguson Form Board (p. 43). 16 + on the former and 18 on the latter.

A non-verbal intelligence test would be preferable, but the Sleight Tests (p. 18) only range up to 10 years and the Cattell Scale I up to 11 years, though both will, if necessary, give useful measures up to 15 or 16 years. In this instance, since a university career is contemplated, the measurement must be thorough.   The Cattell Culture-Free Test, which is well adapted to the university entrance level, was therefore used, with a check on verbal level by Burt's Northumberland Test, since in both he could work on his own, with stimulation at intervals.   I.Q. given respectively as 128 and 120.   Advised to stay at school and to receive special coaching, especially in English.   Character (C) tests (p. 252) shows moderately low ' p ' and this in agreement with general opinion that he is of very steady, serious character.   Hence advised might confidently be expected by steady plodding to get a university degree.

Case 7.—Vocational selection of workers for a large business: (1) Packers and sorters (only one-third of applicants needed); (2) clerical workers.   Testing not to take more than half an hour of applicant's time.

(1) *Packers and Sorters.*—Selected partly on intelligence and partly on dexterity.   As educational attainment of applicants seemed very low, a non-verbal test was indicated.   Mental age also probably low, so three sub-tests from Sleight's non-verbal test were used.   Upper two-thirds according to this test then given Eye-board Test (p. 65) and Leake-Smith Form Board, which appears to involve sorting skill (p. 39).   Other qualities by very brief standard interview (p. 221).

(2) *Clerical Workers.*—Selected by (i) intelligence test; (ii) perseveration to indicate reliability, drive, and attention to detail (moderately low ' p ' wanted); (iii) test of English and Arithmetic attainment.   Intelligence on abridged form of Scale IIIA (two sub-tests only—suitable for adults rather above average) (p. 21).   Perseveration by adult battery (p. 232).   This cannot be abridged, because norms would be invalidated and reliability dangerously reduced.   The whole half-hour is taken up by these tests, so attainment test must be brief.   Midland test of English Comprehension, Spelling, and Arithmetic Knowledge, each started not at beginning but at 12-year level.   Elimination first by I.Q. (it was possible to reject below 105), then by attainment (elimination of those impossibly low in one or both

subjects), and finally by perseveration (last because least dependable of tests).

Case 8.—Social research scheme. Comparison of students in a university who have matriculated: (1) from schools segregating sexes; (2) from co-educational schools; with regard to (*a*) frequency of neurotic tendencies; (*b*) general knowledge; (*c*) attitude to social questions, particularly regarding position of women; (*d*) general character development; (*e*) temperament.

Self-ratings to be made on Psychoneurotic Questionnaires: (*a*) each syndrome separately, and (*b*) with results pooled (p. 270). General Knowledge by test (p. 117), and by Ballard's test of Geography, History, Algebra, Academic Knowledge, and other attainment tests (p. 84), and by Watson's test of General Knowledge, Thurstone Attitudes tests (p. 158), selected items. Character by rating scale (pp. 212–13), filled in by committee of fellow students, and by ' C ' factor tests (p. 232). Degree of Surgency (extraversion) by rating scale (p. 174).

Case 9.—University woman student, aged 20, complaining of nervous symptoms of an obsessional type, though actually the physical illnesses which she also describes indicate an hysterical pattern. Disabling tremor of right hand, liability to over-excitement, vague illnesses, and threatened ' appendicitis ' which medical man considers to have no physical foundation. Some anxiety about university examinations; both parents and lecturers doubt whether she ought to continue at university.

Two intelligence tests, with an interval between, were given, since it was necessary to have an accurate measure on which to base advice as to degree. In such circumstances, it is generally as well to have tests by different designers, to diminish overlap of special factors. N.I.I.P. Test 33 and Cattell Scale IIIA. I.Q. 114.

' C ' factor, ' A ' factor, and surgency (' F ' factor) measures of personality structure were used and spot-dotting test to check indications of obsessional make-up (p. 258). Second decile, fifth decile, ninth, and tenth decile respectively on former and very high score on latter test, showed neurotic, specifically hysterical constitution type, with obsessional expression.

General history brings out other obsessional traits and their possible origin.   Detailed psychotherapeutic examination begun with Jung's Association Test (p. 282) in conjunction with the P.G.R., followed by free association (in later sittings) on five key issues discovered in the sitting.   Two of these lead up to origin of hand tremor.   The free association procedure is shortened, and put on a surer foundation, through a single examination with these objective aids.   On grounds of I.Q., advised vocationally to give up university course.   This, together with essential psychotherapy, caused symptoms to clear up in four months.

Case 10.—A ' problem ' child.   Secondary school boy, aged 13, referred by school and parents for repeated disregard of authority, taking money from other boys and from strangers by false pretences, causing trouble by fabricating stories, etc.   School work described as very poor relative to his apparent intelligence.

Physical examination reveals no defect except digestive weakness.   Hyperthyroid in appearance with slightly protuberant eyes.

Whilst history and home enquiry are being followed up by social worker, he is tested as follows.   Since he shows signs of not settling down well at first, the investigation is begun with a number of performance tests.   Enjoys Koh's Block, M.A. 12·0 (p. 50), and Knox Cube, M.A. 13·0 (p. 39).   Shows some lack of planning capacity in Passalong, M.A. 12·6.   As he is still markedly distractable, is given as intelligence test Spearman's ' Measure of Intelligence ' (p. 20) as an individual test.   I.Q. 112. (Given Cattell Scale II some weeks later, attained I.Q. 114.)

On second visit and prior to discussing difficulties with psychologist, is given Perseveration test (p. 232).   Result: extreme score, decile 10, indicating deep, long-standing, emotional frustration, and conflict.   As he is said to have ' no stable interests,' is given Interests test (p. 134), which shows high interest in mechanical matters, in parents and home, and in social life, low on sport, artistic, naturalistic, and religious interests. It is significantly higher than average (2 deciles) on the whole, i.e. wide general knowledge relative to his I.Q.

A temperamental test of fluency (p. 176) gave a middle value, decile 5, i.e. not substantiating his apparently highly surgent temperament, which may therefore be temporary.

On third visit he is given Jung's Word Association Test. Significant words are ' disobey,' ' dreaming,' ' helpless,' ' jealous,' ' run away,' ' stay-at-home,' ' stubborn,' ' stories.' The following-up of these words led to an evaluation of his emotional problems. These are too complex a subject to be discussed in the space here available, but, simply stated, the main roots turned out to be a rejection by the mother from the time of his birth and a jealousy of a delicate (favoured) younger brother. His intelligence was such that direct therapy was possible, beginning with his being given insight into his own problem. At the same time the social worker discovered factors in the mother's history accounting for the rejection and for certain maladjustments between the parents. Thereby it was possible to improve these matters, and so to bring about some real alteration in the relations to and management of the child. On the school side a demonstration of the boy's actual I.Q. resulted in the staff modifying their belief that he was slacking. His incipient interests in science were fostered, and a revival of attention began which spread to other school subjects. His character improved immediately on the adjustment of the home situation. For three months there were sporadic recurrences of the old trouble, but after six months his case was closed as adjusted, and there has been no recurrence.

2. Interpretation and Synthesis of Results

The significance of the measurements from any single test is fully discussed in the sections which deal with that test. Before reading the present chapter, therefore, the experimenter should make a thorough study of those sections, as indeed he probably will have done already in the process of choosing tests suitable for the particular purposes he has in mind. In the case of tests still in the experimental stage, e.g. perseveration tests, fluency tests, the psychogalvanic reflex, this reading should extend to the literature given in the references, if any extensive use and interpretation of the test is to be attempted.

Here we can only discuss the interpretation of the more common interrelations of test results. First let us face the not unusual situation of finding a performance test mental age significantly above or below that obtained by the intelligence test. In such circumstances, if only one performance test has been given, it is well to give another. If these agree in being higher than the intelligence test, one should first ask whether the latter has been properly chosen having regard to the educational attainment of the child. Or has the child had practice in something very similar [1] to the performance test? These simple possibilities being ruled out, one must look to special aptitudes (rarely) or to temperament-character effects.

It is difficult to generalise about performance tests, since they have so little in common, but it is the experience of most psychologists that a high score relative to intelligence test mental age is frequently achieved by children of good, persistent, determined character. Conversely, where the performance test mental age is below the I.Q. indication, one may suspect that the child or adult is not making good use of his intelligence—is perhaps temperamentally not capable of making good use of it.

Qualitative differences in handling performance tests are also well worth recording, for it is generally true that the foresight, perseverance, or emotional instability shown in the test situation are equally characteristic of the individual's behaviour in more important or social situations. But not invariably: one must take into account the part which that momentary test situation plays in the

---

[1] The cumulative indication of research on transference of training is to the effect that the practice must be *very* similar to produce any effect.

individual's purposeful life plan. Some adults, for example, will come with a play attitude or a suspicious or a lazy and half-hearted approach, so that their behaviour is no indication of what they would do with anything touching a major sentiment. Marked persistence in a performance test situation may also arise from a strong self-assertive instinct, and be no indication of continuous persistence in the large affairs of life, such as arises from a well-integrated self-regarding sentiment. Some tests, notably Mazes, the Passalong, Koh's Block, seem to be better done by boys than by girls, and evidently involve some temperamental factor of initiative and emotional stability, but other tests involving manipulative skill, e.g. the Seguin, show no such difference. Bearing such points in mind one should watch for differences in performance test scores.

With regard to attainment tests, it is necessary to point out that discrepancies between the subdivisions of the same test, as between speed of reading, spelling, and grammatical habit are by no means uncommon, and often throw interesting light on the past education, on reading habits, and on the atmosphere of the home (good speech, much or little reading). Differences between arithmetic attainment age in "mechanical skill" and in "method knowledge" are equally prevalent and equally instructive. A child of 13 or 14 years in a special (dull) class, having a mental age of, say, 8 years, will generally have a ' method ' age of about 8 also, but in ' skill ' may be at 13 or 14 yrs. or even higher. Such a child, interested in his work and well-instructed, may make very great progress in the speed and accuracy of the simple processes, but it is very rare to find him ahead in ' knowledge.'

In general, attainment in arithmetic follows closely the mental age, and is very rarely above it, but attainment in English, at least in reading and vocabulary, can be pushed well above the mental age, and the writer has known more than one instance of a Mongolian imbecile, with a mental age of 4 or 5, getting a reading attainment age of 9 or 10.

The relations of I.Q., A.Q. (p. 87), and E.R. (p. 87), are well worth studying in the interests of attaining a sound picture of the individual's adjustment, his sentiments, and on that of energy, etc.

It is the experience of all psychological clinics that low attainment (relative to mental age) is frequently associated with emotional difficulties or instability. Observations suggest that this is particularly true of specific, chronic disability in arithmetic, which is often associated with an hysterical kind of emotional instability; but there is no true research evidence on the matter. Some backwardness in arithmetic, on the other hand, is due merely to school absence, often occurring in early school life, which has caused the child to miss some particular step on which all later advance depends. Backwardness then engenders dislike for the subject, and dislike backwardness. Always one should distinguish backwardness through absence or accidental causes from backwardness through systematic chronic disability. The latter is much more likely to be linked with emotional causes: attitude to the first teacher, retraction of libido from social activities. (Hence general English disability may be associated with a desurgent temperament.) The writer has seen some cases of spelling disability, in which the deficient attention to peculiarities of word form was just part of a general absence of function of the ' reality principle ' in the individual's dealing with the external world. Attention to the emotional confusions, obstinacies, or regressions of the subject should then precede or accompany whatever coaching and analysis of intellectual difficulties take place in remedial work on special disabilities.

The implications of the intelligence test itself, i.e. mental age (more properly "intelligence age") are perhaps already sufficiently clear from the earlier discussions on ' g ' and ' s.' One may perhaps point out, however, that the power measured is not always conterminous with the popular conceptions of intelligence. One of the most popular notions of intelligence involves also an activity, an ingenuity, a creativeness which is not part of ' g,' and which is probably measured to some extent by ' fluency of association.' In most instances, where the person fails to live up to the predicted level of intelligence, some factor of this kind—low surgency or high perseveration—is working to cause the ' g ' to be merely latent or spasmodically employed, though it will always be revealed again in a test situation or anything requiring passive comprehension of complexities.

On the other hand, ' g ' is operative in fields where ' intelligence ' in the popular sense is not usually thought to be important, notably in all kinds of actual sense percep- tion, judgment of shape and distance, of relative pitch, etc. It should also not be overlooked in measuring special aptitudes. Most measures of special aptitudes already con- tain some amount of ' g,' so that there is no need to take the person's intelligence into account in addition to the test result when predicting his performance in particular fields. Where special aptitude tests do not, however, correlate with 'g'—as in the case of some manual dexterities— it is best, in predicting the success in any job, to take 'g' into account too. Whether this should be done additively or by multiplication is not yet entirely clear either theoretically or practically, so that the person engaged in vocational selection will need to combine the scores in some way sug- gested by his knowledge of the particular job. Usually the special aptitude can well be given much greater weight, at any rate in all sorts of routine work.

The effect of interest upon the expression of intelligence should never be left out of account. For example, effective use of intelligence in social situations—so-called ' Social Intelligence '—is probably largely a function of social interest (as measurable by the interests test) and surgency of temperament, both of which conduce to the acquisition of social experience, plus good intelligence.

To predict the suitability of a person for inclusion in a given educational or vocational group, certain persistent selective effects in the group concerned should always be taken into account, over and above the I.Q itself. Even before these are considered one needs, of course, to have an accurate idea of the average I.Q. and the scatter of I.Q. which normally exist in the class, school, or vocational group concerned. The diagram on p. 26 should be useful in this respect. Among the selective effects one must consider age—e.g. the lower I.Q.s in a class are usually among the oldest boys, whose mental age therefore is often as high as or higher than that of the ' brightest ' boys. The highest I.Q.s will not therefore necessarily come out at the top of the class. The longer that group is kept together, however, the more will the high I.Q.s come to the top, since their mental age is increasing more rapidly. Classification according to I.Q. in the first place avoids this spreading of the field which is so upsetting to effective class teaching.

Among the vocations, as the writer has argued elsewhere,[1] the general effectiveness of members of a given calling probably does not vary as much as the I.Q. Those with I.Q.s in the lowest quartile seem to have compensatory gifts in character, temperament, or special aptitude, whilst those who apparently have exceptionally high intelligence for the job are lacking in these. This must be taken into account when deciding, from a comparison of I.Q. with a given occupation level, the fitness of the person for that occupation.

Occasionally this selection produces even an inverted relation of I.Q. to effectiveness. Thus, among students who have passed with equal success the various examinations necessary to reach a degree, those with lower I.Q.s necessarily have had to have temperament-character advantages absent among the brighter but only equally successful. If one attempts to select, say, good practical teachers from such a group by means of intelligence tests, one finds the correlation of ' g ' with teaching success very low or even negative; for those temperament-character qualities which have become inversely related (in this particular group) to intelligence are actually

[1] " Occupational Norms of Intelligence," *Brit. J. Psychol.*, 1934.

more important in teaching than in the examination, and now determine the order of teaching success.

One special occasion for intelligence test interpretation which perhaps needs comment here is that which involves advising the secondary school leaver as to his fitness for taking a degree, or as to the type of degree and the subject in which he may best take it. The average I.Q. and I.Q. scatter of successful (London) degree students is given on p. 32 (which also gives figures for Cambridge students). Columbia University results show that I.Q. has a fairly close relation to class of degree obtained, so that one may to some extent foresee, from a comparison of the given I.Q. with the above scatter, whether a first or third class is likely. The surveys of Dale[1] and White[2] show that certain academic subjects require a higher I.Q. than others. The order of ' g ' saturation for various subjects obtained in these surveys is in general agreement with that obtained by mathematical analysis of the amount of ' g ' in such subjects at school level, but is different in a few particulars, because the subject is not necessarily the same in matter and form at the university level as at the school level. Dale found the following order of decreasing intelligence demand: Mathematics, Classics, Natural Sciences, English, Modern Languages, History; while White, classifying according to Faculties, found the decreasing order Arts, Science, Medicine, Laws, Librarianship, Engineering, Journalism, Architecture, Fine Arts. At the school-leaving level the intelligence test is a valuable help in prognosis and in avoiding misplacement, but in the more highly selected groups of second- or third-year students, already at the university, emotional maladjustment seems rather more important in determining failure and success.[2]

These notes on the interpretation of intelligence test results would not be complete without reference to those

[1] Barbara Dale, " The Use of Mental Tests with University Women Students," *Brit. J. Educ. Psychol.*, February 1935.
[2] H. D. J. White, " An Application of Mental Tests to University Women Students," *op. cit.*, November 1931.

instances, happily rare in good tests, when considerable disagreement exists between the verdict of the component sub-tests. It used to be said that high variability in the Binet test, i.e. absence of a sharp failing point, with resulting scatter of pass and fail items over several years, was indicative of emotional instability in the subject tested. It was never proved, however, that the connection was at all a close one, neither was the theoretical basis clear. Presumably it indicated at least an abnormal educational background and possibly high ' oscillation ' of attention and capacity.

Big differences between sub-tests should always be investigated further ; the subject may have failed, through some slip on the part of the examiner, to get a fair grasp of the instruction. Some valuable sidelights on the subject's temperament may be gained by comparison of the tests particularly well done and particularly badly done. Certain sub-tests, though they correlate in general well with intelligence, admit of being upset completely on rare occasions by the lack of some special (but very normal) aptitude. Thus, in one instance a child who scored 8 out of 12 on Line's test in the Dartington Scale and who, therefore, definitely could not be lacking in intelligence, scored only 3 on the Substitution (Symbol digit) test. On further examination this proved to be due to inability to handle a pencil (a rare degree of muscular inco-ordination) which had caused the child to spend undue time and effort merely in making the circles and crosses. True oscillation effects, as shown by scatter of fail and pass items in a graded sub-test, in which most subjects proceed so far and then fail, are certainly frequently found in emotionally unstable subjects. It sometimes appears strikingly in performance tests. Occasionally the normal rapid decline of test-time on the three successive trials of the Seguin Form Board may be replaced by a rise and fall. With young children (below 6) this is not so uncommon, but among older children it often accompanies defective powers of concentration and nervous instability. From

Spearman's original work, as yet inadequately followed up, it seemed likely that this oscillation of performance would be particularly high among epileptics. Certainly three of the highest oscillations on the Seguin-Goddard test recorded by the present writer were by epileptics, one of whom had a slight attack of ' petit mal ' in the middle of the test, so that the cause of the unusually long time score was definitely observable. With young children and invalids, marked differences on sub-test scores often arise from fatigue, and indicate nothing more than that the experimenter has failed to notice premonitory signs of it and adjust his testing programme accordingly.

At the present time, owing to the chaotic state of research in the temperament-character field, it is the temperament tests and character probes that offer the greatest difficulties in interpretation; indeed, a really fruitful use of these tests is only possible to the psychologist who has through experience obtained an artist's skill in applying them, and who is fully versed in the relevant research literature.

Thus, for example, the reasons for discrepancy between ' fluency of association ', as tested, and ' surgency ' of temperament, as observed, are still matters for research, yet the total picture in cases of high fluency and low surgency sometimes indubitably points to maladjustment crippling a natural surgency. In one instance a secondary school boy, referred for obstructiveness and offences against authority, proved to have a fluency score in the ninth decile, yet was described as being dour and unsociable. This boy also had an I.Q. of 139, so that his school difficulties were not at all due to intellectual factors, whilst his perseveration score was moderately low, suggesting no systematic character defect. His father proved to be a man sadistically attached to this boy (for reasons too complex to describe here), and took a pleasure in shackling him with all sorts of exacting restrictions. The boy's reaction to this authority was being carried over to all authority. Whilst treatment was going on, the headmaster was persuaded to give the boy opportunities for social expression and leadership in spite of his apparent lack of the necessary qualities. Within a surprisingly short time he became a thoroughly surgent type and a leader, exhibiting, to the great surprise of the school, the qualities which the tests indicated as being present, but which had hitherto been conspicuously absent.

Just because no single temperament, interest, or character test can as yet be wholly depended upon, it is necessary to glean temperament indications from as many and varied tests as possible, whilst making them brief. A youth of 18, hitherto of entirely good repute in school and out of it, was referred for behaviour superficially very much like a manic-depressive psychosis. He would have prolonged periods of excitability, would stay out all night, and would react violently if attempts were made to control him. At other times he was silent and depressed, refusing to get out of bed. He was said to be quite a social figure, but an interest test pointed to a distinct lack of social and human interests. Tested with a perseveration test he was at the eighth decile on the first occasion and beyond the tenth on the second. These findings indicate a schizophrenic rather than a manic-depressive disorder. The experimental criteria of Kretschmer (p. 190) also agreed with this and the patient's build was emphatically of a leptosomatic type. Thus, in spite of his accessibility at that time, his periods of complete normality, and his atypical behaviour when considered as schizophrenic, he was considered to be in all probability an incipent dementia præcox case, who should be recommended to go as a voluntary patient to the mental hospital. This diagnosis was in time confirmed at the mental hospital.

In spite of many instances where the perseveration test result neatly dovetails into the rest of the picture which one is constructing, this test remains least certain of any in its indications. Thus, although most very low perseverators have the unduly quick excitability, the tendency to nag, and the active instability of mood noted on p. 209, some are among the most model characters. It is quite possible that there are two types of low perseverators: (1) those with too great mental energy—the unruly type mentioned above, and (2) those who are as defective in mental energy as many high perseverators, but who force themselves to live up to an exacting standard of will function (in psychoanalytic terms a hyperactive super-ego). These are very critical with themselves and with others, put great emphasis on the will, and are often silent and anxious in bearing. It is possible that these are the persons who constitute cases of fluctuation between the extremes of perseveration, creeping up to the tenseness of extreme low perseveration and then snapping and falling to the extreme of high perseveration with melancholic or schizophrenic accompaniments. These are speculations based on close observation of only one or two cases; yet in the interpretation of temperament tests at the present time such clinical impressions must be borne in mind as possible guides. After some experience, one does in fact get a very definite understanding of the personality which these tests indicate, even if it is not possible always to make the conception fully explicit in our present verbal terms. A low perseverator is, in spite of brusque reactions and arbitrary behaviour, a fundamentally likeable person who will respond to personal loyalties and do his best to be dependable. A high perseverator is usually a much more difficult person to get hold of and never entirely calculable. High fluency with high perseveration gives at once an impression of extreme rascality, just as high fluency with moderately low perseveration brings out the attractive qualities which make for natural leadership.

The use and interpretation of temperament interest and character tests should also assist in following the course of treatment. The tests of ' w ' used by Hartshorne and May with large groups have been used successfully with individuals and smaller groups in tracing the changes in honesty and reliability resulting from various applied influences. The further discussion of the significance of these tests in individual and group situations is, however, in the present stage of their evolution, beyond the scope of a book of this size.

3. The Complete Case Study

Sometimes the bare test results are alone a sufficient basis to enable the psychologist to decide upon a change in a child's school classification, the selection of an employee, or the necessity for treatment, but in other instances the test is only a part of a comprehensive interview or series of interviews in which the interpretation of the tests is determined by the whole picture.

There are two principal types of interview, the planning of which requires discussion here: the psychiatric interview and the employment interview (which in a sense cover the vocational interview and the psychological or social research interviews). Much has been written about the second of these,[1] and it is only the first which needs to be set out in any detail.

Of all interviews, however, one can say that:

(1) They should follow a definite scheme in the mind of the interviewer (or be a standard interview on paper), since only in that way are fair comparisons of individuals to be made; and

(2) The interview plan should be flexible, especially in the psychiatric interview, permitting the subject to display his lines of interest. It is the interviewer's ultimate aim to appeal to the subject's hidden fears, prejudices, and ambitions, in order to bring them into the open. Nevertheless, the interviewer needs to keep control, if only to avoid dawdling in irrelevant places. He should lead up to what he wants to talk about and interject a direct question when the facts he wants are finally not forthcoming.

(3) The subject should be given time to get accustomed to his surroundings. For this reason it is often best, as indeed it is frequently on other grounds necessary, to let the routine part of testing precede the interview. With neurotic adults or difficult children it is particularly neces-

---

[1] Principally: H. W. Bingham, " The Three Functions of the Interview in Employment," *Management Review*, xv, 1926; *How to Interview* (New York). J. J. Crawford, " The Art of Interviewing," *Industrial Management*, lxi, 1921. P. M. Symonds, *Diagnosing Personality and Conduct*. Woodworth, " Psychological Experience with the Interview," *J. Person. Res.*, 1925.

sary that the surroundings should be æsthetically pleasant
and not contain stimuli which normally condition a de-
fensive or emotionally-disturbed state.   Notably, one must
avoid a too formal, police-court-like setting.   Thus
children who are unhappy at school will be far more responsive in a room that is most unlike a classroom—preferably a room with toys and a certain amount of untidiness.
Always the room should be such as to give complete
privacy.

(4) It is best to begin with pleasant topics which are,
however, of real interest to the subject.   With children
these are usually play interests; with adults they vary
greatly according to class, etc.   A social worker interviewing working-class mothers may even find that the subject's
health or rather her illness and physical complaints form
the most attractive opening subject.

With children referred for problem behaviour, as also
with adults who are not familiar with the objects of a
psychological clinic, it is best to remove strangeness by
saying a few words about how the clinic tries to help, what
it is for, and why the person has been sent.   To leave a
question-mark standing in the mind of the patient too long
is to give opportunities for an obstructive attitude to grow
up around it.   It is illuminating to find out what the child
or parent has heard about the clinic, or the employee about
the selection methods, and to correct caricatures.   In all
interviews the interviewer and the interviewed must have
some common goal and purpose, if the conversation is to
proceed rapidly and fruitfully, and though this direction
may be of the most general kind, to wit, the improvement
of the patient's condition, it must be jointly envisaged.

(5) The interviewer should show as early as possible that
he is able at once to verify the truth of statements, or that he
is prepared to do so.   For that purpose he should be entirely sure of his own facts relevant to the case before the
interview, and should verify fresh facts between interviews.
Valuable evidence on home conditions is often obtainable
by interviewing parents and children independently and

before they have had time to influence each other, and by comparing purely factual statements.   Generally, the findings of the first interview will suggest definite facts for the social worker to enquire about before the second interview.

(6) With delinquents the facts of the delinquency should be taken for granted.   The child should not be given confirmation in his expectation that he is to be morally reproved once more and that demonstrations of repentance are required.   But he may be given to understand later that his motives for the action are of interest; that a problem remains unsolved, and that he must be helped to realise what dissatisfactions are behind the actions which led up to his delinquency.   In all this, a detached but kindly interest, without censure, superior amusement, or condonation is proper to the stages of investigation, though the psychologist may enter more feelingly into the situation at the later stage of therapy when transference and suggestion are employed.

(7) Although theoretically self-evident, it is necessary in practice to warn against implying answers to one's own questions, i.e. against leading questions, particularly among children, of whom 99 per cent. will say what they think is expected or wanted.   Likewise, the interviewer must guard against premature interpretations forming in his mind during the first interview, before all aspects are known.   Rice,[1] in his experimental study of the methods of a number of skilled interviewers interviewing (for a social enquiry) a number of ' down and outs ' found that one interviewer, a prohibitionist, recorded that 62 per cent. imputed their position to drink and 7 per cent. to industrial conditions; another interviewer, a socialist, questioning the self-same group, found 22 per cent. attributing their position to drink and 39 per cent. to industrial conditions. Each was a trained and conscientious investigator. Psychiatric interviews, unless improved, can match this in variation of interpretation of case-histories.

(8) Various devices must be cultivated with the taciturn,

[1] " A Contagious Bias in the Interview," *Amer. J. Soc.*, xxxv, 1929.

suspicious, or diffident person.   Normally, questions should
be framed briefly and clearly.   They should suit the vocabulary of the person interviewed, so that they mean what one
intends them to mean, and, since children have little power
of interpretation in general terms, questions of a generalised nature are usually wasted.   But in these circumstances
they need occasionally to be provocatively ambiguous, to
call forth discussion.   Or, failing to get a response, the
interviewer may suggest alternative answers, making sure
that both will be unacceptable to the subject.   Usually,
too, the person interviewed should be encouraged to qualify
his answers, not merely to answer yes or no.   The influences
of primitive passive sympathy should not be neglected.
Some volubility on the part of the interviewer is the best
stimulant to talkativeness in the person interviewed, though
it must necessarily be controlled at the right moments.   For
similar reasons the interviewer should be genuinely at his
ease, frank and friendly, encouraging by nod, gesture, and
smile.   (Naturally this applies more to the psychiatric
than the business interview.)   Again, the interviewer needs
to be a good listener with an expectant (but not too in-
quisitive) air and an occasional offer of inviting or
insistent silences.   With children, if any depth of acquaint-
anceship is desired, the adult must quickly indicate that he
is not to be classed with the typical ' adult-in-authority.'
He must, moreover, remove the child's inferiority barrier
by penetrating into fields where the child knows more than
he does himself, so that the child is able to accept him on a
basis of give and take.   It is valuable even to abdicate
from the physically superior position of sitting in a big chair
behind an impressive desk and to join the child in floor
games or in an informal chat sitting on the table.   He
must show that he is ' with the child ' and possessed of
common enjoyments and concerns.   For this reason he
may well parallel experiences recited by the child with
similar experiences recounted from his own childhood.
There is little danger of this fraternisation being overdone;
indeed, much work with children fails through the psycho-

logist being unable, in the time at his disposal, to separate himself emphatically enough from the parent or teacher image with which the child is in difficulty.

Further discussion of the technique of ' rapport ' in the psychiatric type of interview would take us into questions of ' transference,' for the adequate treatment of which the psychologist must be referred to his text-books on psycho-analysis. Most maladjusted individuals, whether children or adults, readily acquire such a transference or emotional dependence upon the psychologist if the latter is really rendering assistance in emotional problems. It is a thing passively to be encouraged in the early stages, because it renders easier the bursting of emotional barriers and causes the subject to be much more fundamentally responsive to the psychologist's suggestions. Nevertheless, its growth must always be carefully watched, since the psychother-apist's aim must eventually be to make this dependence unnecessary. Its eventual dissolution may unintentionally be rendered unduly difficult. This is admittedly a greater danger with adults than with children, who are in any case normally psychologically dependent on parents during childhood, but even with the latter it is necessary for the psychologist who deals with large numbers of children to shift the transference from himself to other personalities able to act as wise mother or father substitutes. The supply of such willing and capable persons is an important concern of any child psychologist dealing with an extensive list of cases.

(9) For certain purposes it may be valuable to include tests within the interview, without the person interviewed being subjected to any formal testing. Great as is the demand for such techniques, the difficulties of devising anything which can at the same time satisfy the psycholo-gist's demands for reliability is even greater, and only one or two tentative and none-too-reliable essays have yet been produced (see pp. 8 and 22). These are Snedden's " Measuring General Intelligence by Interview " (*Psychol. Clinic*, xix, 1930), a vocabulary test with a validity

reaching 0·8, and Lester and Hewlett's "Measuring Introversion and Extraversion," by rating the amount of overt reaction (mainly talking) when twelve provocative statements (some virtually questions) are made.

(10) The results of the interview need to be adequately recorded and dated. In a business interview this may be done during the proceedings, but when matters very intimate to the individual are being discussed in the psychotherapeutic interview, the right atmosphere is all too readily destroyed by the sight of such taking down of evidence and, with children originally referred for delinquency, it may excite suspicion and distrust. Then the record should be written or, better, dictated, immediately after the sitting, and should preserve mainly the actual responses, the psychologist's conclusions or impressions being clearly separated. Alternatively, and particularly with adults, the psychologist may remain screened from the reclining patient, whose free associations he may take down verbatim unobtrusively. Children's play in the clinic play-room is similarly best observed from behind a one-way screen.

There are standard forms for most employee selection interviews, and some good standard approaches have been similarly developed for psychiatric interviews [1] (see e.g. p. 192 and Tjaden's *Analytical Interview* (p. 221), or any text-book of psychiatry, e.g. Stoddart's *Mind and its Disorders* (p. 533)).

With the latter, however, such rigidity should not extend farther than the first 'case taking,' for it is in the free pursuit of patients' conversational trends that the study eventually lies.

The following scheme has been found a useful one in interviewing (for the first time) nervous, difficult, and delinquent children. It is intended to act both as a guide to procedure and a framework for recording.

---

[1] For more detailed schemes see H. W. Bingham, *How to Interview*; S. I. Franz, *Handbook of Mental Examination Methods* (Macmillan, 1920); and G. H. Kirby, *Guides for History-taking and Clinical Examination of Psychiatric Cases*, 1921.

Scheme for Initial Interviewing of Delinquent or Nervous Children

Opening remarks on why child has come to the psychologist.

Ask child first why he thinks he has come, in case he has been brought on some fraudulent misunderstanding which requires correction.   Explain aim to help child; he is one of a great many.   Doubtless good reasons for what he has done.   Anything he tells one will be entirely in confidence. Necessity for frankness.   (The psychologist will need to be on his guard against inadvertently betraying information about parents or teachers given by the child through confusing it with the social worker's reports which may need to be discussed with parents, teachers, or in a police court.) Notice general bearing of child (especially fidgeting, nail-biting, degree of fatigue, steadiness of attention, etc.).

Questions on play life, or observations of child's play with toys with which he has been supplied, or talk with him about jokes in a comic paper he may be reading.   Social or individual games preferred ?   Active or passive ? Older or younger boys or girls ?   Leader ?   Reading preferences. Love of animals.

Questions on companions.   Which he admires?   Why? Especial chums? Are they good scrappers? Have they a gang? Do they outwit their parents? Fond of books or games? Indulge in swearing or bad habits? (Get initial slant on child's own nature from his comments on friends and the nature of his friends.) Has he many friends? Do people tease him? Do his parents like his friends and let him bring them home?   How often can he go out?

Questions on illnesses and absence from school.   Headaches or sickness? Fainting or dizziness? Eating and sleeping habits (if necessary to discuss masturbation, best done among physical habit questions).

School life.   Liking for school?   Does he do well or badly ? (cf. teacher's account).   What teachers he likes or dislikes and why.   School societies or teams.   Subjects liked or disliked.

Attitude towards family.   What do parents think of

school work? Of delinquencies or nervousness concerned? What punishments, and are they deserved? Father or mother better liked? Get an idea of actual amount of time spent by either parent with child. Peculiarities of parents or hints of criticism of parents. Favouritism, and if so, of which child? Rules and restrictions and how much enforced?

Fears and emotional conflicts. Nightmares. Ordinary dreams and of what. (Detailed in subsequent interview.) Day-dreams. Sleep walking or talking. Nervousness of standing before class. Other fears. Bullying by other children. Shame in regard to sex matters or to physical inferiorities. Tics. Enuresis. Thumb-sucking or nail-biting. Early emotional memories. Left-handed. Stuttering. Accidents or operations. First day at school. Death of relatives. Degree of conscientiousness in details. Liking for lonely activities, cycle rides, etc.

Delinquencies or minor misconduct. What have people said? What is subject's attitude? What was the real beginning of the difficulty? Early lying, stealing, or revolt. Were these treated rightly? Is subject likely to feel the same again? Has he ever had similar impulses which he has succeeded in restraining?

Plans for the future. Vocational interests. Results of tests. Would subject like to come again to talk about things?

Except in unusual circumstances the interview on these lines is preceded by whatever testing of intelligence, attainment, and temperament is deemed necessary, but the more complex probing of character through word association tests, miniature situations, free association tests, play situations, etc., described in Chapter VI (especially Section 4b (ii)) dovetails naturally into the later stages of the interview. Indeed, until the psychologist has begun the preliminary interview survey, he cannot know which of these probes he will need.

The above scheme may take from one to four interviews. It is always necessary to keep in mind, however, that the course of events should be adapted in response to the perceived needs of the situation, since treatment is bound to begin, to some extent, even in the first interview. With the fuller course of treatment as such, however, this book is not concerned.

NOTES ON MATHEMATICAL FORMULÆ

THIS appendix is intended to provide practically all the formulæ needed in simple routine work in handling scores and some of the formulæ needed in research work. It is an aid to memory ; not an introduction to statistics. Consequently, the accompanying notes are very scant, and sufficient only to remind the psychologist of the purpose and range of use of the formulæ.

For a regular introduction to statistical methods in connection with such tests the reader is referred to P. E. Vernon's *The Measurement of Abilities*, University of London Press ; to Garrett's *Statistics in Psychology and Education*, Longman's Green, New York ; or to Wynn Jones's *Introduction to the Theory and Practice of Psychology*. Those who wish to go more deeply into statistical theory as it relates to test construction should read Burt's *The Factors of the Mind*, Holzinger's *Statistical Methods for Students in Education*, the present writer's *Description and Measurement of Personality*, World Book Co., 1945. For the derivation of formulæ the reader is referred to G. Udny Yule, *An Introduction to the Theory of Statistics*. Also *Statistical Methods for Research Workers*, by Fisher, and the research articles of Pearson and Spearman (see e.g. Appendix to *The Abilities of Man*).

Statistical Terms

The Mean is the value obtained by adding up all the individual measurements and dividing by the number of measures.

The Median is the value of the middle item in a collection of measurements, or that point above which and below which are 50 per cent. of the measurements.

The mean may be upset by a few extreme scores, whilst the median is not ; but the median cannot be employed in most computations in the way that is possible with the mean.

357

The Mode is the value at which most cases occur, i.e. the most frequent measurement among all the measurements.

Expressing the Degree of Variability or Scatter of Measurements

It should be noted that the attempt to define range by quoting the extreme values is practically valueless since these vary greatly from sample to sample. We may use:

(1) *Mean Deviation* or average deviation obtained by adding the absolute values (neglecting signs) of all the deviations from the mean and dividing by the number of cases:

$$M = \frac{\Sigma d}{N}$$

(2) *Standard Deviation*, obtained by squaring the deviations from the mean, adding them together, taking the average, and finding its square root, i.e. :

$$\sigma = \sqrt{\frac{\Sigma d^2}{N}}$$

(3) *Quartile Deviation.*—The position of the lower quartile Q_1 is established by finding the value that has one-quarter of the measurements below it and three-quarters above. Similarly, the upper quartile Q_3 is the value that has only one-quarter of all the measurements falling above it. The *Quartile Deviation* or *Semi-inter-quartile range* is half the distance between these two points. It is one of the simplest measures of dispersion to work out, and conveys at once a rough notion of the amount of scatter.

$$Q = \frac{Q_3 - Q_1}{Q}$$

(4) *Pearson's Coefficient of Variation.*—This expresses variability independently of the general magnitude and nature of the measurements, so that with its aid one might compare variability in size of mice with that of elephants, or the variability in weight of commercial pounds of butter with the variability in volume of pints of milk:

$$V = \frac{100\,\sigma}{M},$$

where σ and M have the meanings indicated above.

Normality or Skewedness of Distribution of Measurement

Any large number of measurements may have the general nature of their distribution graphically expressed by means of a histogram. This is constructed by taking a certain interval in the measurements and erecting rectangles at this interval along a base line, each rectangle being proportionate in height to the number of cases that fall within that interval. A best fitting curve may later be fitted to this histogram. For most psychological measurements this curve follows the normal probability curve (see references above for formula and purpose of the normal

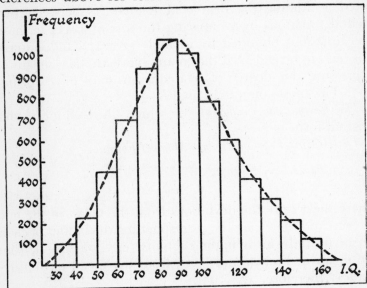

Fig. 63.—Distribution diagram, showing method of constructing histogram and distribution polygon or curve.

probability curve). Most psychological measurements on a sufficiently large population fit into this normal symmetrical probability curve approximately,[1] but sometimes the curve is lopsided or skewed, and it is necessary to express the amount of skewedness. This can be done by means of :

[1] Actually they form a leptokurtic curve superficially resembling a normal probability curve, but the latter has mathematical properties which make its use generally convenient.

Pearson's Measure of Skewedness:

$$Sk = \frac{M - Mo}{\sigma},$$

where M is the mean ; Mo is the mode;

$$or \ Sk = \frac{3(M - Md)}{\sigma},$$

where M*d* is the median.

Measures of Association of Two Sets of Measurements

Since a considerable amount of time in psychology is devoted to finding the degree of relatedness between two mental functions by comparing the lists of scores in those two functions obtained by a single group of individuals, it is only to be expected that many mathematical means of expressing this degree of relatedness should have sprung up. The most commonly used is:

The Correlation Coefficient, of which the soundest and original form is:

The Bravais-Pearson Product Moment Formula :

$$R = \frac{\Sigma \, xy}{\sqrt{\Sigma x^2 \Sigma y^2}},$$

where the *x*'s are the deviations from the mean in the one activity and the *y*'s are the corresponding deviations of each person from the mean in the *y* activity (e.g. Jones is -5 from the mean in French and -13 from the mean on mathematics; therefore, $xy = 65$).

Σxy is the sum of the *xy*'s of all the people in the group and Σx^2 the sum of the squares of the deviations.

To save working out the deviations, the same formula may be expressed in a way which permits the use of the scores as they stand:

$$r = \frac{\Sigma XY - NMx \, My}{\sqrt{(\Sigma X^2 - NM^2x) \, (\Sigma Y^2 - NM^2y)}},$$

where N equals the numbers of cases, and where M*x* is the mean of X, and M*y* the mean of Y.

As Stephenson has shown, this formula, if used with measurements that have been scaled down to the same mean and standard deviation in both sets of measurements, can be simplified to:

$$r = 1 - \frac{\Sigma(X - Y)^2}{2\Sigma(X^2 - NM^2)}$$

Where all possible inter-correlations have to be worked out between a half-dozen or more performances, a considerable saving of time and trouble is generally made by investing in the little extra time at the beginning required to scale the results to the same distribution.   The denominator in the above equation then becomes the same for all correlations, so that the formula becomes:

$$r = 1 - \frac{\Sigma D^2}{K},$$

where D is the difference between the individual's raw score in x and y, and K is the constant denominator obtained from the formula above.

Rank Correlation Coefficient.—The above formulæ are based on calculations with actual scores or measurements. When dealing with smaller numbers of cases, say, not more than fifty, it saves time to ignore the measurements and to work on ranks.   One arranges individuals in their rank order, and carries out subsequent calculations on these ranks.   With certain kinds of material the results are in any case first given in ranks, measurements not being possible.   One may then use:

Spearman's Rank Formula :

$$\rho = 1 - \frac{6\Sigma d^2}{N(N^2 - 1)},$$

where d is each individual's difference in rank order between the two rankings.

Since this formula assumes equal spacings between the ranks, it needs a correction to make it strictly comparable with the product-moment coefficient as follows:

$$r = 2 \sin \frac{\pi}{6} \rho$$

The correction is so slight as to be scarcely worth making except in research work.

A still more simple rank formula is:

Spearman's Foot Rule :

$$R = 1 - \frac{6\Sigma D}{N^2 - 1},$$

where D represents the positive differences of rank only. This gives very rough values, but is useful in preliminary surveys.

Correlation Ratio.—The above correlation coefficients are strictly only to be used when a linear relationship exists between the two series, i.e. when a regular increase in one produces a regular increase or decrease in the other. Two series of measurements may be closely related and yet not have these linear correlations, e.g. Perseveration and Will Character (see p. 208). The correlation coefficient will then yield a much lower figure than the true correlation deserves. With such material a proper estimate of the degree of relatedness is obtained better by the correlation ratio:

$$\eta_{xy} = \frac{\sqrt{\Sigma f y \; \overline{xy}^2}}{\sigma x} \; ; \; \text{or}$$

$$\eta_{xy} = \sqrt{1 - \frac{\sigma^2 ax}{\sigma x^2}},$$

where σax is the standard deviation of the differences from the position assumed by the regression line.

Coefficients of Association, Colligation, and Contingency

It is often desired to find the amount of association between results which are not expressed in a series of measurements or ranks, but are simply divided into one or two categories in respect to one matter and the same number of categories in respect to the other with which it is required to find the degree of association, e.g. presence or absence of motor accidents related to drinking or teetotalism. We may then use:

Yule's Coefficient of Association :

$$Q = \frac{ad - bc}{ad + bc},$$

where
   a is the number of cases in which both attributes are present;
   b the number in which the first attribute is present and the second absent;
   c the number in which the second is present and the first absent;
   d the number in which both attributes are absent.

Another measure yielding results more numerically comparable with the correlation coefficient is:

Yule's Coefficient of Colligation

$$\omega = \frac{\sqrt{ad} - \sqrt{bc}}{\sqrt{ad} + \sqrt{bc}},$$

the symbols meaning the same as in the above.

When there are more than four or five categories on each side, a useful device is:

Pearson's Contingency Coefficient (Coefficient of Mean Square Contingency) :

$$C = \frac{\sqrt{S - 1}}{S},$$

$$\text{where } S = \Sigma\left(\frac{f^2xy}{fxfy}\right),$$

fxy being the frequency of cases in any one box below; *fx* the frequency of cases in the column in which that box occurs, and *fy* the frequency of cases in the row in which that box occurs. After the cases have been distributed in the boxes, therefore, this fraction is worked out for each box and summed for all the boxes to get the value ' S.'

	Low P.	Mod. Low P.	Mod. High P.	High P.	fy
High 'w'		6	4	1	11
Medium 'w'	2	1	3	4	10
Low 'w'	5	1	3	9	18
fx	7	8	10	14	

FIG. 64.—Showing relation between scores in character ('w') and in perseveration ('p'), arranged for calculating the contingency coefficient.

Thus, for the box indicated by heavy underlining,

$$\frac{f^2xy}{fxfy} = \frac{3^2}{10 \times 10} = \cdot 09$$

Correlation with Three Variables

When the correlations have been found between three variables (in three pairs), it is sometimes required to find the amount of correlation which would exist between two of them if the third were kept constant, e.g. the relation between school attainment and estimations of character, intelligence being kept constant. Such an estimation may be obtained by the following:

Partial Correlation Formula :

$$r_{12 \cdot 3} = \frac{r_{12} - r_{13} \cdot r_{23}}{\sqrt{(1 - r^2_{13}) (1 - r^2_{23})}}$$

$r_{12 \cdot 3}$ = the correlation of 1 with 2 when 3 is kept constant.

Effects of Chance Errors in Measurements

In many measurements it is necessary to allow for effects due to chance errors of experiment, or to decide whether a given mean, difference of means, correlation coefficient, etc., is one which, as likely as not, could be obtained by chance, or one which is definitely significant. For the latter purpose the notion of ' Probable Error ' has been developed. The probable error of a measurement will depend, among other things, upon the size of the sample taken, relative to that of the total population.

The meaning of the probable error value is best illustrated by saying that if the probable error of a measurement is 4·5, there is an even chance of the measurement being within 4·5 units (above or below) the true measurement (i.e. that from the whole population). Unless a measurement is bigger than its probable error, therefore, there is only a fifty-fifty probability that it means anything at all (i.e. that it is not purely a product of chance factors).

The probability of getting a measurement, by sheer chance, twice as big as the P.E. is only ·1773 (in 1), three times as big, ·0430, four times, ·0070, and five times, about ·0007. Consequently, the general convention has been adopted that a measurement can be regarded as significant if it is at least four times its P.E. A measurement even two or three times the P.E. is, however, an indication of the need for further enquiry as to significance.

(1) *Probable Error of the Mean:*

$$\text{P.E.}_m = \frac{·6745\sigma}{\sqrt{N}}$$

(2) *Probable Error of the Differences between two Means, when Uncorrelated:*

$$\text{P.E.}_{m1-m2} = \sqrt{(\text{P.E.}_{m.1.})^2 + (\text{P.E.}_{m.1.})^2}$$

(3) *Probable Error of Correlation Coefficient:*

$$\text{P.E.} = \frac{·6745(1 - r^2)}{\sqrt{N}}$$

(4) *Probable Error of Rank Correlation Coefficient:*

$$\text{P.E.} = \frac{·7063(1 - \rho)}{\sqrt{N}}$$

(5) *Probable Error of Correlation Ratio:* precisely as that for Correlation Coefficient.

(6) *Probable Error of Coefficient of Association:*

$$\sigma\, Q = \frac{1 - Q^2}{2} \sqrt{\frac{1}{a} + \frac{1}{b} + \frac{1}{c} + \frac{1}{d}}$$

(7) *Probable Error of Contingency Coefficient:* too complex to be given here. See Holzinger, *op. cit.*

It should be noted that the general effect of chance errors on a correlation coefficient is not to raise or lower it by a chance amount, but rather to produce a definite diminution. If the consistency coefficients for the tests concerned are known, it is possible to correct the coefficients for the attenuating effect of errors, and to discover the value which the correlation between the two abilities would have if the test for these abilities were perfectly reliable. This correction for attenuation is as follows:

$$r_{ab} = \frac{r_{a1\,b1}}{\sqrt{r_{a1a2} \times r_{b1b2}}}$$

where $r_{a1\,a2}$ is the consistency coefficient of the A test, $r_{a1\,b1}$ is the observed correlation between the two tests, and r_{ab} is the corrected coefficient (i.e. correlation between ' true ' scores).

There is also a formula which would enable one to allow in the correlation coefficient for the effects of any selection which has previously taken place with the group concerned. It is well known that a reduction in scatter tends to reduce the correlation coefficient. This formula will be found in Wynn Jones, *op. cit.*

Another cause of the correlation coefficient being below its true value is an undue shortness in the test itself. An idea may be obtained of the size that the correlation coefficient would have had, had the tests been longer, by means of:

The Spearman Brown Prophecy Formula Figure for Predicting the Consistency of Lengthened Tests :

$$R = \frac{nr}{1 + (n - 1)\,r},$$

where r is the original consistency coefficient and n is the amount by which the length of the test is multiplied. The standard error of the above formula is

$$\sigma n = \frac{n(1 + r)}{r \sqrt{N}}.$$

A similar formula may be used to discover what the validity of a lengthened test would be, viz. :

$$R = \frac{n\,(r_1)}{\sqrt{n + n\,(n - 1)\,r_2}},$$

where r_1 is the original validity and r_2 is the consistency coefficient of the test.

Factor Analysis

The Tetrad Difference Equation is as follows:

$$r_{12} \cdot r_{34} - r_{13} \cdot r_{24} = 0.$$

If this equation is satisfied, we may suppose that the abilities concerned in these correlation coefficients are divisible into a general factor and factors specific to each test. Naturally, this condition, owing to experimental errors, is never exactly fulfilled, and it suffices if the tetrad differences arrange themselves approximately in a normal probability curve with a standard error not significantly greater than the standard error calculated according to formula. A very rough formula for this probable error is:

$$P.E. = \frac{1 \cdot 349}{N^{\frac{1}{2}}} r\,(1 - r),$$

where r denotes the mean of the correlation coefficients taken into account.

This tends to give values rather too small. A fuller range of suitable but much more complex formulæ will be found in the Appendix to Spearman's *Abilities of Man*, whilst a discussion of tetrad difference calculations and the theory of ' g ' will be found in Appendix I of Thomas's *Ability and Knowledge* (see p. 1).

QUESTIONNAIRE FOR PERSONALITY FACTORS

CERTAIN serious defects of the questionnaire method have been indicated above, but for special purposes, and while objective tests are being developed and standardised, the questionnaire can be useful. The chief conditions for valid use of a questionnaire are (1) mature subjects, (2) subjects of at least average education, and (3) subjects willing to co-operate fully and capable of doing so.

The following is a combined questionnaire and test form for measuring the ten most important personality factors—including general mental ability (B or 'g'), and general education (K)—as listed in Chapters V and VI above. It employs some projective and interest type questions. In the case of seven factors the validity of the items has been established by previous factor analyses of questionnaires, but in the remainder it depends on the soundness of the designer's matching of questionnaire items with the behaviour described in the rated factors (Chapters V and VI). Because of these untried features the score for each factor is at present allowed to rest only on the twenty questions which were specifically inserted for its estimation, but when the questionnaire has itself been factor analysed it is probable that each factor will be assessable from as many as thirty or forty items, because some items will be found sufficiently loaded with a second factor to permit their use also in assessing other factors than those for which they were originally known to be valid. At present there is very little overlap of items— only such, in fact, as reduces the total number of items required from 200 to 190.

This number of items is the absolute minimum possible for any sort of reliable estimate of ten factors. In fact, the questionnaire is intended to be used only as a preliminary screening device, to get a general idea of the total personality and ability in circumstances when any fuller testing is quite impossible, or to indicate the cases in which more substantial testing of particular aspects of personality would be desirable. A more lengthy questionnaire (595 questions in three parts), testing thirteen factors (four or five the same as the above and the rest established in questionnaire material only, being therefore of unknown relative importance), is available in the Guilford-Martin Questionnaires. These are based on more extensive factor analytic research than any of their predecessors in the questionnaire field, and are standardised for American college students. (Obtainable from the Sheridan Supply Co., Beverly Hills, California, U.S.A.)

The questionnaire set out below is actually both a questionnaire and its key. The letters at the extreme left indicate to which factor or factors each item contributes (one point if 'correct,' o if not), and the underlined answer indicates which is 'correct' in the sense of contributing to a positive loading in the factor concerned. Naturally these should not be reproduced in the actual test form! The scores on any factor could thus range between o and 20, and the percentile score (or, more coarsely, appropriately to the roughness of the instrument, the decile score) is to be obtained from the raw score of the given individual by consulting the tables of norms. The interpretation of the decile score must be made in accordance with the discussions of the meanings of these factors given in Chapters V and VI. It will be noticed, in looking at the scoring key, that the factors repeat themselves throughout the questionnaire in roughly cyclic order. This is not made precise, because the additional ease in scoring thus obtained would be offset by ease of cheating!

It is hoped that copies of this questionnaire, with separate stencil key and norms, will soon be available from the University of London Press.

PERSONALITY QUESTIONNAIRE FOR
FACTORS A, B ('g'), C, D, E, F, G, I, K, AND L

Directions.—This is designed to give you more knowledge of your own personality. It is not just a test of intelligence, and in general there are no *right* and *wrong* answers, but only answers indicating varieties of temperament and personality. Answer each as thoughtfully and as honestly as possible, for the answers will be kept confidential. It is sometimes difficult to answer definitely ' Yes ' or ' No,' for you may be average on the trait concerned, but in such cases remember that you must be *slightly* to one side of average and answer accordingly.

A Yes (1) At social gatherings do you tend to keep in
E No   the background (e.g. avoiding the task
           of introducing people) ?

B   (2) Which one of the numbers on the left is
 2, 8, 6, 3, 4   different from all the rest ?

C Yes (3) Do you rather frequently feel in low
F No   spirits (depressed) ?

D Yes (4) Are your feelings rather easily hurt by the
   No   chance remarks of others ?

E Yes (5) Do you feel that you lack self-confidence ?
   No

G Yes (6) Do you find that your interests tend to
   No   change rapidly and unpredictably ?

I Yes (7) Are you easily startled, by sudden sounds,
   No   etc. ?

K Yes (8) Are you in general more interested in
   No   intellectual questions than in athletics or
           sports ?

L Yes (9) Do you think that most people are self-
   No   seeking beneath a veneer of goodwill ?

A   Yes (10) Are you much troubled with shyness?
      <u>No</u>

B   <u>Stone</u> (11) Which of these things is not the same as the others? Dog, cat, stone, cow.

C   Yes (12) Do you have frequent occasions when you feel lonely?
      <u>No</u>

D⟋ Yes (13) Do you find that you easily get over-excited and 'rattled' in exciting situations?
L   No

E   Yes (14) If you find your opinions differ from those of the people you are with, do you tend to feel discouraged?
      <u>No</u>

F╳Yes (15) Do you often feel just miserable for no reason at all?
C   No

G   <u>Yes</u> (16) Can you claim to be of decidedly more than average stability and persistence?
      No

I   <u>Yes</u> (17) Do you rather often find difficulty in getting to sleep?
      No

K   <u>Yes</u> (18) Do you take pleasure in analysing and studying the motives of people?
      No

L   <u>Yes</u> (19) Do you think that the average person gets a certain amount of pleasure from being malicious in personal relationships?
      No

A   Yes (20) Are you rather slow to make new friends?
      <u>No</u>

B 1, 4, 9, (21) Underline the number that does not belong.
   <u>11</u>, 16

C   Yes (22) Do you often feel remorseful over unwise impulses to which you have given way in the past?
      <u>No</u>

D   <u>Yes</u> (23) Do you get too easily upset?
      No

E Yes (24) Do you unhesitatingly complain to the
   No   waiter if served unsatisfactory food in a
              restaurant ?

F Yes (25) Are you inclined to worry unduly about
G No   possible misfortunes ?

G Yes (26) Do you like best a job that provides you
   No   with pretty constant change of work and
              scene ?

I Yes (27) Are you easily distracted from what you
   No   are doing by conversation, sudden noises,
              etc. ?

K Yes (28) When you have a problem, do you prefer
   No   to work it out in your own way ?

L Yes (29) Do you find that there are an appreciable
   No   number of people in your environment
              whom you feel compelled actively to
              dislike ?

A. Yes (30) Do you find it difficult to start up a con-
   No   versation with a stranger in a train or
              store ?

B Hand (31) ' Spade ' is to ' Dig ' as ' Knife ' is to
  Sharp   —— ? Underline the best word on
  Cut   the left.
  Shovel

C Yes (32) Do you frequently feel lonely, even when
   No   in a group ?

D Yes (33) Do you have frequent ups and downs of
   No   mood ?

E Yes (34) Are you troubled by feelings of inferiority ?
   No

F Yes (35) Would you describe yourself as a meditative
   No   and introspective person ?

G Yes (36) Do you find yourself often suspicious of
L No   other people's motives ?

I   Yes / No   (37) As a child (or still) have you been much troubled by night terrors?

K   Yes / No   (38) Do you prefer to plan and lead in a group undertaking?

L   Yes / No   (39) Do you believe that you tend to be found fault with more than you deserve?

A   Yes / No   (40) Do you prefer to read about eventful things rather than have them happen to you personally?

B   Grass / Milk / Tree / Puppy   (41) 'Dog' is to 'Bone' as 'Cow' is to —— ? Underline best word among those on the left.

C   Yes / No   (42) Do you often feel unsure of being able to see a job through and get discouraged easily by difficulties?

D   Yes / No   (43) Do you express your emotions readily and directly?

E   Yes / No   (44) Do you readily sell things or solicit funds for a cause in which you are interested?

F   Yes / No   (45) Can you carry a load of responsibilities and still feel comparatively carefree all the time?

G / D ×   Yes / No   (46) Do you sometimes feel pretty sorry for yourself and rather mistreated?

I   Yes / No   (47) Do you sometimes experience a nervous restlessness, which shows itself in mannerisms, e.g. tapping with the foot, twiddling a pencil, biting nails?

K   Yes / No   (48) Are you usually aware, and objectively critical, when some person or newspaper tries to get across what is really propaganda?

L Yes   (49) Do you usually trust people until it is
     <u>No</u>   proven to you that your trust is mis-
                  placed, as opposed to being wary from
                  the beginning ?

A <u>Yes</u> (50) Are you apt to be self-conscious and
     <u>No</u>   embarrassed when speaking to those in
                  authority in your business ?

B <u>Wise</u> (51) 'Own' is to 'Rich' as 'Know' is to
    Kind   —— ? (Underline on left.)
    Conceited
    Old
    Absent-minded

E Yes   (52) Do you find it difficult to tell a salesman
     <u>No</u>   firmly that you are too busy to listen to
                  him ?

F Yes   (53) Do you find it difficult to make decisions
     <u>No</u>   on questions that are troubling you, so
                  that you tend to postpone doing any-
                  thing about them ?

G Yes   (54) As a rule, do you enjoy the situation of
     <u>No</u>   having to work out a job with several
                  other people, rather than being left to do
                  as you like ?

I   <u>Yes</u> (55) Are you fairly often aware of being
     No   bothered by indigestion, heartburn, and
                  suchlike disturbances ?

K <u>Yes</u> (56) Do you enjoy tackling puzzles and prob-
     No   lems for their own sake—even pretty
                  difficult ones ?

A Yes   (57) In most parties and social groups generally,
     <u>No</u>   do you prefer to keep quietly in the
                  background ?

B   Colours   (58) 'Combine' is to 'Mix' as 'Team'
    Liquids   is to —— ?   (Underline correct
    Enemies   word on left.)
    Army
    <u>Crowd</u>

C   Yes   (59) Are you discouraged by a sense of not
    <u>No</u>   being adjusted to your job, friends, and
                     general environment?

D   <u>Yes</u>   (60) Do you find that you cannot take criticism
    No   without getting upset?

E.   <u>Yes</u>   (61) Are you ready, when occasion demands,
    No   to bluff your way past a guard or door-
                     man?

F   Yes   (62) When you have some unfinished duties on
    <u>No</u>   your mind, do you find it difficult to
                     relax in between times?

G   Yes   (63) Would you describe yourself as slow and
    <u>No</u>   deliberate in manner and in the way you
                     go about any undertaking?

I   <u>Yes</u>   (64) Have you been known to walk or talk out
    No   loud in your sleep?

K   <u>Yes</u>   (65) Do you give thought to looking at present-
    No   day problems in the light of history, in
                     order to see them in perspective?

L   <u>Yes</u>   (66) Do you get very angry when you discover
    No   that people have planned to take advan-
                     tage of your ignorance or good nature in
                     some matter?

A   Yes   (67) Are you given to being absent-minded and
    <u>No</u>   not much in touch with all that goes on
                     around you?

B   Suit   (68) 'Clock is to 'Time' as 'Tailor' is to
    Cloth   ——? (Underline correct word on
    Scissors   the left.)
    Tape
    Pattern

C   Yes   (69) Do you find that your moods are unstable,
    No   so that you cannot be sure what you are
    going to want to do a day or so ahead of
    time ?

D   Yes   (70) Have you sometimes got unduly con-
    No   cerned about what afterwards turned out
    to be a trifling physical illness or dis-
    ability ?

E   Yes   (71) Do you think you get better results if you
    No   upbraid an assistant severely sometimes
    when he fails to get work done as you
    like it ?

F   Yes   (72) Do you think that the average person's
    No   degree of optimism about prospects of
    social and political progress is justified ?

G   Yes   (73) When you make up your mind on some
    No   personal matter, have you generally
    thought around it so well that you find
    you don't have to change it because of
    what other people tell you later ?

I   Yes   (74) Do you get annoyed by people cleaning
    No   finger-nails in public (or chewing loudly,
    or similar defaults) ?

K   Yes   (75) Do you take a carefree, happy-go-lucky
    No   attitude to the social problems that seem
    to worry many people ?

L   Yes   (76) Do you always want a sound theory on
    No   which to base your actions, rather than
    doing things just because other people
    do them ?

A   <u>Yes</u>   (77) Do you feel that only an insensitive person
     No   would discuss his innermost thoughts and
                 convictions with casual acquaintances ?

B   Yes   (78) Is ' Find ' a better opposite to ' Reveal '
     <u>No</u>   than ' Hide ' is ?

C   Yes   (79) Do you get emotionally disturbed if you
     <u>No</u>   stand near the edge of the roof of a high
                 building ?

D   <u>Yes</u>   (80) Do you like to have pleasant, sociable
     No   company when you are working ?

E   <u>Yes</u>   (81) At public meetings have you ever got up
     No   and heckled the speaker with awkward
                 questions ?

F   <u>Yes</u>   (82) Are you a rather talkative person who
     No   enjoys telling plenty of anecdotes when
                 the company is sympathetic to your
                 doing so ?

G   Yes   (83) If you know you are doing the right thing,
     <u>No</u>   are you nevertheless apt to be emotionally
                 affected by the various opinions expressed
                 by other people about what you are
                 doing ?

I   <u>Yes</u>   (84) Are you inclined to express your emotions
     No   easily ?

K   <u>Yes</u>   (85) Do you think the problem as to whether
     No   æsthetic education and experience are
                 being neglected in the modern world is
                 vital ?

L   <u>Yes</u>   (86) Have you often been troubled by the con-
     No   viction that you are being watched by
                 people all along the street ?

A   <u>Yes</u>   (87) Do you keep up a rather large circle of
     No   friends in preference to confining yourself
                 to only two or three intimates ?

B   Any   (88) Look at the words on the left and under-
    Few   line the one that does not properly
    Some   belong with the others.
    Most
    All

C   Yes   (89) Do you feel that quite a number of your
    No   friends are disappointingly undependable?

D   Yes   (90) Do you take as prominent a part as you
    No   should in social affairs in your circle?

E   Yes   (91) Do you find it embarrassing to be called
    No   upon in an interview to recite a list of
                 your accomplishments, e.g. when apply-
                 ing for a job.

F   Yes   (92) Do you prefer company that discusses
    No   serious questions in a sober fashion to a
                 gay, frivolous crowd?

G   Yes   (93) Do you have a rooted dislike to putting a
    No   job aside before you have thoroughly
                 finished it, i.e. to turning in a half-
                 finished job?

I   Yes   (94) Would you agree that a man's best friend
    No   is a good bank balance?

K   Yes   (95) Do you ponder a good deal over questions
    No   that are considered to be of importance
                 for social progress?

L   Yes   (96) Have there been many instances in your
    No   life where people have planned to do
                 you harm?

A. Yes   (97) Do you readily enter into arrangements for
    No   co-operative work or play with others
                 (if so, underline ' Yes '), or has experi-
                 ence taught you to be very cautious of
                 making such arrangements (if the latter,
                 underline ' No ')?

B   Wise   (98) Underline the one word on the left that
      <u>Lovely</u>   does not properly go with the others.
      Base
      Kind
      Dishonest

C   Yes   (99) Do you find that in the things you are
      <u>No</u>   doing nowadays your interest falls away
                     rather quickly and sometimes un-
                     expectedly ?

D   <u>Yes</u>   (100) Have you rather often said things in the
      No   heat of the moment that you have
                     thought unwise afterwards ?

E   <u>Yes</u>   (101) Do you feel that you could do almost any
      No   job if you really set your mind to
                     accomplish it ?

F   <u>Yes</u>   (102) Do you find yourself ' artistically ' elabor-
      No   ating little incidents that have happened
                     to you, so that you have amusing stories
                     to tell your guests ?

G   Yes   (103) Do you sometimes get extremely angry
      <u>No</u>   when crossed in your purposes and find
                     difficulty in controlling your temper ?

I   <u>Yes</u>   (104) Do you generally trust opinions you have
      No   arrived at by swift intuition (if so, answer
                     ' Yes '), or do you prefer to go step by
                     step with cold logic (if so, answer ' No ')?

K   <u>A</u> B   (105) The name ' Pre-Raphaelites ' is given
      <u>C</u> <u>D</u>   to a school of :
      <u>E</u> F   A. painters   in C. Italy   in the E. 19th cent.
            B. philosophers   D. England   F. 17th cent.
            (Underline three letters in the column
            on the left.)

L   <u>Yes</u>   (106) Do you think that actually the majority
      No   of politicians are people who are out for
                     their own good under pretence of look-
                     ing after the people ?

A—Yes (107) As you recall matters, when you have
L—No done a good turn for people you know, has it generally been returned ?

B Peculiar (108) ' Surprise ' is to ' Strange ' as ' Fear ' is to ——? (Underline the correct word on the left.)
Angry
Dirty
Anxious
Terrible

C. Yes (109) Do you sometimes find yourself getting unduly emotional over an issue in argument, although you had started out without any great interest in it ?
No

D Yes (110) Has it always been a cause of suffering with you that you are too sensitive to what other people say ?
No

E Yes (111) When you watch other people doing a job, do you sometimes have a strong urge to take it out of their hands because you feel you could do it so much better ?
No

F Yes (112) Do you rather often suffer from black spells in which you feel that nothing will ever be right again ?
No

G Yes (113) Do you think that to be always kind on principle is more important than to indulge in spontaneous generosity ?
No

I Yes (114) Do you have a feeling that you use up more energy than most people in getting things done ?
No

K Contralto (115) Which of these singers is able to reach the highest note ?
Baritone
Tenor
Soprano

L Yes (116) Is a good piece of advice for anyone starting out in business, " Trust nobody much and your closest acquaintances least of all " ?
No

A Yes (117) If you had to take a job with an engineer-
   No   ing firm, would you prefer that of being
                out selling the machine to that of sitting
                down to design machinery ?

B Once (118) Underline the one word which does not
   Only   belong.
   Alone
   First
   Second

D Yes (119) Are you considered a somewhat tempera-
   No   mental person ?

F Yes (120) Do you get worried rather easily about
   No   financial matters and wonder often
                whether you have set aside ' enough for
                a rainy day ' ?

I Yes (121) Do you try to avoid the sight of a bad
   No   accident in the street ?

K Doric columns   (122) Which one of the items
   Flying buttresses   on the left is char-
   Rounded, decorated   acteristic of the Norman
     arches   style of architecture ?
   Pointed windows

A Yes (123) As a hobby would you be more interested
   No   in astronomy than in running the
                entertainments for a social club ?

B Discomfort (124) ' Black ' is to ' Grey ' as ' Pain '
   Wound   is to —— ? (Underline word on
   Anger   left.)
   Illness
   Pleasure

D Yes (125) Are you sometimes accused of trying to
F No   take charge of the conversation, because
                you are more lively and quick than
                others ?

G Yes   (126) Are you rather above the average in
   No   tidiness, punctuality, and general de-
                 pendability ?

I Yes   (127) Do you feel that you are quicker than
   No   most people in your reactions and
                 responses ?

K Ancient Greece   (128) Leonardo da Vinci lived at
   The 19th Century   the time of —— ? (Under-
   The 18th Century   line one period at left.)
   The Renaissance

L Yes   (129) Do you object to modifying, for ' practi-
   No   cal ' considerations, or to please con-
                 ventional people, ideas at which you
                 have arrived by your own reasoning ?

A Yes   (130) Do you dislike people who express emo-
   No   tions too freely and are too familiar with
                 their emotional life more than you do
                 people who are over-cautious, thrifty,
                 and obstinate ?

B Monotonous   (131) Underline the item on the left
   Uneven   which does not belong with
   Zigzag   the rest.
   Wide
   Regular

C Yes   (132) Do you have many periods of dissatis-
   No   faction when you feel you want to get
                 away from everything (or go to a play
                 or out for a riotous evening or some
                 such distraction) ?

D Yes   (133) Do you frequently reflect that you have
   No   not had as much good luck in life as
                 most people ?

F   <u>Yes</u>   (134) When you start some new undertaking,
      No   do you generally feel so enthusiastic that you see mainly the rosy side of things (if so, underline ' Yes '), or are you inclined to dwell on the pitfalls and dangers which many people do not see (if so, underline ' No ') ?

G   <u>Yes</u>   (135) If you say you will have a piece of work
      No   done by a certain time, does it distress you very much not to be able to deliver it on time ?

I   Yes   (136) When you meet a stranger, do you feel
      Certainly   (apart from any shyness) that it would be interesting to know all about him (underline ' Yes,' if so), or do you feel that one can waste too much time talking to people who are of no practical consequence to one (underline ' Certainly,' if so) ?

K   <u>David Copperfield</u>   (137) Underline two characters
      Orlando   on the left who are from
      Mrs. Malaprop   stories by Dickens.
      <u>Mr. Micawber</u>
      Sir Roger de Coverley

L   <u>Yes</u>   (138) Do you sometimes brood a long time over
      No   things that upset you ?

A   <u>Yes</u>   (139) If you find two of your acquaintances
      No   have quarrelled, do you step in and find ways of smoothing out the difficulties, or do you think it best to leave them to come to their senses ? (If the latter, underline ' No.')

B   Not far   (140) ' Soon ' is to ' Never ' as ' Near ' is
      Seldom   to ——— ? (Underline word on left)
      Far away
      <u>Nowhere</u>
      Widely

C Yes
  <u>No</u>

(141) Do people who are extreme in doing everything just right, and who are scrupulously correct, annoy you more than those who are careless, untidy and unpunctual ?

D <u>Yes</u>
  No

(142) Do you sometimes get so ' worked up ' in a social situation that you feel you cannot trust yourself to speak, for fear of being *too* emphatic ?

E Yes
  <u>No</u>

(143) Do you often feel so critical and dissatisfied with regard to something you are doing that you throw it aside unfinished ?

F Yes
  <u>No</u>

(144) Are there fairly frequent occasions when you avoid company because you do not feel lively enough to be able to participate with the others ?

G <u>Yes</u>
  No

(145) Do you think people should be extremely careful and conscientious in their remarks about acquaintances, to avoid starting incorrect impressions, even if this makes conversation dull ?

I <u>Yes</u>
  No

(146) Do you think it is frequently the adults who are really at fault when children get punished for being peevish and at a loss for something to do ?

K Arnold
  Huxley
  <u>Darwin</u>
  Wallace

(147) Underline the name of the man who wrote *The Origin of Species*.

L <u>Yes</u>
  No

(148) Have you ever written letters to the editors of newspapers or to prominent people, when you felt that a certain issue was being misunderstood ?

A Yes (149) Would you prefer a job with a fixed,
   <u>No</u>   secure (even if modest) salary to one in
                which you work on a commission basis,
                earning according to your enterprise
                and luck?

B Growl (150) Underline the one word on the left
   <u>Speak</u>   that does not belong with the rest.
   Hum
   Whistle
   Whine

C Yes (151) Do you sometimes carry out what you
   <u>No</u>   feel in the mood to do, regardless of
                later consequences?

D <u>Yes</u> (152) Among your friends, do you value most
   No   those who are of a solid kind, on whom
                one can lean and to whom one can turn
                when in real difficulties?

E <u>Yes</u> (153) On occasions when your plans have gone
   No   wrong, has it happened on at least half
                the occasions that this turned out to be
                due to the failure of assistants and in-
                competence on the part of others
                essential to the plan?

F Yes (154) When you have some difficulty ahead of
   <u>No</u>   you, do you often tend to get strained
                and worried long before it actually has
                to be met?

G <u>Yes</u> (155) Do you think that a man should be
   No   esteemed for his dependability and con-
                scientiousness above most other traits,
                e.g. sociability, intelligence, energy?

I <u>Yes</u> (156) Does the sight of someone in pain inevit-
   No   ably distress you almost as much as if
                you were in pain yourself?

K Parallel lines   (155) Pythagoras' Theorem has to do
    Circles   with —— ? (Underline correct
    Chords   ending on left.)
    <u>Right Triangles</u>

L <u>Yes</u>   (157) Do you sometimes find yourself wondering
    No   a good deal as to what other people are
                    thinking about you ?

A Yes   (158) If you were a teacher, would you rather
    <u>No</u>   teach adult students, seriously interested
                    in their science, than a bunch of bright,
                    interesting, but irrepressible children ?

B Candle   (159) Underline on the left the item which
    Sun   is not in the same class as the rest.
    <u>Moon</u>
    Electric light
    Gas light

C <u>Yes</u>   (160) Do you consider yourself on the whole a
    No   calm, phlegmatic person rather than an
                    impatient, emotional type ?

D <u>Yes</u>   (161) Does it annoy you when people sit around
    No   and do not do anything about conditions
                    which you find intolerable and unjust ?

E Yes   (162) Would you sometimes forgo your rights
    <u>No</u>   rather than have a loud difference of
                    opinion with someone before other
                    people ?

F Yes   (163) Do you tend to grumble and grouse about
    <u>No</u>   things more than most ?

G <u>Yes</u>   (164) Do you consider yourself a quite highly
    No   self-controlled individual, able to con-
                    trol your impulses and to do as you
                    think best in any situation ?

I <u>Yes</u>   (165) Are you inclined to ' doodle ' and to
    No   waste time doing trivial things when
                    more important ones are awaiting you ?

K Paris (166) Underline two of the cities listed at
  Madras   the left which lie between longitude
  Chicago   20° East and 180° East.
  Pekin

L Yes (167) Have you sometimes thought a person
  No   has taken a dislike to you—from certain
  slight signs you have noticed—and discovered later that the person in fact had
  really liked you ?

A Yes (168) Do you like to plan as much of your life
  No   as possible, so that you know just what
  you are doing at certain times, rather
  than leave things to chance or to be
  decided by your feelings at the time ?

B Tune (169) 'Statue' is to 'Shape' as 'Song' is
  Beauty   to —— ? (Underline correct answer
  Notes   on the left.)
  Words
  Poetry

C Yes (170) Are there often times in your life when
  No   everything you do just seems to make
  matters worse, so that you feel like giving
  up and leaving things to solve themselves?

D Yes (171) Do you feel that people are often less
  No   considerate of one another's feelings than
  they should be ?

E Yes (172) If you are reproved by a superior in your
  No   job for some trivial and doubtful issue,
  do you apologise and explain, or do
  you justify yourself and if possible prove
  that you are right ? (Answer 'Yes' if
  you do the former.)

F Yes (173) Do you enjoy parties which give you a
  No   chance to show your resourcefulness in
  witty sallies or high-spirited practical
  jokes ?

G Yes (174) Do you find that you can meet most
  No   practical emergencies—e.g. unusual and
                 uncongenial tasks—without much diffi-
                 culty, or do such situations confuse and
                 upset you ? (Answer ' Yes ' to the first
                 part of this.)

D Yes (175) Do you find it difficult not to be rude to
  No   certain kinds of people who ' set you on
                 edge ' ?

E Yes (176) Do you find it quite difficult to go up and
  No   speak to the important guest at a
                 reception ?

I Yes (177) Does the sight of large insects give you a
  No   creepy feeling ?

E Yes (178) Does it embarrass you to have servants
  No   waiting on you ?

L Yes (179) Do you have many ideas on which you
  No   find extremely few people to agree with
                 you ?

K Pericles   (180) Which of the men named on the
  St. Augustine   left lived after Julius Cæsar
  Lord Nelson   and before Jenghis Khan ?
  Abraham Lincoln

A Book-keeper (181) Underline the one occupation
  Chemist   on the left which you would
  Advertising and   prefer to follow (if you had
    publicity man   to follow one of them).

B Words   (182) ' Justice ' is to ' Laws ' as ' Idea ' is
  Feelings   to —— ? (Underline one word on
  Principles   the left.)
  Judges

C   Yes   No   (183) Do you find that sometimes your notion of what you want to do with your life differs pretty considerably from what you have thought a short time previously?

D   Yes   No   (184) Do you sometimes follow an impulse to get into the limelight, even though you know it will annoy some people present?

E   Yes   No   (185) If you know someone has told a lie about you, do you prefer to ' have it out ' with him face to face, explicitly taxing him with having said it, rather than go about the matter indirectly?

F   Yes   No   (186) Have there been quite a number of occasions when you have felt that life is hardly worth living?

G.   Yes   No   (187) Do you think that with a properly trained will most people could achieve far more than they at present think they can?

I   Yes   No   (188) Do you find that your mind often wanders away from what you are doing, even when it is an important task that you want to get done?

K   Trotsky   Lenin   Czar Nicholas   Pavlov   Marx   (189) Which one of the names listed on the left is that of a person who might be said roughly to have played the same rôle in the Communist Revolution that Rousseau played in the French Revolution?

L   Yes   No   (190) Do these questions seem to you designed in a manner to give a tolerably complete and fair picture of your particular personality?

G.M.T.—14*

GENERAL INFORMATION TEST

THE following test is designed to test information (and, by inference, interest) in a complete circumference of possible (general) knowledge. The sectors—3 items to each—are as follows :

1. Travel, geography (1, 2, 3).
2. Sport and athletics (4, 5, 6).
3. Commerce, business (7, 8, 9) (monetary).
4. Mechanical, constructive (10, 11, 12) (carpentry, plumbing).
5. Scientific (13, 14, 15).
6. Philosophy, theory, mathematics (16, 17, 18) (things of the mind).
7. Rural, naturalistic (19, 20, 21) (farming, gardening).
8. Religious (22, 23, 24).
9. Literary, dramatic (25, 26, 27) (journalism).
10. Artistic (28, 29, 30) (painting, sculpture).
11. Decorative (31, 32, 33):
    a. Physical improvement of residence.
    b. Dress, dressmaking, grooming.
12. Sensual pleasures (34, 35, 36) :
    a. Food.
    b. Drink.
13. Sex, dating (37, 38, 39).
14. Social community, friends (40, 41, 42) (dancing, gossip, clubs, charity).
15. Home, i.e. family (43, 44, 45).
16. Children (46, 47, 48).

17. Fine arts (49, 50, 51) :
    a. Music.
    b. Architecture.
18. Clerical interests (52, 53, 54).
19. Manual and repetitive labour (55, 56, 57).
20. Political, national, historical (58, 59, 60).
21. Sedentary pastimes (61, 62, 63).
    a. Sedentary games, cards, gambling.
    b. Collecting hobbies.
22. Education (64, 65, 66).
23. Communication and transport (67, 68, 69).
24. Miscellanous (70, 71, 72).
    a. Protection—police, fireman.
    b. Cooking.
    c. Military.

For British subjects there are three or four items which will need to be recast in appropriate local information, monetary terms, etc.

The test is presented with the following instructions :

TEST I. INFORMATION

You have, at most, 30 minutes for the following 72 questions concerned with general information, so do not waste time on those you cannot answer at once but *guess*, i.e. make an attempt *in every case*. Do not get discouraged ; few people answer more than 50 per cent. correctly.

Whenever a series of numbered alternatives are offered underline one unless specifically asked to underline more. Some questions, like (3) below, require underlining at two places.

1. The national park located in Wyoming is :
   1. Yosemite.
   2. Yellowstone.
   3. Mt. Rainier.
   4. Mt. McKinley.

2. In going from San Francisco to the Philippine Islands by plane, at which island would you probably stop for refuelling ?   1. Tarawa.
   2. <u>Guam.</u>
   3. New Guinea.
   4. Solomon Islands.

3. A common way of representing the globe on a flat map is called :   1. Cartographer's   projection.   It
   2. Columbus'
   3. <u>Mercator's</u>
   exaggerates the spaces near the   1. Equator.
   2. First Meridian.
   3. <u>Poles.</u>

4. Which *two* of the following are true ?
   1. A field goal in hockey is worth three points.
   2. <u>A free throw in basketball counts one point.</u>
   3. There are ten players in a curling match.
   4. <u>A safety is worth two points.</u>

5. Which of the following is the name of a famous (horse) race track ?
   1. Chequers.
   2. Kentucky Oaks.
   3. <u>Aqueduct.</u>
   4. Lido Park.

6. The crawl stroke in swimming requires, in comparison with other strokes, more attention to :
   1. Synchronising arm and leg movements.
   2. The development of a scissors kick.
   3. <u>Breathing.</u>
   4. The manner of bringing down the upper arm.

7. What would be the least amount of capital with which one could reasonably expect to make a start in the grocery business?   1. $ 500 or £120.
   2. <u>$1500 or £350.</u>
   3. $3000 or £750.
   4. $5000 or £1000.

8. A man who aims to depress the stock market is known as a : 1. bull.
   2. contango.
   3. bear.
   4. chequer.

9. Gold at the present time is priced at :
   $10 (or £2) an ounce.
   $25 (or £5) ,,   ,,
   $35 (or £8) ,,   ,,
   $100 (or £20) ,,   ,,

10. In an internal combustion engine the
    1. Connecting rod
    2. Crank shaft
    3. Cam shaft
    is immediately responsible for operating the
    1. Cylinder.
    2. Valves.
    3. Magneto.

11. In sewing, which one of the following is used to prevent seams from ravelling ? 1. scissors.
    2. hooks and eyes.
    3. zipper.
    4. pinking shears.

12. For fastening two pieces of wood or metal together which *two* of the following means would be used ?
    1. Cotter.
    2. Pendick.
    3. Dowel.
    4. Last.
    5. Landau.

13. Which of the following minerals consists chiefly of silica, magnesia, and lime ? 1. asbestos.
    2. carborundum.
    3. mica.
    4. selenium.

14. The acceleration of a falling body due to gravity is about :   5 ft. per second.
    10 ,, ,,   ,,
    12 ,, ,,   ,,
    28 ,, ,,   ,,
    <u>32 ,, ,,   ,,</u>

15. The term ' mitosis ' in biology has to do with :
    1. breathing.
    2. oxygen consumption.
    3. <u>cell division.</u>
    4. circulation of the blood.
    5. the pancreas.

16. The empirical line of development of thought in philosophy started with :   1. <u>Bacon</u>
                                                    2. Plato
    and was continued by which two of the following philosophers? 1. Spinoza.
                                                    2. <u>Locke.</u>
                                                    3. Leibnitz.
                                                    4. <u>Hume.</u>

17. Which two of the following have been systems of philosophy or ethics?   1. rationalisation.
                                                    2. agrarianism.
                                                    3. <u>utilitarianism.</u>
                                                    4. <u>nominalism.</u>

18. A syllogism is a :   1. small fresh-water animal.
                         2. form of speech.
                         3. philosophical system.
                         4. <u>form in logic.</u>

19. A Guernsey is a breed of   1. sheep   which   1. is
                               2. <u>cow</u>   2. <u>is not</u>
                               3. pig
    famed principally for its meat value.

20. A larch is one of the few   1. conifers
                                  2. varieties of cedar
                                  3. trees
     that is not   1. found in America.
                    2. a hardwood.
                    3. evergreen.

21. Which two of the following make good thick hedges
     for gardens ?   1. Rhododendron.
                      2. Palmetto.
                      3. Privet.
                      4. Box.
                      5. Azalea.

22. Which of the following are Protestant Churches ?
     1. Methodist.
     2. Church of England.
     3. Greek Church.
     4. Bahai.

23. A famous son of Jacob was :   1. Esau.
                                  2. Isaac.
                                  3. Joseph.
                                  4. Joshua.

24. Which two of the following are religions followed by
     some millions of people ?   1. Zoroastrianism.
                                  2. Baludism.
                                  3. Mahdism.
                                  4. Bahai.

25. Who was Othello's wife ?   1. Clytemnestra.
                               2. Eurydice.
                               3. Miranda.
                               4. Desdemona.

26. Emerson was a   1. Southern
                     2. New England
     writer noted for his   1. Transcendentalism.
                            2. Humour.
                            3. Graphic portrayal of living
                               conditions among the poor.

27. *Of Human Bondage* was written by :
    1. Upton Sinclair   about a   1. wage slave.
    2. John Steinbeck   2. <u>young medical student.</u>
    3. <u>Somerset Maugham</u>
                                    3. war prisoner.

28. ' The Last Supper ' was painted by :
    1. Raphael.
    2. Landseer.
    3. <u>Da Vinci.</u>
    4. Rembrandt.

29. Which two of the following are famous for sculpture ?
    1. Goya.
    2. <u>Michelangelo.</u>
    3. Picasso.
    4. <u>Epstein.</u>
    5. Gauguin.

30. Which two of the following are famous painters ?
    1. <u>Ver Meer.</u>
    2. <u>Giotto.</u>
    3. Pagliacci.
    4. Renan.
    5. Von Beck.

31. To correct the impression made by a small badly-lit room, which one of the following would you recommend ?
    1. <u>Paint it cream and use one large plain rug.</u>
    2. ,, ,, ,, ,, ,, two small bright rugs.
    3. ,, ,, red ,, ,, a gaily flowered rug.
    4. ,, ,, ,, ,, ,, two richly decorated rugs.

32. A short fitted skirt attached to the waist by a 1. <u>yoke.</u>
                                                2. tunic.
    is called a   1. peplum.
                    2. <u>kilt.</u>
                    3. dress.

33. Which *two* of the following are names of period furniture ?   1. Duncan Phyfe.
      2. Sandwich.
      3. Gregorian.
      4. Chippendale.

34. A side dish or relish is sometimes called :
      1. demitasse.
      2. à la reine.
      3. hors d'œuvre.
      4. à la vent pré.

35. French dressing is a   1. salad dressing
                           2. kind of icing for fancy cakes
    made of   1. oil, whipped cream.
              2. olive-oil, vinegar.
              3. sugar and gelatin.

36. A Tom Collins contains :   1. rum.
                               2. whiskey.
                               3. Scotch.
                               4. sauterne.
                               5. gin.

37. When a girl wears a corsage to a *dance* she :
      1. pins it on the right side.
      2. buttons it up the middle.
      3. wears it on the left side.
      4. removes it when dancing.

38. List the names of a few movie stars of the opposite sex to yourself :

    _____   _____
    _____   _____
    _____   _____
    _____   _____

    (Count ' passed ' if four or more listed.)

39. Which two of the following are characteristics popularly ascribed to :

1. Men	2. Women
(Women answer these only)	(Men answer these only)
Charitableness.	Talkativeness.
Egotism.	Devotion to duty.
Lesser emotionality.	Caprice.
Attention to detail.	Cynicism.
Quickness of apprehension.	Persistence.

40. ' Modern ' ballroom dancing does *not* include which *two* of these?   1. rhumba.
2. square dance.
3. waltz.
4. conga.
5. quadrille.

41. Which two of the following are the names of men's and women's clubs?   1. Eastern Star.
2. Elks.
3. Knights of Commerce.
4. R.A.K.B.

42. Which *three* of the following are names of local restaurants?

The Arcade.	(Experimenter should sub-
Perry's Café.	stitute three moderately
Anderson's Café.	well-known local restau-
Court House Café.	rants and three false
The Huddle.	names in irregular
The Co-ed Restaurant.	order.)

43. The grocery bill (i.e. total food expenditure) per week for a family of three people (in a lower middle-class home) would be nearest which of these?

1. $6.00 (or £1 10s. 0d.).
2. $7.50 (or £2 0s. 0d.).
3. $12.00 (or £2 15s. 0d.).   (Adjust to cost of
4. $15.50 (or £3 15s. 0d.).   living.)
5. $21.00 (or £5 0s. 0d.).

44. Suppose yourself to be a housewife confronted at
    9 a.m. with the following tasks :
    A. Some clothes to be ironed and prepared for
       ironing.
    B. Some breakfast dishes to be washed.
    C. Some shopping to be done.
    Which would you touch first ?   B
    „   „   „   „* second ?   A

45. *Women answer this :*
    How long does it take a man to shave :
    a. With an electric razor ?   B   A. 3 minutes.
    b. With an ordinary razor ?   B   B. 8   „
                                          C. 16 „
                                          D. 20 „
                                          E. 30 „

    Men answer this :
    If you were buying the average girl a pair of gloves,
    which of the following sizes would be most likely to
    fit ?   2. $5\frac{3}{4}$
       (In the   3.   (In $6\frac{3}{4}$
       U.S.A.)   4.   Britain) $7\frac{1}{2}$
                   6. $8\frac{1}{4}$
                  ___

46. Before a baby begins to teethe he can usually :
    1. Eat some cooked foods.
    2. Crawl.
    3. Sit up easily.
    4. Drink from a cup alone.

47. The size of shoe for an average three-year-old child is :
                        0.   1.
       (In the   2.   (In   2.
       U.S.A.)   3.   or   Britain)   3.
                        4.   4.
                        5.   6.

48. You have : A. one baseball game set ; B. one tinker
    toy ; C. one cowboy suit with toy pistol. Indicate
    by the appropriate letters for which of the following

children you would consider these most suitable. (One child will be left unmatched with a toy.)

John, aged 5 B
Harry, ,,   7 C
Tom, ,,   9
Will,   ,,   11 A

49. The 'Moonlight Sonata' was written by :
  1. Haydn.
  2. Bach.
  3. Mozart.
  4. Beethoven.
  5. Strauss.

50. Which two of the following refer to the style specifically of the head of a column?   1. Doric.
                    2. Rococo.
                    3. Gothic.
                    4. Ionic.

51. The best name for the horizontal beam or stone over a doorway is :   1. Transept.
                    2. Lintel.
                    3. Cornice.
                    4. Foyer.
                    5. Entablature.

52. Pica is a name that refers to a :
  1. kind of mountain flower.
  2. species of baboon.
  3. size of type.
  4. South American musical instrument.

53. Which two of the following are standard paper sizes ?
  1. $8\frac{1}{2}$ by 11 inches.
  2. $8\frac{1}{2}$ by 14 inches.
  3. $7\frac{1}{2}$ by 11 inches.
  4. $8\frac{1}{2}$ by 12 inches.

54. Stenographic notes can be taken by which two of the following? 1. Pitman.
   2. Gregg.
   3. Regent.
   4. Esperanto.
   5. Dictaton.

55. A block and tackle is used in :
   1. Fishing.
   2. Lifting heavy loads.
   3. Wiring a house.
   4. Spreading grain.
   5. Producing concrete blocks.

56. A person who uses a hod is employed in which of the following trades?
   1. baking.
   2. bricklaying.
   3. carpentry.
   4. house painting.

57. The price of a professional plasterer's trowel is about :
   1. $.75 (or 3s.).
   2. $2.50 (or 10s.).
   3. $4.00 (or £1).
   4. $6.00 (or £1 10s.).

58. In the U.S.A. each : 1. State
   2. County
   3. City
   sends one member to 1. The Federal Senate
   2. The Federal House of
   Representatives
   for each: 1. 100,000 people or more.
   2. 200,000 ,, ,, ,,
   3. 300,000 ,, ,, ,,
   4. 400,000 ,, ,, ,,

59. Commodore Perry compelled the : 1. Mexicans
                                      2. Algerians
                                      3. <u>Japanese</u>
    to open their country to foreign trade in :
                                      1. 1775.
                                      2. 1812.
                                      3. <u>1854.</u>
                                      4. 1881.
                                      5. 1909.

60. In the United Nations Organisation (Security Council)
    the U.S.A. has 1. fewer   votes 1. than
                   2. <u>the same number of</u>   2. <u>as</u>
                   3. more
    Russia (excluding Ukraine). A veto on military
    action against an aggressor: 1. <u>can</u>   be imposed
                                  2. cannot
    by one nation only.

61. In poker, five cards in one suit is known as a :
    1. full house.
    2. straight.
    3. <u>flush.</u>
    4. two pairs and a single.
    5. run.

62. The term ' vulnerable ' is used in : 1. rummy.
                                          2. whist.
                                          3. poker.
                                          4. <u>bridge.</u>
                                          5. 500.

63. The collector of antique glass seeks which two of
    these ?
    1. Sheraton.
    2. <u>Daisy and button.</u>
    3. <u>Whitefriars.</u>
    4. Glaser crystal.

64. Hutchins is a name which has been in the papers a good deal recently in connection with :
    1. Bridge games.
    2. Chess.
    3. <u>College education.</u>
    4. Military training.
    5. The veterans' education programme.

65. In the U.S.A. about 30 per cent. of people
    $$\frac{60}{85}$$
    graduate from high school and about 5 per cent.
    $$\frac{8}{13}$$
    (of the 18 to 24 age-group) attend college.

66. Which two of the following are famous writers on the philosophy of education ?
    1. Beard.
    2. Gray.
    3. <u>Dewey.</u>
    4. <u>Rousseau.</u>

67. Which two of the following are names of railway companies either in Britain or the U.S.A. ?
    1. <u>G.W.R.</u>
    2. <u>O.P.R.</u>
    3. <u>Coastline.</u>
    4. Oregon and Californian.
    5. G.E.R.

68. Indicate the approximate cost of the following long-distance calls (3 minutes) by writing the letters A, B, and C opposite the appropriate sums.   (Station-to-station, night calls, tax not included.)

Urbana to New York	(A)	$0.40	<u>B</u>
Urbana to Chicago	(B)	$2.50	<u>C</u>
Urbana to Los Angeles	(C)	$1.30	<u>A</u>
		$1.90	

(Substitute local town for Urbana and in Britain substitute London, Bristol, Manchester for N.Y., Chicago and Los Angeles.)

69. Books may be sent through the mail at :
   1. <u>4 cents for the first pound.</u>
   2. 8   ,,   ,,   ,,   ,,
   3. 10   ,,   ,,   ,,   ,,
   4. 20   ,,   ,,   ,,   ,,

70. A city of 100,000 inhabitants has a police force numbering about : 1. <u>100</u>   and a fire brigade of
   2. 150
   about : 1. 50.   3. 200
   2. <u>90.</u>
   3. 250.

71. Sour milk is usually employed in making a cake when the recipe also calls for :   1. <u>baking soda.</u>
   2. chocolate.
   3. baking powder.
   4. cream of tartar.

72. To which rank in the army does the rank of captain in the navy correspond ?   1. Captain.
   2. Major.
   3. Lieut.-Colonel.
   4. <u>Colonel.</u>

INDEX

'A' factor, 162, 169, 189
Abilities and factors, 55
Accomplishment quotient, 87
Achievement test in biology, 116
Acquisitiveness of disposition, 196
  test, 199
Adaptation board, 49
Aggressiveness by test, 260
Alexander, W. P., 42, 81
  performance test, 43
Algebra attainment tests, 115
Allport's ascendance-submission test,
  129, 209
American Council on Education:
  economics test, 116
  European history test, 119
  French test, Alpha, 117
    Beta, 117
  German test, Alpha, 118
  Italian test, 125
  psychological examination for high-
    school students, 18
  college freshmen, 21
  Spanish test, Alpha, 126
    Beta, 126
  trigonometry test, 126
Anxiety hysteria, 262, 266
  personal questionnaire, 272
  rating scale, 266
Anxiety neurosis, 215, 262
  personal questionnaire, 272
  rating scale, 265
Anxiety neurotics in spot-dotting test, 258
Aptitude tests, 58–83
Arithmetic attainment tests, 109–115
  knowledge of methods, 109
  mechanical skill, 114
Arithmetic facility, 54
Arithmetical ability and intelligence
  level, 339
Arthur, G., 36
  performance tests, 47
Artistic ability, 58
Ascendance-submission test, Allport,
  129, 209
Assertiveness-submissiveness of disposition, 196
  test, 197
  physiological test, 301
Atkins's 'object fitting' test, 50
Attainment quotient, 87
Attainment tests, 84
  discrepancies in, 339
  material available, 89–127
  purpose of, 84
  technique of construction, 86, 158

Attitude tests, 158
Aveling, F., 261
Ayres' handwriting scale, 118
Ayres' spelling scale, 99

'B' factor, 162, 218
Babcock, E., 22
Ballard, P. B., 84, 87, 90
  Arithmetical reasoning test, 110
    mechanical test, 114
  Chelsea test, 18
  Columbian test, 19
  Crichton test, 21
  English comprehension test, 100
    construction test, 103
  Group Tests of Intelligence, 99
  junior test from *The New Examiner*,
    17
  one-minute reading scale, 96
  silent reading test, 91
  The New Examiner, 84
Basedowoid type, 299
Benge's clerical aptitude test, 61
Bennett-Fry mechanical comprehension
  test, 70
Binet, 5, 13, 77, 221
Binet-Simon scale and revisions, xiv, 12,
  48, 327
Biology attainment tests, 116
Body sway test, 257, 261
Bravais-Pearson product-moment for-
  mula, 360
Bridges' emotional development rating
  scale, 221
Bristol group reasoning tests, 23, 68
Brogden, H. E., 222, 228
Brown, W. W., 261
Buros, O. K., xiv
Burt, Sir Cyril, xvi, 81, 84, 92, 213
  arithmetic test, 109
  composition test, 103
  drawing of a man test, 62, 116
  goodness of cursive handwriting,
    test, 119
  graded reasoning tests, 68
  mechanical graded test, 114
  ungraded test, 114
  Mental and Scholastic Tests, 48, 84,
    127
  Northumberland Standardised Tests,
    13, 118, 119, 333
  No. 1. Arithmetic, 113
  No. 2. English, 95, 96
  No. 3. Intelligence, 20
  test in æsthetics, 59
  vocabulary test, 99

405

2 years
- **65 to 85%.** Pile *four* blocks in a stable pillar (see above).
- **,, ,, ,,** Make single vertical stroke, with pencil, in imitation (see above).
- **50 to 65%.** Obey propositions:
  - Put the ball on the box.
  - Put the ball in the box.
  - Put the ball behind the box.
  - Put the ball in front of the box (or chair).
  - Put the ball under the chair.
  - (getting *three* correct.)
- **20 to 50%.** Make tolerable drawing of a circle after seeing one drawn.
- **,, ,, ,,** Build ' bridge ' with three bricks after seeing one made.
- **,, ,, ,,** Can name *three* objects in a picture (Dutch Home Scene, (" Tell me what you can see ").

3 years
- **65 to 85%.** Use pronouns, plurals, and past tense in speech.
- **,, ,, ,,** Presented with several cubes and cup. " Put just *one* block into the cup." Respond correctly.
- **50 to 65%.** " Put *two* blocks in cup " (as above and after doing one successfully). Respond correctly.
- **20 to 50%.** Copy a cross just recognisably from a model + presented (but not drawn in their presence).
- **,, ,, ,,** Can carry out three commissions without asking further. " Here's a key; I want you to put it on that chair over there; then I want you to shut that door, and then bring me the box which you see over there." (Pointing in turn to these objects.) Repeat, stressing: *First* put the key on the chair; *then*, etc.

4 years
- **65 to 85%.** Successfully respond to instructions to put only two cubes in cup. (See 3-year test above.)
- **,, ,, ,,** Answer reasonably two out of three:
  - " What must you do when you are sleepy ? "
  - " What ought you to do when you are cold ? "
  - " What ought you to do when you are hungry ? "
- **20 to 50%.** Copy a square (recognisably) from a model (but not drawn in their presence).
- **,, ,, ,,** Provide two oblong cards, one divided by a diagonal cut into two triangles. Child presented with two triangles and asked to " Put them together so that they look exactly like this (pointing to rectangle).' Allow three attempts of 1 minute each. Pass if two of three are successful.
- **,, ,, ,,** Give an answer to " What must you do if you have lost something ? " which shows that expression ' lost ' is fully understood.
- **0 to 20%.** Give a correct answer on three out of four ' missing feature ' pictures. " What is left out of the face ? " (Four pictures of faces as in Binet 7 year. One with mouth, one with nose, one with ear, and one with eye missing.)

The percentages on the left indicate the number of children found by Gesell to pass this test at the age concerned. A child should have the mental age indicated on the left when he passes the tests on which 50% (say 40–60%) of the children of that age succeed. But unfortunately Gesell's norms are not arranged in 50% categories. With the arrangement of items made above a child should pass for a given year when he succeeds in more than a half of the items for that year (except in the Fourth year, when just a half will suffice).

The Measurement of Intelligence in Infants and Pre-school Children. Psyche Cattell, Psychological Corporation, 1940.

This is a test which, in part, is developmental, as in Gesell's scale, and in part describes tests requiring some apparatus. It is, perhaps, the most useful and generally valid set of tests yet proposed for the 0–4-year range, and is well standardised.

Merrill Palmer Test for children of 21 to 63 months (effective range 2–6 years). Time required ¾ hour to 1¼ hours, according to child.—A medley of some 38 verbal and non-verbal tests, giving 93 separate diagnostic items. The test is not constructed on intelligence test principles in so far as the constituents are selected on grounds of *low* mutual correlation (see Stutsman, *Mental Measurement of the Pre-School Child*, 1922). Probably not a very sound measure of ' g,' but rather of general development. Interesting to children and highly practicable to administer. Correlates ·78–·79 with Binet score. Recently standardised for this country by Hilda Bristol (details published in Prof. Hamley's section [1] on " Mental Tests " in the *Education Year Book*, 1935), on 530 children, with the following results:

Age in Months:	21	24	27	30	33	36	39	42	45	48	51	54	57	60	63	66	68
Points:		11	17	23	30	34	44	51	57	63	69	73	76	79	62	64	66	67

The American norms, on 631 cases, are about 5 points lower than these over the whole range. Apparatus (fairly extensive) obtainable from Messrs. Stoelting, or from Raper, Psychological Laboratory, University College, Gower St., London.

Minnesota Pre-School Scale (Goodenough, Foster, Van Wagener). Range 18 months to 6 years.—Not so attractive to children as is the Merrill Palmer. Available, Educational Test Bureau, Minneapolis.

The California First-year Mental Scale.—A series of test items selected from various sources. Standardised on 61 infants over range 1 to 21 months. Consistency coefficient ·62 (0–3 months) to ·86 (4–18 years). Validity unestablished. Described in University of California Syllabus Series, 1933, No. 243.

---

[1] Or " The Testing of Intelligence," H. R. Hamley. Evans Bros., 1935.

On the whole, one is forced to admit that there are as yet no very satisfactory tests of ' g ' over the 0–4-year age-range.

Kindergarten Period: 4–8 years

Dartington Intelligence Scale (Cattell Intelligence Tests, Scale 0). Individual test, 4–8 years.—Eight validated sub-tests.[1] 96 pass or fail items. Standardisation slender, but on well-sampled group. American standardisation by Psyche Cattell. Time required—$\frac{3}{4}$ hour; shortened form, 25 minutes. Obtainable from Messrs. G. Harrap & Co.

Junior School Range: 8–11 years

Ballard's Junior Test (*New Examiner*, p. 236).—A mixture of test types, some of which involve a certain amount of general knowledge. 100 items. No time limit. Norms for elementary school children of 8–14 years.

Cattell Test, Scale I. Non-verbal. Group or Individual. For ages 8–11 years.—Eight sub-tests of good validity. 106 pass or fail items. Standardised on 620 selected cases, including individuals of known mental age. Time required, 45–50 minutes. A and B Forms provided. The test can be given in a shortened form requiring 20 minutes. Stencil key. Preliminary practice given in test itself. Obtainable from Messrs. G. Harrap & Co. (This test replaces the verbal Scale I, the verbal test having been found not entirely satisfactory for children of 8–11.)

Otis Primary.—Eight non-verbal subjects of good validity. Ages 6–10 years. Norms too low for English children (about 11 points of I.Q.). English norms recently prepared. Results expressed in Indices of Brightness which are not comparable with Intelligence Quotients, and generally not so useful. Time required, about 35 minutes. Obtainable from Messrs. G. Harrap & Co.

Simplex Junior.—Group or Individual. An ' omnibus ' type of test. Age-range rather large (7–14 years) for accur-

[1] See " Intelligence Tests for Children of 4–8 years," by R. B. Cattell and H. Bristol, *J. Educ. Psychol.*, iii, 1933.

ate sorting of junior children.   Time required, 45 minutes.
Well standardised.   Stencil keys.   Obtainable from
Messrs. G. Harrap & Co.

Sleight. Non-verbal.—Ten short sub-tests of good
validity.   Age-range 6–11 years.   Time required, about 35
minutes (18¼ minutes' testing time, remainder instructions,
etc.).   Soundly standardised.   Obtainable from Messrs. G.
Harrap & Co.

Senior and High School School Range: 11–17 *years inclusive*

(Tests for scholarship examinations at 11 years should be
chosen from the 11–14 mental age-range, since most
scholarship candidates between whom it is desired to distinguish finely fall at a 12–13 mental age.)

*American Council on Education Psychological Examination for
High School Students.*—Companion test to adult form (see
below).   Designed by L. L. and T. G. Thurstone and
revised each year.   High validity as tested by internal
factorial composition.   One hour.   Machine scorable.
Obtainable Co-operative Test Service (see below).

Cattell Test, Scale II.   Verbal with non-verbal items.
Group or Individual.   Ages 11–15 years.   (Quite suitable
for average and sub-average adults.)—Six sub-tests, giving
151 pass or fail items.   The validity of these individual
sub-tests ranges [1] from 0·65 to 0·85.   Standardised on
2,070 cases supplied from various parts of Great Britain.
Time required, 70 minutes.   The first sub-tests have a
generous time limit to give subjects a sense of confidence.
A and B Forms provided.   Preliminary ' practice ' test
supplied to eliminate ' test sophistication.'   The test can
be given in a much shortened form requiring 24 minutes
and correlating with the full scale [1] 0·88.   Stencil key.
Obtainable from Messrs. G. Harrap & Co.

Chelsea Tests.   (P. B. Ballard.)   Verbal ages 11–14
years.   Group or Individual.—Four sub-tests giving 100
pass or fail items.   First test timed, but others unlimited.
Total time therefore varies, but about an hour generally

---

[1] Halstead, H., and Chase, V. E., "Review of a Verbal Intelligence Scale on
Military Neurotic Patients," *Brit. J. Med. Psychol.*, xx, 195–201, 1944.